OVID RECALLED

*...le plus gentil et le plus ingénieux
de tous les poètes grecs et latins.*

GASPAR BACHET, SIEUR DE MÉZIRIAC (1626)

OVID
RECALLED

BY

L. P. WILKINSON

*Fellow of King's College
and Lecturer in Classics in the
University of Cambridge*

CAMBRIDGE
AT THE UNIVERSITY PRESS
1955

PUBLISHED BY

THE SYNDICS OF THE CAMBRIDGE UNIVERSITY PRESS

London Office: Bentley House, N.W.1
American Branch: New York

Agents for Canada, India, and Pakistan: Macmillan

Printed in Great Britain at the University Press, Cambridge
(Brooke Crutchley, University Printer)

TO

Dennis Proctor

CONTENTS

CONTENTS

PREFACE

COMPARATIVELY little has been written about Ovid lately, considering the volume of his work and its historic as well as intrinsic interest. In Büchner and Hofmann's survey, published in 1951, of work done on Latin language and literature since 1937 he claims only two pages out of two hundred and forty. It so happened also that Sellar, composing his classic *Roman Poets of the Augustan Age* (1892), died with the section on Ovid alone incomplete, and this gap has never really been made good. There is Ripert's charming *Ovide, Poète de l'Amour, des Dieux et de l'Exil* (1921), and Rand's all too brief *Ovid and his Influence* (1925) in the series 'Our Debt to Greece and Rome'; and more substantial, there is Hermann Fränkel's *Ovid, A Poet between Two Worlds* (1945). This last work suffers from what most critics seem to agree to be fanciful interpretation, and also from the convention that in the Sather Lectures quotation should be in English, which cannot do justice to Ovid of all poets; but it is based on wide reading and up-to-date knowledge, and I gladly acknowledge my debt to its informative notes in particular. Anyone approaching the study of Ovid must also be grateful to E. Martini's *Einleitung zu Ovid* (1933), with its reliable information on each work as well as on various aspects of him, and its select bibliographies.

The present book is not intended as a contribution to scholarship. It is addressed primarily to the Latinate reading public; but I hope it may also be of interest to students of the classics who are not experts on Ovid, for whom the references at the end of the volume (indicated by catch-figures in the text) are supplied, and still more, on the other hand, to readers who have forgotten their Latin or never had any, for whom I have provided the translations. These last are nearly all in heroic couplets, not because I have any illusions about the possibility of reproducing in English verse the streamlined neatness of Ovid's Latin, even when the full sense can be fitted into the shorter medium in the more verbose language and fortune proffers appropriate rhymes, but simply from a hope that rhyme and metre of any kind may prove more palatable to the non-classical reader than plain prose would be. I have stuck to this traditional medium because it is the closest counterpart we have to the Ovidian elegiac (indeed, a direct descendant, as I shall indicate), compact, subject to clear restrictions, and familiar to all educated readers. Anything modern, such as *vers libre* or sprung rhythm, would be wholly foreign to the spirit of the original. And I have not scrupled to use various poetic licences and words that belong to the convention of heroic couplets.

It is true that our Augustan Age made translations into this medium of almost all Ovid's works; but these are sometimes so free or diffuse as to be more like paraphrases, and thus not very helpful to those who want a crib; and, moreover, their vocabulary tends to be artificial, whereas Ovid's was usually plain and direct, or to be outmoded now, whereas Ovid's was in the main contemporary. I do not mean that his diction was not poetic; but it was not quaint or recherché or archaic. As regards the *Ars Amatoria* I have less excuse, for two notable versions in couplets have appeared in our time. Mr Phillips Barker's (1931) is brilliant, not to say flashy, but he helps himself out with feminine rhymes, which lend variety but are not quite true to the Ovidian discipline; Mr B. P. Moore's (1935), more chaste artistically, maintains a high standard of excellence. I am therefore driven to confess that I have made my own versions partly because the attempt has been so enjoyable in itself, though partly also, as already stated, with the object of keeping as closely as I could to the Latin, couplet by couplet, for the benefit of those who need a crib. So they represent a compromise for which I must ask indulgence.*

Ovid's writings are voluminous and too repetitive. As in the case of Wordsworth or Tennyson, only a selection can do him

---

* Mr A. Watts' elegant translation of the *Metamorphoses* into heroic couplets, with reproductions of the etchings of Picasso, appeared while this book was in the Press; also Mr R. Humphries', and Miss Mary Innes', neither of which I have seen.

justice. There is much in him that we can enjoy today, but the casual reader might well be discouraged in the search. References could be given to the selected passages, but it would be tedious for the reader to keep looking things up in separate volumes, even if he possessed the complete works. For these reasons I have quoted at length most of the passages that seem to me to deserve it, so that the book is somewhat in the nature of an anthology with running commentary.

I have added two chapters and an epilogue on the posthumous fortunes of the poet. The study of these from original sources could be the work of more than a lifetime, and I have pieced together my account from a limited number of secondary authorities who have dealt with various aspects. It seemed better to do even this than to leave the reader with a wholly false impression of Ovid's status by ending at his death. No ancient author, not even Cicero, has had so great a posthumous importance in proportion to his intrinsic merits. Ovid has been part of the cultural history of Western Europe; and the study of the classics is shorn of a great deal of its interest and justification if we overlook what it has meant to others down the ages, and how they have turned it to peculiar uses of their own, as Dante did in the case of Virgil, to the enrichment of the heritage passed on to us. For these chapters I must acknowledge a particular debt to F. J. E. Raby's *Secular Latin Poetry* (1934), R. R. Bolgar's *The Classical Heritage and its Beneficiaries* (1954) and Douglas Bush's *Mythology and the Renaissance Tradition in English Poetry* (1932). The part of Rand's book that deals with *Nachleben* is tantalizingly short. To my great disappointment I have found W. Brewer's *Ovid's Metamorphoses in European Culture* (1933) unusable. It contains a mass of information, but this is wholly undocumented apart from a bibliography, and in many cases it is patent that the author is interpreting any similarity as influence.

I wish to thank friends who have read all or most of this book in typescript and made valuable suggestions, Mr George Rylands, Dr R. R. Bolgar, Mr W. A. Camps, Mr A. G. Lee and Mr D. W.

Lucas. They are in no way responsible for the faults that remain. Others have kindly given me help in various ways, notably Professor W. B. Stanford, Professor M. L. Clarke, Mr E. J. Kenney, Mr A. M. Jaffé, Mrs R. Bromwich, the staffs of the Warburg Institute and Stanford University Libraries. The Society of Authors as A. E. Housman's literary executor has given permission to quote the extract from an article of his in the *Journal of Philology*; and the frontispiece appears by permission of the Trustees of the National Gallery. To my College I am grateful for generous help with typing expenses, and to the staffs of the University Typewriting Office and University Press at Cambridge for their patient skill.

L. P. W.

CAMBRIDGE

May 1955

INTRODUCTION

IF you ask anyone whether he likes Ovid, the chances are that he will reply that he did not care for what he read of him at school and has read nothing since. Further inquiry may elicit the fact that he was introduced to him by way of selections from the *Heroides* or *Fasti* or *Tristia*, works which have this in common, that they are not 'unsuitable' for schoolboys. But what are the preferences of a mature reader? Macaulay may serve as a witness, since he read Ovid all through at least once during his residence at Calcutta, and his biographer has obligingly assembled his opinions for us.* Well, 'He was evidently surfeited by the *Heroides*, but pleased by the *Amores*. Of the *Ars* he said, "Ovid's best".' 'The *Fasti* were almost too much for him', the *Tristia* he found 'a very melancholy set of poems'. With the *Metamorphoses*, though they contained 'some very fine things', he was disappointed at first reading, though he liked them better on reperusal. So the works that are commonly set before schoolboys are precisely those which a literary man of the world found least palatable. I should myself be inclined to begin my order of preference *Metamorphoses*, *Amores*, *Ars*, but the point remains: there is a case for offering the individual reader a reintroduction to Ovid.

And in a wider sense also there is, I venture to think, a case for offering our generation a reintroduction. For nearly two centuries Ovid has been out of fashion.† Suggested reasons for this, which are cumulative, I will postpone to where they belong chrono-

---

* Sir G. O. Trevelyan, *Life and Letters of Lord Macaulay* (1908 edn.), p. 725.

† A crude test is provided by references in the *Cambridge History of English Literature*, where comparative figures are approximately as follows:

	Before Dr Johnson	Since Dr Johnson
Virgil	127	41
Horace	92	34
Ovid	66	5

logically—in the Epilogue; here we are only concerned with the fact, and with posing the question whether the attitude of recent generations has not been, in a temporal sense, rather provincial. For six centuries, roughly from 1075 to 1675, Ovid's position as one of the greatest poets, comparable with that of Virgil, was scarcely challenged.* Thus in the fourteenth century at one end of Europe Maximus Planudes was rendering the *Metamorphoses* and *Heroides* into Greek prose for Byzantine readers, a unique distinction in an age when all the cultural traffic was going the other way, while at the other his name was one to conjure with in the poetry of Dafydd ab Gwilym, who, though he may only have known him at second hand, invokes as his source of inspiration a fictitious 'Book of Ovid'.†

It is perhaps significant that Ovid has always appealed most to the young. The *Metamorphoses*, read at the age of seven or eight, before he knew French, was the first work of literature to delight Montaigne.‡ Petrarch, Boccaccio, Shakespeare and Milton are among those who seem to have enjoyed him especially in their youth. More surprising is the testimony of Wordsworth: 'Before I read Virgil I was so strongly attached to Ovid, whose *Metamorphoses* I read at school, that I was quite in a passion when I found him in books of criticism placed below Virgil.'§ At Eton Swinburne, about 1850, wrote Ovidian poems on Byblis, Clytië, and Apollo and Daphne; and there, a few years later, Robert Bridges' eyes were first opened to poetry by reading some elegies of Ovid.|| The most striking evidence, however, of his power to affect the young is Goethe's recollection in *Dichtung und Wahrheit*

---

* In Miss H. R. Palmer's *List of English Editions and Translations of Greek and Latin Classics Printed before 1641* (1911), Latin poets figure in the following order: Ovid 74, Virgil 63, Horace 36, Terence 33, Seneca 30, Juvenal 15, Lucan 13, Persius 10, Martial 5, Plautus 2. Of course the figures are affected by the number of works each poet wrote.

† Cf. Chaucer's 'Lollius'. Dafydd uses 'ofyddiaeth' to mean love-poetry. For his relationship to Ovid see T. M. Chotzen, *Recherches sur la Poésie de Dafydd ab Gwilym* (1927), p. 143.

‡ Essays, I, 25.   § Note on *Ode to Lycoris*.

|| G. Gordon, *Robert Bridges* (1946), p. 14.

of how he had struggled to vindicate him against Herder's strictures:*

'Try as I might to take my favourite under my protection, saying that for a youthful imagination there could be nothing more delightful than to linger with gods and demigods in those gay and glorious surroundings and be a witness of their actions and their passions,...all that was not allowed to count: there was no genuine, first-hand truth to be found in these poems: here was neither Greece nor Italy, neither a primitive nor a civilised world, but mere imitation throughout of what already existed, such as one could expect only of an over-cultivated man. And when I finally tried to establish that whatever an outstanding individual produces is also 'Nature', and that among all peoples, old and new, it is always only the poet who has succeeded in being a poet, these facts were allowed to count for absolutely nothing in my favour, and I had to endure much, indeed I was nearly put off my Ovid by it.'

Again and again it is clear that the qualities in Ovid which appealed to these young poets were his fertility in invention, his power of conjuring up vivid pictures, his unphilosophic gusto, his preoccupation with love, and his knowledge of the human heart. They were also enchanted by the wild, free, romantic world he had imagined as background for his *Metamorphoses*, careless whether it was *Natur* or not. I would not suggest for a moment that we should put him back on his pedestal beside Virgil; indeed, I have tried to remain conscious throughout of the danger of overpraising through eagerness to redress the balance. It was absurd of Landor, reacting against his contemporaries, to say that Ovid's contest of Ajax and Ulysses is 'the most wonderful thing in the whole range of Latin poetry', and that it 'has more continued and unabated excellence than anything in Dante'.† But

---

* I, p. 50; cf. p. 167 (Sophien Ausgabe, Bd. 26).
† Works VII, p. 240; IX, p. 271.

has not the time come for the exile to have his case impartially reviewed, to plead at any rate to be brought nearer home—

non ut in Ausoniam redeam, nisi forsitan olim,

but at least

ut par delicto sit mihi poena suo?

Is it not possible that a poet who could say so much to Shakespeare, Milton and Goethe may still be able to say more than we have realized even to us?

LIST OF ABBREVIATIONS

A.A.	Ovid's *Ars Amatoria*.
Abh.	Abhandlungen.
A.J.P.	*American Journal of Philology*.
Am.	Ovid's *Amores*.
A.P.	*Anthologia Palatina*.
Ber.	Bericht.
C.H.E.L.	*Cambridge History of English Literature*.
C.I.L.	*Corpus Inscriptionum Latinarum*.
C.Q.	*Classical Quarterly*.
C.R.	*Classical Review*.
Cl. Phil.	*Classical Philology*.
F.	Ovid's *Fasti*.
G.L.	*Grammatici Latini*.
Her.	Ovid's *Heroides*.
Hum. Gym.	*Humanistisches Gymnasium*.
J.P.	*Journal of Philology*.
J.R.S.	*Journal of Roman Studies*.
M.	Ovid's *Metamorphoses*.
P.	Ovid's *Epistulae Ex Ponto*.
Ph. Qu.	*Philological Quarterly*.
P.L.	*Patrologia Latina*, ed. Migne.
P.M.L.A.	*Publications of the Modern Language Association of America*.
R.A.	Ovid's *Remedia Amoris*.
R.-E.	Pauly-Wissowa-Kroll, *Real-Encyclopädie*.
Rev. ét. lat.	*Revue des études latines*.
Rev. hist. rel.	*Revue de l'histoire des religions*.
Rh. Mus.	*Rheinisches Museum*.
S.P.	*Studies in Philology*.
St. It. Fil.	*Studi Italiani di Filologia Classica*.
T.A.P.A.	*Transactions of the American Philological Association*.
Tr.	Ovid's *Tristia*.
Wien. Stud.	*Wiener Studien*.

NOTE

Superior figures in the text refer the reader to the Appendix of References beginning on p. 445. An index of the passages quoted will be found on p. 471 and a list of modern works cited will be found on p. 463.

CHAPTER I

EARLY YEARS[1]

INTEGER ET LAETUS

F EW of the poets of Rome were natives of the city. They came from all over Italy—in later times, from all over the Empire. Inevitably, however, they gravitated to the capital, there to find the life and audience that suited them; only the shy, sensitive Virgil could keep away for long. But even when their name was made they did not forget the humbler town of their origin, Mantua or Verona or Venusia, proud to have added fresh laurels to it, and not ashamed to say so. And the towns in turn were proud of their sons.

Less than a hundred miles east of Rome, on the railway to Pescara, the Apennines enclose a small, undulating plain watered by many streams and graced with poplars:

> Here Sulmo lies amid Pelignian hills,
> Small, but for ever fresh with watering rills.
> Though sun draw near and soil begin to crack
> Under the Dogstar's merciless attack,
> Pelignian fields with trickling streams abound,
> And luscious herbage clothes the softened ground.
> Corn-crops are grown, and vines surpassing these,
> With here and there a patch of olive-trees,
> And where the brook glides softly through the reeds
> Thick tufts of grass cover the watermeads.*[2]

One is not surprised to find a Corso Ovidio among the streets of the modern Sulmona, and a renaissance statue of Ovid in the

---

* The unfailing water and greenness were what remained in Ovid's memory. He recalls them quite irrelevantly at *F.* IV, 686, for instance.

courtyard of the Palazzo del Convitto;* for who (save some prisoners in the last war) would ever have heard of Sulmona, *bel paese* though it is, or gone out of his way to visit it, if the poet had not been born there?

> Atque aliquis spectans hospes Sulmonis aquosi
> moenia, quae campi iugera pauca tenent,
> 'quae tantum', dicet, 'potuistis ferre poetam,
> quantulacunque estis, vos ego magna voco.'³

> *So shall the stranger, gazing on the walls*
> *That watch o'er Sulmo's plots and waterfalls,*
> *Cry, ' Thou that such a poet didst beget,*
> *Small though thou be, yet will I call thee great.'*

One detail may puzzle the uninitiated. At Rome the letters S.P.Q.R. appear on trams, public buildings, civic documents and so forth, and we know what they mean; but what is the meaning of the letters S.M.P.E. which we read everywhere here? The answer does credit both to the municipality and to its poet who boasted, 'Sulmo Mihi Patria Est'.†⁴

To most Greek authors it had not occurred that their readers might wish to know about themselves as well as about their message. If they became autobiographical, as Plato did in his *Seventh Letter* or Isocrates in his *Antidosis*, it was generally for some ulterior purpose. Roman *humanitas* knew no such reticence. It is true that Horace's accounts of his early life in *Satires* I, 6 and II, 6 are given to support an argument, but in the First Book of the *Epistles* he sometimes tells of himself because he assumes that the recipient of the letter, and the general public after him, will be interested; and at the end he gives a miniature self-portrait, much as a modern poet might supply his publisher with a photograph for

---

* Bindi, *Monumenti degli Abruzzi*, says that this statue is really of Marco Barbato, poet friend of Petrarch, who was born at Sulmona and died in 1362. But no matter; to the people of the place it is Ovid.

† This device, found on the cathedral apse, goes back at least to the thirteenth century.⁵

the frontispiece. The publication of Cicero's correspondence in all its mass of unsifted detail is evidence enough of a public interest in individuals as intense as ours today.

From time to time in the course of his works Ovid tells us this or that about his life. At *Amores* I, 3, 10, for instance, he mentions that both his parents find it necessary to economize, or to make him economize (it is not clear which); and he begins an account of a festival at Falerii, just as some modern journalist or broadcaster might do in order to add a touch of human interest, by saying that he only chanced to witness it because his wife comes from there.[6] In the nostalgia of exile he becomes still more reminiscent, and in *Tristia* IV, 10 he gives us an unusually detailed piece of autobiography.

Publius Ovidius Naso was born on March 10, 43 B.C., exactly a year after his brother.[7] The equestrian status of his family was of long standing, not recently acquired in the ups and downs of the civil wars like that of so many others.[8] The name Ovidius, common on inscriptions in that Pelignian neighbourhood but not found elsewhere, would attest his origin from that race even if he had not himself claimed to be its glory.[9] The sturdy Pelignians had been ringleaders in the Social War, when their town of Corfinium was selected as capital by the Confederates and renamed Italica. Ovid rejoiced in the free spirit in his race,

> Quam sua libertas ad honesta coegerat arma,
>   cum timuit socias anxia Roma manus.[10]

> *Whom love of freedom drove to righteous arms*
> *When Allied bands filled Rome with dire alarms.*

All this was long happily over. The Pelignians were proud of the Roman status they had fought to gain; and some recent forebear distinguished for his nose had earned for Ovid's family the Latin *cognomen* of Naso.

Ovid's father, without being rich, was reasonably well off. He sent his two sons to Rome, probably about 31 B.C., the year of the

Battle of Actium,[11] and put them under distinguished teachers—
insignes urbis ab arte viros. Let us see what kind of education they
were likely to have had.[12]

After learning, from the age of seven to eleven or twelve, to
read and write under an elementary schoolmaster (*litterator, ludi
magister*), the more favoured Roman boy proceeded to secondary
education. In theory, since the Roman system was simply the
Hellenistic transplanted, a boy's curriculum comprised the whole
ἐγκύκλιος παιδεία (*artes liberales*); but in practice the mathematics, music and the rest appear to have been very much subsidiary subjects, taken only by a few, and it was the *grammaticus*
who dominated the scene.*[13]

The *grammaticus* was a man such as the celebrated Orbilius, who
held the rod over Horace while he studied the old Latin version of
the *Odyssey* by Livius Andronicus. He taught formal grammar
on Greek lines, explained authors word by word, supplied mythological and historical background, commented on points of
literary or philosophical interest, and imparted a correct intonation
and delivery.[14] We may also assume with some confidence that
before a promising boy left his *grammaticus* he was at home in the
Greek language and literature. (When Cicero began to give
lessons in rhetoric to his son and nephew, he preferred Greek to
Latin as the medium of instruction.[15]) Finally, there were prescribed exercises on themes, which served as a prelude to the higher
courses in rhetoric.†[16]

The Romans did not make the mistake of having a fixed age for
passing from one school to another any more than for assuming
the gown of manhood, realizing that individual boys differ both
in their capacities and in their rate of development. We do not
know when Ovid, no doubt precocious, passed on from the

---

* The course proposed by Vitruvius (I, 1, 3) for budding architects, including
drawing, optics, history, philosophy, music, medicine, law and astronomy, sounds
utopian.

† Greek as an element of Roman education began in the days of Scipio the
Younger, reached its peak with Cicero, and then gradually declined with the
growth of Latin literature.

grammaticus to the *rhetor*. But we may now turn to examine the rhetorical schools of his day.

When Cicero was young, at the beginning of the first century, it was still the custom to put a promising boy in the hands of some distinguished statesman or speaker, whom he accompanied everywhere, thereby obtaining not only an apprenticeship in oratory but an invaluable introduction to public life. There were also, however, schools of rhetoric. Hitherto these had been run by Greeks in the Greek tongue, but about that time one Plotius Gallus first began to teach rhetoric in Latin.[17] Cicero's conservative mentors advised him to stick to Greek, as being a better training, apart from the consideration that the new school had an odour of radicalism;[18] but by the end of the Republic schools of Latin declamation were dominant.

After the establishment of the principate the Forum lost much of its importance as the centre of political as distinct from juridical life. More and more public work was undertaken by the Emperor's own staff of freedmen. Decisions were taken by the Emperor himself, or by influential civil servants, while the Senate and the Rostra became largely a façade. The intense controversies of the late Republic had no longer any place. Henceforward, in the well-known words of Messalla in Tacitus' *Dialogus de Oratoribus*,[19] 'the long quiet of the times, the continual calm of the people, the unbroken tranquillity of the senate, and in particular the discipline imposed by the Emperor, reduced eloquence itself, like everything else, to a state of peace'.

It was not merely that eloquence had now a diminished role in public life: its subjects were restricted to the uncontroversial, unobjectionable, and therefore academic. At the beginning of the first century the themes of the schools had included subjects of burning topical interest: 'Should Italians receive the rights of citizenship?' or 'Scipio Nasica is impeached for the murder of Tiberius Gracchus'.[20] But now the issues that occupied men's thoughts and hushed conversation, the really interesting topics, could not be handled at all in public. What rhetorician would have dared to announce such a subject as 'Caesar Octavian deliberates whether to institute proscriptions on his return from Alexandria', or 'Cornelius Gallus defends himself on a charge of treason'? No doubt the logical course would have been to admit that rhetoric had little future and to reform the educational system accordingly. But men do not readily appreciate fundamental changes of situation where most of the externals are unchanged; they tend rather to modify existing institutions and later, if pressed, to find new arguments in their favour. Thus when printing was invented, University lectures, which existed mainly because of the inadequate supply of manuscript books, lost much of their *raison d'être*. But there were the class-rooms and the lecturers, and a University without lectures was unthinkable; so the institution has continued to this day, while other grounds of justification have been emphasized or discovered.

Two kinds of exercise were practised in the schools and coteries of rhetoric, the *suasoria* and the *controversia*. A *suasoria* was a theme for soliloquy, generally of a historical nature, though historical facts could be treated as cavalierly as they are in a modern film,[21] especially where ancient Greek history was concerned. The elder Seneca has left us specimens of the treatment of seven such themes by Augustan rhetoricians of his youth. The two most interesting to us are, 'Cicero deliberates whether to beg Antony for mercy' (No. 6), and 'Cicero deliberates whether to burn his writings, Antony having promised him safety on that condition' (No. 7). Clearly these are subjects for impassioned declamation, not for serious argument: they 'expect the answer "no"'.

A *controversia* was the discussion of a complicated imaginary law-suit. The situations were bizarre, the details were vague, and the law given as a basis for the argument may occasionally have been either obsolete or Greek or factitious.* These features would suggest that approximation to the conditions of real life was not the primary concern of the exercise. For this it has been roundly

---

* The old idea, however, that the laws used were *mainly* factitious has been strongly contested recently by F. Lanfranchi,[22] and by Bonner.[23]

6

abused, both in ancient and modern times. Petronius' hero maintains that the unreal world of the schools unfits young men for practical life: they live in a world of 'pirates standing in chains on the beach, tyrants pen in hand ordering sons to cut off their fathers' heads, oracles in time of pestilence demanding the blood of three virgins or more, honey-balls of phrases, every word and act besprinkled with poppy-seed and sesame'.[24] Petronius himself was writing a picaresque novel, a form of literature which earlier ages had lacked; and, as Boissier suggested,[25] it was perhaps just because the Augustans were somewhat starved of romance in their literature that their rhetoric took on these romantic colours.*

There is much indeed to be said against the schools of declamation. Quite apart from any sensationalism in the subject-matter, pressing one side of a question for victory is not the best form of education for those who have not learnt 'to seek for truth in the company of friends'. But surely we have heard too often that argument about academic studies having no relation to 'real life', and the kind of person who uses it nowadays should be a warning against condemning the rhetoricians out of hand. If one is setting an essay question, one may rightly avoid choosing a topical subject which the pupil is likely to have seen or heard discussed; one wants to make him think for himself. We should therefore hesitate before we criticize Roman educators who thought that if you teach a boy to think for himself at all, he will be able to think straight about any given subject.† By keeping the details vague they gave more scope for variety and imagination; and by introducing pirates and tyrants they made the questions more exciting (what harm, if mind-training, not truth to life, were the object?); while the complications and coincidences were essential if the problem was to afford more than a simple and obvious line of treatment.

And after all, are we so different? Dip into recent Cambridge

---

* *Alitur enim atque enitescit velut pabulo laetiore facundia*—Quintilian.[26]
† *Instruit etiam quos non sibi exercet*—Seneca.[27]

examination papers and you may come across such a question as this:

'Hay, Wheat and Corn walk down the street on the way to the Cromwell Arms. Hay, while bending down to tie his shoe laces, is injured when the sign attached to the side of the public house unexpectedly collapses. Wheat endeavours to assist him, but is knocked unconscious by a barrel of beer which rolls out of an open doorway on the upper floor of the building. Corn hurries off to call Dr Barley, but falls into a bear-pit in the private drive of the doctor's surgery and breaks his arm.

Advise Hay, Wheat and Corn according to the principles of (*a*) Roman, (*b*) English law.'[28]

In some Latin countries the historical declamation continued to play a part in education almost up to the present century. M. Émile Ripert, who as Hannibal had spoken to his troops on the Alps and as Bossuet had directed the thoughts of the Dauphin, found the recollection of his training far from dull:

'Puéril et passionnant exercice ! Pour un instant nous échappions aux réalités scolaires et bourgeoises qui nous entouraient. Petits écoliers de rhétorique en quelque sous-préfecture, nous étions les maîtres du monde, les généraux vainqueurs, les poètes illustres: nous donnions des conseils, nous faisions des remontrances aux grands de la terre. Enivrement de la seizième année ! Notre enthousiasme livresque nous plaçait de plainpied avec ce que l'humanité a porté de plus glorieux.'[29]

The declamation was the ancient counterpart of our essay. It taught young men both how to arrange their thoughts in a logical and orderly manner and how to express them forcefully and with careful art, though it suffered from two not intrinsic faults, the prevailing bad taste and the Roman indifference to truth. In addition, it taught elocution and delivery in general, virtues in which we are apt to be miserably deficient. The Romans had more respect for their language than we have for ours; few people today express themselves so well on paper as the general run of Cicero's correspondents, let alone Cicero himself.

The *rhetor* whom Ovid admired most was a flamboyant Spaniard of highly individual talent, Marcus Porcius Latro. He borrowed from him ideas and epigrams for his poems, but finding his style unsuitable as a model for himself, he joined the class of the 'Asiatic' Arellius Fuscus, another of the four outstanding virtuosos of the day. Even as a student he was considered a good declaimer. It is not surprising to hear that he preferred the *suasoria*, which demanded chiefly imagination and the expression of emotions, to the *controversia*, which involved reasoning from a given law. 'His genius was for neatness, elegance and charm. Already at that time his style seemed nothing else than free verse.'[30]

If ever he did declaim a *controversia*, it was liable to be one with an ethical flavour; and it so happens that it is from his treatment of such a theme that Seneca gives us illustrative excerpts. This document[31] is so curious and so significant that I will quote from it at some length. The theme was as follows: 'A man and wife have sworn an oath together that if anything happens to either, the other will die. The husband, having gone abroad, has sent a messenger to the wife to say that he is dead. The wife has thrown herself down from a height; but her life has been saved, and she is being ordered by her father to leave her husband. She refuses, and is disowned.' It is easy to see how this subject might appeal to Ovid: the faithfulness of a woman to a man who has risked killing her to test her devotion is one of those paradoxes of love's psychology which fascinated him. Here are some relics of what he put into the husband's mouth, odd sentences that remained stored up in the prodigious memory (if we may believe him) of Seneca:

'My whole task consists in this, to get you to agree that a wife may love her husband and a husband may love his wife. It follows that, if you permit them to love, you must permit them to take such an oath. And what oath do you think we took? It was in your name that we swore: she invoked the wrath of her father, I of my father-in-law, in the event of our proving untrue. Father, have mercy. We did not break our oath.... In love you may more easily demand an end than a limit. Do you then expect to ensure that they keep to the limits you have approved, do nothing inconsiderately, promise nothing that they will not feel bound to perform, and weigh every word in the scales of reason and honour? That is how old men love.... You know, father, what our few transgressions were: we sometimes quarrelled and struck one another, and believe it or not, we sometimes broke our vows. What concern of a father are lovers' oaths? Why they do not even concern the gods.... You have no cause, my wife, to pride yourself, as though you were the first to sin thus: there have been wives who perished with their husband, and wives who perished for their husband; but every age will honour them, every genius celebrate them....'

There speaks the future author of the *Heroides*, albeit with the crudity and banality of a schoolboy. We have heard so much about the effect (assumed to be bad) of rhetoric on his poetry, that we ought to make sure what is meant by this.* Seneca tells us that Ovid was bored by argumentation,[32] and he says himself that, while his brother succeeded at the bar, his own bent was always for the Muses.[33] Among his contemporaries the rhetoricians counted him among the poets, and the poets among the rhetoricians.[34] He himself, writing from his exile to the rhetorician Cassius Salanus, finds a common element between them in ardour or intensity (*calor*):

> Distat opus nostrum, sed fontibus exit ab isdem,
>   artis et ingenuae cultor uterque sumus;
> thyrsus enim vobis, gestata est laurea nobis,
>   sed tamen ambobus debet inesse calor.
> utque meis numeris tua dat facundia nervos,
>   sic venit a nobis in tua verba nitor.
> iure igitur studio confinia carmina vestro
>   et commilitii sacra tuenda putas.† [35]

* Fränkel has some admirable remarks on this subject.[36]
† In line 3, which is corrupt, *vobis* and *nobis* should perhaps be interchanged.

Our works are twain, but from one fount they start;
We're each devoted to a liberal art.
You bear the thyrsus, branch of laurel we,
But ardour equally in both should be.
Your eloquence gives sinews to my line,
While my example makes your diction shine.
With justice then you kinship claim with song:
Allies are we, and bound by treaties strong.

We should never forget that Roman poetry was written primarily to be declaimed, not read. 'To compose poems when you have no one to read them to is like dancing in the dark', says Ovid in the loneliness of his exile:

> Excitat auditor studium, laudataque virtus
> crescit, et immensum gloria calcar habet.[37]

> *A listener fires you; merit thrives on praise:*
> *Fame is a mighty spur the spirit to raise.**

The rhetorical art claimed to teach both what to say (*inventio*) and how to say it (*elocutio*), figures of thought (σχήματα διανοίας) and figures of expression (σχήματα λέξεως). The rhetoricians had built it up by examining works or passages of literature which they admired, in order to find out why they were effective. The authors they studied included Homer and the early writers who lived long before rhetoric became a recognized art, and who, speaking from the heart and using ideas and words in the way they found most expressive, unconsciously provided material for generalizations about modes of thought and figures of speech. These the rhetoricians organized under headings and subheadings, in the orderly manner inherited from Aristotle.

The fourth book of the *Saturnalia* of Macrobius is devoted to illustrating these rules from the works of Virgil. Thus emotion (*pathos*) is subdivided into anger and pity (the former befitting the accuser and the latter the defender); in angry passages the

---

* I have adapted Milton's line because Ovid's may well have been in his mind.

beginnings must be abrupt, and all must consist of short sentences
with frequent changes in figures of speech, indicating a mind
fluctuating on a tide of indignation.*[38] Of course *ars rhetorica*
could not make a man a poet, any more than Aristotle's *Poetics*
could make a man a dramatist. But it is perfectly true that Virgil's
style is more 'rhetorical' than Homer's. The Augustans had
rhetoric in their bones. Nor is it by any means certain that Virgil
was not a better writer for this. At all events, it is a little unfair
that Ovid should so often be singled out as 'rhetorical' and therefore bad.† Fränkel's conclusion is most pertinent: 'Let us, then,
try to explain Ovid's poetry in terms of poetry rather than dump
upon it our grievances against the school rhetoric of his time.
After this is done, there will still be ample scope for scolding as
well as commending the poet. First of all, however, let us try to
understand Ovid as he wanted to be understood.'[39]

Whether the casuistical atmosphere of the rhetorical schools
had a bad effect on his character we cannot know; but we may
suspect that he would never in any case have been a Virgil, or
even a Horace. What he was, and what he has given us, is perhaps
the best that could ever have been hoped of him. At all events it
could never do anyone harm to be taught to arrange his thoughts
on a given subject, while an ability to make epigrams, unless it
becomes an obsession, does at least enliven social intercourse and
literary style.

Ovid tells us that from his earliest days he felt the urge to write
poetry, incurring from his father the censure that fathers reserve
for sons who lift their eyes from lower ambitions.[40] Whether
because of his own promise or through some other connexion,
he was drawn into the ambit of a great patron of literature, the
noble M. Valerius Messalla Corvinus, almost as soon (it appears)
as he reached Rome, when he was scarcely more than twelve years

---

* Scholia dealing with Virgil as an exponent of rhetorical principles were used
by Servius, and Claudius Donatus wrote a work on the subject.[41]

† For some good instances of figures in Ovid which can fairly be said to show
rhetorical influence, see Bonner.[42]

old.*[43] Messalla was then at the height of his prestige, having recently commanded the centre of Octavian's fleet, as consul, at the Battle of Actium. The poets under his patronage tended to be superior in birth to those who gathered round Maecenas, the knight who, as Horace tells us,[44] cared nothing for such distinctions. But there is no question of rivalry or ill-feeling between the two circles. Horace, whose charming hymn to a Wine-Jar (*Odes* III, 21) was written for Messalla, liked his protégé Tibullus, while finding Propertius, a fellow-member of Maecenas' circle, antipathetic. Ovid made friends with Propertius, but only began to know Messalla's Tibullus; and Maecenas himself composed a Symposium in which Virgil and Horace were given parts and Messalla made a speech in praise of wine.[45] It would seem that elegy was the popular verse-form in Messalla's circle, for besides Tibullus it contained Sulpicia and possibly Lygdamus, from whom we have poems preserved in Book III of 'Tibullus'.

It was not at school that Ovid was initiated into the latest mysteries of the Roman Muse, for the first Roman schoolmaster to comment on *recent* Latin poets was Quintus Caecilius Epirota, a freedman of Cicero's friend Atticus, who was intimate with the ill-fated poet Cornelius Gallus, and Suetonius tells us that he began to do this after Gallus' suicide,[46] which took place in 26 B.C. By that time Ovid would have got beyond the *grammaticus*. However, he would not lack contemporary stimulus, for during the first year or two after his arrival at Rome several events of great importance occurred in the world of poetry: Horace collected and published in book form the remainder of his satires and iambic pieces which he thought worth preserving and began to recite in the circle of his friends the earliest of the *Odes*; Virgil published his *Georgics*, and embarked on the *Aeneid*; and Propertius brought out the first book of his elegies. During the next few years Propertius published two more books of elegies, and Tibullus his two books; Horace published *Odes* I–III and *Epistles* I; and the *Aeneid* was

---

* Messalla's circle, which probably originated at Athens in the days before Philippi, is the subject of an article by Ullman.[47]

nearly completed. Few decades of literature can compare with the years 30–20 B.C. The fact that a poem had not yet been finally published did not mean that work in progress was unknown to other poets. Propertius had presumably heard portions of the *Aeneid* read when he proclaimed:

Cedite, Romani scriptores, cedite, Graii:
nescioquid maius nascitur Iliade.[48]

Yield, Roman, yield, Greek writers: something greater then the Iliad *is being born.*

In a famous passage Ovid recalls in exile his associations with the poets of that time.[49] Four he knew well, Aemilius Macer, Propertius, Ponticus and Bassus. Virgil, who rarely came to Rome, he had only seen, and whether the phrase

et tenuit nostras numerosus Horatius aures

means literally that he heard Horace recite or metaphorically that his ear was charmed by the *Odes,* we cannot determine. He laments that the early death of Tibullus in 19 B.C. prevented their friendship from ripening. This may seem surprising, given the time available, but during the preceding decade Messalla was absent from Rome for a large part of the time,[50] while there is no need to suppose that his circle was closely knit, and there is some evidence that Tibullus was liable to illness.[51] Moreover, Ovid himself went at some period—his early twenties would be the natural time—to study at Athens,[52] and he also completed the Grand Tour, spending the greater part of a year in Sicily and visiting the famous cities of Asia Minor in company with Pompeius Macer,[53] a poet of Greek antecedents to whom Augustus was later to entrust the organization of the imperial libraries. With what excitement must he have contemplated the scenes of the many legends he was later to recount so vividly! Like Catullus, he visited the site of Troy,[54] and like him also had the great grief of losing his beloved brother, who died at the age of twenty.[55]

Meanwhile he acquired a wide knowledge of both Greek and Roman poetry. So long as books were in papyrus rolls, it was laborious to look up a passage, the left hand rewinding as the right unwound. Even after the place was found, the entire process had to be repeated backwards. Consequently people relied on their memories, and though they might not always remember or quote accurately,* the amount they kept in their head seems to have been remarkable. Ovid's literary allusions range so widely within short poems or passages that we may infer that he was drawing on a well-stocked memory.

Messalla, as Ovid himself tells us,[56] encouraged his early poetic efforts. Already his 'Corinna' was the talk of the town by the time he first gave his public recitation, presumably of early pieces destined to form part of the *Amores*.[57] He tried to tell us exactly when this was by saying that he had then had his beard cut only once or twice. Unfortunately, scholars do not agree as to the interpretation of this, but Wheeler may well be right in thinking he would still be in his teens.[58]

He was originally destined for a public career, and as an earnest of this assumed the *laticlave*, the broad-striped tunic.†[59] Indeed, he held some judicial offices (creditably, he claimed), being at one time a *tresvir* of some sort,‡ and a *decemvir stlitibus iudicandis*, i.e. a member of a board who presided over the centumviral courts, besides acting sometimes as arbitrator.[60] But he soon abandoned his *laticlave*, and with it any ambition for a public career (which in any case was losing substance under the principate), preferring to live at ease and write, dividing his time between Rome and his garden villa on the pine-clad slopes between the Clodian and Flaminian Ways.§[61] Henceforward he adopted in real life, possibly under the influence of his friend Propertius, what had

---

* There are three points in *Her*. 1 (Penelope to Ulysses) which seem to indicate that Ovid was relying on a slightly inaccurate memory of the *Odyssey*. At *R.A.* 783–4, he attributes to Agamemnon Achilles' oath by the sceptre (*Il*. 1, 234).

† It was worn by sons of Senators and Knights who aspired to be candidates for office.　　　　　　　　　　　　　　　‡ Either *capitalis* or *monetalis*.

§ He says he did some gardening himself.[62]

become the traditional attitude of the elegist, a polite respect for the successful man of action combined with a firm refusal to have anything to do with action himself. Even the polite respect tended to shade into agreement to differ, and from that into open contempt. Not attached to Maecenas, he never really became, what Virgil, Horace and Propertius became in turn sooner or later, an Augustan.

When he was scarcely grown up he had been given a wife (presumably by his father), but she was 'neither worthy nor useful' (*nec digna nec utilis*) and the union did not last for long. His second wife 'had nothing against her' (*sine crimine*). She was probably the mother of the poet's only child, a daughter; but again the union was destined, for whatever reason, to be short-lived.[63] And here we may leave his life for a while and turn to his poetry.

CHAPTER II

LATIN EROTIC ELEGY

HIS COMES UMBRA TUA EST

To give a full account of Latin erotic elegy would be beyond the scope of this book; but something must be said about its traditions, and then about the nature of the love affairs it purports to reflect.

It used to be assumed that that 'subjective' love-elegy in which a poet told of his own experience was an invention of the Greeks. Had not Propertius claimed to be a disciple of Callimachus and Philetas?[1] The loss of the great bulk of Greek elegy, an important genre especially in Hellenistic times, made it difficult to check the assumption, which in itself was natural enough; but in the last half-century it has been generally abandoned.* Nevertheless, the Alexandrians did write ostensibly subjective *love-epigrams*, as Plato had done, and by the end of the second century B.C. these were being adapted in fumbling Latin by aristocratic amateurs at Rome.† Half a century later we find Catullus writing in elegiac verse which, though technically not much superior to theirs (at least as regards the pentameter), is often highly effective because he was a true poet venting his own experience. Most of his poems in this metre (65–116) are short enough to be classed as epigrams, but some can only be called elegies.‡[2] Propertius names Catullus, followed by Calvus, Varro of Atax and Gallus, as his predecessors in Roman elegy; and two at least of Catullus' poems, 68 (*Quod mihi fortuna*) and 76 (*Siqua recordanti*), give him as good a claim as

---

* There is, however, an element of love in some of the personal elegies attributed to Theognis; and some doubt must remain while we have so little of Philetas, who was described as 'singing of swift Bittis' by Hermesianax.[3]

† Catulus, Aedituus, Porcius Licinus.[4]

‡ His friend Calvus wrote at least one elegy, on Quintilia.

any known poet to be called the inventor of subjective love-elegy. He was not, however, ranked with the elegists in later years, no doubt because he was better known for his lyrics. Some fifteen years after him, about the time of the Battle of Philippi, Cornelius Gallus wrote four books of erotic elegies to 'Lycoris' (the celebrated stage artiste Cytheris). Of these only one colourless pentameter survives; but by a curious chance we possess a handbook of stories in prose about legendary lovers dedicated to Gallus by the Greek poet Parthenius for use in his epic and elegiac verse. The interest of the elegiac poets in such love-stories is most marked. At the end of his epyllion on the *Marriage of Peleus and Thetis**5 Catullus laments that 'the world is too much with us', human nature is degenerate and gods and heroes no longer walk the earth. To him, and to the sensitive poets who followed him, the imaginary world of Greek mythology became a refuge from the corruption and banality of modern life. In his Allius elegy[6] Catullus compared with his divine Lesbia, 'mea candida diva', the heroine Laodameia, and so inaugurated one of the chief features of Roman elegy, the parallel from Greek legend (παραδεῖγμα or *exemplum*).†7 Turn to Propertius and begin the opening elegy: the first eight lines state the theme, his constant devotion to Cynthia, the next eight give the parallel, the story of Milanion's devotion to Atalanta.

Throughout his work Propertius constantly used this device, and Ovid, without being so much obsessed with it, followed suit. To us it is apt to seem a tiresome substitute for thinking of something to say: we may find it hard to recapture the romantic aura, to feel the thrill that a Roman elegist may have felt in comparing his present situation with that of fabled heroes half-divine. Yet even in our own poetry it occurs, sometimes most effectively, as in Dryden's elegy to the memory of Mr Oldham:

> To the same goal did both our studies drive;
> The last set out, the soonest did arrive.

---

* For the nature of epyllia see pp. 144–7.

† As a feature of poetry it goes back at least as far as the Theognidean Corpus.[8]

> Thus Nisus fell upon the slippery place,
> Whilst his young friend perform'd, and won the race.

Here the reminiscence of the *Aeneid* prepares the reader's mind for the intensely moving allusions to Roman poetry in the concluding lines:

> Once more, hail, and farewell; farewell, thou young,
> But ah too short, Marcellus of our tongue!
> Thy brows with ivy, and with laurels bound;
> But fate and gloomy night encompass thee around.

Catullus in his Lesbia poems had generally written straight from the heart, but all the other Roman elegists made frequent use of traditional motives. As to the sources there has been much controversy.*[9] As regards Ovid, coming as he did after Gallus, Propertius, and Tibullus had established the genre, this question is of secondary significance.

Source-hunting has occupied a great deal of scholars' time, and it is important to be clear about the extent of its usefulness. The fact that a poet can be shown to have taken much from others, consciously or unconsciously, need have little bearing on his originality. This has been illustrated most clearly by J. L. Lowes in his celebrated examination of Coleridge's *Ancient Mariner* and *Kubla Khan* entitled *The Road to Xanadu*. Classical poets had no idea of copyright. They prided themselves not on originality of thought, but on originality of treatment and on perfection of form. Brandt remarked of Ovid: 'There is no motive of any importance in the *Amores* to which one cannot point out a literary predecessor.'[10] But the knowledge that some detail is traditional can sometimes save us from falsely taking it as autobiographical evidence; and Ovid will sometimes echo his predecessors with

---

* It is agreed that Menander and the New Comedy are the ultimate source of many motives, though some are older, but it is disputed to what extent the lost Hellenistic elegy and Roman comedy acted as a clearing-house. The epigrams of Meleager's *Garland* and those of Philodemus may be further sources, and also the commonplaces of the rhetoricians and mythological handbooks.

obvious intent to recall the associations of their poems, or in a spirit of contrast or burlesque. But when all is said, most of Ovid's poems can and should be read simply for themselves, regardless of their debt to tradition.

Two examples will suffice, one to show how hard-worked a motive could be, the other to show how many traditional motives could be woven into a single poem. In the famous love-story of Acontius and Cydippe told by Callimachus in his *Aetia* the love-sick youth withdraws to the lonely forest and carves on the bark of the trees 'Cydippe is beautiful':

ἀλλ' ἐνὶ δὴ φλοιοῖσι κεκόμμενα τόσσα φέροιτε
γράμματα, Κυδίππην ὄσσ' ἐρέουσι καλήν.[11]

But may you bear letters cut in your bark enough to tell that Cydippe is beautiful.

This motive was probably already a feature of popular pastoral poetry. It reappears in Virgil's *Eclogue* x, with a rhetorical conceit added at the end: as the letters will grow, so will the lover's passion:

Certum est in silvis, inter spelaea ferarum,
malle pati tenerisque meos incidere amores
arboribus: crescent illae, crescetis, amores.

I am resolved that it is better in the woods, amid wild beasts' dens, to suffer and carve my love on the saplings: they will grow, and thou wilt grow, my love.

Who is the lover here? There is little doubt that it is the poet Cornelius Gallus himself. For it has been urged with considerable plausibility that this poem in his honour contains a number of reminiscences from his own works.[12] Propertius took up the theme (I, 18, 21):

A quotiens teneras resonant mea verba sub umbras,
scribitur et vestris Cynthia corticibus!

Ah, how often my words echo under your shades, and 'Cynthia' is written on your bark!

And what should Ovid's Paris do, in love with Oenone in the vales of Ida? Inevitably he carved in the bark of a young poplar on the bank of the Xanthus lines which could later be used in evidence against him (*Her.* v, 29–30):

> Cum Paris Oenone poterit spirare relicta
> ad fontem Xanthi versa recurret aqua.

> *Should Paris leave Oenone and not die,*
> *Back to their source shall Xanthus' waters hie.*

Moreover, this very formula, the σχῆμα ἐκ τοῦ ἀδυνάτου or oath of constancy until all nature goes awry, occurs in endless forms throughout ancient literature, a famous chorus in Euripides giving especial currency to the flowing back of rivers.*[13]

And now let us take a single, quite typical, poem from the *Amores*, II, II, and observe its antecedents. It is a *propempticon*, or 'send-off', a familiar type of which we have previous examples from Erinna (fr. 1), Theocritus (VII, 52–89), Propertius (I, 8 a) and Horace (*Epode* I).† Here is the opening:

> Prima malas docuit, mirantibus aequoris undis,
>   *Peliaco pinus vertice* caesa vias,
> quae concurrentes inter temeraria cautes
>   conspicuam fulvo vellere vexit ovem.
> o utinam, nequis remo freta longa moveret,
>   Argo funestas pressa bibisset aquas!

> *It was the pine felled on Pelion's summit that first taught*
> *men evil voyages, to the wonder of the waves, which*
> *hardily between the clashing rocks bore the shining fleece*
> *of gold. Ah, would that Argo had been drowned deep in*
> *waters of doom, that no one more should vex the ex-*
> *panse of sea with oars!*

---

* ἄνω ποταμῶν ἱερῶν χωροῦσι παγαί.

† *Epode* x is a burlesque *anti-propempticon* for Maevius. *Odes* I, 3 and III, 27 may also be anterior to Ovid's poem. Cinna wrote a *propempticon* for Pollio.

The first couplet has an echo of the opening of Catullus' *Peleus and Thetis* (64),

> *Peliaco* quondam prognatae *vertice pinus,*

the second gives one incident from the saga of the Argonauts, recounted by Apollonius Rhodius (IV, 922 ff.) and lately in Latin by Varro of Atax, and the third recalls the famous opening of Euripides' *Medea*. Corinna, like Cynthia in Propertius I, 8, is going on a sea-voyage. She will have to face the traditional perils, Scylla and Charybdis, the Syrtes, and the ill-famed Acroceraunian cliffs which Horace feared for Virgil in his *propempticon*, *Odes* I, 3. Line 34,

> aequa tamen puppi sit Galatea tuae,
>
> *yet may Galatea be kindly to your ship*

is a reminiscence of Propertius (l. 18),

> sit Galatea tuae non aliena viae,

and line 35,

> vestrum crimen erit talis iactura puellae,
>
> *the loss of such a girl will be your crime*

may be a reminiscence of Propertius II, 28, 2:

> tam formosa tuum mortua crimen erit.

As Propertius stands on the shore to deplore Cynthia's departure (15–16), so Ovid stands to welcome Corinna's return (43 ff.); and he ends with the couplet

> Haec mihi quamprimum caelo nitidissimus alto
>   Lucifer admisso tempora *portet equo,*
>
> *These times may Lucifer, brightest in high heaven, bring me apace with horse unreined,*

a clear echo of the final couplet of Tibullus' *propempticon* for Messalla,

> Hoc precor, hunc illum nobis Aurora nitentem
>   *Luciferum* roseis candida *portet equis.*[14]

Most of these parallels are pointed out in the commentaries. A more industrious search, or the rediscovery of lost works of earlier poets, might reveal further influences. There is also the likelihood that the Suasoria *An navigandum* (Should one go to sea?) contributed ideas. Yet the poem remains essentially Ovid's from the notorious line 10,

> et gelidum Borean egelidumque Notum,

(which his friends, according to the anecdote,[15] unanimously wished away, while he impenitently clung to it) to the lovely line 15,

> litora marmoreis pedibus signate, puellae,
>
> *maidens, with marble feet the shore imprint,*

delightful alike to the inward ear and eye. How exquisite too is the preceding couplet,

> Nec medius tenues conchas pictosque lapillos
> pontus habet: bibuli litoris illa mora est.
>
> *No pebbles gay, no shells mid-ocean has,*
> *Charms that on drying sands detain our gaze.*

That eye for beautiful things is essentially Ovidian. No less characteristic is the couplet 31-2,

> Tutius est fovisse torum, legisse libellos,
> Threïciam digitis increpuisse lyram,
>
> *Safer to read a book, all snug in bed,*
> *To run your fingers o'er a lyre instead,*

which he liked so much that he repeated it almost word for word at *Heroides* III, 117.

* * *

The ancients did not set the object of their love on a pedestal: the 'ever-feminine' did not draw them upwards. The attitude of medieval chivalry, still not without its effect today, would have been incomprehensible to them, let alone the attitude of Dante to Beatrice. The idealism of Plato's Academy remained unique, aside from the main stream of literature, and probably also of life. In Homer, indeed, love is much as we know it today. Odysseus, though he has no hesitation in yielding to the divine charms of a Calypso or a Circe when war has kept him ten years and more from home, is fundamentally faithful to his wife Penelope. Andromache and Hector behave in the face of war like any devoted married couple today. And Nausicaa, falling in love with Odysseus at first sight, wishes he might be her husband. But when we emerge from the Dorian Invasions and the Dark Age we find a curious change. Whatever feelings husbands and wives may then have had for one another, love as expressed in poetry has become homosexual. The passion of Alcaeus, Anacreon, Ibycus, Solon, Theognis and Pindar was largely for boys, as Sappho's was for girls, and the inscriptions on vases of the period tell the same story. This new orientation was of Dorian origin. The gymnasium became the centre of erotic life.

In the Athens of Pericles a wife's place, as he himself reminded her in Thucydides, was in the home: outside the home, to provide men with stimulating companionship, there were cultivated *hetaerae* like the beautiful Laïs or the clever Aspasia. Moral criticism of homosexuality at Athens began in this period;[16] here, though not in Dorian states like Sparta and Thebes, the affairs which we find taken for granted in the Socratic literature were fashionable only in upper class or 'advanced' circles, to judge from the reactions Aristophanes and the Attic Orators expected from their audience of average citizens. The result was sublimation in the case of Socrates himself, suppression in the general run.

The fourth century was the golden age of the *hetaerae*, whom the ever-popular New Comedy introduced as characters into literature; but in the third, when the literary centre of gravity shifted to the eastern Mediterranean, the love of boys emerged again, in the Ionic-Alexandrian epigram and lyric, and in the idylls of Theocritus. It was these last two phases that set the tone for the Greco-Roman world. There was little thought of Platonic sublimation: most ancients would have agreed with Donne:

> Whoever loves, if he do not propose
> The right true end of love, he's one that goes
> To sea for nothing but to make him sick.

Hetaerae could not be expected to remain constant, and boys could not to be expected to bloom for long. And yet there may often have been in these affairs something which it would be fairer to call love than merely lust.

At Rome things were somewhat different. Paederasty, though it remained a fit subject for literature, was considered by many to be no fit mode of behaviour. It is noteworthy that, whereas Propertius and Tibullus, not to mention Virgil and Horace, dealt on occasion with the love of boys, Ovid not only omitted it altogether, but went out of his way once to deprecate it, for the sympathetic reason that the parties do not derive equal enjoyment.*[17] Moreover, wives at Rome did not lead a cloistered existence: they played much the same part in society as they do today, and it followed that they might become the subject of love-poetry. Catullus' Lesbia was a consul's wife. Nevertheless, the cultivated, or at least accomplished, *hetaerae*, usually Greek freedwomen, were not displaced, though a Cicero might feel obliged (not very seriously) to explain how he came to be at table with Cytheris,[18] the mistress successively of Volumnius and Mark Antony, whom Virgil's friend Gallus was later to celebrate in his elegies under the name of Lycoris. To this class belonged also the Cynthia-Hostia of Propertius, the Delia-Plania and the Nemesis of Tibullus, and the various mistresses, whether real or fictitious, of Horace. As such too is Ovid's Corinna envisaged.

In their treatment of old material the three Roman elegists were as individual as the three Attic tragedians were in their treatment

---

* The tone of his references to effeminate men tends to be hostile, as one would expect from such a sympathizer with women; e.g. *A.A.* I, 524:

> et si quis male vir quaerit habere virum.

of the Electra story. Propertius gave his elegy a romantic, Tibullus an idyllic, Ovid a realistic and humorous colouring. Through the veil of conventional matter the differences in their temperament make themselves apparent. Propertius was an aesthete—passionate, neurotic, imaginative, intense, sometimes morbid and abject, sometimes triumphant, occasionally noble and even tragic. Tibullus was a milder spirit—refined, fastidious, hypochondriac, sentimental, not without wit and humour, in his less plaintive moods as fitting a friend for Horace as Propertius was not. But Ovid is no more passionate, romantic or sentimental than Chaucer. However much he may affect to be the victim of the erotic situations he depicts, we feel, and are surely meant to feel, that he is really, like the Horace of the *Odes*, a detached observer of the tragi-comedy of sex, a witty connoisseur, no doubt experienced himself, but steeped in the literature of his subject. As such he came before the world in his first poems, the *Amores*, which are more often intended to entertain us by their art and wit than to move us as a record of personal experience.

CHAPTER III

THE ELEGIAC COUPLET

BLANDA ELEGEIA

IN order to explain how Ovid's favourite metre came to be
what it is, a short but somewhat technical exposition is
necessary.*

When Ennius, in the second century B.C., introduced the hexameter from Greek into Latin, his ear forbade him simply to copy
Greek practice. His surviving verses show two very marked
metrical tendencies which were new, and it seems that both were
due to the fact that Latin had a stress accent which cut across the
beat of the quantitative metre. In the first place no less than
80 per cent have a caesura in the middle of the third foot, as in

Mūsāē | quāē pĕdĭ|būs ‖ māg|nūm pūl|sātĭs Ŏ|lȳmpŭm;

and of the remainder over 80 per cent have a caesura in the middle
of both the second and fourth foot, as in

pōstīl|lā, ‖ gēr|mānă sŏ|rōr, ‖ ēr|rārĕ vĭ|dēbăr.

The effect of these caesuras is that in the first four feet of the line
taken together the stress accent tends to conflict rather than
coincide with the metrical beat (*ictus*).† And in the second place
there is reason to believe that the preference he shows for ending
with a word of either two or three syllables exceeds what is
natural in proportion to the existing number of such words. The

---

* In what follows (pp. 27–9) I have drawn freely on my article on 'The
Augustan Rules for Dactylic Verse', *C.Q.* 1940, pp. 30–43. To save footnotes the
reader is asked to refer to this for amplification of the figures and conclusions
quoted. For further analysis see E. Sturtevant, *T.A.P.A.* 1923, pp. 51–73, and
1924, pp. 73–85.

† Or more strictly, *expectation* of beat.[1]

effect of this is to make stress accent and metrical beat coincide in the last two feet. If ' ' ' may symbolize accent where ictus coincides, and 'x' accent where it conflicts, we get this result (*quae* having no accent):

Músae | quae pĕdi|bus || măg|num pul|sátis O|lýmpum;
postĭl|la || ger|mána sŏ|ror, || er|ráre vi|débar.

By the next century we find that these tendencies have become rules in the hexameters of Cicero and Catullus. The Romans, as Bentley insisted,* must have read poetry naturally according to stress-accent of their daily speech, just as we read English poetry; fortunately, for without what Ritschl† called the 'harmonious disharmony' of ictus and accent it would be very monotonous, whereas the varied interplay of these is delightful. But they seem to have felt that if ictus and accent did not coincide at the end of the line, the ear would lose the metre altogether; so they made rules of what Ennius had instinctively felt, and ensured interplay in the first four feet and harmony in the last two.

But what about the pentameter? This proved less tractable. The earliest Greek pentameters already had a fixed caesura in the middle; the difficulty was to get coincidence of ictus and accent in the latter half; and in fact it could only be completely secured if the last word were a monosyllable. This seems to have been felt to be intolerable‡—too much of a bump, perhaps—and in any case it could only have been an occasional remedy. So Catullus apparently resigned himself to the risk that the reader's ear might lose the metre at the end of each couplet. It was much that so spontaneous a poet still had freedom to end it with a word of any number of syllables; and only 38 per cent of his pentameters end with a dissyllable.

Propertius, writing a generation later and some years after Gallus, begins his First Book (29–28 B.C.) with three couplets in

---

* 'Schediasma' prefixed to his edition of Terence, p. xvii.

† Ritschl, following some hints of Hermann, first formulated the theory here outlined.

‡ Instances are very rare.[2]

which there is still no attempt at coincidence of ictus and accent
in the second half of the pentameter:

> contactum nullis ‖ ánte cŭpidĭnibus.
> et caput impositis ‖ préssit Ãmor pĕdibus.
> improbus, et nullo ‖ vívere consĭlio.

But 64 per cent of the pentameters in this book end with a dissyllable, a marked increase over Catullus' figure. The reason seems
to be this. The impulse to bring out the metre at the end of the
line was so strong, that he felt that to end with a dissyllable, which
ensured a normal proportion of two coincidences to one conflict,
was a gain, despite the restriction in freedom of choosing words:

> cum tamen adversos ‖ cógor habére dĕos.
> et facite illa meo ‖ pálleat óre măgis.[3]

Indeed, once the effect had been demonstrated by Propertius'
use of the dissyllabic ending in the majority of cases in this book,
Roman poets seem to have become convinced that the metrical
advantage outweighed the severe disadvantage in loss of freedom;
and whatever view we take of the desirability of imposing this
restriction on young English composers (a restriction the more
galling because, being generally unexplained, it seems grossly
arbitrary), we must assume that artists of the calibre of Propertius,
Tibullus and Ovid knew their business.* The odium has fallen
upon Ovid, and who knows how many schoolboy composers have
taken a dislike to him for this rather than for the individual
qualities of his poetry? Yet Tibullus' First Book, published while
Ovid was still at school (c. 26 B.C.), has a dissyllable at the end of
93 per cent of its pentameters; while in Propertius III (c. 22 B.C.)
the percentage is 97·6, and in IV (? 16 B.C.) it is 99.† In fact, this
had become practically a rule by the time Ovid began to write;
he was merely following current practice.

---

* There has been too much tendency to exclaim with W. Meyer, 'Wer möchte
behaupten dass diese Regel nicht thöricht war?'

† Figures for Propertius in M. Platnauer, *Latin Elegiac Verse* (1951), p. 17. For
polysyllabic endings in Ovid's later works see p. 85 n.

The adoption of this rule had an indirect but far-reaching effect on the nature of Latin elegiac poetry—else I should not have inflicted this technical explanation on the reader.* Catullus wrote elegiacs like those of the Greeks, in which the sense often ran on from couplet to couplet. Here is an instance covering six couplets (LXVIII, 105–16):

> Quo tibi tum casu, pulcherrima Laodameia,
>   ereptum est vita dulcius atque anima
> coniugium? tanto te absorbens vertice amoris
>   aestus in abruptum detulerat barathrum
> quale ferunt Graii Pheneum prope Cylleneum
>   siccare emulsa pingue palude solum,
> quod quondam caesis montis fodisse medullis
>   audit falsiparens Amphitryoniades,
> tempore quo certa Stymphalia monstra sagitta
>   perculit imperio deterioris eri,
> pluribus ut caeli tereretur ianua divis
>   Hebe nec longa virginitate foret.

As far as treatment goes, that might just as well have been written in hexameters. But turn to Tibullus and we find that almost all his couplets are self-contained; a complete change has come over Latin elegy. Here is a specimen (II, 1, 37–46):

> Rura cano rurisque deos. his vita magistris
>   desuevit querna pellere glande famem;
> illi compositis primum docuere tigillis
>   exiguam viridi fronde operire domum;
> illi etiam tauros primi docuisse feruntur
>   servitium, et plaustro supposuisse rotam.
> tum victus abiere ferae, tum consita pomus,
>   tum bibit irriguas fertilis hortus aquas;
> aurea tum pressos pedibus dedit uva liquores,
>   mixtaque securo est sobria lympha mero.

* The next two paragraphs are taken from my article in C.Q. 1940, pp. 40–1.

What had happened may best be explained and illustrated by a comparison with the English heroic couplet. The new rule which ensured that the metre should be supported by the stress in the second half of the pentameter marked off the couplets rhythmically from one another and gave the verse a more regular flow and ebb. The parallel development in English poetry is well described by Lytton Strachey in his Leslie Stephen Lecture on Pope (1925):

'It was not until the collapse of blank verse, about 1630, that the essential characteristics which lay concealed in the couplet began to be exploited. It was Waller who first fully apprehended the implications of regularity; and it is to this fact that his immense reputation during the succeeding hundred years was due. Waller disengaged the heroic couplet from the beautiful vagueness of Elizabethanism. He perceived what logically followed from a rhyme. He saw that regularity implied balance, and that balance implied antithesis; he saw that balance also implied simplicity, that simplicity implied clarity, and that clarity implied exactitude. The result was a poetic medium contrary in every particular to blank verse—a form which, instead of being varied, unsymmetrical, fluid, complex, profound and indefinite, was regular, balanced, antithetical, simple, clear and exact.'[4]

How well these last words describe the elegy of Tibullus as contrasted with the hexameters of Virgil! The regularization of the second half of the pentameter had much the same effect as rhyme; the couplet became an artistic unit. Catullus had used no tricks of style, not even anaphora.* Tibullus was the Waller of the Latin elegy; he paved the way for Ovid, its Pope. Elegiacs now become affected by the new rhetoric, with its short sentences of parallel, antithetical members. Pentameter restates hexameter; the roughness of elision is almost gone; assonance and alliteration tune the verse. Listen to the play of sounds in this:

> Ne tibi neglecti mittant mala somnia Manes,
> maestaque sopitae stet soror ante torum.[5]

* For anaphora see p. 36.

The couplet has become a plaything, fascinating in itself, liable to become an end in itself; *loci communes* tend to supply the place of thought and feeling. It has been well said that Tibullus was more a musical composer than a poet.[6]

Ovid absorbed the stock-in-trade of his predecessors; but whereas Tibullus tended to insipidity and Propertius to outbursts of temperament, his wit, always in control, gave individuality to his style. Lytton Strachey, in the same lecture, maintained that Pope's heroic couplet was itself his 'criticism of life'; and to some extent the same may be said of Ovid's elegiac couplet, at any rate in his erotic elegies. Its intricate subtleties and surprises reflect the paradoxes and complications of love's psychology. Let us take, for example, *Amores* III, 11 *b*, Ovid's rhetorical expansion of Catullus' *Odi et amo*:[7]

> Luctantur pectusque leve in contraria tendunt
>   hac amor hac odium, sed, puto, vincit amor.
> odero, si potero; si non, invitus amabo.*
>   nec iuga taurus amat; quae tamen odit, habet.
> nequitiam fugio—fugientem forma reducit;
>   aversor morum crimina—corpus amo.
> sic ego nec sine te nec tecum vivere possum,
>   et videor voti nescius esse mei.
> aut formosa fores minus, aut minus improba, vellem;
>   non facit ad mores tam bona forma malos.
> facta merent odium, facies exorat amorem—
>   me miserum, vitiis plus valet illa suis!
> parce, per o lecti socialia iura, per omnes
>   qui dant fallendos se tibi saepe deos,
> perque tuam faciem, magni mihi numinis instar,
>   perque tuos oculos qui rapuere meos!
> quicquid eris, mea semper eris; tu selige tantum,
>   me quoque velle velis, anne coactus amem!
> lintea dem potius ventisque ferentibus utar,
>   ut quam, si nolim, cogar amare, velim.†

> * This line was found scratched on a wall in Pompeii.[8]
> † Munari's text here is as emended by Madvig.

A tug-of-war distracts my wavering breast,
Love versus hate: methinks love comes off best.
If hate I cannot, grudging I will love:
Ox bears the yoke he hates but cannot move.
I flee from sin—I look, and flee no more:
Your ways I shun—your body I adore;
Nor with you nor without you can I live,
And scarcely know for what my prayers should strive.
Would you less lovely or less vicious were!
Fair form belies so foul a character.
When I should hate, your looks implore my love;
Alas that looks should then the stronger prove!
O spare me, by our bed's confederate ties,
By all the gods that tolerate your lies,
By your fair face, to me a power divine,
And by your own eyes which have ravished mine,
Whate'er you be, I'm yours! But would you have
Me love you, choose, a volunteer or slave?
Nay rather, with the wind I'll trim my course,
And will to love whom else I'd love perforce.

The fascination of elegiacs is hard to define. There are times when we seem to hear them 'like Ocean on a western beach': every successive billow gathers in the first four feet of the hexameter, curls over in the dactylic fifth and breaks on the final spondee, to ebb again with the backwash of the pentameter.* On another occasion we may conceive of them as horses, trotting, cantering, galloping or weaving intricate patterns like those in the time-honoured Troy game of the mounted Roman boys described by Virgil in the Fifth *Aeneid* (580–7):

> Olli discurrere pares atque agmine terni
> diductis solvere choris, rursusque vocati
> convertere vias infestaque tela tulere.
> inde alios ineunt cursus aliosque recursus

---

* In this respect its movement is analogous to, though more rapid than, that of Horace's Alcaic stanza.

adversi spatiis, alternosque orbibus orbes
impediunt pugnaeque cient simulacra sub armis;
et nunc terga fuga nudant, nunc spicula vertunt
infensi, facta pariter nunc pace feruntur.*

*They gallop apart in pairs, and open their files three and three
in deploying bands, and again at the call wheel about and bear
down with levelled arms. Next they enter on other charges and
other retreats in opposite spaces, and interlink circle with
circle, and wage the armed phantom of battle. And now they
discover their backs in flight, now turn their lances to the
charge, now plight peace and gallop side by side.*

(Tr. J. W. Mackail.)

Turn to another poem and we may find still lighter verses, tripping
like dancers who now advance boldly, now gracefully retire again;
or we may see with the mind's eye of Schiller,† as reproduced by
Tennyson:

In the hexameter rises the fountain's silvery column,
In the pentameter aye falling in melody back.

As a sequence of rise and fall it was felt by Ovid himself:

Sex mihi *surgat* opus numeris, in quinque *residat*.⁹

Let my work rise in six feet and sink back in five.

Perhaps no other verse-form generates of its own mere motion so
haunting a melody. For a while it can be sheer delight. The fatal
thing is for it to go on too long; for then it becomes as cloying as
the later stages of the dance 'Sir Roger de Coverley' when there
are too many couples on the floor.

Some particular rhythms have an abstract charm of their own.
I have always liked the pentameter in which the second word is

---

* That Virgil himself felt an analogy between writing his verse and driving
a team of horses is clear from *Geor.* II, 541–2.

† Im Hexameter steigt des Springquells flüssige Säule,
   Im Pentameter drauf fallt sie melodisch herab.

(Also rendered into English by Coleridge.)

of the form ∪ – – – and the third – ∪∪ – ∪, coiling itself up slowly in the first half to uncoil smoothly and rapidly in the second; as in

> venit inornatas dilaniata comas.[10]
> fertur inadsueta subsecuisse manu.[11]
> vecta peregrinis Hippodamia rotis.[12]
> sumque repentinas eiaculatus aquas.[13]

In Propertius, although the couplets are normally self-contained, the sense of the hexameter is often incomplete without the pentameter, which is therefore weighty and important. But in Tibullus, and still more in Ovid, the unit tends to be the line, and as far as sense goes the pentameter may be only an echo or variant of the hexameter. There can be virtue however in this, for it produces the effect known as parallelism. Why this effect should be pleasing is a mystery of aesthetic psychology, but its appearance in many literatures is sufficient evidence that men feel it to be so:

> When Israel came out of Egypt,
> And the house of Jacob from among the strange people,
> Judah was his sanctuary,
> And Israel his dominion.
> The sea saw that, and fled;
> Jordan was driven back;
> The mountains skipped like rams,
> And the little hills like young sheep.[14]

There is something soothing and satisfying in the leisurely antiphony. The English heroic couplet likewise lends itself to parallelism:

> Learning and Rome alike in empire grew,
> And arts still followed where her eagles flew;
> From the same foes, at last, both felt their doom,
> And the same age saw learning fall, and Rome.[15]

On the other hand, the compact form of the pentameter makes it a better vehicle for epigram and wit even than the hexameter,

III. THE ELEGIAC COUPLET

which sometimes seems to exist only to compère its brilliant young partner. What could be neater than lines such as these?

> sint mea, sint dominae fac rata vota meae.[16]
>
> et quae non puduit ferre, tulisse pudet.[17]
>
> et quae clam facias, facta referre palam.[18]

But the subject-matter of elegy, often trite enough, required heavy spicing to make it palatable. The spice was provided in a multitude of ways. First there are the recognized rhetorical figures of speech, which impart life and energy—*anaphora*, *apostrophe* and the rest.[19] For instance, anaphora (repetition of a word, generally at the beginning of clauses) can act as a link to bind couplets together. It can also be used for emphatic insistence, as in

> *quam* vir, *quam* custos, *quam* ianua firma, tot hostes
>   servabant, nequa posset ab arte capi,[20]

or

> *ipse* tuus custos, *ipse* vir, *ipse* comes.[21]

The Romans particularly liked it with variation of case or number (*adnominatio*),* as in

> *Medeam* timui; plus est *Medea* noverca;
>   *Medeae* faciunt in scelus omne manus;[22]

or more diffusely:†

> *Carmina* sanguineae deducunt cornua lunae,
>   et revocant niveos solis euntis equos;
> *carmine* dissiliunt abruptis faucibus angues,
>   inque suos fontes versa recurrit aqua;
> *carminibus* cessere fores, insertaque posti,
>   quamvis robur erat, *carmine* victa sera est.[23]

But there are other devices not so easy to name which contribute no less. One of these we may call syntactical pattern. Its effect

---

* Greek πολύπτωτον.[24]

† This is a development of Tibullus I, 8, 19–22, where the word *cantus* is thrice repeated.

can best be illustrated once more by analogies from the heroic couplet of Pope, but the much greater flexibility of Latin word-order gave a great advantage to the Roman poet.*

First there are patterns of symmetry, as in 'that verse which they call Golden, of two substantives and two adjectives with a verb betwixt to keep the peace'†; this is found both in hexameters—

> aurea sanctorum potuissent templa deorum;[25]
> nulla recantatas deponent pectora curas;[26]
> grandia per multos tenuantur flumina rivos;[27]

and in pentameters—

> callidus in falsa lusit adulter ave;[28]
> roscida purpurea supprime lora manu;[29]
> frigidaque arboreas mulceat aura comas.[30]

The corresponding type in heroic couplets (less effective because English obliges the adjective to come next to its noun) is very common. Here are a few examples from Pope's *Windsor Forest*:

> The lonely woodcocks haunt the wat'ry glade;
> The clam'rous lapwings feel the leaden death;
> Her buskin'd Virgins trac'd the dewy lawn.

At other times the symmetry may be chiastic, perhaps emphasized by the repetition of words, as in

> Memnona si mater, mater ploravit Achillem;[31]
> Romulus Iliades Iliadesque Remus;[32]
> sive tuas, Perseu, Daedale, sive tuas;[33]

---

* English, for instance, could not compass exquisite interweaving such as we find in *Tr.* IV, 10, 65–6:

> Molle, Cupidineis nec inexpugnabile telis.
> Cor mihi, quodque levis causa moveret, erat.

† Dryden, Preface to *Sylvae*. See L. P. Wilkinson, *Horace and His Lyric Poetry* (1944), pp. 146–7. Syntactical pattern—*Wortstellung*, as the Germans call it—plays a greater part in Horace's Odes than in Ovid's Elegiacs. For the whole subject see E. Norden, *Aeneis* VI, App. III.

or in English (a few examples from many in the *Dunciad*),

> Prose swell'd to verse, verse loit'ring into prose;
> A wit with dunces and a dunce with wits;
> Cross as her sire, and as her mother grave.

It may extend throughout a couplet, as in

> tu, pinnas gemma, gemma variante capillos,
> ibis in auratis aureus ipse rotis;[34]

or in Pope (*Essay on Criticism*, 635–6):

> Though learn'd, well-bred; and though well-bred, sincere:
> Modestly bold, and humanly severe.

The symmetry need not, of course, be exact: indeed, it is often more pleasing artistically when the balance is not perfect, as in

> haec tibi sunt mecum, mihi sunt communia tecum;[35]

> culte puer, puerique parens Amathusia culti.[36]

This chiastic form is particularly common in our heroic couplet. Here are six lines from Pope's *Messiah* (33–8) containing three examples:

> Lo, earth receives him from the bending skies!
> *Sink down, ye mountains, and ye valleys, rise;*
> With heads declin'd ye cedars, homage pay;
> *Be smooth, ye rocks; ye rapid floods, give way!*
> The Saviour comes, by ancient bards foretold:
> *Hear him, ye deaf, and, all ye blind, behold!*

These effects occur only by chance, if at all, in early Greek elegy. It was the Sophist orator Gorgias at the end of the fifth century who began to experiment, in prose, with syntactical patterns. Among his scanty fragments we have phrases such as τοὺς πρώτους τῶν πρώτων Ἕλληνας Ἑλλήνων and τὸν χρόνον τῷ λόγῳ τὸν τότε τῷ νῦν ὑπερβάς.[37] But word-order in Greek was less flexible than in Latin, and this experiment did not come to much. Nevertheless, when a century later the Hellenistic poets went back to elegy, we do find among the few surviving couplets of Philetas, who with Callimachus was to become Propertius' model, one or two which suggest that he may have been feeling after what became so common in Latin elegy:

καὶ γάρ τις μελέοιο κορεσσάμενος κλαύθμοιο
κήδεα δειλαίων εἷλεν ἀπὸ πραπίδων.[38]

and again (playing with sounds rather than syntax),

οὔ μέ τις ἐξ ὀρέων ἀποφώλιος ἀγροιώτης
αἱρήσει κλήθρην, αἱρόμενος μακέλην.[39]

The artistic grouping of clauses (*cola* and *commata*) into 'periods', which Virgil introduced from oratory into epic and Horace into lyric, plays a part also in the structure of elegy, though the regular division into end-stopped couplets precludes great variety. The couplets are grouped according to sense in sections of suitable length, and within these sections the clauses or sentences are sometimes built up into periods on aesthetic principles approved by experience. Here is an example. Demetrius, the writer on style, remarks that in composite periods the last member should be longer than the rest and should, as it were, sum up and embrace them.[40] A favourite arrangement was the *tricolon* of three limbs,[41] and in its most pleasing form either the first two were equal or the second was longer than the first, the third being longer than either (a principle familiar enough from music). Let us turn once again for illustration to Ovid's Elegy on Tibullus (*Am.* III, 9). Within the bounds of a couplet we have this arrangement (ll. 21–2):

> Quid pater Ismario,
> quid mater profuit Orpheo?
> carmine quid victas obstupuisse feras?

and again, in double form, within the bounds of two couplets (ll. 37–40):

Vive pius—
    moriere;

pius cole sacra—

    colentem | mors gravis a templis in cava busta trahet;
carminibus confide bonis—

    iacet, ecce, Tibullus; | vix manet e toto parva quod urna
        capit.*

The separation of adjective and noun, and the principle of balance which tended to make the one occur before the caesura and the other at the end of the line, produced, in these inflected languages, something very like rhyme, as can be seen in the first couplet of Philetas quoted above. Of the 49 pentameters in the only surviving fragment of his successor Hermesianax no fewer than 26 have this form of assonance. The proportion in Latin pentameters is probably well over 20 per cent. Propertius II, 34 contains 38 examples in 94 lines (hexameters and pentameters), including six in succession (85–90), though the figures for Ovid would be lower than this. It seems likely that such rhyme was an accidental by-product;[42] but it must have had its effect,† and in course of time it became regularized in the naïvely charming 'Leonine' hexameters of the Middle Ages, such as

hac sunt in *fossa* Baedae Venerabilis *ossa*;

mundum *iucundum* cognovimus esse *rotundum*.

This is only one form of the assonance which imparted melody to elegiacs as to other forms of Latin poetry. I find particularly

---

* Cf. Lincoln, *Gettysburg Address*, quoted in this connexion by G. Highet, *The Classical Tradition* (1949), p. 334:

'But, in a larger sense,

        we cannot dedicate,
        we cannot consecrate,
        we cannot hallow this ground.'

'We here highly resolve that these dead shall not have died in vain; that this nation, under God, shall have a new birth of freedom; and that government of the people, by the people, for the people, shall not perish from the earth.'

† It is easy to fancy with Raby (*Secular Latin Poetry* I, p. 28) that Ovid was pleased with his 'Leonine' hexameter *A.A.* I, 59:

    quot caelum *stellas*, tot habet tua Roma *puellas*.

attractive pentameters in which the first two words in the second half are assonant (especially where they are also alliterative), as in

> vivent, dum meretrix *blanda, Menandros* erit.[43]
>
> instruat, Aoniam *Marte movente* lyram.[44]
>
> qui quod es, id vere, *Care, vocaris,* ave.[45]

Assonance and alliteration are indeed inseparable in discussion. It is hard to believe that such an elaborate pattern as the following with its interplay of alliterative *f, v* and *m, fac, for* and *or,* is fortuitous:

> Aut formosa fores minus, aut minus improba, vellem;
> non facit ad mores tam bona forma malos;
> facta merent odium, facies exorat amorem:
> me miserum, vitiis plus valet illa suis![46]

And how much the splendid outburst at the climax of the epilogue to *Amores* I owes to the alliterative *c* and *r, v* and *m* and *p,* the assonance of *re* and *ri, mi* and *po,* and the internal rhyme of the pentameters!

> Cedant carminibus reges regumque triumphi,
> cedat et auriferi ripa benigna Tagi;
> vilia miretur vulgus; mihi flavus Apollo
> pocula Castalia plena ministret aqua.[47]

I have always felt that the ensuing couplet

> sustineamque coma metuentem frigora myrtum,
> atque a sollicito multus amante legar,

though blameless in itself and germane to the periodic structure, is something of an anticlimax musically just because, despite the alliterative *m*'s, it lacks the vivid sound values of its predecessor, which Shakespeare chose as superscription to his *Venus and Adonis,* 'the first heir of my invention'.*

---

* Octavianus Mirandula evidently had some such feeling, for the excerpt in his *Flores Poetarum* ends at *aqua.*

The perfect blending of vowels and consonants is, however, one sign of the true poet which ultimately defies analysis. It is surely not so much the metaphor, trite enough in all conscience, as something in the sounds, that makes us thrill when the curtain goes up and Gloucester begins to speak:

> Now is the winter of our discontent
> Made glorious summer by this sun of York.

What is it that makes some chance line stick in the memory?—

> amnis harundinibus limosas obsite ripas,[48]

or

> ensiger Orion adspiciendus erit,[49]

or

> movit inauratae pollice fila lyrae.[50]

(Each individual reader will recall examples from his own experience.) Why is there such virtue, as the Romans felt themselves,[51] in the blending of Greek words with Latin, especially proper names?—as in

> Isi, Paraetonium genialiaque arva Canopi
> quae colis et Memphin palmiferamque Pharon*[52]

or in this pageant of Aegean isles:

> Iam Samos a laeva (fuerant Naxosque relictae
> et Paros et Clario Delos amata deo),
> dextra Lebynthos erat silvisque umbrosa Calymne,
> cinctaque piscosis Astypalaea vadis.[53]

---

* Ovid clearly liked these sounds, and repeated them in varied form at *M.* IX, 773–4. Horace, *Odes* I, 1, 32–4, is another example:

> si neque tibias
> Euterpe cohibet nec Polyhymnia
> Lesboum refugit tendere barbiton.

None of these stylistic devices may seem of much importance in itself; but taken together they represent a genuine art, analogous to music, bearing indeed much the same relation to the meaning of a poem as the music of a song does to the words. How much we owe to the orators, to Cicero perhaps above all, for initiating the Augustan poets into the mysteries of *elocutio*, which, becoming instinctive, have enabled many, both then and since, including even some whose 'message' may not be particularly striking or original, to delight us with their masterpieces of verbal art!

CHAPTER IV

THE 'AMORES'

TENERORUM LUSOR AMORUM

IT is not surprising, from what we can gather about his natural
bent, that Ovid should have decided to devote himself to elegy
rather than to some other form of poetry. When he was in his
teens the *Cynthia* of Propertius was being 'read all over the
Forum', while within Messalla's circle there was the example of
Tibullus, not to mention Lygdamus and Sulpicia. Propertius,
who would have found congenial spirits in nineteenth-century
Paris, once wrote in a mood of unconscientious objection to
military glory,

> Me sine, quem semper voluit natura iacere,
> hanc animam extrema reddere nequitia.[1]

> *Let me, whom Fortune willed a profligate,*
> *Breathe my last breath in unregenerate state.*

One side of Propertius seems to have been really like that, a blend
of *nostalgie de la boue* and defiant moral nihilism. (A certain
attitude of moral and political non-conformity had already
appeared in Catullus.) Ovid, I believe, saw the literary possibilities
of a pose on these lines, and deliberately adopted it, styling himself

> ille ego nequitiae Naso poeta meae.*[2]

> *I, Naso, that poet of my own naughtiness.*

Might it not repel readers? A few perhaps. But Ovid knew human
nature well. We often have erotic feelings which we suppress as

* Tibullus never uses *nequitia*: Propertius uses it seven times, in two cases
referring to his affair with Cynthia: I, 6, 26; 15, 38; II, 5, 2; 6, 30; 24, 6; III, 10, 24;
19, 10.[3]

discreditable; all the better when someone else confesses, *praeterito pudore*, to giving the same feelings free rein. The confession may earn sympathy or contempt, according to the rigidity of the reader's moral censorship; but in either case the underlying impulse receives vicarious satisfaction. The character of Don Juan was invented as a dreadful warning; in due course he became a popular hero.* Some Sunday papers expose vice under pretext of cleaning it up, others simply expose it; in either case sales prove equally good.

There is, in fact, no need for anyone to be shocked. Human nature has an apparently infinite capacity for not applying what it reads to how it lives. The world of Roman love-elegy can be taken as a 'conventional' world, like that of Restoration comedy, and there is a good deal of sense in Lamb's remarks in his essay *On the Artificial Comedy of the Last Century*, for all Macaulay's strictures:

'I confess for myself that (with no great delinquencies to answer for) I am glad for a season to take an airing beyond the diocese of strict conscience—not to live always in the precincts of the law-courts—but now and then, for a dream-while or so, to imagine a world with no meddling restrictions.... I come back to my cage and my restraint the fresher and more healthy for it. I wear my shackles more contentedly for having respired the breath of an imaginary freedom. I do not know how it is with others, but I feel the better always for the perusal of one of Congreve's—nay, why should I not add even of Wycherley's—comedies. I am the gayer at least for it; and I could never connect those sports of a witty fancy in any shape with any result to be drawn from them to imitation in real life.'

Naturally Ovid pretended that this world was real, and himself its hero—*usus opus movet hoc*; but he pathetically abandoned his

---

* 'No wonder the opera pleased the general public; their sympathies, which would naturally be with Don Giovanni in any case, were kept carefully concentrated upon him. We do not care in the least what becomes of the ladies any more than he does' (E. J. Dent, of Bertati's version, *Mozart's Operas*, p. 207). 'It is impossible not to regard him as a fascinating hero, unless we take a severely puritan view of the whole opera' (*ibid.* pp. 213–14).

bravura when trouble forced him to do so: 'Believe me, my conduct is different from my verse; my life is pure though my Muse be wanton. A large part of my work is fiction and imagination: it allows itself liberties its author denies himself. My book is no evidence of character, but an innocent diversion: you will find in it much to beguile the ear.'[4]

Indeed, the enjoyment to be derived from this vicarious wickedness is enhanced by the pleasing shocks of blasphemy. The more blandly impudent and unconscionable the rascal is, the more we laugh in spite of (indeed, because of) the affront to any censor we may have within. It must be emphasized, however, that the mere fact of having a mistress would not have shocked a Roman. In all countries where marriages have been made for reasons of convenience and often at the instigation of parents the husband at least has been pardoned a certain amount of amusement with the *demi-monde*, still more so the young bachelor.

It is beside the point to seek for autobiography in Ovid's erotic elegies. Even in Propertius genuine experience was thickly overlaid with traditional motives: Tibullus' mistresses might seem purely fictional, were it not that one or two details seem too singular even to have been invented merely to give an air of verisimilitude—for instance, the mention that Nemesis' sister had been killed by falling out of a window.[5] But there is nothing to persuade us that Ovid's Corinna really existed. Even his statement to her that he knows someone who is spreading it round that *she* is really Corinna, whereas none but herself will be sung by him, need only be a characteristic piece of Ovidian fun—assuring an imaginary character of his unswerving loyalty. It is hard to believe that even the least reticent genuine lover would have had the face to publish *Amores* II, 8, the outrageous blackmail of Cypassis, or III, 7, the complaint of his own temporary impotence. And Apuleius, who can tell us confidently the real name of Lesbia, Cynthia, Delia and others,[6] does not even mention Corinna, though he is obviously recalling every identification of a poetic pseudonym he can.

The clue to the *Amores* is a passage in the proem to Book II (7-10):

> Atque aliquis iuvenum, quo nunc ego, saucius arcu,
>   agnoscat flammae conscia signa suae,
> miratusque diu, 'quo', dicat, 'ab indice doctus
>   composuit casus iste poeta meos?'

> *And may some youth whose wounder is the same*
> *Perceive the signs and recognize the flame,*
> *And, musing long, demand, 'What tell-tale spy*
> *Has told this poet all my history?'*

Ovid is bent on representing every phase and situation of love, every twist and paradox of love's psychology. No doubt he was not without amorous experience, but reading and talk could have given him most of the motives that occur. To try to fit a Corinna episode into the framework of his authentic biography with its three marriages is labour lost.*

It is all represented as a great game, played seriously at times, but regarded by the player between-whiles with amused and indulgent astonishment. The introductory epigram, written for the second edition of the *Amores*, is suitably light-hearted and disarming:

> Qui modo Nasonis fueramus quinque libelli
>   tres sumus; hoc illi praetulit auctor opus.
> ut iam nulla tibi nos sit legisse voluptas,
>   at levior demptis poena duobus erit.

> *The five small books of Naso once we were:*
> *Now we are three, for so he did prefer.*
> *Granted we still may not appeal to you,*
> *You'll be relieved to find us minus two.*

Next follows a literary squib. When first the Alexandrian poet Callimachus set the tablets on his knee, Apollo spoke to him:

---

* As is done, for example, by Owen, *Tristia* I, Introd. p. xvi. For a useful analysis of the ideas found in Roman love-elegy see E. Burck, 'Römische Wesenszüge in der Augusteischen Liebeselegie', *Hermes*, 1952, pp. 163–200.

'Poet, you must always offer me the fattest possible victim, but song that is slender.' So he tells us in the famous prologue to the *Aetia* against the poets of grand epic, of all passages in Greek poetry the one most quoted by the Romans.[7] Since then no reputable poet ever began right; he invariably embarked on some epic theme, only to be interrupted by a pinch on the ear from Apollo and an admonition to do what he had really wanted to do all along.* Not to be outdone, Ovid claimed to have begun an epic about martial deeds, when Cupid with a laugh stole a foot from the second line and turned hexameters into elegiacs.† The poet protested, in true Propertian style, with a string of arguments from Olympus *ad hominem*, but to no purpose: Cupid chose a shaft,

> Lunavitque genu sinuosum fortiter arcum,
> 'quod' que 'canas, vates, accipe' dixit 'opus'.

> *Firm with his knee he flexed the sinuous bow,*
> *And crying, 'Poet, here's your theme!', let go.*

(How smoothly and deftly that hexameter draws the bow! How smartly, with the detached word *opus*, the arrow loosed at *dixit* strikes home!—And how hopeless it is to attempt to reproduce the effect in English! Ovid may have had in mind a statue of Cupid in this attitude—several examples have survived.) So love is to be the theme, and elegiac, of course, the metre must remain.

A slight piece, perhaps, but already there are touches of a distinctive, rococo wit: and, sure enough, in the piece that follows

---

* Virgil, *Ecl.* VI, 3–5; cf. Horace, *Odes* IV, 15, 1–4; Propertius III, 3. At II, 1, 11–22 Ovid professes that his chosen theme had been one accepted as typical of grand epic, the Battle of the Gods and Giants. He was deterred not by Apollo, but by his mistress, who slammed her door in his face! For the Gigantomachia as typical cf. Propertius II, 1, 19 f., 39 f.; III, 9, 48. S. G. Owen has a whole chapter (edn. *Tristia* II, pp. 63–81) on Ovid's supposed *Gigantomachia*. But its reality receives no support from *Tr.* II, 71–2 and 333–4, where the example is purely typical; and Ovid does not mention it at *Tr.* II, 547 ff. when reviewing his serious works. I fully share the scepticism of F. Pfister, *Rh. Mus.* 1915, pp. 472–4, and E. Reitzenstein, *Rh. Mus.* 1935, pp. 87–8, about its ever having been more than a literary fiction.

† This conceit is kept up, recurring at ll. 17–18, 27–30.

we have the whole paraphernalia of Hellenistic baroque—the Triumph of Love, the golden boy, in a car drawn by doves. There he stands, driving elegantly, his head bound with myrtle, his wings and hair sparkling with jewels; at his golden chariot wheels follows a long train of captive youths and girls, among them Ovid with his wounds yet fresh and such obvious enemies as Sanity (*Mens Bona*[8]) and Modesty, while Charms, Error and Madness act as escort. Venus looks down with approval from heaven, and scatters roses from her altar offerings. Thus tricked out he passes through the throng, dealing many a wound with flame or shaft. The conventional elegiac metaphor of love as a form of soldiering is here carried to its impudent extreme.[9] The first poem is an introduction to the *Amores* as a whole, an intimation that in them love will be treated not seriously, as in Propertius and Tibullus, but in a half-humorous, detached, Hellenistic spirit; the second well illustrates this programme: whereas Propertius introduced his Third Book with a poem in which he himself, crowned with laurel, is driving in proud triumph with his Muse, Ovid makes Cupid the Triumphator, and himself one of the captives in his train. We are being introduced to a new mood of Latin elegy;[10] we are to be entertained, not moved.

Cupids can be charming if kept in their proper sphere, as in Propertius' description of how he fell in with a band which haled him to his mistress' house (II, 29). But a few go a long way, and the intrusions of such symbolism into realistic descriptions of love can be tiresome, as any reader of the First *Aeneid* must feel.* Ovid generally, though not always, avoids this pitfall. The fact that Cupid, owing to the unfortunate incident described by Demodocus in *Odyssey* VIII, could be called Mars' stepson was a godsend for the manufacture of conceits, while the other fact that, as Aeneas' half-brother, he was related to the Emperor, gave good scope for baroque, and perhaps faintly mischievous, flattery.[11]

But for the most part the *Amores* are realistic enough. The rules of the game are that 'All's fair', and the character of the lover is

* The substitution of Cupid for Ascanius in Dido's bosom, ll. 657–722.

represented on this assumption. He is a real lover, of Mediterranean temperament. Though he never speaks of anything so irrelevant as marriage, he can contemplate a liaison sufficiently long for the end not to need thinking of, sometimes even for life; but at other times he can love two women at once, or even be distracted between twenty different types. He is potent enough for anything—and yet on another occasion he fails inexplicably. He is comparatively poor, and it kills his love if his mistress asks for money; not even beasts, but only prostitutes, do that. The union he wants is one on equal terms, based on the assumption that both parties get equal pleasure from the act:

> Cur mihi sit damno, tibi sit lucrosa, voluptas
> quam socio motu femina virque ferunt?

If money passes, the transaction is completed, and there survives none of the mutual gratitude which cements love affairs. As a lover he hates war and soldiers (how can Corinna bear the feel of hands stained with blood?); indeed, he hates all men of affairs, who ruined the Golden Age of Saturn with their ploughing, sailing and gold-digging that lead to war. Their only use is to supply Roman girls with false hair from captured Germans. But let them have their reward—if only they do not use it to tempt away the girls of poor, innocent poets. Not that he has no gift to bring; a poet's gift, rightly valued, surpasses all money—the hope of an immortal name.

He is jealous, of course, sometimes insanely jealous. In a fit of passion he is capable of pulling his mistress' hair and slapping her face, only to suffer violent remorse. He fears that his praise of her has attracted rivals. Yet jealousy and variability are sauces his love requires, and he inveighs against her complacent official lover for spoiling the sport by providing a sitting bird. At another time, infuriated by her open infidelities, he meditates revolt; but though he hates her character, he still loves her face:

> sic ego nec sine te nec tecum vivere possum.
>
> *Thus I can neither live with you nor without you.*

He knows he must be her slave eternally, and only prays she will make it easy and not degrading for him. He does not want to be free from love; life would be empty without it. If necessary, he will share his mistress with rivals, if only she will take pains to deceive him:

non peccat quaecumque potest peccasse negare;
She sins not who can feign she has not sinned;

she will find him a most willing dupe. To sum up, his greatest desire is to have her love; failing that, to find her ever worthy of his love; at worst, to be allowed to love.

And what of the girl? Her status is left vague, but she may be taken to be an amateur of the kind that receives a generous allowance for expenses. She is not a common prostitute ('she-wolf'—*lupa*), but more like the educated and accomplished *hetaerae* of Athens. Her relations are only mentioned once, when the bawd suggests they too should cadge from her lovers, and so increase the family resources. Sometimes we hear of her 'vir'. In I, 4 he seems to be something very like a husband, who can shut her in at night and claim her favours *de jure*. The term (American 'boy-friend') can mean any reigning lover, and at times Ovid seems himself to claim this position. A janitor keeps the door of her house; she is also guarded by a eunuch, who cannot be expected to sympathize with the suitor, and she walks abroad with a dusky chaperone. At such times a furtive tablet may be slipped to her in the new Portico of the Danaids, or at Isis' temple, with a space left in the wax for her reply. But there are times when her husband is careless: a bawd can give her corrupting advice, while Ovid eavesdrops from a cupboard; she can visit him alone at noon, and go alone to the theatre or circus.

She is, of course, beautiful. She has highly skilled maids to do her hair. This is remarkably fine, with a natural wave, but on one occasion it all comes out through injudicious use of hair-dye, where-upon Ovid teases her with the prospect of a German wig (well knowing that it will in fact grow again). Once she has recourse to abortion on her own and makes herself dangerously ill, the poet's reaction being a mixture of indignation and solicitude, untempered by any sympathy for her motives or sense of personal responsibility.

Her feelings are seldom revealed. She is capable of jealousy, not without cause. She is keen on racehorses and their drivers, rather than literary or artistic like Propertius' Cynthia. Ovid does not expect anyone so lovely to be chaste, but only discreet. However, even discretion does not seem to be one of her strong points. And the gods laugh at her perjuries.

These portraits should not be taken seriously as such; they are simply convenient devices for assembling motives. The man indeed has a shadow of reality, because, though variability of mood is his chief characteristic, he is not without singleness of purpose; and after all, the pretence at least is that he represents Ovid of Sulmo.* But the woman is a composite figure, or a number of incompatible figures. In twelve elegies she is named Corinna, probably after the Boeotian poetess, as Catullus named his Lesbia in honour of another Greek poetess; these pieces may be survivors of the first edition. In the rest she may or may not be envisaged as the same person. All that matters is that the variety of moods and situations be such that every lover who reads may recognize much of his own experience. So we are free to take each poem on its merits and enjoy it without ulterior speculation.†

* F. Lenz, *St. It. Fil.* 1935, pp. 227–35, thinks that III, 14 is exceptional in springing from genuine experience of Ovid himself, and that for this reason it was reserved for the last place before the Epilogue.

† R. P. Oliver, *T.A.P.A.* 1945, pp. 191–215, maintains that Corinna was real on the ground that, had she not been, the poet would not, in a serious autobiographical poem written when he was fifty-three, have kept up the pretence (*Tr.* IV, 10, 60):

nomine non vero dicta Corinna mihi.

He thinks the first edition in five books may have revealed much of their story chronologically, whereas in the edition we have the Corinna poems selected are jumbled to efface her identity. I find his arguments ingenious rather than convincing.

Let us begin with a straightforward account of a successful act of love (*Am.* I, 5).* It is surprising how rarely poets have felt urged to communicate so intense and universal an experience; since many can scarcely be credited with reticence, one can only suppose that, when content and gratified, they lose the itch for verbal self-expression. 'Lips only sing when they cannot kiss.' Propertius, however, did write more than one such poem (II, 14 and 15), and his success in communicating his felicity may well have encouraged Ovid.

Aestus erat, mediamque dies exegerat horam;
    adposui medio membra levanda toro.
pars adaperta fuit, pars altera clausa fenestrae;
    quale fere silvae lumen habere solent,
qualia sublucent fugiente crepuscula Phoebo,
    aut ubi nox abiit nec tamen orta dies.
ille verecundis lux est praebenda puellis,
    qua timidus latebras speret habere pudor.

ecce, Corinna venit, tunica velata recincta,
    candida dividua colla tenente coma—
qualiter in thalamos formonsa Semiramis isse
    dicitur, et multis Laïs amata viris.
deripui tunicam—nec multum rara nocebat;
    pugnabat tunica sed tamen illa tegi.
quae cum ita pugnaret, tamquam quae vincere nollet,
    victa est non aegre proditione sua.

ut stetit ante oculos posito velamine nostros,
    in toto nusquam corpore menda fuit.
quos umeros, quales vidi tetigique lacertos!
    forma papillarum quam fuit apta premi!
quam castigato planus sub pectore venter!
    quantum et quale latus! quam iuvenale femur!

---

* The text used for the *Amores* is that of F. Munari (Florence, 1951), except for a few places where I have taken the advice of Mr E. J. Kenney.

singula quid referam? nil non laudabile vidi,
    et nudam pressi corpus ad usque meum.
cetera quis nescit? lassi requievimus ambo.
    proveniant medii sic mihi saepe dies!

It was full noontide on a sultry day;
Taking siesta on my bed I lay;
One shutter closed, the other open stood,
Making a half-light much as in a wood,
Like the dim gloaming at the set of sun,
Or when night's gone but day's not yet begun:—
A light beloved of timorous girls and shy
That seek to veil their maiden modesty.

Sudden, Corinna comes: ungirt her dress:
On either side her neck a braided tress.
E'en so, methinks, into her chamber moved
Semiramis, or Laïs much-beloved.
I snatched the dress, so fine, it half revealed;
Though e'en with this she strove to be concealed;
Yet strove she not as one intent to win:
Easily, self-betrayed, she soon gave in.

So there she stood all naked to my gaze.
In all her body not one fault there was.
What shoulders and what arms I saw, I held,
What dainty nipples, asking to be felt,
Beneath the shapely breast what belly smooth,
Hips large and beautiful, the thighs of youth!

Why single out? No part but stood the test.
Her naked to my naked form I pressed.
All know the sequel. We relaxed in swoon.
O, oft may Fortune grant me such a noon!

The erotic elegist is so single-minded, he imposes on himself such limitations, that he cannot be read for long without tedium.

But Ovid does find ways of keeping us amused, and his glimpses of Roman life are particularly delightful. His account of laying siege to a girl at a race-meeting (III, 2) is surely one of the most witty and spirited poems in all Latin. It is a dramatic monologue, except for the stage direction given in the penultimate line. The sudden transitions from the intense to the banal are worthy of Byron.* Long though the poem is, it deserves quotation in full.

> 'Non ego nobilium sedeo studiosus equorum;
>   cui tamen ipsa faves, vincat ut ille, precor.
> ut loquerer tecum veni, tecumque sederem,
>   ne tibi non notus quem facis esset amor.
> tu cursus spectas, ego te; spectemus uterque
>   quod iuvat, atque oculos pascat uterque suos.
>
> o, cuicumque faves, felix agitator equorum!
>   ergo illi curae contigit esse tuae?
> hoc mihi contingat, sacro de carcere missis
>   insistam forti mente vehendus equis,
> et modo lora dabo, modo verbere terga notabo,
>   nunc stringam metas interiore rota.
> si mihi currenti fueris conspecta, morabor,
>   dequc meis manibus lora remissa fluent.
> at quam paene Pelops Pisaea concidit hasta
>   dum spectat vultus, Hippodamia, tuos!
> nempe favore suae vicit tamen ille puellae.
>   vincamus dominae quisque favore suae!
>
> quid frustra refugis? cogit nos linea iungi.
>   haec in lege loci commoda circus habet—
> tu tamen a dextra, quicumque es, parce puellae:
>   contactu lateris laeditur illa tui.

---

* Byron had more than a touch of Ovid. For Corinna struggling, *male pertinax* and *facili saevitia*, in I, 5 cf. Julia in *Don Juan*:

> A little while she strove and much repented,
> And whispering 'I will ne'er consent'—consented.

tu quoque, qui spectas post nos, tua contrahe crura,
   si pudor est, rigido nec preme terga genu!
sed nimium demissa iacent tibi pallia terra.
   collige—vel digitis en ego tollo meis!
invida vestis eras, quae tam bona crura tegebas;
   quoque magis spectes—invida vestis eras!
talia Milanion Atalantes crura fugacis,
   optavit manibus sustinuisse suis;
talia pinguntur succinctae crura Dianae,
   cum sequitur fortes, fortior ipsa, feras.
his ego non visis arsi; quid fiet ab ipsis?
   in flammam flammas, in mare fundis aquas.
suspicor ex istis et cetera posse placere,
   quae bene sub tenui condita veste latent.

vis tamen interea faciles arcessere ventos,
   quos faciet nostra mota tabella manu?
an magis hic meus est animi, non aëris, aestus,
   captaque femineus pectora torret amor?
dum loquor, alba levi sparsa est tibi pulvere vestis.
   sordide de niveo corpore pulvis abi!

sed iam pompa venit—linguis animisque favete!
   tempus adest plausus—aurea pompa venit.
prima loco fertur passis Victoria pinnis—
   huc ades et meus hic fac, dea, vincat amor!
plaudite Neptuno nimium qui creditis undis.
   nil mihi cum pelago! me mea terra capit.
plaude tuo Marti, miles: nos odimus arma:
   pax iuvat, et media pace repertus amor.
auguribus Phoebus, Phoebe venantibus adsit.
   artifices in te verte, Minerva, manus.
ruricolae Cereri teneroque adsurgite Baccho.
   Pollucem pugiles, Castora placet eques.
nos tibi, blanda Venus, puerisque potentibus arcu
   plaudimus: inceptis adnue, diva, meis,

daque novae mentem dominae; patiatur amari.
  adnuit, et motu signa secunda dedit!
quod dea promisit, promittas ipsa, rogamus:
  pace loquar Veneris, tu dea maior eris.
per tibi tot iuro testes pompamque deorum,
  te dominam nobis tempus in omne peti!

sed pendent tibi crura. potes, si forte iuvabit,
  cancellis primos inseruisse pedes.

maxima iam vacuo praetor spectacula circo
  quadriiugos aequo carcere misit equos.
cui studeas, video. vincet, cuicumque favebis.
  quid cupias ipsi scire videntur equi.
me miserum, metam spatioso circuit orbe!
  quid facis? admoto proximus axe subit.
quid facis, infelix? perdis bona vota puellae;
  tende, precor, valida lora sinistra manu.
favimus ignavo—sed enim revocate, Quirites,
  et date iactatis undique signa togis!
en, revocant—at ne turbet toga mota capillos,
  in nostros abdas te licet usque sinus.

iamque patent iterum reserato carcere postes;
  evolat admissis discolor agmen equis.
nunc saltem supera spatioque insurge patenti!
  sint mea, sint dominae fac rata vota meae.

sunt dominae rata vota meae, mea vota supersunt.
  ille tenet palmam; palma petenda mea est.'
risit, et argutis quiddam promisit ocellis.
  'hoc satis hic: alio cetera redde loco.'

'*For thoroughbreds I do not care a pin,*
Although I pray that he you back may win!
I came to talk to you, with you to sit,
Lest I should love and you not know of it.
You watch the horses, I watch you; and thus
Let's feast our eyes each on what pleases us.

Thrice happy he, the driver you support!
So that's the lucky one who holds your thought?
Let me be he, right from the very start
I'll urge my horses on with fearless heart,
Now give the rein, now searing lashes deal,
Now graze the turn-post with my near-side wheel;
But, sighting you, in full career I'll stop
And from my heedless hands the rein let drop.
How nearly Pelops fell in Pisa's chase
Through gazing on Hippodameia's face!
Yet sure his lady brought him victory:
So may we each to ours beholden be!

Why edge away? The line must keep us close*
(These rules are not entirely otiose!).
You on the lady's right, sir, please keep clear:
She does not care to feel your side so near.
And you behind, sir, please control your legs:
Don't stick your knees into her back, she begs.
But look, your skirt is trailing here below:
Lift it—or rather, let me lift it so.
O jealous dress to hide such comeliness!
The more you look, the more—O jealous dress!
Such were the legs Milanion longed to raise
When Atalanta bared them for the chase;
So artists paint the limbs of Artemis
That of brave beasts the braver huntress is.
With these still hid I burned, but seeing these
Is adding flame to flames, or sea to seas;
From these can I those further joys infer
Which lurk beneath that robe of gossamer.

But would you, while we wait, care to be fanned?
My programme, I will wave it with my hand.
Or is this heat not in the air around
But in my burning heart, to woman bound?

---

* In the Roman circus the individual seats were marked off by a line.[12]

Look, there's a speck of dust upon your dress:
Off, dust! How dare you soil such loveliness?

But hush! Attend! the great procession draws
Near us, the pomp of gold: prepare applause!
In front, with wings outstretched, is Victory;*
Hail, goddess! Grant my love victorious be.
Cheer Neptune, you that brave the billows rough;
No seas for me: my land is room enough.
You soldiers, clap for Mars: I hate alarms;
Peace is my love, and love in peace's arms.
Phoebus, aid augurs; Phoebe, hunters aid;
Pallas, to thee the craftsman's court be paid;
Farmers, for Ceres rise and Bacchus dear;
Boxers, cheer Pollux; horsemen, Castor cheer.
For thee, sweet Venus, with thy archer-son,
Is our applause: give me thy benison;
Bend my new mistress to accept my love—
She bowed in favour! Did you see her move?
Come, then, the goddess' promise ratify,
And you shall be the greater deity.
I swear by all this witness-train divine,
For all eternity I wish you mine.

But look, your feet are dangling: would you care
To put your toes up on the railing there?

Now for the chief event. The course is clear.
The praetor signs. The chariots appear.
I spot your favourite—certain of success:
The very horses seem your wish to guess.
O agony! How wide he took the post!
What are you at? Your lead will soon be lost!

---

* The procession started from the Capitol and came by the Forum and the
Forum Boarium to the Circus Maximus, the whole length of which it traversed,
while the ivory statues of the gods received applause especially from those whose
patrons they were. On one occasion, in 45 B.C., the crowd withheld applause for
the statue of Victory because it was accompanied by one of Caesar. Cicero
expressed his delight at this in a letter to Atticus.[13]

What are you at? You're ruining apace
My lady's hopes: pull at your left-hand trace!
We've picked a loser, sure;—but call them back,
Spectators, wave your togas round the track.*
See, back the togas wave them—Oh! Take care!
Here under mine there's shelter for your hair.

Once more the starting-boxes open wide.
Out fly the horses in a motley tide.
This time at least an open lead secure:
Make sure my lady's hopes, and mine make sure.

My lady's hopes have triumphed, mine not yet:
He gets his prize, but mine is still to get.'
She smiled, and shot a glance of promise fair.
'Enough for here: grant me the rest elsewhere.'

The way in which the wooer turns the favoured driver to account, first using him to establish a tie of common sympathy with the girl, then, when he is doing badly, contriving to shine by imaginary contrast, and finally exploiting her mood of enthusiasm when he wins, is as ingenious as it is true to life. It deserved to succeed.

Scarcely less witty and brilliant is the jealous lover's anticipation of a party (I, 4). Here the girl is officially the mistress of another, but has already given her favours to the poet:

Vir tuus est epulas nobis aditurus easdem—
ultima cena tuo sit precor illa viro!
ergo ego dilectam tantum conviva puellam
adspiciam? tangi quem iuvet, alter erit,
alteriusque sinus apte subiecta fovebis?
iniciet collo, cum volet, ille manum?
desine mirari, posito quod candida vino
Atracis ambiguos traxit in arma viros.
nec mihi silva domus, nec equo mea membra cohaerent—
vix a te videor posse tenere manus.

* The spectators could by this means claim a fresh start.

quae tibi sint facienda tamen cognosce, nec Euris
　　da mea nec tepidis verba ferenda Notis.
ante veni quam vir—nec quid, si veneris ante
　　possit agi video; sed tamen ante veni.
cum premet ille torum, vultu comes ipsa modesto
　　ibis ut accumbas, clam mihi tange pedem.
me specta nutusque meos vultumque loquacem;
　　excipe furtivas et refer ipsa notas.
verba superciliis sine voce loquentia dicam;
　　verba leges digitis, verba notata mero.
cum tibi succurrat Veneris lascivia nostrae,
　　purpureas tenero pollice tange genas.
siquid erit de me tacita quod mente queraris,
　　pendeat extrema mollis ab aure manus.
cum tibi quae faciam, mea lux, dicamve placebunt,
　　versetur digitus anulus usque tuis.
tange manu mensam, tangunt quo more precantes,
　　optabis merito cum mala multa viro.

quod tibi miscuerit, sapias, bibat ipse, iubeto;
　　tu puerum leviter posce quod ipsa voles.
quae tu reddideris ego primus pocula sumam,
　　et qua tu biberis, hac ego parte bibam.
si tibi forte dabit quod praegustaverit ipse,
　　reice libatos illius ore cibos.
nec premat indignis sinito tua colla lacertis,
　　mite nec in rigido pectore pone caput;
nec sinus admittat digitos habilesve papillae;
　　oscula praecipue nulla dedisse velis.
oscula si dederis fiam manifestus amator,
　　et dicam 'mea sunt!' iniciamque manum.

haec tamen adspiciam, sed quae bene pallia celant,
　　illa mihi caeci causa timoris erunt.
nec femori committe femur, nec crure cohaere,
　　nec tenerum duro cum pede iunge pedem.
multa miser timeo, quia feci multa proterve,

61

exemplique metu torqueor ipse mei:
saepe mihi dominaeque meae properata voluptas
    veste sub iniecta dulce peregit opus.
hoc tu non facies; sed, ne fecisse puteris,
    conscia de tergo pallia deme tuo.

vir bibat usque roga—precibus tamen oscula desint!—
    dumque bibit furtim, si potes, adde merum.
si bene compositus somno vinoque iacebit,
    consilium nobis resque locusque dabunt.
cum surges abitura domum, surgemus et omnes,
    in medium turbae fac memor agmen eas.
agmine me invenies aut invenieris in illo:
    quicquid ibi poteris tangere, tange mei.

me miserum! monui paucas quod prosit in horas:
    separor a domina nocte iubente mea.
nocte vir includet, lacrimis ego maestus obortis,
    qua licet, ad saevas prosequar usque fores.
oscula iam sumet, iam non tantum oscula sumet;
    quod mihi das furtim iure coacta dabis.
verum invita dato—potes hoc—similisque coactae;
    blanditiae taceant sitque maligna Venus.
si mea vota valent, illum quoque ne iuvet opto;
    si minus, at certe te iuvet inde nihil.
sed quaecumque tamen noctem fortuna sequetur,
    cras mihi constanti voce dedisse nega.

Tonight your lover will be at the feast;
Your lover there! Would it may choke the beast!
So I'm to watch, a fellow-guest (no more),
Another clasp the girl whom I adore;
See you another's bosom nestling fill
And let his arm creep round your neck at will!
No wonder fair Hippodameia's charms
Made those wine-heated Centaurs fly to arms,
When I, no savage, no half-horse Yahoo,
Can scarce refrain from laying hands on you!

Yet may we scheme. Mark closely what I say,
Nor let the breezes bear my words away.
Be there before him; not that I can see
How that will help us—still, before him be.
When he reclines and you demurely go
To join him, touch my foot with covert toe;
Watch me, my nods, the language of my eyes;
Receive, return, these furtive gallantries;
Words without sound my speaking brow will sign;
Words framed with fingers note, or traced with wine.
When you recall the scenes our love has played,
On blushing cheek let tender thumb be laid;
Or if you would reproach me silently,
Hold with your hand your ear's extremity;
If what I say or do have favour found,
Finger your ring and turn it round and round;
Just touch the table, as men do in prayer,
          To show you execrate that fellow there.

The cup he pours you bid him drink (take heed),
Then softly tell the waiter what you need.
The one you order I will first take up,
And where you'll drink my lips shall press that cup.
If he should give you food he's tasted first,
Spurn food once tasted by that mouth accurst.
Let not those arms upon your shoulders rest,
Nor lay your soft head on his bony chest;
From bosom and from tempting paps dismiss
His fingers. Most of all—allow no kiss;
For should you kiss him, I'd my love betray,
Cry 'those are mine' and hands upon you lay.

So much is all in view: where cloaks conceal,
There lie the roots of the blind fears I feel.
Then lay not leg to leg, nor thigh to thigh,
Nor let your soft foot press his hard foot nigh.

Much do I fear who much have wantonly
Performed: my own experience tortures me:
I and my lady oft beneath a dress
Have hastily achieved love's sweet success.
I know you won't; but lest you seem to have tried,
Come, lay that guilty-looking cloak aside.

Coax him to drink (though not to kisses' length),
And as he drinks add slyly to the strength.
When soundly sleep and wine his limbs entrance,
We'll take our cue from place and circumstance.
You'll rise, break up the party, homeward bound;
Remember, seek the densest crush around.
There will I find you soon, or you find me:
Touch me at any opportunity.

Alas, I plan what soon must be denied.
Night bids me sternly leave my mistress' side.
Her lover closets her; my tearful fate
To follow only to that cruel gate.
He'll take your kisses, more than kisses too;
What I may steal he can require of you.
But grudge it—that you can—and forced appear;
Breathe no endearments, let the rite be drear.
Pleasure for neither—that's the most I pray;
If less, for you no pleasure anyway.
But oh, whatever deeds the night may bring,
To-morrow swear to me you gave him not one thing.

This poem has an amusing echo in II, 5, where the poet's advice proves a boomerang. They are all three at the party, and the girl and his rival think he is in a drunken sleep; but he sees it all, the significant movements of the brow, the communicating nods, the speaking looks, the words framed with fingers or traced with wine, the prearranged code-signs. The couplet (29-30)

'Quid facis?' exclamo, 'quo nunc mea gaudia defers?
iniciam dominas in mea iura manus!'

intimates that the situation has come about which he sought to forestall with ll. 39–40 of I, 4:

> Oscula si dederis, fiam manifestus amator,
>   et dicam 'mea sunt' iniciamque manus.

There can be no doubt, the correspondence in detail being so exact, that Ovid intended this irony, the laugh being against himself. There are other such cross-references in the *Amores*: III, 7 is a wry pendant to the bragging confidence of II, 10; III, 11 *b* brings the poet to heel after the incipient show of independence in III, 11 *a*.*

Sometimes the ironical twist occurs in the middle of the poem, in a somewhat Horatian manner. The reader is invited to laugh at the poet's unguarded self-revelation. III, 4 begins with a sermon to a husband in a high moral tone. Why set a watch upon your wife, he asks:

> Siqua metu dempto casta est, ea denique casta est;
>   quae, quia non liceat non facit, illa facit!
> ut iam servaris bene corpus, adultera mens est;
>   nec custodiri, ne velit, ulla potest.

> *Where fear leaves off, there chastity begins;*
> *Who does not sin because she may not, sins.*
> *Body in ward, the mind may wanton still:*
> *Guard as you may, you cannot guard the will.*

This is the wisdom of the ages. We hear it in Tiresias' reply to the prurient Pentheus: 'Even in the Bacchic orgies she who is sound of heart will not be corrupted':

> καὶ γὰρ ἐν βακχεύμασιν
> οὖσ' ἥ γε σώφρων οὐ διαφθερήσεται.[14]

From Theophrastus' lost book *On Marriages* it passed to St Jerome: 'Verum quid prodest etiam diligens custodia, cum uxor servari

---

* With most editors, I take it that l. 33 begins a new poem. The idea of presenting the same circumstances as affecting a lover and his rival had been exploited by Meleager in two epigrams on the appearance of Dawn.[15]

impudica non possit, pudica non debeat? Infida enim custos est castitatis necessitas; et illa vere pudica dicenda est, cui liceat peccare si voluit.'* It is in the Gospel: 'Whosoever looketh on a woman to lust after her, hath committed adultery with her already in his heart'; and in Milton's *Areopagitica*: 'I cannot praise a fugitive and cloistered virtue.'

All the more outrageous is Ovid's *nequitia*, which does not reveal itself at first. From the sermon he goes on to prudential advice: by shutting her up you only suggest to rivals that she is particularly worth having, and everyone knows that forbidden fruit is the most tempting; in any case, a guard is degrading to a free-born woman. It is not until line 37 that his real intention slips out:

> Rusticus est nimium, quem laedit adultera coniunx,
> et notos mores non satis urbis habet.

> *Only a boor minds if his wife betrays,*
> *A country boor unversed in city ways.*

Why marry a beautiful wife if you insist on having a faithful one? The two are incompatible. Come, don't be a puritan; cultivate all those friends her charms produce for you, and win a lot of good will with a minimum of trouble. How nice to be always asked by the young to their parties, and to see many presents in your home that others have had to pay for!

How shameless! But what fun! Just like Restoration comedy. And how pleasantly the theme is reversed in II, 19! There the 'husband' is spoiling the game by *not* forbidding the fruit. Ovid provides him with a list of suspicious circumstances which ought to put him on his mettle. And then, at line 47, comes a delightful twist: 'I give you due warning: unless you begin to set a watch on your lady, she will begin to cease to be mine'; and he proceeds

---

* 'But what is the use even of careful watching, when a vicious wife cannot be guarded, and a virtuous one should not be? For compulsion is but a deceptive guardian of chastity; and only she can truly be called virtuous who is free to sin if she will' (*Adv. Iovinianum*, I, 47. Fränkel, *op. cit.* p. 187, note 62. He also gives the passage quoted from Matt. v, 28.)

to argue from his own feelings to the husband's, assuming that the latter needs him no less, to add a spice of piquancy to his conjugal love. The familiar complaints of lovers are neatly reversed, and he ends, 'If you want to keep me as your rival, forbid it.' With his rhetorical training Ovid loved to use arguments on one side and then reverse them for use on the other.

In one poem, I, 10, there is a marked shift of ground, and yet I am doubtful whether such irony is intended. In lines 1–52 the poet protests that cadging for gifts kills love, at great length and with apparent sincerity; but at lines 53–6 he says there is no harm in asking gifts of the rich. The cynical drop in standards is startling, but since he returns in the last couplet to his former theme, I suspect that the rich man's gifts were only introduced to lead up by contrast to the poor man's offering, service, zeal, faithfulness, and a name made famous in poetry;—though one could interpret this poem too as ironical, the poet's real reason for protest emerging as, not that cadging spoils love, but that he cannot afford to pay the market price.

But for sheer, breath-taking impudence the pair of poems on Cypassis takes the palm (II, 7 and 8). Bursting with plausible self-righteousness, the poet shows Corinna how inconsistent and absurd her jealousies are. If he looks round in the theatre, or if a good-looking woman looks at him, she's jealous. If he praises a girl, it's obvious; if he decries one, it's suspicious. If he looks well, he must be indifferent to her; if he looks ill, he must be in love with someone else. And he hasn't even the consolation that the accusations are true! And now the last straw—he's accused of seducing Cypassis, the African maid who does her hair. He hopes, if he has a mind to err, it won't be with a slave. Besides, is it likely he would risk an attempt on a faithful servant who is in favour with her mistress, with the prospect of both repulse and exposure? By Venus and her son he swears it is untrue!

Convinced by such unanswerable logic, we proceed to the next poem. It is to Cypassis. Ovid compliments her first on her hair-dressing, and then on her technique in bed, and asks how Corinna

got wind of their secret love-making. Hastily he forestalls any
protest about his derogatory remarks on loving slaves with a
recantation and a reference to Achilles and Agamemnon, and
proceeds to chide her for having blushed when accused, contrasting the composure with which he had sworn by Venus ('may
the goddess pardon the perjuries of an innocent heart!'). As a
reward for this service he asks her to go to bed with him again that
day. She shakes her head, and pretends to be afraid? But surely
it is enough to win the approval of either, master or mistress. If
she persists, he will confess and so betray her (with details so
minute that they will both convince and enrage her mistress):

> Quoque loco tecum fuerim, quotiensque, Cypassi,
> narrabo dominae, quotque quibusque modis.

> *Where and how oft we lay I'll tell to her,*
> *How many modes we used, and what they were.*

English cannot reproduce the relentless blackmail of those ac-
cumulated pronouns beginning with 'q'.

Ovid's sly, Callimachean humour is seldom far away. It peeps
out in his charming and famous protest to the Dawn (I, 13),*
which will be dealt with later. In its less satirical form it appears
at its best in the sentimental burlesque elegy on the death of
Corinna's parrot (II, 6). The Greek Anthology contains a number
of epitaphs on animals and winged creatures, wild or tame, which
are the ancestors of Catullus' lament for Lesbia's sparrow, a poem
which provided Ovid with his framework.[16] The effect of burlesque
is achieved by following the set form of funeral elegy: the bidding
to mourners (1–16); the regrets—'Ah, what avails—' (17–24);
the outburst against the powers responsible—σχετλιασμὸς—with
a list of those who could have been better spared (25–42); the
deathbed scene (43–8); the hopes of a suitable future life (49–58);
the committal (59–62).† The parrot ends as a sort of Orpheus,
charming with his talk an Orphic bird's paradise.

---

* E.g. ll. 29–30, and the final couplet: 'scires audisse—rubebat'. See pp. 388–91.

† Compare his Elegy on the death of Tibullus (*Am.* III, 9): bidding to mourners

Psittacus, Eois imitatrix ales ab Indis
  occidit; exequias ite frequenter, aves.
ite, piae volucres, et plangite pectora pinnis
  et rigido teneras ungue notate genas;
horrida pro maestis lanietur pluma capillis,
  pro longa resonent carmina vestra tuba.

quod scelus Ismarii quereris, Philomela, tyranni,
  expleta est annis ista querela suis;
alitis in rarae miserum devertere funus—
  magna sed antiqua est causa doloris Itys.
omnes quae liquido libratis in aëre cursus,
  tu tamen ante alios, turtur amice, dole.
plena fuit vobis omni concordia vita,
  et stetit ad finem longa tenaxque fides.
quod fuit Argolico iuvenis Phoceüs Orestae,
  hoc tibi, dum licuit, psittace, turtur erat.

quid tamen ista fides, quid rari forma coloris,
  quid vox mutandis ingeniosa sonis,
quid iuvat, ut datus es, nostrae placuisse puellae?
  infelix, avium gloria, nempe iaces!
tu poteras fragiles pinnis hebetare zmaragdos,
  tincta gerens rubro Punica rostra croco.
non fuit in terris vocum simulantior ales:
  reddebas blaeso tam bene verba sono.

raptus es invidia—non tu fera bella movebas:
  garrulus et placidae pacis amator eras.
ecce, coturnices inter sua proelia vivunt;
  forsitan et fiant inde frequenter anus.
plenus eras minimo, nec prae sermonis amore
  in multos poteras ora vacare cibos.
nux erat esca tibi causaeque papavera somni,

(1–16); regrets (21–34); σχετλιασμός (17–20, 35–46); death-bed (47–58); future
life (59–66); committal (67–8). Horace achieves an analogous effect in his
burlesque hymn to a wine-jar (III, 21), where he closely follows the set form of
'cletic' hymns.

pellebatque sitim simplicis umor aquae.
vivit edax vultur ducensque per aëra gyros
  miluus et pluviae graculus auctor aquae;
vivit et armiferae cornix invisa Minervae—
  illa quidem saeclis vix moritura novem;
occidit ille loquax humanae vocis imago
  psittacus, extremo munus ab orbe datum!
optima prima fere manibus rapiuntur avaris;
  implentur numeris deteriora suis.
tristia Phylacidae Thersites funera vidit,
  iamque cinis vivis fratribus Hector erat.

quid referam timidae pro te pia vota puellae,
  vota procelloso per mare rapta Noto?
septima lux venit non exhibitura sequentem,
  et stabat vacuo iam tibi Parca colo.
nec tamen ignavo stupuerunt verba palato:
  clamavit moriens lingua, 'Corinna, vale!'

colle sub Elysio nigra nemus ilice frondet,
  udaque perpetuo gramine terra viret.
siqua fides dubiis, volucrum locus ille piarum
  dicitur, obscenae quo prohibentur aves.
illic innocui late pascuntur olores
  et vivax phoenix, unica semper avis;
explicat ipsa suas ales Iunonia pinnas,
  oscula dat cupido blanda columba mari.
psittacus has inter nemorali sede receptus
  convertit volucres in sua verba pias.

ossa tegit tumulus—tumulus pro corpore magnus—
  quo lapis exiguus par sibi carmen habet:
COLLIGOR EX IPSO DOMINAE PLACUISSE SEPULCRO.
ORA FUERE MIHI PLUS AVE DOCTA LOQUI.

The parrot, mimic bird from Indian skies,
Is dead. All fowls, flock to the exequies.
Go, faithful fowls, and beat the breast with wings

And tear the cheek with claw-hooked harassings;
Instead of hair, dishevelled plumage rend,
And for the funeral trump your voices lend.

Why, Philomela, wail for Tereus' crime?
That plaint has long ago fulfilled its time.
For this rare bird thy mournful dirges pour;
Great was the loss of Itys, but of yore.
Grieve, all that wing the limpid air above,
But chiefly thou, devoted turtle-dove.
Yours was a life of perfect harmony;
Firm to the end was your fidelity;
As Pylades to his Orestes clove,
So to his parrot faithful was the dove.

But what could faith avail, or gorgeous hues,
Or voice of varied mimic sounds profuse,
Or to have won straightway my lady's heart?
Glory of birds, unhappy! dead thou art!
Thy plumes could dim the emerald's brittle pride,
Thy crimson beak in tawny saffron dyed.
For mimicry was never such a bird,
So well it lisped in echo of each word.

Not fighting, sure—fate's envy brought decease
To such a talker, such a friend of peace;
Pugnacious quails in constant strife engage
('Tis hence, maybe, they oft attain old age).
Thy wants were frugal: talking was so sweet,
Thy mouth had very little time to eat.
Nuts were thy fare, and poppy's drowsy seed;
For drink, the purest water all thy need.
The greedy vulture and the wheeling kite
Live on, and daws live on that rain invite;
The raven too, for all Minerva's hate:
Nine ages pass and scarce he meets his fate.
But gone that echo of each human sound,
The parrot, gift from earth's most distant bound!

All that is best soon falls to envy's force;
The worst is suffered to run out its course;
Thersites saw Protesilaüs' urn,
And Hector's brethren watched his body burn.

Where are the vows my lady made for thee?
The gusty winds have swept them out to sea.
The seventh dawn, thy last to be, appeared,
And Fate stood over thee with distaff cleared;
And yet that tongue no langour stultified:
Dying, 'Corinna, fare thee well!' it cried.

Neath an Elysian hill a grove is found,
Dark ilex; ever green and fresh the ground.
There faith believes the good birds have their heaven,
And far from thence all noxious fowls are driven.
There spotless swans may feed at large, and eke
The long-lived phoenix, ever bird unique;
There Juno's peacock spreads his plumes abroad;
The pleasing dove kisses her eager lord.
Lodged in this grove amid these pious birds
The parrot draws them all to hear his words.

His bones a mound of fitting size inters,
With gravestone large enough to bear this verse:
MY LADY'S LOVE FOR ME THIS TOMB WILL TEACH.
MORE THAN A BIRD I HAD THE ART OF SPEECH.

Of course there is much in the *Amores* that is conventional and tedious *to us*. This is not always the poet's fault; his very success has helped to popularize his themes. Thus the motive

> I would I were the glove upon that hand
> That I might touch that cheek

has become a little hackneyed by now, so that we may do less than justice to the conceits of that charmingly phrased poem (II, 15) which accompanies the gift of a ring to his mistress. He envies it, and pictures how, if he could take its place, he would work himself loose and contrive to fall into her bosom; how she would moisten him at her lips before using him to seal wax; and wear him, he devoutly hopes, in her bath.* But the complaint outside the closed door (παρακλαυσίθυρον), which we find in I, 6, had long been poetic stock-in-trade,[17] and is hardly redeemed by such traits as the humour of lines 5–6, where Ovid assures the janitor that he has grown so conveniently thin with love that the door need only be opened a few inches, or the wan beauty of lines 65–6,

> Iamque pruinosus molitur Lucifer axes,
>   inque suum miseros excitat ales opus.

And now the rimy Morning Star is setting his wheels in motion, and the bird of dawn is rousing wretches to work.

In I, 9, *Militat omnis amans*, the familiar parallel between the lover and the soldier is worked out in rather tedious detail; and II, 12, celebrating the bloodless victory in love's siege, is trite for all its enthusiasm.

One of the troubles is that Ovid could rarely refrain from sowing with the sack instead of the hand, a fault which one at least of his own contemporaries noted.† Thus in I, 5, the poem translated above, the comparison in lines 3–4 between the chiar-oscuro in a room at noon with one shutter open and the half-light in a wood is excellent; the further comparison with the twilight after sunset or before sunrise adds nothing, and in fact slightly changes and spoils the picture. Having occasion to mention that even rivers have been in love, Ovid feels constrained to expend twenty lines in mentioning all the instances he can think of;[18] and in III, 12 he takes twenty-two lines to give instances of marvels told by the poets, when two or three would have established the point. This is a fault from which other great Roman poets are not entirely free.[19]

---

* The tone is not unlike that of Callimachus' *Coma Berenices*, mostly lost but known to us from Catullus' version (LXVI).

† *Nescit quod bene cessit relinquere*, 'he cannot let well alone'.[20]

It is, however, true that genuine feeling can make a triumphant poem out of the most conventional forms, traditional details and rhetorical devices. We may divine that one subject on which Ovid really felt strongly was the claims of *otium* as against *negotium*, leisure against practical activity, as Fränkel well puts it.* In this he is at one with Horace: leisure, so far from being disgraceful, is the only begetter of culture, including poetry, and the men of action are Philistines and enemies of the Muse:

et quisquam ingenuas etiamnunc suspicit artes?[21]

Does any still respect the purer arts?

The elegy on the death of Tibullus (III, 9) is as conventional as could be in form;† it is full of traditional artificialities (so, after all, is *Lycidas*); and yet it pulses with indignation and pity. It is a passionate vindication of the value of poets in the world, all the more intense because it is the treatment of Ovid no less than of Tibullus that evokes it; just as Shelley's *Adonaïs* is a lament not only for Keats, slain by the Edinburgh reviewers, but also for Shelley,

A herd-abandoned deer struck by the hunter's dart.

The feeling of solidarity among poets comes out in the closing lines, where Tibullus is conceived as meeting in Elysium the great elegiac poets of the past, Catullus and Calvus, and Gallus whose tragic death was a recent memory. Can we doubt that there was also in his mind Gallus' friend, the great poet who is not mentioned, perhaps because he did not write elegy, but whom fate had snatched away in his prime, with his masterpiece unfinished, not long before Tibullus:‡

* *Op. cit.* p. 9. 'In Rome poetry had no proper standing because the spirit had none.' Fränkel quotes the well-known remark of even so enlightened a person as Cicero, that if the span of his life were doubled he would still refuse to waste his time in reading lyric poets (Seneca, *Epist.* 49, 5).

† See p. 68, n.

‡ He mentions Virgil and Tibullus together at *Tr.* IV, 10, 51-2. The wording of Domitius Marsus' epigram,

Te quoque Vergilio comitem non aequa, Tibulle,
mors iuvenem campos misit ad Elysios,

suggests that Virgil died first, though not by much.

Memnona si mater, mater ploravit Achillem,
 et tangunt magnas tristia fata deas,
flebilis indignos, Elegeia, solve capillos.
 a, nimis ex vero nunc tibi nomen erit!
ille tui vates operis, tua fama, Tibullus,
 ardet in extructo, corpus inane, rogo.

ecce, puer Veneris fert eversamque pharetram
 et fractos arcus et sine luce facem;
aspice demissis ut eat miserabilis alis
 pectoraque infesta tundat aperta manu!
excipiunt lacrimas sparsi per colla capilli,
 oraque singultu concutiente sonant.
fratris in Aeneae sic illum funere dicunt
 egressum tectis, pulcher Iule, tuis.
nec minus est confusa Venus moriente Tibullo
 quam iuveni rupit cum ferus inguen aper.

at sacri vates et divum cura vocamur;
 sunt etiam qui nos numen habere putent!
scilicet omne sacrum mors importuna profanat,
 omnibus obscuras inicit illa manus!
quid pater Ismario, quid mater, profuit Orpheo,
 carmine quid victas obstupuisse feras?
'aelinon!' in silvis idem pater 'aelinon!' altis
 dicitur invita concinuisse lyra.
adice Maeoniden, a quo ceu fonte perenni
 vatum Pieriis ora rigantur aquis:
hunc quoque summa dies nigro submersit Averno.
 effugiunt avidos carmina sola rogos.
durat, opus vatum, Troiani fama laboris,
 tardaque nocturno tela retexta dolo.
sic Nemesis longum, sic Delia nomen habebunt,
 altera cura recens, altera primus amor.

quid vos sacra iuvant? quid nunc Aegyptia prosunt
 sistra? quid in vacuo secubuisse toro?
cum rapiunt mala fata bonos—ignoscite fasso—

sollicitor nullos esse putare deos.
vive pius—moriere; pius cole sacra—colentem
    mors gravis a templis in cava busta trahet;
carminibus confide bonis—iacet, ecce, Tibullus:
    vix manet e toto parva quod urna capit.
tene, sacer vates, flammae rapuere rogales,
    pectoribus pasci nec timuere tuis?
aurea sanctorum potuissent templa deorum
    urere, quae tantum sustinuere nefas!
avertit vultus Erycis quae possidet arces;
    sunt quoque qui lacrimas continuisse negant.

sed tamen hoc melius quam si Phaeacia tellus
    ignotum vili supposuisset humo;
hic certe madidos fugientis pressit ocellos
    mater, et in cineres ultima dona tulit;
hic soror in partem misera cum matre doloris
    venit inornatas dilaniata comas;
cumque tuis sua iunxerunt Nemesisque priorque,
    oscula nec solos destituere rogos.
Delia discedens, 'felicius' inquit 'amata
    sum tibi: vixisti dum tuus ignis eram';
cui Nemesis, 'quid', ait, 'tibi sunt mea damna dolori?
    me tenuit moriens deficiente manu.'

si tamen e nobis aliquid nisi nomen et umbra
    restat, in Elysia valle Tibullus erit.
obvius huic venies hedera iuvenalia cinctus
    tempora cum Calvo, docte Catulle, tuo;
tu quoque, si falsum est temerati crimen amici,
    sanguinis atque animae prodige Galle tuae.
his comes umbra tua est; si qua est modo corporis umbra,
    auxisti numeros, culte Tibulle, pios.
ossa quieta, precor, tuta requiescite in urna,
    et sit humus cineri non onerosa tuo!

If for Achilles, if for Memnon slain,
Their goddess-mothers wept with human pain,

Mourn, Elegy, this wrong, and loose thy hair.
Alas too apt thy name shall now appear! *
Tibullus, bard and glory of thy lyre,
An empty corse, lies burning on his pyre.

Lo, Venus' son his quiver bears reversed,
His torch extinguished and his bowstring burst;
See how he goes with drooping wings distrest,
Beating with savage palm his naked breast.
Tears wet the locks that o'er his neck abound,
And from his lips the shaking sobs resound.
Thus, brother at Aeneas' funeral,
Men say he passed, Iulus, from thy hall.†
Nor less did Venus for this death lament
Than when the boar Adonis' body rent.

So 'sacred bards' and 'wards of heaven' are we,
And some would grant ourselves divinity!
Surely rude Death mars every sacred thing,
On all alike his murky hand doth fling!
Could e'en his mother Thracian Orpheus save,
His sire, his song that did the beasts enslave?
'Ah Linus!' in the forest that same sire
'Ah Linus!' mourned to his reluctant lyre.‡
And what of Homer, that Pierian spring
All poets' lips for ever freshening?
He too one day to dark Avernus came:
Only our verse escapes the insatiate flame.
By poets sung, the tale of Troy lives on,
And that slow web with nightly stealth undone;
So Delia, so shall Nemesis have praise,
Sung in Tibullus' first and latest lays.

* Deriving her name from the Greek ἒ λέγειν, to cry 'woe'.

† Aeneas also was son of Venus, by Anchises, Iulus (= Ascanius) being his son and heir.

‡ Orpheus was son of Apollo and the Muse Calliope (Milton: 'What could the Muse herself that Orpheus bore, the Muse herself for her enchanting son?', no doubt thinking of this passage). Linus was another singer son of Apollo; Ovid accepts the derivation of the Greek cry of woe *ailinon* from *ai* ('alas') and his name.

Ah what availed Egyptian Isis' rites,
Her timbrels, and those chaste, unpartnered nights?*
When good men perish—may I be forgiven!—
By fate malign, I doubt of gods in heaven.
Live righteously—you die; those gods revere—
Death drags you from the altar to the bier;
Trust in good verse—Tibullus there lies cold:
All that remains a little urn can hold.
How could the flames devour thee, poet blest,
Nor fear to feed upon that sacred breast?
Flames that shrank not from such impiety
Could burn the temples of the gods on high!
The Queen of Eryx turned her face away,†
Scarce able to restrain her tears, men say.

Yet better thus than if Phaeacia's land
Thy nameless corpse had sunk in common sand;‡
For here thy mother closed thy swimming eyes
And gave thy ashes their last obsequies;
Thy sister here, her mother's grief to share,
Came with dishevelled, unadornèd hair;
And with thy kin to add their kisses came
Thy lovers both, and watched beside the flame;
Said Delia, parting, 'Happier didst thou live
As mine; while I enflamed thee, thou didst thrive';
But Nemesis, 'What is my loss to thee?
His hand in death declining clung to me.'

And yet, if aught survives but name and shade,
Tibullus, sure, dwells in the Elysian glade;
There, wreaths of ivy on their youthful brow,
Shall Calvus and Catullus greet him now;

* Tibullus' Delia, like Propertius' Cynthia, was a devotee of Isis, and as such observed periods of ritual abstinence from intercourse.

† Venus, who had a famous shrine on Mt Eryx at the western tip of Sicily.

‡ Corfu, identified with the Phaeacia of the Odyssey; Tibullus (I, 3, 3–10), taken dangerously ill there, prayed not to die away from his mother, his sister and Delia. L. 58 echoes Tibullus I, 1, 60.

Thou too, if falsely men thee traitor call,
Gallus, of life and spirit prodigal.*
These are thy friends: if man hath any soul,
Tibullus, thou hast joined this blessed roll.
Peace for thy bones in quiet urn I crave,
And may the earth weigh light upon thy grave.

The motive that the poet, however poor, can give his lady a gift beyond price, the hope of an immortal name, had been used by Propertius, and occurs several times in the *Amores*. Horace had already written his *Exegi monumentum*, and his sense of the power of poetry was even now inspiring the Fourth Book of the *Odes*. In the epilogue to the First Book of the *Amores* Ovid throws down the gauntlet to the Philistines, and in a splendid sweep of rhetoric proclaims the triumph of poetry and his own *non omnis moriar*. As so often, the list round which the poem is built, here a list of poets, is too long; the temptation to bring in everyone, if possible with an echo of some words of theirs, proved too much for him. Nevertheless it is a fine poem, for once again sincerity breathes life into the dry bones (I, 15):

Quid mihi, Livor edax, ignavos obicis annos,
    ingeniique vocas carmen inertis opus;
non me more patrum, dum strenua sustinet aetas,
    praemia militiae pulverulenta sequi,
non me verbosas leges ediscere, non me
    ingrato vocem prostituisse foro?
mortale est quod quaeris opus: mihi fama perennis
    quaeritur, in toto semper ut orbe canar.

vivet Maeonides, Tenedos dum stabit et Ide,
    dum rapidas Simois in mare volvet aquas;
vivet et Ascraeus, dum mustis uva tumebit,
    dum cadet incurva falce resecta Ceres.

---

* Calvus and Catullus, inseparable friends, occur here as writers of elegy; their successor Gallus, as first Governor of Egypt, committed suicide in 26 B.C. when summoned to answer some charge of disloyalty to his friend Augustus.

Battiades semper toto cantabitur orbe;
    quamvis ingenio non valet, arte valet.
nulla Sophocleo veniet iactura cothurno;
    cum sole et luna semper Aratus erit;
dum fallax servus, durus pater, improba lena
    vivent et meretrix blanda, Menandros erit;
Ennius arte carens animosique Accius oris
    casurum nullo tempore nomen habent.
Varronem primamque ratem quae nesciet aetas,
    aureaque Aesonio terga petita duci?
carmina sublimis tunc sunt peritura Lucreti
    exitio terras cum dabit una dies;
Tityrus et fruges Aeneïaque arma legentur
    Roma triumphati dum caput orbis erit;
donec erunt ignes arcusque Cupidinis arma
    discentur numeri, culte Tibulle, tui.
Gallus et Hesperiis et Gallus notus Eois
    et sua cum Gallo nota Lycoris erit.
ergo cum silices, cum dens patientis aratri
    depereant aevo, carmina morte carent.

cedant carminibus reges regumque triumphi,
    cedat et auriferi ripa benigna Tagi!
vilia miretur vulgus: mihi flavus Apollo
    pocula Castalia plena ministret aqua,
sustineamque coma metuentem frigora myrtum
    atque a sollicito multus amante legar!
pascitur in vivis Livor: post fata quiescit,
    cum suus ex merito quemque tuetur honos.
ergo etiam cum me supremus adederit ignis
    vivam, parsque mei multa superstes erit.

Why, rodent Envy, call my life a waste,
My verses, only idle wit misplaced,
Bid me go seek, ere feeble age forbid,
War's dusty prizes, as our fathers did,

Or memorize long laws, and mid the noise
Of thankless law-courts prostitute my voice?
Your aim is low, mine of transcendent worth—
Fame, to be ever sung throughout the earth.

Homer shall live while Tenedos shall stand
And Simoïs roll from Ida to the strand;
And Ascra's poet, while the vintage swells*
And swathes of corn the curving sickle fells.
Battiades shall every land resound:†
Though not in genius, great in art he's found.
Sophocles' drama need not fear decline;
Aratus lives while sun and moon shall shine.
While cheating slave, stern father, harlot smart
And bawd are with us, thou, Menander, art.
Ennius the rugged, Accius the sublime,
Have won a name that shall outlast all time.
The fame of Varro's Argo ne'er shall cease,
Of how Prince Jason sought the Golden Fleece.
Never shall perish high Lucretius' verse
Till one last day destroy the universe.
The Shepherd, Crops, Aeneid shall be read
While Rome remains the world's triumphant head.
While Cupid lights his fire or aims his dart
Men will peruse Tibullus' polished art.
Gallus from East to West shall still be famed,
And with him his Lycoris shall be named.
Yea, flints with age may crumble, rust away
The ploughshare's tooth, but verse knows no decay.

Let kings and royal triumphs yield to song
Let Tagus yield that bears rich gold along;
Let baubles draw the vulgar, but to me,
Apollo, grant full draughts of Castaly;
Crown me with myrtle-leaves that shun all frost,
Fit reading for the lover tempest-tossed.

* Hesiod.   † Callimachus, son of Battus of Cyrene.

Envy the living gnaws; in death, it sleeps;
Then each his own deservèd honour keeps.
So I, when death my body gives to fire,
Shall live, and my best part survive the pyre.

There are foretastes in the *Amores* of Ovid's future development.* Lines 13–58 of I, 4, the instructions to his mistress about how to behave at the feast, are in the vein of the *Ars Amatoria*, as is the appeal to the chaperone Bagoas in II, 2 and the bawd's advice to Corinna in I, 8. The story-telling of the *Fasti* and *Metamorphoses* is presaged by the fable of Ilia and the Anio (III, 6, 45–82) and of the love of Ceres for Iasius (III, 10, 25–42); while the interest in old ceremonies which gave rise to the *Fasti* finds expression in a poem which has no contact with erotic elegy at all, the description of a festival of Juno at Falerii in southern Tuscany, which Ovid happened to witness because his wife came from there (III, 13). But for the moment he turned to another form of erotic poetry, the *Letters of the Heroines*.

* The fact that the *Amores* as we have it is a revised edition forbids us to lay much stress on chronological sequence as between *Amores*, *Heroides* and *Ars Amatoria* (see next chapter).

CHAPTER V

THE 'HEROIDES'

DOLOR IRA MIXTUS

THE dating of Ovid's earlier works, covering together about twenty-five years, presents insuperable difficulties, partly because their nature almost precludes topical references, partly because the *Amores* as we have them are a revised, rearranged and possibly supplemented selection, in three books published together, from five books originally issued singly.* The *Ars* as we have it is also apparently a second edition, in which Book III and at least the final couplet of Book II have been added to the original two books. We know that Tibullus, mourned in *Am.* III, 9, died some time in 19 B.C., and that *Ars Amatoria* I (here we have a useful topical reference)† was being composed early in 2–1 B.C., presumably after the *Amores*. At *Am.* II, 18, 19–34 (presumably a passage belonging to the second edition) Ovid intimates that, besides the 'artes amoris',‡ he is engaged on the *Letters of the Heroines*, and that his friend Sabinus, returned from his wanderings abroad, has with remarkable speed composed replies from some of the heroes.§ There would be no need to deduce from this that *Heroides* I–XV had yet been published in book form, for Romans often recited

---

* *Am.* I, prologue. Evidence for issue singly: II, 1, 1–3; III, 12, 7; for rearrangement: an event of 19 B.C. (Tibullus' death), is treated in a poem now in Book III (9), an event of 16 B.C., or later (defeat of Sygambri) in a poem now in Book I (14).

† L. 177; cf. *R.A.*, l. 155: departure of young C. Caesar for the East.

‡ Rand suggested that this phrase might refer to the partly didactic *Amores*, not the *A.A.*[1]

§ He mentions his epistles from Penelope (I), Phyllis (II), Oenone (V), Canace (XI), Hypsipyle (VI) or Medea (XII), Ariadne (X), Phaedra (IV), Dido (VII) and Sappho (XV); Sabinus has replied for Ulysses to Penelope, Hippolytus to Phaedra, Aeneas to Dido, Demophoön to Phyllis, Jason to Hypsipyle, and Phaon to Sappho. The first list is not complete, and the second need not be.

and circulated their poems first to friends; nevertheless, *Ars Amatoria* III does mention *Amores* I–III and the *Heroides* together as though by now they had been so published.[2] We can do no more than conclude tentatively that by the year I B.C. Ovid had issued the first, if not also the second, edition of the *Amores*, and the first fifteen epistles of the *Heroides*, whether singly or in book form, and begun the *Ars*, this being the general order though there was some overlapping.[3]

The nineteenth century laid arrogant hands on the work of many ancient authors. Large portions of the traditional texts were bracketed as interpolations simply because a particular editor felt them to be unworthy of the author, subsidiary 'arguments' being easily discovered *a posteriori*.* The *Heroides* have received much attention of this kind. Scholars such as Lachmann[4] and Lehrs[5] did not scruple to bracket passages or whole poems on almost purely subjective grounds. Thus Lachmann, acute though many of his observations are, condemns the whole of No. III because of the repeated *epanalepsis* in ll. 3–10.

> Quascumque aspicies, lacrimae fecere lituras:
>   sed tamen hae lacrimae pondera vocis habent.
> si mihi pauca queri de te dominoque viroque
>   fas est, de domino pauca viroque querar.
> non, ego poscenti quod sum cito tradita regi,
>   culpa tua est—quamvis haec quoque culpa tua est:†
> nam simul Eurybates me Talthybiusque vocarunt,
>   Eurybati data sum Talthybioque comes.

But how could anyone be certain that these lines were not the work of the juggler with words who clung to his

> semibovemque virum semivirumque bovem?

He was surely *capable de tout*. Who denies that Virgil, even Virgil,

---

* Peerlkamp's edition of Horace is a curious example.
† The change of mind in this line is at least highly Ovidian.

at the mature age of thirty-one, wrote *Eclogues* VIII, 47–50, lines no less artificial?—

> Saevus amor docuit natorum sanguine matrem
> commaculare manus; crudelis tu quoque, mater;
> crudelis mater magis, an puer improbus ille?
> improbus ille puer: crudelis tu quoque mater.

It is true that, once the formula has been disclosed, it is not beyond the wit of an ingenious man to fabricate an Ovidian Heroine's Epistle from hints provided by pre-Ovidian writers; nor have there been lacking poets in antiquity, or scholars since the Renaissance, capable of writing elegiac verse hardly distinguishable from Ovid's. It is also true that alterations in Ovid's text were made during the Middle Ages, including the insertion or substitution of whole lines and couplets. * But there is really no evidence sufficient to discredit the authenticity of any poem as a whole.[6] Nos. XVI–XXI differ from the *Heroides* proper in that they consist of pairs, letters from heroes with the heroine's replies. This development might have been suggested by Sabinus' replies to the original single epistles, though Ovid makes the man in each case take the initiative. They contain a few metrical peculiarities, but these do not amount to much. In particular, there are three pentameters which end with a word of more than two syllables; but that is no larger a proportion than Ovid admitted in his later work.† True, he never mentions having written such pairs, but why should he? To anyone not on the look-out for evidence of spuriousness they seem anything but inferior to Nos. I–XV. They may have been written by Ovid at the time when he was writing the *Fasti*, shortly before his exile.‡ I propose in any case to treat all twenty-one poems as Ovidian, and deal with them together.

* See Purser's Introduction to Palmer's edition, pp. xxxvii–xlii. I have used Palmer's text in this chapter, except where otherwise indicated.

† XVI, 290; XVII, 16; XIX, 202. There are two such endings in the later books of the *Fasti*: V, 582; VI, 660. In the poems from exile there are 20 of four and 9 of five syllables, excluding proper names.[7]

‡ They had apparently not yet been composed when *Am.* II, 18 was written, and the increased role of narrative in them is consonant with the later period.

Although Ovid may write about women often with amused cynicism, he seems to have had an unusual inclination to see things from their point of view. He had a masculine and Mediterranean conviction that any woman could be had for the asking—*casta est, quam nemo rogavit*—but he had also a tender side to his nature which gave him an interest in the weaker sex and a certain insight into what their feelings might be. As Sellar well remarks, he treats the love of a woman for a man as serious, but not *vice versa*. Nevertheless, he can see that men are often cads when it comes to relations with women, and in their way the *Heroides*, as much as Euripides' Alcestis or Virgil's Dido, may have served to make some of his male contemporaries search their consciences.

Thus the predisposition was there; but in view of the extent to which Ovid was influenced, both in detail and in choice of subjects, by his friend Propertius, it is probable that the idea of writing elegiac letters from deserted heroines was suggested by Propertius IV, 3, an imaginary letter in which a real person, under the name of Arethusa, is conceived as writing to her husband, who has gone to the wars, under the name of Lycotas. There had been poems entirely concerned with legendary heroines before, notably the Hesiodic *Eoeae*, and imaginary letters may possibly have been used already as a literary form at least in the rhetorical schools.* Ovid's claim to originality ('ignotum hoc aliis ille *novavit* opus't[8]) was for having combined the two, or for having seen the possibilities, such as they were, of developing Propertius' charming invention into a genre.

The choice of the epistolary form for what are really tragic soliloquies was not entirely happy. Of course it gives an opportunity for a certain amount of 'business', especially at the beginning and end. Penelope tells Ulysses not to reply, but to

---

* There is however no evidence for this earlier than the third century A.D.; Theon, *Prog. c.* 10, Rhet. Gr. II, p. 115 (Spengel). There are also lyric poems by Catullus and Horace that have the appearance of letters, and may in fact have been intended for despatch.[9]

† H. Peter takes *novavit* to mean 'revived'.[10] But there is no trace of such a genre in extant Alexandrian poetry.

come back in person; she does not know his address, so must hopefully give a copy of her letter to every traveller who touches at Ithaca.[11] Any blots are attributed to tears, or even to the anticipated effects of a suicide's life-blood.[12] Poor Briseïs, a captive from Mysia, can hardly write Greek at all.[13] Grief makes lettering unsteady, and pens drop from nerveless fingers.[14] * Leander's having to write is in itself sufficient proof that the sea is unsafe for swimming; only one sailor could be found brave enough to embark from Abydos with his letter.[15] Oenone is able to open with a double-barbed shaft:

> Perlegis? an coniunx prohibet nova? perlege—non est
>   ista Mycenaea littera facta manu.

> *Read you? Or does your latest bride forbid?*
> *Read without fear: I am no Atreïd.*†[16]

And Cydippe, plighted irrevocably to Acontius through inadvertently reading an oath aloud, begins her reply with telling effect:

> Pertimui, scriptumque tuum sine murmure legi,
>   iuraret ne quos inscia lingua deos.[17]

> *Trembling I read your note without a sound,*
> *For fear my tongue by some new oath be bound.*

But in general the letters make little attempt at realism, and the shackles of the fiction are easily cast aside. Dido turns from Aeneas at the end to address her sister;[18] and Deïaneira, hearing as she writes that Hercules is dying in the poisoned robe, continues her letter as a lament, with a refrain every six lines.[19]

One drawback is the necessity of choosing a point in the story when it would be plausible for a letter to be sent. This prejudices the letter from Laodameia to Protesilaüs (XIII). According to the story, an oracle had said that the first man of the Greek army to

---

* Hypermnestra's hand is burdened with her shackles (XIV, 130).

† She is hinting that Paris, never noted for bravery, is living in terror of receiving a letter from Menelaus or Agamemnon, besides being under Helen's thumb.

touch Trojan soil would straightway be killed. Protesilaüs of Phylace leapt ashore first and was promptly slain by Hector. On hearing of this his wife Laodameia prayed, and was granted, that his shade might visit her for a short while. Her devotion and refusal to be separated from him cost her her life (the authorities differ as to how she died, but some say she embraced him and refused to part from him when he returned to Hades). She became the type of wifely devotion, and both Catullus[20] and Propertius[21] had shown the imaginative possibilities of this beautiful tale. Now the whole interest begins with Protesilaüs' leap, and the great moment is the return of his shade; but in order to make the sending of a letter plausible, Ovid had to envisage Laodameia as writing it when the last news was that the fleet was still detained at Aulis. He can portray her wifely devotion, but with regard to the unique parts of the story the best he can manage is elaborate tragic irony: may her husband beware of Hector, she writes: may he be the last to land; she seems to see him before her in the night, and dreams of clasping him in her arms, as now she clasps the waxen image she has made of him.*[22]

But the intrinsic objection to the *Heroides*, from our point of view, is one which a modern might more easily anticipate than an ancient. Recounting in the *Ars Amatoria* how the eloquence of Ulysses won Calypso, Ovid says with evident approval,[23]

> ille referre aliter saepe solebat idem.
>
> *he often used to tell the same story in a different way.*

But we are much more interested in originality of content, and much less in form, than the Romans. How could anyone, we ask, hope to make a series of poems readable which should represent the feelings of a number of not very markedly differentiated characters in a situation which, for all the variety of circumstances, was emotionally the same, even granted that they were originally circulated one by one? If such a poem is to be moving, it must

---

* One tradition here adapted by Ovid concerned an image she made of her husband *after* his death.[24]

convince. The poet must feel genuinely for the suffering woman, and must beguile us to enter into his feeling. He may succeed once, but when he solicits our sympathy for one woman after another, we begin to suspect his. And this suspicion is increased when, for instance, the supposedly naïve Phyllis, *et amans et femina*, comes out with a verbal conceit such as this (II, 25-6):

> Demophoön, ventis et verba et vela dedisti;
> vela queror reditu, verba carere fide.

> *Demophoön, both promises and sails you gave to the winds:*
> *I complain that your sails have no return, your promises no*
> *faith.*

The sources used for the *Heroides* range throughout Greek and Latin literature, from Homer and Sappho to Catullus and Virgil, probably including prose mythographers. Ovid was a great reader, using books both to stimulate his Muse and to provide her with provender. Like Catullus at Verona, he was to find separation at Tomis from his library an obstacle to poetic composition.* To study his method it is best to take a letter that has a single and extant source. Such is that of Briseïs to Achilles (III), which can hardly have any source save the *Iliad*. Here at least there is a suitable moment for an effective letter—the return of the embassy in Book IX which had gone to Achilles to offer her restoration.

Ovid sets himself to imagine what Homer only hints at, the feelings of Briseïs from the time when Agamemnon announced his intention of taking her from Achilles. She is a barbarian princess, a captive among strangers; but she has come to love her heroic captor, and goes unwillingly with the two heralds when they come to his tent and lead her away—

> ἡ δ' ἀέκουσ' ἅμα τοῖσι γυνὴ κίεν.[25]

She cannot blame him for acting under *force majeure*—and yet, need he have surrendered her so soon, without so much as a kiss, as

---

* Catullus LXVIII, 33; Ovid. *Tr.* III, 14, 37: *non hic librorum per quos inviter alarque copia.*

though she were once more being captured?[26] (*Achilles* in Homer forbore to blame *the heralds* for doing what they could not help, and bade Patroclus hand over Briseïs without more ado.)[27] Ovid adds a good and characteristic touch: the heralds, she says, exchanged a look, amazed that he showed no indication of his old love for her:

> Alter in alterius iactantes lumina vultum
> quaerebant taciti noster ubi esset amor.

Often she wished to steal back to him by night, but she was afraid of being captured by some marauding Trojan (perhaps the Doloneia put this idea into Ovid's head), and enslaved to one of Priam's many daughters-in-law (17–20). Besides, she expected Achilles himself to come and rescue her: had not Patroclus whispered to her as she was led away, 'You will soon be here again'? (21–4). (This idea was suggested by her lament over Patroclus at *Iliad* XIX, 297–300, where she recalls how, at the sack of her home, it was he who had comforted her, saying he would make her Achilles' wife.) And now he is not only not coming to rescue her, but positively refusing her when her return is offered! (25). When, in his speech in the *Iliad* rejecting the overtures of Agamemnon (IX, 308–429), Achilles comes to Briseïs (336), in his first bitter words he expresses longing for 'his beloved wife', and in the same breath brutally adds that Agamemnon may sleep with her, for all he cares,

> ἔχει δ' ἄλοχον θυμαρέα, τῇ παριαύων
> τερπέσθω,

but he adds pertinently that he loves her, captive though she be, just as Menelaus loves Helen. Ovid realized that Briseïs would not understand that, while she was Achilles' beloved bed-fellow, she was still more his γέρας, the symbol of his honour; that he could genuinely love her, yet sacrifice her with scarcely a qualm if he thought it would enhance the assertion of his honour. Her incomprehension increases her pathos. She enumerates the gifts offered by Agamemnon through his three ambassadors, the last straw being the women,[28]

> Quodque supervacuum est, forma praestante puellae
>   Lesbides, eversa corpora capta domo,
> cumque tot his—sed non opus est tibi coniuge—coniunx,
>   ex Agamemnoniis una puella tribus.

> *Then, for full measure, Lesbian girls as well,*
> *Rare beauties, captured when their country fell;*
> *And last, a wife—fine superfluity!—,*
> *Your choice of Agamemnon's daughters three.*

Could he not have accepted the other gifts and used them to ransom her? Then she turns to the tragedy of her home, Lyrnesus, recalled later in the *Iliad* in her lament for Patroclus; how Achilles himself had sacked the town, killed her husband and her three brothers, and taken her, a princess in her own country—

> et fueram patriae pars ego magna meae—

to be his concubine; and how she had yet come to forget all this for his sake, having found in him what Homer's Andromache found in Hector:

> tu dominus, tu vir, tu mihi frater eras.[29]

> *you were my lord, my husband and my brother.*

She has heard, as Odysseus reported, that he is threatening to sail home on the morrow.[30] Anything rather than that—or at least let him take her too; she will not claim to go as his wife; she will be a slave, even a handmaid to the noble wife he has boasted that Peleus will provide for him.[31] Only let him protect her from her mistress and not speak slightingly of their past love—yet even that she will endure, if only she be not left behind (77–82).

Nevertheless, she appeals to him to lay aside his incomprehensible wrath: *vince animos iramque tuam*—ἀλλ᾽, Ἀχιλεῦ, δάμασον θῦμον μέγαν.[32] She still imagines that she in herself is the whole cause of it, just as Helen was of the war:

> propter me mota est, propter me desinat ira.

> *for my sake your anger was stirred, for my sake let it cease.*

And lest he be ashamed to yield to a woman, she repeats the story already told him by Homer's Phoenix, how the great Meleager had at length yielded to the entreaties of his wife Cleopatra and gone out to fight.[33] (Here Ovid has an advantage, for the tale is doubly effective in the mouth of a 'wife' herself.) She swears a great oath, by the bones of her husband and brothers and himself and his sword that killed them, just as Homer's Agamemnon swore a great oath by Zeus and Earth and the Sun and the Furies, that there had been no intercourse between him and her, and as Homer's Priam kissed the dread hands of Achilles which had slain so many of his sons.[34] Achilles, she adds, cannot boast of such fidelity: he is not even unhappy, but spends his time singing to the lyre and sleeping with a concubine (Homer relates that the embassy found him doing the former, and left him to do the latter).[35] She begs the Greeks to send her as ambassador; surely he will not be able to resist her kisses, her well-known touch and look (127–34). There are two more Homeric references, to Peleus' spear, which even Patroclus could not throw,[36] and finally to Achilles' sword, with which he would have slain Agamemnon himself if Athena had not stayed his hand.[37]

It will be seen that there is hardly a hint in Homer's story that Ovid has not turned to account, and he has added some good touches of his own. This is one of the best pieces, almost free from his besetting faults. It is not too long, and achieves an affecting pathos. Perhaps it was just because Homer did not dwell on Briseïs' feelings that Ovid, forced to rely on developing imaginatively such hints as he gave, produced something worth while.

Let us now consider another poem in which we may be fairly certain that Ovid used a single source provided by a supreme poet. Here, by contrast, the heroine's feelings had already been imagined;

they had been expressed in magnificent, if rhetorical, verse only a few years before. We can only suppose that it was Ovid's passion for leaving nothing out that made him venture to express the reproaches of Dido to Aeneas (VII).* He keeps close to his model, and echoes him from time to time.

For the sending of the letter he chose the moment in *Aeneid* IV when Dido has made her two passionate speeches in vain and the Trojans are preparing to sail; her mood was expressed in her words to Anna (433):

> tempus inane peto, requiem spatiumque furori.
>
> *all I ask is a breathing-space, relief and respite for my frenzy.*

But the more Ovid strives to excel, the less he succeeds. The forced epigrams creak—Aeneas is giving both sails and promises to the wind; he is casting off his pledges and his ships together; he is forsaking what's done to seek what's yet to do—*facta fugis, facienda petis*. We are not really convinced when Virgil's Dido, exaggerating a curse that had come naturally in Homer, less naturally in Catullus, raves that Aeneas was the son of a Caucasian crag, nurtured by Hyrcanian tigresses; still less, when Ovid's Dido attributes his origin to stone and mountain-oaks, wild beasts or, better still, the sea in storm as now it is.[38] She tries to frighten him with this storm, adding that even in calm the sea has many perils, and, as the element from which Venus sprang, is especially hostile to perjured lovers. She fears for the safety of Ascanius too, and of the Trojan Penates.

So it goes on, argument after weary argument, conceit after strained conceit (to our way of thinking), for close on two hundred lines.

But more often than epic, Greek tragedy provided Ovid with his sources for the *Heroides*.† There were extant then many more

---

* He himself says that the Dido episode was one of the best known in the *Aeneid*.[39]

† Hermione from Sophocles, perhaps *via* Pacuvius; Deïaneira from Sophocles' *Trachiniae*; Phaedra from the lost earlier version of Euripides' *Hippolytus*, also

of these dramas than now, and he speaks of them with enthusiasm and apparent familiarity at *Tr.* II, 381–406. Indeed, as far as their spirit goes, the true ancestor of these outbursts, *dolor ira mixtus*, is Euripides. He, like Ovid, had tended to see things from the woman's point of view, and although he was accused of maligning the sex, he was the forerunner of its emancipation in the Hellenistic age. An obvious case in point is the speech of his Medea when confronted with Jason, which directly influenced Ovid's treatment (XII). She reviles him (465–74), recites the things she has done for him (475–88), reproaches him for ingratitude and breaking his oath (489–98), brings home to him the extent of her present plight (499–515), and finally appeals to Zeus (516–19). On such lines are the *Heroides* constructed. There are other speeches in Euripides by women who have been wronged in one way or another which are similar in conception. The fine and moving outburst of Andromache in the *Troades* comes near in places to what we should call rhetoric, and it is surprising with how little alteration it can then be translated into Ovid's medium:*

> ὦ βάρβαρ' ἐξευρόντες Ἕλληνες κακά,
> τί τόνδε παῖδα κτείνετ' οὐδὲν αἴτιον;
> ὦ Τυνδάρειον ἔρνος, οὔποτ' εἶ Διός,
> πολλῶν δὲ πατέρων φημί σ' ἐκπεφυκέναι,
> Ἀλάστορος μὲν πρῶτον, εἶτα δὲ Φθόνου,
> Φόνου τε Θανάτου θ' ὅσα τε γῆ τρέφει κακά·
> οὐ γάρ ποτ' αὐχῶ Ζῆνά γ' ἐκφῦσαί σ' ἐγώ,

used by Seneca; Canace from Euripides' *Aeolus*; Laodameia from Euripides' *Protesilaüs*; Hypermnestra partly from Aeschylus' *Danais*. From Homer come Ovid's Penelope and Briseïs, from Apollonius Rhodius his Hypsipyle; from Callimachus his Phyllis (? *Aetia*), Acontius and Cydippe (*Aetia* III), perhaps also Hero and Leander; from Hellenistic works Ariadne (cf. Catullus LXIV) and Oenone (W. Kraus, 'Ovidius Naso' in *R.-E.*, col. 1928).

* 764–73: 'Greeks that have devised barbarities, why do you kill this innocent child? And thou, offspring of Tyndareus, never of Zeus wast thou begotten, but of many fathers, I say—Vengeance, and Envy, and Murder, and Death, and all the woes the earth brings forth; for never will I own that Zeus begot thee, bane of many barbarians and Greeks. Curses upon thee! For with those eyes so beautiful thou hast shamefully destroyed the fair plains of Troy.'

πολλοῖσι κῆρα βαρβάροις Ἕλλησί τε.
ὄλοιο· καλλίστων γὰρ ὀμμάτων ἄπο
αἰσχρῶς τὰ κλεινὰ πεδί᾽ ἀπώλεσας Φρυγῶν.

O mala degeneres meditati barbara Grai,
  quem puer hic laesit? cur nece dignus erat?
tuque, O Tyndareo, neque enim Iove, nata propago—
  immo te plures progenuisse reor,
scilicet Eumenides Mortemque Iramque ministrum
  Mortis, et in terris quicquid ubique nocet;
rebor enim numquam genitam te de Iove summo,
  hostibus et sociis exitiale nefas!—
a pereas oculis cum resplendentibus istis,
  pro quibus indigne Dardana regna iacent!

But Euripides can carry it off where Ovid cannot. His heroines'
outbursts do not occur until the progress of the drama has
heightened the tension, so that we do not feel them to be over-
strained; and his iambic verse, being flexible, can be realistically
expressive:

ἀλλ᾽ ἄγετε, φέρετε, ῥίπτετ᾽, εἰ ῥίπτειν δοκεῖ,
δαίνυσθε τοῦδε σάρκας,

So Andromache continues, in a wild rhythm of frenzy now beyond
the reach of the compact, end-stopped elegiacs of the Roman, in
which one couplet will make a point, and the next few develop it,
and then the poet's unflagging *inventio* will think of another point
—everything in neat and watertight compartments.

Whatever their origin as an idea, and whatever their varied
sources, in treatment the *Heroides* are influenced by the rhetorical
ethopoeïa.* It is they, no doubt, which have given Ovid the
reputation of being more rhetorician than poet. The situation is

---

* School exercises involving impersonation of some legendary or historical
character. Fränkel is more indulgent to the *Heroides* than most readers may feel
inclined to be. He does well to remind us, however, that they are true to life in
that slighted lovers often do write such letters, whether or not they post them,
'silently arguing out the issue with our remote and unwitting partner' (*op. cit.*
p. 36).

given, and the pupil of Arellius Fuscus, assuming the character of the heroine, proceeds to make every point that can be made.* The familiar commonplaces (τόποι) are pressed into service. Thus time and again the heroine traces her plight back to its origins by a chain of causality, just as the Nurse had done in the opening lines of Euripides' *Medea*: 'I wish the Argo had never rowed between the Symplegades on the way to Colchis, I wish the pines had never been felled in the glens of Pelion to furnish oars for the heroes who went in quest of the Golden Fleece for Pelias; for then—.'† These stock themes are supplemented by motives peculiar to the particular story. The literary sources are scrutinized for any hint, and the circumstances of the heroine and hero, their life and their family connexions, are fully exploited. For instance, Demophoön was a son of Theseus, which enabled Phyllis to say that the only deed in his father's long career that seemed to have impressed him was his desertion of Ariadne on Naxos.[40] The heroines are mainly concerned, like the rhetoricians, with scoring points, whether argumentative or emotional. Ovid makes little attempt to conceive them as belonging to a more primitive civilization (what ancient writer would?). In so far as they are not embodiments of *das Ewig-Weibliche*, they are Roman women of his own day.

So much was due to rhetorical education; but Ovid himself seems to have had a fundamental trait in his own psychology which pushed its effect to extremes. He was 'puzzle-minded'. He loved to set himself a problem and then treat it exhaustively, fitting in all the pieces provided by the subject. He cannot select; he must go on to the end, even if it spoils his poem. Deïaneira must recite all the amours of Hercules, not excluding the grotesque story of his obliging the fifty daughters of Thespius, and follow this with a complete catalogue of his labours, of which he was no doubt even now boasting to her rival![41] *Nescit quod bene cessit relinquere,*

---

* A good example of legalistic argument is VIII, 31–48 (Hermione).

† Tr. D. W. Lucas. This passage was much admired in antiquity (see D. L. Page *ad loc.*). Ovid found it imitated in Ariadne's complaint in Catullus, LXIV, 171–7. Cf. Ennius, fr. 246 V.

as Seneca said. Nearly all the *Heroides* are too long; the shortest extends to 116 lines, and the average is about 190.

With our modern background we expect such poems to be moving individually, or at least collectively to provide penetrating psychological studies of how various women would behave in a similar situation. It is true that Ovid takes some pains over both *pathos* and *ethos* and varies his *color*, but the heroines are little differentiated except to the extent that their situations differ. Psychological subtlety is not one of the characteristic excellences of ancient literature, though Ovid excels his predecessors in this respect. We may be fairly sure that his audience read these poems as connoisseurs of rhetoric; they did not weep for Ovid's Dido as Augustine was to weep for Virgil's. They would derive particular pleasure from recognizing the details in the traditional story and observing how dexterously Ovid had made use of them; they would burst into applause at a telling couplet; and of course they would delight, as modern practitioners do, in the easy mastery of the verse, the ingenious tricks and periphrases, the grace, the inevitability. The *Heroides* were probably not intended to move; they are a display of virtuosity designed to entertain.

We can at least appreciate the terse, quotable aphorisms—*tarde, quae credita laedunt, credimus*, or *abeunt studia in mores*—;[42] the fine expressions of *ethos*:

> qui bene pro patria cum patriaque iacent,*
>
> *who nobly for their country and with their country fell,*

or

> rustica sim sane, dum non oblita pudoris;[43]
>
> *by all means call me simple, so long as mindful of my honour;*

the irony when Hypsipyle says she thought of sending her two children by Jason as envoys to him, but was deterred by the thought that Medea might kill them—Medea who was to kill her

---

* Briseïs, of her brothers.[44]

own children;[45] the double irony when Penelope imagines Ulysses telling some love that his wife is 'rustica' and only fit to stay at home and weave, whereas she is preserving her fidelity to him precisely by the trick of her weaving, while in reality he for his part is even now telling a goddess that he wishes to leave her for home because he prefers his wife, homely though she be by comparison.[46] We can admire (not without a smile) the verbal jugglery of

> Si, nisi quae facie poterit te digna videri
> nulla futura tua est, nulla futura tua est,[47]

> *If none in beauty not a match for thee*
> *Shall be thy love, then none thy love shall be,*

or of the hardly translatable

> Non sum qui soleam Paridis reprehendere facta
> nec quemquam qui, vir posset ut esse, fuit,[48]

> *Nor Paris nor another blame I can*
> *Who, to obtain a wife, has played the man.*

But such conceits can be incongruously absurd, as when Medea complains that, though she could put a dragon to sleep, she cannot put herself:

> quae me non possum, potui sopire draconem;[49]

and we can only laugh outright when Ariadne says that she is not surprised that the horns of the Minotaur (whom she insists on calling her brother) could not pierce Theseus' breast, his heart is so hard.[50] There are, indeed, plenty of examples of κακοζηλία, what we should consider bathos or bad taste, if we were to take these letters seriously; such as Hero's suggestion that, if Leander feels he cannot manage the double journey, she will swim out and meet him half-way to kiss on the crest of a wave.[51] The heroines are not too miserable to make puns—*non honor est sed onus* (IX, 31), *verbera cum verbis* (x, 38), *hospes an hostis* (xvii, 10). I feel sure that in the *Heroides* Ovid, a baroque spirit before his time, was prepared to risk seeming comic if only he could seem clever.

Here and there, amid the desert of debating points, we do come across cases of what seem genuine feeling or pathos, when the poet forgets himself and his audience. Canace, doomed to die herself for her incest with her brother Macareus, laments for their new-born child, exposed to die on the mountains, as many an innocent mother must have lamented in times when this barbarity was the normal form of birth-control (xi, 111–18):

> Nate, dolor matris, rabidarum praeda ferarum,
>   ei mihi! natali dilacerate tuo;
> nate, parum fausti miserabile pignus amoris,
>   haec tibi prima dies, haec tibi summa fuit.
> non mihi te licuit lacrimis perfundere iustis,
>   in tua nec tonsas ferre sepulcra comas;
> non super incubui, non oscula frigida carpsi.
>   diripiunt avidae viscera nostra ferae.

> *My son, your mother's sorrow, born this day,*
> *Born and cast out to ravening beasts a prey,*
> *My son, poor pledge of love, alas, unblest,*
> *This day your first, this day shall be your last.*
> *With no due tears may I your body lave*
> *Nor bear shorn locks in mourning to your grave,*
> *Nor may I kiss your cold lips, bending o'er:—*
> *Wild beasts are tearing what my body bore.*

Medea, rejected by Jason, vividly describes her anguish:[52]

> Iussa domo cessi natis comitata duobus
>   et, qui me sequitur semper, amore tui.
> ut subito nostras Hymen cantatus ad aures
>   venit, et accenso lampades igne micant,
> tibiaque effundit socialia carmina vobis,
>   at mihi funerea flebiliora tuba,

pertimui nec adhuc tantum scelus esse putabam:
    sed tamen in toto pectore frigus erat.
turba ruunt et 'Hymen' clamant 'Hymenaee' frequenter.
    quo propior vox haec, hoc mihi peius erat.
diversi flebant servi lacrimasque tegebant;
    quis vellet tanti nuntius esse mali?
me quoque, quicquid erat, potius nescire iuvabat,
    sed tanquam scirem, mens mea tristis erat,
cum minor e pueris iussus studioque videndi
    constitit ad geminae limina prima foris:
'huc mihi, mater, abi! pompam pater' inquit 'Iason
    ducit et adiunctos aureus urget equos.'

Thrust from our home, I took our children two,
And, ever present still, my love for you.
Sudden the wedding-song assailed my ears,
I saw the wedding-torches through my tears;
The pipes began to sound your marriage-lay,
More drear to me than funeral-trumpets they.
Foreboding much, yet disbelieving still
In guilt so black, my heart with fear ran chill.
The crowd approaching 'Hymen, Hymen' sing,
The nearer they, the worse my suffering.
My slaves in corners strive to hide their tears,
None willing to confirm such hideous fears;
I too strive fondly not to know 'tis true,
And yet my heart is rent, as though I knew;
When, eager for the sight, our younger boy
Placed at the door,* calls out to me with joy,
'Mother, come here! A great procession, led
By father: all in gold he drives ahead!'

---

* Palmer misconceives the scene. He thinks Medea is in the street, but surely she must be in some dower-house. The MSS read *iussus studioque videndi*: she cannot bear to look out herself, but she tells her little boy to do so, he is so eager to see what is happening. Most MSS also read *hinc*, but some inferior ones read *hic*; the true reading is probably *huc*; cf. M. III, 454, *quisquis es, huc exi*.

Hermione tells of her bewilderment in her girlhood when her
mother Helen left Sparta with Paris, and of her embarrassment
when she was brought back, ten years later, after the fall of Troy:[53]

Vix equidem memini, memini tamen: omnia luctus,
    omnia solliciti plena timoris erant.
flebat avus Phoebeque soror fratresque gemelli,
    orabat superos Leda suumque Iovem.
ipsa ego, non longos etiam tunc scissa capillos,
    clamabam, 'sine me, me sine, mater, abis?'...

parua mea sine matre fui, pater arma ferebat,
    et duo cum vivant, orba duobus eram.
non tibi blanditias primis, mea mater, in annis
    incerto dictas ore puella tuli,
non ego captavi brevibus tua colla lacertis,
    nec gremio sedi sarcina grata tuo;
non cultus tibi cura mei, nec pacta marito
    intravi thalamos matre parante novos.

obvia prodieram reduci tibi, vera fatebor,
    nec facies nobis nota parentis erat;
te tamen esse Helenen, quod eras pulcherrima, sensi;
    ipsa requirebas, quae tua nata foret.

I scarce recall—and yet I do recall:
Foreboding, grief and fear were over all;
My mother's father, sister, brothers there
Were weeping; Leda sought her Jove in prayer.
Myself, with girlish tresses torn in woe,
Cried 'Mother, will you leave me, leave me so?'...

My mother gone, my father with the host,
Though both yet lived, I felt that both were lost.
Your baby, mother, never in your ears
Lisped the sweet prattle of her tender years;

No little arms around your neck I threw
Or climbed upon your lap to comfort you.
You did not bring me up, you were not there
The promised bride for wedlock to prepare.

When you came back I met you on the shore,
But, truth to tell, remembered you no more,—
Yet knew you straight for Helen, none so fair,
While you must ask, 'Which is my daughter here?'

These three passages have one element in common, they all introduce children: the innocent, unconscious baby of Canace, the naïve little boy of Medea, the lonely child Hermione. *Maxima debetur puero reverentia*: Ovid's attitude to women, even suffering women, might sometimes be equivocal, but the pathos of childhood touched him as it had touched the Alexandrian poets.

The passage about Medea derives its effect also from his exceptional skill in narrative. The heroines are far more pathetic when they simply tell their story than when they utter strings of reproaches and arguments, regrets and lamentations. The story of Ariadne, told against a romantic background of shore and cliffs and trees, is one of the best things in the whole collection.[54]

Tempus erat, vitrea quo primum terra pruina
  spargitur et tectae fronde queruntur aves;
incertum vigilans, a somno languida, movi
  Thesea prensuras semisupina manus:
nullus erat: referoque manus iterumque retempto,
  perque torum moveo bracchia: nullus erat.
excussere metus somnum; conterrita surgo,
  membraque sunt viduo praecipitata toro.
protinus adductis sonuerunt pectora palmis,
  utque erat e somno turbida, rapta coma est.

luna fuit: specto siquid nisi litora cernam;
  quod videant, oculi nil nisi litus habent.
nunc huc, nunc illuc, et utroque sine ordine, curro;
  alta puellares tardat harena pedes.

interea toto clamanti litore 'Theseu!'
  reddebant nomen concava saxa tuum,
et quotiens ego te, totiens locus ipse vocabat:
  ipse locus miserae ferre volebat opem.

mons fuit; apparent frutices in vertice rari;
  nunc scopulus raucis pendet adesus aquis.
ascendo, vires animus dabat, atque ita late
  aequora prospectu metior alta meo.
inde ego, nam ventis quoque sum crudelibus usa,
  vidi praecipiti carbasa tenta Noto.
ut vidi haud dignam quae me vidisse putarem,*
  frigidior glacie semianimisque fui.
nec languere diu patitur dolor; excitor illo,
  excitor et summa Thesea voce voco.
'quo fugis?' exclamo; 'scelerate revertere Theseu!
  flecte ratem! numerum non habet illa suum.'

It was the hour when earth is glistering
With rime, and leaf-hid birds begin to sing.
Scarce half awake as I lay on my side,
My drowsy hands to clasp my Theseus tried—
In vain! I drew my hands in, tried again,
Stretching my arms to sweep the couch. In vain!
Fear shook off sleep; I sat upright in dread
And flung myself from the deserted bed,
Beat on my breast with palms resounding deep,
And tore my hair still disarranged from sleep.

The moon is up. I search if I can spy
Aught but the shore: shore only meets my eye;
Now here, now there, I run, and all unplanned;
My tender feet sink deep into the sand;
And 'Theseus!' all along the beach I cry,
'Theseus!' the rocks and hollow caves reply;

---

* See Housman, *C.R.*, 1897, p. 240. His emendations in the *Heroides* are conveniently summarized by Purser on pp. liv–lix of Palmer's edition.

Oft as I call, they call in sympathy:
As if to aid me in my agony.

A hill there is, crowned with a fringe of trees,
Its side a cliff carved out by angry seas.
Strong in my frenzy I ascend, and sweep
With searching eyes the wide-unfolded deep,
And thence—for e'en the breezes are unkind—
I spy your sail flying before the wind.
Then at that sight, which ne'er did I deserve
To see, I freeze like ice, unstrung my nerve;
Yet pain allows no rest; I spring upright,
Spring up, and 'Theseus!' shout with all my might,
'Where are you fleeing? Wicked man, turn back:
Reverse your ship for one her crew doth lack!'

There is one touch here that jars, to my feeling: the fine conception of inanimate nature sympathizing with Ariadne's plight is blurred by the rather trite parenthesis about the winds being heartless as her lover. But how many touches there are which are fresh and true! Her gradual awakening, her sleep-dishevelled hair, her feet sinking in the sand, the hill so vividly pictured in a few strokes.*

The plight of a deserted heroine can indeed inspire a moving and beautiful poem if these elements that Ovid used all too sparingly—narrative, romantic setting and pathos—are given their due place, and reproaches (wherein lies the danger of rhetorical excess) are not multiplied till they become tedious. Tennyson has demonstrated this in his *Oenone*, a poem which may have been suggested by *Heroides* v and certainly takes some hints from it, but which is steeped in romanticism. Theocritus, indeed, might have

---

* There is a wall-painting in the House of the Tragic Poet at Pompeii which shows Theseus embarking and Ariadne on top of a cliff with a few trees on it, holding her hand to her eyes and gazing after him; reproduced, e.g., by G. E. Rizzo, *La Pittura Ellenistico-Romana* (1929), Tav. xxxix; K. Schefold, *Pompeianische Malerei* (1952), Taf. 52. It was painted in Vespasian's time, probably after a Greek original of *c.* 400 B.C. (Schefold, p. 33).

written such a poem, but one can scarcely imagine Ovid sustaining, or wishing to sustain, such a level of romantic and lyrical beauty throughout a whole piece. His genius was for wit.

It is not surprising that we feel a certain relief when we come upon a piece in the *Heroides* which is not one more version of the now familiar complaint. If we cannot be moved, we may perhaps be amused. The specious arguments of Phaedra designed to allay the scruples of Hippolytus (a real *suasoria* this) are worthy of the bawd Dipsas in *Amores* I, 8. Ovid is here once more in his element, the poet of amorous intrigue, of brazenness and *nequitia* (IV, 129–48):

> Nec, quia privigno videar coitura noverca,
> terruerint animos nomina vana tuos.
> ista vetus pietas, aevo moritura futuro,
> rustica Saturno regna tenente fuit.
> Iuppiter esse pium statuit quodcumque iuvaret,
> et fas omne facit fratre marita soror.
> illa coit firma generis iunctura catena
> imposuit nodos cui Venus ipsa suos.
> nec labor est celare, licet peccemus, amorem:
> cognato poterit nomine culpa tegi.
> viderit amplexos aliquis, laudabimur ambo;
> dicar privigno fida noverca meo.
> non tibi per tenebras duri reseranda mariti
> ianua, non custos decipiendus erit:
> ut tenuit domus una duos, domus una tenebit;
> oscula aperta dabas, oscula aperta dabis;
> tutus eris mecum laudemque merebere culpa,
> tu licet in lecto conspiciare meo.
> tolle moras tantum properataque foedera iunge:
> qui mihi nunc saevit, sic tibi parcat Amor!

> *Do not, because I seek my stepson's bed,*
> *Let empty names put fears into your head;*
> *Such antique scruples' days were numbered when*
> *Old Saturn still enjoyed his rustic reign;*

Jove, ruling that what pleased could not be sin,
Sealed it by marrying his next of kin.
The bond of kinship cannot firm remain
Where holy Venus has not forged the chain:
Why strive to veil our passion? Where's the need,
When kinship's name can cloak the guilty deed?
Embraces seen will praise on both confer:
I'll pass for a devoted stepmother.
Not yours to force a husband's bolted door
In darkness, or deceive a janitor:
One house has held, one house shall hold us still,
Openly have we kissed, and kiss we will.
No blame will you receive, but praise instead,
Safe at my side, and even in my bed.
Only make haste and straight our union seal,
Ere you, like me, be broken on Love's wheel.

How shall we assess the *Heroides*? It is undeniable that they have been highly popular throughout the centuries. 'All the world loves a lover', concludes Showerman,[55] 'and all the world has for a long time loved most of the *Heroides*', and Shuckburgh[56] says much the same. But taste has changed considerably in the past hundred and fifty years, and it is most important that traditional judgements should not be accepted without question. The classics have suffered because their exponents have too often felt it their duty to be propagandists, with the inevitable result that un-prejudiced readers are disappointed and become sceptical. The proof of the pudding is in the eating. To me the single *Heroides* (i–xv) are a uniform plum pudding with a fair admixture of glittering rings and sixpences. The first slice is appetising enough, but each further slice becomes colder and less digestible, until the only incentive for going on is the prospect of coming across an occasional ring or sixpence. It seems a pity that so many school-boys should first be introduced to Ovid through this work. Few of them can ever have been deserted by a lover, and one suspects that the choice is due to the unobjectionableness rather than the interest of the subject-matter. Yet even with this restriction one would have thought the *Fasti* or *Metamorphoses* more suitable.

It is with palates almost ruined by long draughts of the bitter lees of love in the *Heroides* proper (I–XV) that we come to the living wine in XVI–XXI, three letters from heroes with the heroines' replies. Here the passion is either awakening or at its height. The epistolary fiction is maintained, but instead of 'half a dialogue' we have something approaching a love scene. It is a considerable improvement.* Hero is waiting in her tower for Leander as he swims the Hellespont by night, and the setting is no less romantic than the dawn on Naxos:[57]

> Haec ego, vel certe non his diversa, locutus
>   per mihi cedentes sponte† ferebar aquas.
> unda repercussae radiabat imagine lunae,
>   et nitor in tacita nocte diurnus erat;
> nullaque vox usquam, nullum veniebat ad aures
>   praeter dimotae corpore murmur aquae;
> alcyones solae, memores Ceÿcis amati,
>   nescioquid visae sunt mihi dulce queri.
> iamque fatigatis umero sub utroque lacertis
>   fortiter in summas erigor altus aquas;
> ut procul aspexi lumen, 'meus ignis in illo est:
>   illa meum' dixi 'litora lumen habent'.

> *While thus, or nearly, to the moon I spoke,*
> *The friendly water yielded to my stroke;*
> *The billows gleamed with her reflected light*
> *Which clear as day illumed the silent night.*

---

* Shuckburgh's much-used school edition omits XI (Canace) as unsuitable and XV–XXI because unfortunately in his day (1879, 2nd edn. 1885) 'the last seven have been now pretty generally pronounced to be by another hand. And without entering further into the question we may without difficulty acknowledge their inferiority in many ways' (p. xxiv); whereas E. K. Rand, writing in 1925 (*Ovid and his Influence*, p. 27) says: 'If they are not from Ovid's pen, an *ignotus* has beaten him at his own game'.

† *Sponte*, Francius, Bentley (MSS *nocte*).

No sound, no murmur to my ears there came,
Save where the surface rippled as I swam;
Only the halcyons, still on Ceÿx bent,
Seemed to be uttering a sweet lament.
At length, with effort of my arms distressed,
I reared myself upon a billow's crest,
And saw far off a light that made me cry,
'My flame's own light on yonder shore I spy!'

Narrative skill and the pathos of childhood excitement before a catastrophe combine, as in the passage about Medea, to move us in the account Cydippe of Athens gives of her visit to Delos, surely inspired by recollections of the poet's own youthful tour. The story had formed one of the most famous episodes in the *Aetia* of Callimachus. Acontius of Ceos, a handsome youth, saw Cydippe at a festival at Delos, and straightway fell in love with her. Having no hope of winning anyone so inaccessible by ordinary means, he followed her to Artemis' temple, and rolled in her path an apple on which he had written in verse, 'I swear by Artemis that I will marry Acontius'. Her nurse picked it up and, being illiterate, handed it to Cydippe to read; and she, reading aloud as even adults normally did in antiquity, pronounced the oath before she could realize its import. She told no one, and in due course her father arranged a different marriage for her; but whenever the time came, she was wasted with a mysterious fever. After this had happened three times, the father consulted the oracle at Delphi, and the story of the unwitting vow was revealed. On Apollo's advice she then fulfilled it.

One of the chief contributions gained from the Oxyrhynchus Papyri was a fragment of Callimachus' *Aetia* some eighty lines long including part of this story.[58] It breaks in at the first fever of Cydippe, so that we cannot tell to what extent Ovid was indebted to Callimachus, who in turn had found the story in Xenomedes, a local historian of Ceos.*[59] The narrative style of this poem,

* From what we have it would appear that Ovid borrowed details but was free in his general treatment of the story.

which is several times referred to by Ovid,[60] is not at all like his. It is lively, but factual almost to bareness, unsentimental, even amused, and frequently impeded by learned allusions, periphrases and digressions; Ovid's is swift, fresh and picturesque:[61]

Mota loci fama properabam visere Delon,
  et facere ignava puppe videbar iter;
quam saepe ut tardis feci convicia remis
  questaque sum vento lintea parca dari!
et iam transieram Myconon, iam Tenon et Andron,
  inque meis oculis candida Delos erat,
quam procul ut vidi, 'quid me fugis, insula,' dixi,
  'laberis in magno numquid, ut ante, mari?'

institeram terrae cum iam prope luce peracta
  demere purpureis Sol iuga vellet equis.
quos idem solitos postquam revocavit ad ortus,
  comuntur nostrae matre iubente comae.
ipsa dedit gemmas digitis, et crinibus aurum
  et vestes umeris induit ipsa meis.
protinus egressae superis, quibus insula sacra est,
  flava salutatis tura merumque damus;
dumque parens aras votivo sanguine tingit
  festaque fumosis ingerit exta focis,
sedula me nutrix alias quoque ducit in aedes,
  erramusque vago per loca sacra pede;
et modo porticibus spatior, modo munera regum
  miror et in cunctis stantia signa locis;
miror et innumeris structam de cornibus aram
  et de qua pariens arbore nixa dea est,
et quae praeterea—neque enim meminive libetve,
  quicquid ibi vidi, dicere—Delos habet.

forsitan haec spectans a te spectabar, Aconti,
  visaque simplicitas est mea posse capi.
in templum redeo gradibus sublime Dianae—
  tutior hoc ecquis debuit esse locus?

mittitur ante pedes malum cum carmine tali—
   ei mihi, iuravi nunc quoque paene tibi!
sustulit hoc nutrix mirataque 'perlege' dixit:
   insidias legi, magne poeta, tuas!

Fired by its fame, to Delos I would go;
So keen I was, my ship seemed all too slow.
How oft impatiently did I deplore
The niggard canvas and the sluggish oar!
Myconos, Tenos, Andros now were past
And shining Delos hove in sight at last.
'Island', I cried, 'Why do you flee from me?
Are you once more adrift upon the sea?'

I landed when the day was well-nigh done,
Well-nigh unyoked the horses of the sun.
Soon as they did with daylight reappear,
My mother woke me, bade me dress my hair;
Herself the robe upon my shoulders laid,
Gems on my fingers, gold upon my head.
Then forth we go, the Island's deities
With gifts of wine and incense to appease;
She with a victim's blood the altars dyes
And heaps the flames with solemn sacrifice;
I with my nurse to other shrines repair
And wander through the hallowed places there,
Now pace the colonnades, now in amaze
At royal gifts and countless statues gaze,
Gaze at the altar made of myriad horn,
The tree neath which Latona's twins were born,
And all the rest—I can no longer, no,
Will not recall what Delos has to show.

Acontius, as I looked, you looked on me,
Sure you could prey on such simplicity.
To the high steps of chaste Diana's fane—
Where should be safer?—I returned again.

> *An apple to my feet came rolling, thus*
> *Inscribed—but stay! those words are perilous!*
> *Nurse picked it up, and wondering, 'Read it', said,*
> *And, mighty poet, trapped by you, I read.*

Cydippe's struggle is hopeless, because the goddess will demand fulfilment of the oath; but it is a long time before she betrays the secret that she does not care for her official bridegroom (189–206); and not until the end does she openly capitulate to Acontius (227–48).

Perhaps more interesting than this struggle against destiny is the struggle within the soul of Helen in xvii, a rare opportunity for the poet who coined the phrase *video meliora proboque, deteriora sequor* ('I see and approve the better course, yet choose the worse').* Though here again there is the sanction of a goddess in the background, we are less conscious of it. Helen is depicted as a young and innocent wife. Paris has come to Sparta and been hospitably received. Taking advantage of a temporary absence of Menelaus, he sends his hostess by the hand of a servant a passionate love-letter (xvi). She begins her reply with splendid scorn, answering point for point, and continues so for sixty-four lines; then a slip betrays her real feelings, and gradually she begins to waver until she becomes hopelessly involved:[62]

> Munera tanta quidem promittit epistula dives
>   ut possint ipsas illa movere deas.
> sed si iam vellem fines transire pudoris,
>   tu melior culpae causa futurus eras.
> aut ego perpetuo famam sine labe tenebo,
>   aut ego te potius quam tua dona sequar;
> utque ea non sperno, sic acceptissima semper
>   munera sunt, auctor quae pretiosa facit.
> plus multo est, quod amas, quod sum tibi causa laboris,
>   quod tam per longas spes tua venit aquas.

---

* Spoken by Medea, *M.* vii, 20–1; adapted from Euripides, *Hippolytus,* 380–1; cf. *Medea,* 1078–9.

illa quoque, adposita quae nunc facis, improbe, mensa,
  quamvis experiar dissimulare, noto:
cum modo me spectas oculis, lascive, protervis,
  quos vix instantes lumina nostra ferunt,
et modo suspiras, modo pocula proxima nobis
  sumis, quaque bibi, tu quoque parte bibis.
a! quotiens digitis, quotiens ego tecta notavi
  signa supercilio paene loquente dari!
et saepe extimui, ne vir meus illa videret,
  non satis occultis erubique notis.
saepe vel exiguo vel nullo murmure dixi.
  'nil pudet hunc', nec vox haec mea falsa fuit.
orbe quoque in mensae legi sub nomine nostro
  quod deducta mero littera fecit 'AMO'.
credere me tamen hoc oculo renuente negavi:
  ei mihi! iam didici sic ego posse loqui!

his ego blanditiis, si peccatura fuissem,
  flecterer, his poterant pectora nostra capi.
est quoque, confiteor, facies tibi rara, potestque
  velle sub amplexus ire puella tuos.
altera vel potius felix sine crimine fiat,
  quam cadat externo noster amore pudor!
disce meo exemplo formosis posse carere:
  est virtus placitis abstinuisse bonis.
quam multos credis iuvenes optare, quod optas?
  qui sapiant, oculos an Paris unus habes?
non tu plus cernis sed plus temerarius audes;
  nec tibi plus cordis sed minus oris adest.

The bounty that your letter promises
Might move indeed even the goddesses;
Yet were it in me to transgress my laws,
Yourself had been a more compelling cause;
Either I'll keep my honour ever true
Or follow, not the gifts you bring, but you;
Not that I scorn them; gifts are then, I know,
Most precious when the giver makes them so;

Far more I prize your love, your toil for me,
The hope that brought you leagues across the sea.

Your wanton signs at table in the hall,
Try as I may to feign, I mark them all:
Now you transfix me with lascivious look
Whose urgency my eyes can scarcely brook,
And now you sigh, now take the cup from me
And drink where I have drunk it pointedly.
Oft have your fingers, oft your brow conveyed
Signs clear as any speech could e'er have made.
Oft have I feared lest Menelaus see,
And blushed at gestures made too openly;
Often 'twas on my lips or in my mind,
'This man is shameless'; and 'tis true, I find.
Upon the table-top, my name above,
I read traced out in wine the words 'I love',
But not believing you, my eyes said 'nay'.
(Alas, that I have learned to speak that way!)

These are the charms, had I the mind to sin,
That might seduce me, these my heart could win.
Nay, I confess it: perfect is your face;
Well might a woman long for your embrace.
Let her who may with honour have that joy;
No stranger shall my chastity destroy;
Learn you, like me, to admire and leave alone;
What else is virtue but delight forgone?
How many youths have prized what you now prize?
Have you alone discriminating eyes?
Not more perception have you, but less grace,
Have no more heart, but only show more face.

She wishes she had been unmarried when he came, but warns him against thinking she would leave Menelaus, even if she longed to go as his bride to Troy, adding a moving appeal,

> Desine molle, precor, verbis convellere pectus,
> neve mihi, quam tu dicis amare, noce.[63]

Cease, I implore, to tear this breast apart,
Nor, if you truly love me, break my heart.

She doubts his story of his judging between the three goddesses, and having modestly added that at least she would never have been chosen as Venus' reward, confesses that she is flattered by praise from such a quarter, and finally apologizes for her initial incredulity! Yet still she wavers and struggles, now dwelling on the hopelessness of his plan, now deploring her inexperience in deception:

> Felices quibus usus adest! ego nescia rerum
>   difficilem culpae suspicor esse viam.[64]

Happy the seasoned lover! I, untaught,
Fancy the path of sin with perils fraught.

Her mind is in utter confusion. She feels all eyes are upon her, and confesses that rumours have come to her ears:

> At tu dissimula, nisi si desistere mavis:
>   sed cur desistas? dissimulare potes.
> lude, sed occulte. maior, non maxima, nobis
>   est data libertas, quod Menelaus abest.[65]

But you, deceive them—if you will not cease!—
Why cease, though, when you can deceive with ease?
Make love, but watch! With Menelaus flown
More, but not perfect, liberty we own.

She now admits more than she did before. When Menelaus left and they were exchanging farewells, he told her to look after the house and their Trojan guest; whereat she could hardly restrain her laughter, and could only murmur, 'I will'. And yet she is afraid, for the very fame of her beauty makes Menelaus anxious, and she herself recoils before the untried:[66]

> Et libet et timeo, nec adhuc exacta voluntas
>   est satis; in dubio pectora nostra labant.
> et vir abest nobis, et tu sine coniuge dormis,
>   inque vicem tua me, te mea forma capit;

et longae noctes, et iam sermone coimus,
  et tu, me miseram! blandus, et una domus:
et peream si non invitant omnia culpam;
  nescio quo tardor sed tamen ipsa metu.
quod male persuades utinam bene cogere posses!
  vi mea rusticitas excutienda fuit.

I yearn and fear and know not what I will;
My heart is doubtful and I waver still;
For he is absent, and you sleep alone;
I by your beauty, you by mine, are won;
The nights are long, our talks are intimate,
You such a tempter, and within the gate:
Why, everything invites me to proceed,
And yet some fear restrains me from the deed.
To tempt's unfair: I yearn for fair duress:
Force should have purged me of my prudishness.

But she returns again to thoughts of how to get over her passion. And so it goes on to the end, where she refuses to see him, but agrees to continue negotiations through her handmaids. The whole piece, 268 lines long, is a psychological study presented with masterly wit and insight.

Perhaps it was the study of Greek tragedy for purposes of the *Heroides*, and in particular of Euripides' *Medea* for xII, that inspired Ovid at this period to his only effort at drama.* He heralds it at *Am.* III, 1, 29:

  nunc habeam per te, Romana Tragoedia, nomen.

  now, Roman Tragedy, may I win fame by you.

That poem depicts a struggle for his soul between the Muses of Tragedy and Elegy, at the end of which the former grants him a short respite:

  Mota dedit veniam—teneri properentur Amores
    dum vacat; a tergo grandius urget opus.

* It could, of course, have been the other way round.

Moved, she gave me indulgence—let the tender Loves hasten
while they have time; a nobler work is pressing on their heels.

The tragedy he did produce attained a great reputation in antiquity. Tacitus asserted that no work of Pollio or Messalla was so celebrated as the *Medea* of Ovid and the *Thyestes* of Varius;[67] and Quintilian remarked that Ovid's *Medea* seemed to him to show how much that poet could have achieved if he had only chosen to discipline rather than indulge his genius.[68] Only two lines of it have come down to us:[69]

> servare potui: perdere an possim rogas?
>
> *I was able to save: do you ask if I can destroy?*

and

> feror huc illuc, vae, plena deo.
>
> *hither and thither I rush, ah, full of the god.*

We have no means of assessing its merits. If it achieved contemporary success, it is surprising that Ovid made no further attempt. Quintilian was discussing literature with an eye to oratorical education. We may accept his statement that this play was free from perverted ingenuity; but the taste of theatre audiences had long been debased, and it may not have come into its own until rhetorical drama intended for reading had been established in fashion by Seneca.

Ennius had produced what seems to have been a close version of Euripides' play, and Accius had also treated the story, while Seneca in turn was probably much influenced by Ovid in his version of it. At *Metamorphoses* VII, 1–424 Ovid tells Medea's story in full *except* for her expulsion from Corinth and the murder of her children. The natural inference is that these last events had been dealt with in his tragedy, as in its predecessors.

The Epistle (XII) is conceived at a moment just before the tragedy (at least in Euripides' version) begins. It precedes any interview with Jason, which would have rendered it superfluous, and *a fortiori* the murder of the children, which would have overshadowed everything and shut her out of the line of pathetic and injured heroines. It is, in fact, a sort of introduction to the drama, which may already have been conceived, or even composed. She ends with vague but awful threats, not yet envisaged. 'I will do such things—what they are, yet I know not.' Unlike Lear, she still has power to hurt, and the audience knows it and shudders.[70]

Quos equidem actutum—sed quid praedicere poenam
    attinet? ingentes parturit ira minas.
quo feret ira, sequar. facti fortasse pigebit—
    et piget infido consuluisse viro.
viderit ista deus, qui nunc mea pectora versat!
    nescioquid certe mens mihi maius agit.

Whom I will straight—but why the punishment
Divulge? My wrath is big with dire intent.
My wrath will sway me. I may rue the deed?
I rue the day that I a traitor freed.
God will dispose who now my bosom stirs.
This much I know: I ponder something worse.

CHAPTER VI

THE 'ARS AMATORIA' AND 'REMEDIA AMORIS'

PRAECEPTOR AMORIS

AT some time during Ovid's early period (certainly before he wrote the third book of the *Ars Amatoria*[1]) he tried his hand at didactic poetry of the most prosaic kind—versification of a technical treatise. Precedents for this went back for two or three centuries, to Aratus and Nicander of Colophon, and it would seem that Romans in Ovid's day had written verse treatises, for instance, on games of various kinds, on etiquette, on dyeing fabrics and on making pottery.[2] Most of Nicander's poems (if they may be dignified by that name) were in hexameters, though his *Ophiaca*, a collection of stories about snakes, was apparently in elegiacs. The subject chosen by Ovid was cosmetics (*medicamina faciei*), and after fifty clever and spirited lines of introduction he plunges into a series of versified recipes, presumably taken from some prose treatise by a professional pharmacologist. It is hardly a matter of regret that after a further fifty lines our manuscripts break off.

One would like to think that Ovid broke off too. He tells us that the book was small, but he also indicates that it was published (*A.A.* III, 205–8); and the ending as we have it is too abrupt to be an intentional close. What can have induced him to embark on such a poem? He was not a tasteless bore, as Nicander (to judge from his two extant verse treatises) most certainly was. One may guess that what amused him was, not the subject-matter itself, but the idea of writing a didactic poem on a subject connected with his speciality, love, and in elegiacs, the metre of love-poetry. His unusual tendency to see things through the eyes of the opposite

sex, already exemplified in the *Heroides*, would help to account
for his choice.

There was also the irresistible temptation *épater le bourgeois*.
Cosmetics, then as now, were considered in strait-laced circles to
be a shade unhealthy or improper, though nothing would induce
the girls to give them up—at any rate the girls whose main
business was to attract men, though Ovid also implies that this
work at least is also intended for respectable ladies. Even Propertius, whose primary objection was that such adornments
suggested a desire to attract others besides himself, took a high
line about them to reinforce this: 'So now you are madly
imitating the painted Britons, and flaunting foreign dye upon
your hair? As nature made it is all beauty best: Belgic dye is a
disgrace to Roman faces.'[3] It is the recurrent cry that nature is
right and art wrong, which, sooner or later, is bound to produce
a revolt.* 'Art', said Oscar Wilde, 'is our spirited protest, our
gallant attempt to teach nature her proper place.'† The 'nineties in
England were such a period of revolt,[4] and when they become
self-conscious and articulate in the first number of *The Yellow Book*
(1894), it is no surprise to find a provocative, bantering article by
Max Beerbohm in defence of cosmetics. 'For behold!', he cries,
'the Victorian era comes to its end and the day of *sancta simplicitas*
is quite ended. The old signs are here, and the portents to warn the
seer of life that we are ripe for a new epoch of artifice. Are not
men rattling the dice-box and ladies dipping their fingers in the
rouge-pot?' Ovid, similarly *fin de siècle*—indeed *fin d'ère*—without
knowing it, had said much the same in *his* defence of cosmetics,
the prologue to the *Medicamina Faciei*: the age of Sabine matrons
is passed, who preferred to cultivate their ancestral acres rather
than themselves (11–12); now women go in for every kind of
adornment, and do their hair carefully even in the depths of the

---

* The nineteenth-century revolt was led by Gautier and Baudelaire, and continued by Huysmans and Wilde.[5]

† It was, significantly, Ovid himself who coined the phrase about Nature
imitating Art: *simulaverat artem ingenio natura suo*, he says, of the grotto of Diana.[6]

country; and the bridegroom is himself groomed with no less care than the bride—*nec tamen indignum*. One can imagine him at some party conceiving and throwing out the bright idea that he should write a didactic poem on cosmetics; his friends delighted, and pressing him to do so; and alas, the stifling of what had promised to be a lively squib in the sand-dunes of the intractable material.

But the previous generation at Rome had seen the appearance of didactic poems that were utterly different from the progeny of Nicander, the *De Rerum Natura* of Lucretius and the *Georgics* of Virgil; and elegy itself suggested a subject which could be developed in a true work of literature. Tibullus had shown the way with a witty poem in which the cynical Priapus gave hints on how to win boys; Propertius had passed on for the use of others some fruits of his experience with Cynthia; and Ovid himself had instructed his mistress on the conduct of their affair at a party, and let us overhear the bawd Dipsas putting her worldly wise.*[7] Virgil meanwhile had demonstrated how didactic material could be diversified and made readable. The *Georgics*, indeed, are only pseudo-didactic; in effect they are the first great descriptive poem;[8] and perhaps Ovid's *Ars Amatoria* should also be classed as pseudo-didactic, since it was more likely to be enjoyed by sophisticated readers as satire and the comedy of manners are enjoyed† than used as a handbook by young lovers. It had no comparable predecessor, otherwise Ovid would have mentioned it for certain in his *apologia* (*Tristia* II).[9] It is not a parody, yet its dealing at length and systematically with such a subject in a form associated with serious instruction inevitably generates a pleasing atmosphere of burlesque, and I feel sure that Ovid knew it would.

By now he was in his forties. He was, in fact, exactly as old as

---

* For Propertius as *praeceptor amoris* see A. L. Wheeler, *Cl. Phil.* 1910, pp. 28–40. See also Ovid's own *apologia* for the *A.A.* at *Tr.* II, 447–65. Ovid was original in writing a didactic poem on this scale, and in dealing in it with women. The Hellenistic Ἐρωτικαὶ τέχναι were Cynic or Stoic prose works dealing with boys in a Socratic spirit.[10]

† The New Comedy, with its Latin successors (Plautus, etc.), was full of precepts about love, as well as Hellenistic erotic epigram.

Horace was when he published his first three books of Odes. Both are middle-aged—sympathetic but amused and detached observers of the tragi-comedy of love, sometimes affecting to be singed in the flame but certainly never on fire, giving advice to the young from the maturity of their experience. Here is no reading for the passionate romantic,

> nil praeter Calvum et doctus cantare Catullum.
>
> *trained to sing nothing but Calvus and Catullus.*

There is no sentiment: love is an elaborate game, in which all's fair, a chase which is exciting for hunter and hunted alike. It is assumed that, to begin with at least, the hunter is not in love, for he is advised to act as though he were (*est tibi agendus amans*); but it is equally assumed that the woman's object is to make him fall in love (I, 611–20). The outrageous *nequitia*, the blasphemy against conventional sanctities, that we found in the *Amores* is still the salt of the *Ars Amatoria*.

It is not, however, a pornographic work. The prurient will read on with increasing disappointment, and may never reach their first meagre reward at the end of Book II. It is, in fact, an Art of Courtship or Gallantry, and hardly touches on the act of love itself. When it does, Ovid feels at least the need to feign bashfulness; and he avoids the direct language employed, for instance, by Horace in his eighth and twelfth Epodes.*

Ovid is at pains to emphasize that his poem has nothing to do with married or 'respectable' women.[11] The *demi-mondaines* concerned, mostly freedwomen,[12] do not differ essentially from the Corinna of the *Amores*. They are potential friends and companions, *hetaerae*, not common prostitutes. Even before he embarks on his minute recipes for cosmetics, Ovid reminds his pupils that *mores*, *ingenium*, *probitas*, are the foundation of lasting love, far more than a pretty face.[13] But the girl must be accomplished as well as good,

---

* *A.A.* III, 769; *R.A.*, 359–60. But 'et pudet et dicam': *R.A.*, 407. For an interesting discussion on the subject of whether a spade should be called a spade, see Cicero's letter to Paetus, *Ad Fam.* IX, 22.

able to sing an air from the theatre, to mime an Egyptian ballad, to play the lyre and harp, and to dance;[14] she must know her poets (not excluding Ovid); and the young suitor in turn had best be not only a good talker, but in Greek as well as Latin—a talker, not a declaimer, for no one but a fool addresses a tender girl like a public meeting.[15] The nature of Book II is sufficient indication that Ovid is thinking of fairly permanent liaisons.

The First Book tells where to find a mistress and how to win her; the Second, how to keep her affections. These two form a complete whole, and the Third, instructing the girls in turn how to catch and keep their man, was an afterthought,* though it was characteristic of Ovid to see the other side of the picture. When talking to the men Ovid stresses the importance of good character in both parties, whereas when talking to the women he puts all the emphasis on personal appearance and the arts of seduction; for in psychological matters he was nothing if not a realist.

The artistic problem was, how to create, out of what was bound to be a miscellaneous collection of precepts, a full-scale didactic poem (its ultimate length was 2330 lines) which should be readable. We soon discover one device of embroidery which he was to employ throughout—the old device of mythological parallels that Propertius, perhaps following Gallus, had favoured so much. The first four lines of the poem state the principle that love must be controlled by art—*arte regendus amor*; then—was not Automedon a famous charioteer, Tiphys a famous steersman? Venus has made Ovid tutor to her boy; he will be the Automedon and Tiphys of Love. The next couplet tells us that, as befits his years, Love is wild, but also malleable; then—did not Chiron, tutor to Achilles, tame his fierce nature by teaching him the lyre? Did not the future terror of friend and foe, the slayer of Hector, fear an old man and hold out his hand obediently for the rod? Ovid, like Chiron, is tutor to a mettlesome boy, who is also son of a goddess.

---

* See I, 35–40; cf. II, 733, *finis adest operi*, and the epilogue ending at 744. 745–6 were obviously added later as a transition to the extra book. The three books together were presumably issued as a second edition.

This 'business' occupies eighteen lines, and then we meet the second main form of embroidery, the parallel from nature, generally from animal nature. Does not the ox allow its neck to be subdued to the plough, the horse accept the bridle? *Et mihi cedet Amor.* The fact that in love the female may take the initiative is illustrated by two parallels from the animal kingdom and ten from mythology.[16] Time and again such passages occur throughout the poem, till Ovid himself sighs at last,[17]

quid moror exemplis quorum me turba fatigat?

Why detain you with parallels, the host of which wearies me?

Occasionally one may admire the ingenuity with which the poet finds his parallel, but many are obvious enough; and, however neat the expression may be, it is undeniable that the monotony tells on the modern reader, who begins to feel he knows just what is coming next.

Fortunately Ovid had many other resources. The set pieces which had been inserted sparsely by Hesiod and Aratus into their didactic poems had become one of the main features of Virgil's *Georgics* (not to mention Lucretius, who belongs to a different tradition); and Ovid has a dozen passages that deserve to be so called. A hundred lines from the beginning we come upon an admirable example. He has been describing how all the smartest women flock to the theatre (like trains of ants, inevitably, or like swarms of bees), where one may find girls for every purpose—love, flirtation, a single bout, a long affair—when suddenly he plunges into a delightful burlesque of the Callimachean *aetion* or story told to account for the origin of something (I, 101–30); it is the famous legend of the Rape of the Sabine Women by the Roman soldiery at the instigation of Romulus, which took place (Ovid would have us believe) during a theatrical performance. The story is told in the swift, vivid manner which was later to characterize the *Fasti*. The diversely violent scene, depicted with perfect artistic control, invited the emulation of many a painter of the Renaissance, through whose eyes we are apt to look as we read. Ever since then, says Ovid, love and the theatre have been connected. And he archly adds an aside: 'Romulus, *you* knew how to give gratuities to soldiers; if you offer me such a gratuity, I will turn soldier.'

Another good opportunity for meeting girls had been, he says, a pageant organized recently (2 B.C.) by Augustus, a reproduction of the Battle of Salamis on a specially excavated lake at the foot of the Janiculan Hill. This leads naturally into a set piece (I, 177–228) about the forthcoming expedition to the East of young Gaius Caesar, son of Agrippa and Julia (on which he was in fact to die of a wound). Just when we begin to think that this rhetorical digression has wandered too far and too long from the subject Ovid deftly brings us back to it, with an anticipation of the joyful scene at the boy's return, and the masque with symbolical figures (still a feature of Italian carnival processions) that will accompany his triumph:[18]

> Spectabunt laeti iuvenes mixtaeque puellae,
>   diffundetque animos omnibus ista dies.
> atque aliqua ex illis cum regum nomina quaeret,
>   quae loca, qui montes, quaeve ferantur aquae,
> omnia responde, nec tantum siqua rogabit;
>   et quae nescieris ut bene nota refer:
> hic est Euphrates, praecinctus arundine frontem;
>   cui coma dependet caerula, Tigris erit;
> hos facito Armenios; haec est Danaëia Persis;
>   urbs in Achaemeniis vallibus ista fuit;
> ille vel ille duces—et erunt quae nomina dicas,
>   si poteris, vere, si minus, apta tamen.

> *Mingled with girls shall happy youths look on;*
> *That day shall every barrier be gone;*
> *And if some girl inquire, 'What kings are these,*
> *What places, mountains, rivers, if you please?'*
> *Tell her; and if she ask not, tell her too,*
> *And if you do not know, pretend you do:*

'Euphrates this, with reeds upon his brow;
Those dark green locks—that must be Tigris now;
Call these Armenians; Danaë's Persia this;
Some city of Achaemenus, that is;
There goes a sheik, and there'—trot out a name,
Real or plausible, it's all the same.

Sixty lines later we have another famous story, of how Pasiphaë loved a bull, and produced the Minotaur (289–326). The predilection of Hellenistic poets for stories of monstrous or forbidden love, which sometimes affected Ovid, may seem perverse, but as a psychological phenomenon it is by no means unparalleled. We may find a clue in W. B. Yeats' *Autobiographies*, where he is talking of similar predilections among the poets of the 'nineties with whom he associated in his youth. 'Is it not most important', he says, 'to explore especially what has been long forbidden, and to do this not only "with the highest moral purpose", like the followers of Ibsen, but *gaily out of sheer mischief, or sheer delight in that play of the mind?'*[19] The words I have italicized seem to me to express perfectly what I take to have been the spirit of Ovid, a mischievous spirit like that of Callimachus before him. There was something absurdly piquant in imagining just what a woman would do in this unlikely situation, on the assumption that she would treat the bull like a man, *mutatis mutandis*. Pasiphaë's royal hands undertook the unwonted task of cutting the choicest grass for her love, who for his part was disappointingly unappreciative of her fine apparel. She wished she too had horns, and looked jealously upon the more beautiful cows; she was mortified when she found that some heifer clumsily capering before her lord obviously won his favour, and straightway had her separated from the herd and set to ploughing, or even sacrificed her to the gods with vengeful jubilation.

Later in the First Book (527 ff.) a discussion of the value of wine in love leads into a description of the arrival of Bacchus at Naxos to console Ariadne. The pictorial possibilities of this scene had already occurred to Catullus,[20] but his hexameters seem over-elaborate. Ovid's version is as fresh and colourful as Titian's famous picture, though in treatment more in the manner of Rubens. He takes up the story from where he left it in *Heroides* x. The Latin has a sparkle which for once I will not dim by attempted translation:[21]

Iamque iterum tundens mollissima pectora palmis,
   'perfidus ille abiit. quid mihi fiet?' ait.
'quid mihi fiet?' ait: sonuerunt cymbala toto
   litore, et attonita tympana pulsa manu.
excidit illa metu, rupitque novissima verba;
   nullus in exanimi corpore sanguis erat.
ecce Mimallonides sparsis in terga capillis,
   ecce leves satyri, praevia turba dei;
ebrius, ecce, senex pando Silenus asello
   vix sedet, et pressas continet ante iubas;
dum sequitur Bacchas, Bacchae fugiuntque petuntque,
   quadrupedem ferula dum malus urget eques,
in caput aurito cecidit delapsus asello:
   clamarunt satyri, 'surge age, surge, pater!'
iam deus in curru quem summum texerat uvis
   tigribus adiunctis aurea lora dabat:
et color et Theseus et vox abiere puellae,
   terque fugam petiit terque retenta metu est;
horruit, ut steriles agitat quas ventus aristas,
   ut levis in madida canna palude tremit.
cui deus, 'en, adsum tibi cura fidelior' inquit:
   'pone metum: Bacchi, Gnosias, uxor eris.
munus habe caelum; caelo spectabere sidus;
   saepe reges dubiam Cressa Corona ratem.'
dixit, et e curru, ne tigres illa timeret,
   desilit; imposito cessit harena pede;
implicitamque sinu (neque enim pugnare valebat)
   abstulit. in facili est omnia posse deo.
pars 'Hymenaee' canunt, pars clamant Euhion 'euhoe!'
   sic coeunt sacro nupta deusque toro.

Several other legendary stories are told at length. To illustrate
the fact that violent assault is not always unwelcome to the victim,
Ovid tells (I, 681–706) the story of how the young Achilles, disguised as a girl on Scyros to keep him from the war, assaulted his
room-mate Deïdameia. Or again, how can the poet hope to keep
the winged Love under control? Minos failed to keep Daedalus
and his son Icarus in confinement; and the story of their flight is
recounted in seventy-six vivid lines (II, 21–96). The well-known
Homeric story of Mars and Venus is retold (II, 561–94) to emphasize the point that a lover (as Vulcan could confirm) does not gain
by establishing the infidelity of his love; she simply becomes more
openly instead of stealthily unfaithful. And the sad story of
Procris (III, 687–746) shows what harm can come of believing
things too hastily.

A shorter passage of great charm (II, 123–42) reinforces the
lesson that good talk can compensate for indifferent looks. We
know how Desdemona 'fell in love with that she feared to look
on', hearing Othello speak

> of most disastrous chances,
> Of moving accidents by flood and field,
> Of hair-breadth 'scapes i' the imminent deadly breach,

and so forth. Ovid's Ulysses, *non formosus sed facundus*, held the
love of the divine Calypso by telling her of his part in the Tale of
Troy, with diagrams drawn on the sand. 'He was depicting more
when a sudden wave washed away Pergamus and the camp of
Rhesus with its captain. Then said the goddess, "Those waves to
which you think you can trust your voyage—do you see now
what great names they have destroyed?"'

But most of the poem is naturally occupied with advice.
Usually a general precept will be enunciated, followed by details
of how to apply it. What should the suitor do if he is rebuffed?[22]
He must be patient and submissive. There follows the inevitable
reminder that lions and tigers can be tamed, and bulls broken in,

by patience; and that Milanion, the stock example* of a patient
lover, won Atalanta after prodigies of endurance. The equally
patient reader is then rewarded with a lively list of instructions:[23]

> Cede repugnanti: cedendo victor abibis:
>   fac modo, quas partes illa iubebit, agas.
> arguet, arguito; quicquid probat illa, probato;
>   quod dicet, dicas; quod negat illa, neges.
> riserit, adride; si flebit, flere memento;
>   imponat leges vultibus illa tuis.
> seu ludet numerosque manu iactabit eburnos,
>   tu male iactato, tu male iacta dato.
> seu iacies talos, victam ne poena sequatur.
>   damnosi facito stent tibi saepe canes.
> sive latrocinii sub imagine calculus ibit,
>   fac pereat vitreo miles ab hoste tuus.
> ipse tene distenta suis umbracula virgis,
>   ipse fac in turba qua venit illa locum.
> nec dubita tereti scamnum producere lecto,
>   et tenero soleam deme vel adde pedi.
> saepe etiam dominae, quamvis horrebis et ipse,
>   algenti manus est calfacienda sinu.
> nec tibi turpe puta (quamvis sit turpe, placebit),
>   ingenua speculum sustinuisse manu.

> *Yield to rebuff: yielding will win the day;*
> *Just play whatever part she'd have you play:*
> *Like what she likes, decry what she decries,*
> *Say what she says, deny what she denies.*
> *Laugh when she laughs. She weeps? Be sure you weep.*
> *Let her dictate the rules your face must keep.*
> *When, at her whim, you throw the ivory dice,*
> *Throw ill; if she does, bid her throw them twice;*
> *At dominoes claim not the forfeit due.*
> *Make sure the deuces always fall to you.*

---

* The first of the many *exempla* used by Propertius (i, i, 9).

When in the Soldier-game your marbles go,
See your man falls before his glassy foe.*
Yourself hold up her parasol outspread;
Yourself through crowds make clear her path ahead;
Gladly the footstool at her sofa put,
And ply the slipper for her dainty foot.
Often her hand, though stiff yourself with cold,
To warm within your bosom you must hold;
Nor think it base (to please her, what is base?)
To hold the glass yourself, Sir, to her face.

And now some good advice to women:[24]

Sollicite expectas dum te in convivia ducam,
    et quaeris monitus hac quoque parte meos.
sera veni, positaque decens incede lucerna:
    grata mora venies; maxima lena mora est.
etsi turpis eris, formosa videbere potis,
    et latebras vitiis nox dabit ipsa tibi.
carpe cibos digitis: est quiddam gestus edendi:
    ora nec immunda tota perungue manu.
neve domi praesume dapes, sed desine citra
    quam capis; es paulo quam potes esse minus.
Priamides Helenen avide si spectet edentem,
    oderit, et dicat 'stulta rapina mea est'.
aptius est deceatque magis potare puellas:
    cum Veneris puero non male, Bacche, facis.
hoc quoque, qua patiens caput est, animusque pedesque
    constant; nec quae sunt singula, bina vide.
turpe iacens mulier multo madefacta Lyaeo:
    digna est concubitus quoslibet illa pati.
nec somnis posita tutum succumbere mensa:
    per somnos fieri multa pudenda solent.

---

* I have translated *talos* as 'dominoes', though they were really dice of a larger kind than the *numeri eburni*, simply to avoid the awkwardness caused by there not being two different words in English. In *Latrocinium* (*lusus latrunculorum*) the word *latro* has its old meaning of 'soldier'.[25]

You're anxious I should take you out to dine;
There too you bid me teach you how to shine.
Come late. By lamplight enter gracefully:
Lateness enhances—grand procuress she.
Though you be plain, their cups will lend you grace,
And night itself your blemishes efface.
Eat daintily. Good table-manners please:
No dirty fingers smear your cheeks with grease.
Don't nibble first at home, but stop before
You're sated, when you could perhaps hold more:
Had Paris seen fair Helen eat with greed,
Revolted, he'd have rued his famous deed.
Drinking is more becoming to the fair:
Bacchus and Cupid are no ill-matched pair—
This too, so long as head and brain and feet
Are sound: ere things look double, call retreat.
A fuddled woman is a shameful sight,
A prey to anyone, and serve her right.
Nor is it safe to drowse when table's cleared:
In sleep there's many an outrage to be feared.

At times the precepts merge into satire. What is this but satire
on the character of *demi-mondaines*?[26]

Magna superstitio tibi sit natalis amicae,
    quaque aliquid dandum est, illa sit atra dies.
cum bene vitaris, tamen auferet; invenit artem
    femina, qua cupidi carpat amantis opes.
institor ad dominam veniet discinctus emacem,
    expediet merces teque sedente suas;
quas illa inspicias, sapere ut videare, rogabit;
    oscula deinde dabit; deinde rogabit, emas.
hoc fore contentam multos iurabit in annos,
    nunc opus esse sibi, nunc bene dicet emi.
si non esse domi, quos des, causabere nummos,
    littera poscetur—ne didicisse iuvet.

quid, quasi natali cum poscit munera libo,
  et quotiens opus est nascitur ipsa sibi?
quid, cum mendaci damno maestissima plorat,
  elapsusque cava fingitur aure lapis?
multa rogant utenda dari, data reddere nolunt:
  perdis, et in damno gratia nulla tuo.
non mihi sacrilegas meretricum ut persequar artes,
  cum totidem linguis sint satis ora decem.

Her birthday hold a day of strict taboo:
All giving-days must be black days for you.
Vain all your schemes to dodge: a woman's stealth
Can always fleece a lover of his wealth.
Some vulgar salesman calls while you are by
And spreads his wares before her spendthrift eye;
She'll ask your judgement, as a connoisseur,
Then kiss you, then suggest you buy for her—
One thing for years her soul will satisfy,
Just what she needs, and now's the time to buy.
No use to plead you have no cash in sight:
You'll sign—and curse the day you learned to write.
Now she will beg towards her birthday-cake,
Born when it suits her whim the date to fake,
Now feign a loss and shed a touching tear—
A precious earring fallen from her ear.
She borrows much, but won't repay, of course:
You lose, and get no credit for your loss.
Ten tongues, ten months—still could I not convey
The unholy tricks that all such women play.

Here, on the other hand, satire merges into the comedy of manners:[27]

Sunt tamen et doctae, rarissima turba, puellae;
  altera non doctae turba, sed esse volunt.
utraque laudetur per carmina: carmina lector
  commendet dulci qualiacunque sono;

his ergo aut illis vigilatum carmen in ipsas
    forsitan exigui muneris instar erit.

at quod eris per te facturus, et utile credis,
    id tua te facito semper amica roget.
libertas alicui fuerit promissa tuorum,
    hanc tamen a domina fac petat ille tua;
si poenam servo, si vincula saeva remittis,
    quod facturus eras, debeat illa tibi;
utilitas tua sit, titulus donetur amicae;
    perde nihil, partes illa potentis agat.

sed te, cuicumque est retinendae cura puellae,
    attonitum forma fac putet esse sua;
sive erit in Tyriis, Tyrios laudabis amictus,
    sive erit in Cois, Coa decere puta;
aurata est? ipso tibi sit pretiosior auro;
    gausapa si sumpsit, gausapa sumpta proba.
astiterit tunicata, 'moves incendia!' clama,—
    sed timida, caveat frigora, voce roga.
compositum discrimen erit, discrimina lauda;
    torserit igne comam, torte capille, place.
bracchia saltantis, vocem mirare canentis,
    et, quod desierit, verba querentis habe.
ipsos concubitus, ipsum venerere licebit
    quod iuvat, et laudi gaudia noctis habe.

Yet there are cultured girls, a breed most rare,
And girls not cultured but who wish they were.
Both should be praised in song: a pleasing voice
Can make the meanest poetry sound choice.
Burn midnight oil: both may accept an ode
To her, in lieu of a small gift bestowed.

But what you mean to do in any case,
Contrive she ask, then do it as a grace;
If you have promised freedom to a slave,
Make him this favour through your mistress crave;

Or if some punishment you would remit,
Contrive she plead, and owe you thanks for it:
Yours be the gain: to her the credit pay,
And, losing nothing, grant her fancied sway.

But whoso would a mistress' love retain
Must act as spellbound by her beauty's chain.
Praise Tyrian, if in Tyrian she's drest;
Or if in Coan, Coan suits her best;
If she's in gold, then more than gold's her price,
But if in woollens—'woollens are so nice!'
Stripped to her shift—'you set my heart aflame!',
And then, 'be sure you don't get cold!' exclaim.
Her hair is neatly parted? Praise it thus.
Curled with hot irons? Curls are marvellous.
Her limbs in dance, her voice in song, adore,
And when she stops, complain, and ask for more.
Even the joys of night, her blissful ways
In bed, may be the subject of your praise.

No chance of a paradox, a joke, an aside escapes the witty, resourceful, irreverent mind of the poet. In the very exordium, where conventional poets were wont to claim the inspiration of a god, Ovid disclaims any such thing (25–30). He will not lie about having been taught by Phoebus or meeting the Muses on Helicon:

> usus opus movet hoc: vati parete perito,
>
> *experience is my prompter: trust a poet who knows.*

At the end of a string of injunctions about caring for one's mistress in sickness, he adds: 'There are limits however: don't be the one to cut down her diet, and see that your rival administers any unpleasant medicine she has to take.'[28]

The old *nequitia* of the *Amores* continues outrageous as ever. What could sound more innocently Tibullian than the couplet,

> Tunc aperit mentes, aevo rarissima nostro,
>
> simplicitas, artes excutiente deo,[29]

> *Then does simplicity, most rare in our age, open the heart,*
> *as the god dispels all wiles.*

But the god is Bacchus, the *simplicitas* (alias *rusticitas*) is modesty, and the *artes* are the girl's defences. Ovid blasphemes unconscionably against Homeric sublimity, rebuking the old priest (*quid lacrimas, odiose senex?*) for officiously prejudicing the golden future of his daughter Chryseïs as Agamemnon's concubine, and asserting that the king himself, having rightly enjoyed Briseïs, rightly also swore by his sceptre that he had not done so (a sceptre being no god).* To the girls he recommends a lover's funeral as a good occasion for finding another lover: walking in tears with hair let down is rather attractive.[30]

As in the *Amores*, the intricate play on words brings out the intricacies of love's psychology—the mixture of fear and desire in a girl:

> Quod rogat illa, timet; quod non rogat, optat—ut instes:
> insequere, et voti postmodo compos eris[31]

> *What she asks she fears, what she does not ask, she desires—*
> *that you persist: press on, and soon your prayer will be fulfilled.*

Never give up hope of a girl, however cruel:

> haec quoque, quam poteris credere nolle, volet[32]

> *even she you might believe unwilling will prove willing;*

one should even pray to be the man

> quo sine non possit vivere, posse velit[33]

> *without whom she could not live, but wishes she could.*

There are memorable epigrams, such as

> dos est uxoria lites[34] (*quarrels are a wife's dowry*),

---

* *Il.* I, 8–42, *R.A.* 469–72; *Il.* IX, 133, *R.A.* 777–84; but it was Achilles, not Agamemnon, who swore by the sceptre (*Il.* I, 234), and it was on another occasion.

and

> optima vindictae proxima quaeque dies[35]

> *tomorrow is always the best day for breaking free,*

and

> qui nimium multis 'non amo' dicit, amat[36]

> *who says too often 'I am not in love', is.*

What could more neatly express the dual purpose of girls in attending the theatre than

> spectatum veniunt, veniunt spectentur ut ipsae[37]

> *they come to watch, and to be watched they come*

or the power of wine in love, than

> et Venus in vinis ignis in igne fuit[38]

> *and Venus in their wine is fire in fire?*

The Third Book gives Ovid a chance to show us the reverse side of things, as he loved to do. After a few words on the degradation and unfairness of defeating an unarmed foe, he goes over to the woman's side and gives her advice with remarkably sympathetic insight. Not until line 577 does he affect consciousness of how completely he has betrayed the citadel of his fellow-males, but by now it is too late: he can only go on to the end,

> et sit in infida proditione fides

> *and let me be constant in my faithless treachery.*

There follow some amusing precepts on how to keep a man on the boil. Don't make things too easy. Create an atmosphere of danger. Though the door may be quite safe, make him climb in at the window; and look apprehensive when he appears. Let your maid burst in and cry 'we're undone!', and then hide the trembling youth somewhere.—But let him enjoy you sometimes without alarm, or he may think your nights not worth the candle.[39]

The reverse side from another point of view is given in the *Remedia Amoris*, with which Ovid completed his erotic cycle in

A.D. I.* We should expect him to enjoy turning the precepts of the *Ars Amatoria* inside out, but in fact he only does this to a limited extent.† There were all sorts of sources available: for instance, many of the precepts to be found in Ovid had occurred in a passage in Cicero's *Tusculan Disputations* (IV, 74 f.), based on Chrysippus' *Therapeuticus*,[40] and he certainly had in mind the famous passage in the Fourth Book of Lucretius.[41] The remedies for unhappy love are supposed to be for women as well as men, though the pretence sometimes wears thin. As before, there are set pieces—on the merits of country life as a distraction (169–96), a companion-piece to Horace's Second Epode; on the failure of Circe to hold Ulysses by witchcraft, a remedy both futile and harmful (263–88); on the sad fate of Phyllis, caused by solitude (579–608). Besides the obvious advice there is some quite penetrating psychology. For instance (693–8), do not explain why you wish to separate; do not air your grievance, but nurse it. If you recite her offences, she may clear herself; you may even find yourself helping to excuse her. He who is silent is firm; he who reproaches a woman is asking to be satisfied.

A single specimen of some length will give a fair impression of the work at its best (299–356). One can see that the poet is at least as much intent on amusing the reader as on curing the unhappy lover. The passage about making a rose smell less sweet by calling it by another name is a characteristic reversal of a well-known *locus* about the euphemisms with which men palliate the defects of those they love, which he had used himself at *A.A.* II, 657–62.[42]

* For the date see ll. 155 ff. C. Caesar is in the East by now, but the meeting that settled the conflict there has not yet taken place.

It is fantastic to suppose, with Owen (*Tristia* II, p. 6) that Ovid wrote the *Remedia* as 'a sort of recantation' of the *Ars*, to appease hostile criticism. He goes out of his way to deride his critics (379–96). It is a burlesque of didactic poems about remedies, such as Nicander's Ἀλεξιφάρμακα, and a piquant pendant to its predecessor.

† 16 out of 42 precepts are such, according to the reckoning of K. Prinz (*Wiener Studien*, 1914, pp. 47 ff.), who has explored the sources in so far as they are traceable.

Saepe refer tecum sceleratae facta puellae,
    et pone ante oculos omnia damna tuos.
'illud et illud habet, nec ea contenta rapina est:
    sub titulum nostros misit avara lares.
sic mihi iuravit, sic me iurata fefellit,
    ante suas quotiens passa iacere fores!
diligit ipsa alios, a me fastidit amari;
    institor, heu, noctes quas mihi non dat habet!'
haec tibi per totos inacescant omnia sensus:
    haec refer, hinc odii semina quaere tui.
atque utinam possis etiam facundus in illis
    esse! dole tantum, sponte disertus eris.
haeserat in quadam nuper mea cura puella;
    conveniens animo non erat illa meo;
curabar propriis aeger Podalirius herbis,
    et, fateor, medicus turpiter aeger eram:
profuit adsidue vitiis insistere amicae
    idque mihi factum saepe salubre fuit.
'quam mala', dicebam, 'nostrae sunt crura puellae!'
    nec tamen, ut vere confiteamur, erant.
'bracchia quam non sunt nostrae formosa puellae!'
    et tamen, ut vere confiteamur, erant.
'quam brevis est!' nec erat; 'quam multum poscit amantem!'
    haec odio venit maxima causa meo.

et mala sunt vicina bonis: errore sub illo
    pro vitio virtus crimina saepe tulit.
qua potes, in peius dotes deflecte puellae,
    iudiciumque brevi limite falle tuum.
turgida, si plena est, si fusca est, nigra vocetur:
    in gracili macies crimen habere potest.
et poterit dici petulans, quae rustica non est;
    et poterit dici rustica, siqua proba est.
quin etiam, quacunque caret tua femina dote,
    hanc moveat, blandis usque precare sonis.
exige uti cantet, siqua est sine voce puella:
    fac saltet, nescit siqua movere manum.

barbara sermone est? fac tecum multa loquatur.
    non didicit chordas tangere? posce lyram.
durius incedit? fac inambulet. omne papillae
    pectus habent? vitium fascia nulla tegat.
si male dentata est, narra quod rideat illi.
    mollibus est oculis? quod fleat illa refer.

proderit et subito, cum se non finxerit ulli,
    ad dominam celeres mane tulisse gradus.
auferimur cultu; gemmis auroque teguntur
    omnia; pars minima est ipsa puella sui.
saepe ubi sit, quod ames, inter tam multa requiras;
    decipit hac oculos aegide dives Amor.
improvisus ades, deprendes tutus inermem;
    infelix vitiis excidet illa suis.
non tamen huic nimium praecepto credere tutum est;
    fallit enim multos forma sine arte decens.
tum quoque compositis sua cum linit ora venenis
    ad dominae vultus (nec pudor obstet) eas.
pyxidas invenies et rerum mille colores,
    et fluere in tepidos oesypa lapsa sinus.
illa tuas redolent, Phineu, medicamina mensas:
    non semel hinc stomacho nausea facta meo.

Often your heartless mistress' crimes recall:
The wrongs she did you, oft rehearse them all.
'This thing she took, and that, nor sated yet
She forced me sell my home to pay my debt.
Thus did she swear, and thus herself forswore.
How oft she made me lie before her door!
Others she cares for, but my love disdains:
The nights I forfeit are a salesman's gains!'
Let all this rankle and pervade your sense:
Brood on it all, and breed your hatred thence.
Would you had words to vent your odium!
But hug your pain and eloquence will come.

Lately my thoughts upon a girl were bent
Who was not well-disposed to my intent.
A sick physician, my own herbs I tried
(Shamefully sick, it cannot be denied).
Intently on my mistress' faults to dwell
Helped me, and oft repeated, made me well.
'How ugly are the woman's legs!' I thought,
Though, in all conscience, ugly they were not;
'How far from beautiful the arms of her!'
Though, in all conscience, beautiful they were;
'How dumpy!' (slander); 'How rapacious she!'
(That proved my sharpest spur to enmity.)

Some virtues verge on vices: tip the scales
And even a grace disparagement entails;
So where you can her qualities misprise,
Just cross the borderline and criticize.
If buxom, call her fat; swarthy, if dark;
If slender, on her skinniness remark.
Be she not simple, she's a forward miss,
But be she virtuous, simpleton she is.
Observe, again, her worst accomplishment
And press for that with wheedling compliment:
From her that cannot sing demand a song,
A dance from her whose movements will be wrong.
She has an accent? Let her talk away.
Call for the lyre she has no skill to play.
Her gait's ungainly? Make her walk. Her pair
Of breasts immense? Remove her brassière.
Tell funny stories if her teeth are bad:
Dim lustrous eyes with stories that are sad.

It helps to pay a sudden call at morn,
Ere she has time her person to adorn.
Adornment wins us: gems and gold hide all:
Of her ensemble she's but a fraction small.

One gropes for what one loves 'mid all that show;
Rich Cupid dazzles with his aegis so.
Come unannounced, catch her without those arms:
Ah, her defects will banish all her charms.
But here of over-confidence beware,
For beauty unadorned can oft ensnare.
Go when she smears concoctions on her face,
Go and observe, and don't feel out of place:
Boxes you'll find with myriad varying hues,
And see strange juices down her bosom ooze.
Those drugs recall old Phineus' fabled slime:
Their stench has turned my stomach many a time.

Finally, there is for us an adventitious pleasure in the glimpses of Roman life that these poems afford: the new marble colonnades, adorned with old pictures and with statues, where girls could be picked up; the hot sulphur baths of Baiae; the famous grove of Diana at Nemi;[43] the statues in the theatres, of wood covered with gold leaf;[44] the cushions that relieved the hard seats of the Circus;[45] the wax-tablets on which it was sometimes possible to decipher the previous letter;[46] the girl whose clothes have been stolen by a pretended lover of feminine tastes, shouting 'Stop thief! Stop thief!' all over the Forum;[47] the newer Forum Julium with its temple of Venus Genetrix (called 'Appia' from the Appian Fountain near by,) who laughs to see even the lawyers below caught in the toils of love;[48] the crowds on the Jewish Sabbath; the women thronging to the Lament for Adonis and the mysteries of Isis.[49]

We hear of women's fashions. An oval face calls for a plain coiffure with a parting ('Laodameia' style); a round face should have a small knot on the top of the head, allowing the ears to show; some may prefer to let their hair hang down on either side ('Apollo the Lyre-player'), some to sweep it back ('Diana the Huntress'), some wear it loosely bobbed (*inflatos laxe iacentes*), some tightly bound, some held by a tortoiseshell comb, some waved, and, finally, some artfully dishevelled.[50] There are German hair-dyes, and wig-stalls like that in the Circus in front of the Temple of Hercules and the Muses.[51] There are powder, rouge, eyebrow-pencil, patches, mascara, saffron and cosmetics of all kinds, as prescribed in the *Medicamina Faciei*.[52]

A man, in Ovid's opinion, should be spruce and bronzed by exercise in the Campus. His teeth and nails should be clean, his hair and beard neatly trimmed, his nostrils free from hair, his breath and armpits from smell. His toga should fit well and be spotless, his shoe close-fitting with unwrinkled tongue. Whatsoever is more than this cometh of vanity—leave it to wanton girls. And do not curl your hair either, or smooth your legs with pumice—leave that to Cybele's eunuchs.[53] It might be Beau Nash speaking. Elsewhere we have a vignette of a dandy (*bellus homo*)— hair sleek with scented oil, shoe-tongue tucked in, fine-spun toga, more than one ring.[54] The loosening of the toga seems to have been a sign of desire to attract a woman.[55]

A passage giving advice to girls on how to elude their male-chaperone is full of sidelights on Roman life:[56]

> Scilicet obstabit custos, ne scribere possis,
>   sumendae detur cum tibi tempus aquae?
> conscia cum possit scriptas portare tabellas
>   quas tegat in tepido fascia lata sinu?
> cum possit sura chartas celare ligatas,
>   et vincto blandas sub pede ferre notas?
> caverit haec custos, pro charta conscia tergum
>   praebeat, inque suo corpore verba ferat.
> tuta quoque est fallitque oculos e lacte recenti
>   littera: carbonis pulvere tange, leges.
> fallet et umiduli quae fiet acumine lini
>   et feret occultas pura tabella notas.
> adfuit Acrisio servandae cura puellae:
>   hunc tamen illa suo crimine fecit avum.
>
> quid faciat custos cum sint tot in urbe theatra,
>   cum spectet iunctos illa libenter equos,

cum sedeat Phariae sistris operata iuvencae,
    quoque sui comites ire vetantur, eat?
cum fuget a templis oculos Bona Diva virorum,
    praeterquam si quos illa venire iubet?
cum, custode foris tunicas servante puellae,
    celent furtivos balnea multa iocos?
cum, quotiens opus est, fallax aegrotet amica
    et cedat lecto quamlibet aegra suo?
nomine cum doceat, quid agamus, adultera clavis,
    quasque petas non det ianua sola vias?

You wish to write? Then cheat your escort-spy
When bath-time comes to give you privacy.
Tablets a friend can take on your behalf,
Tucked in her bosom underneath a scarf;
Notes in her garter bound she can conceal,
Or hide your billet-doux beneath her heel.
Should he suspect, bid strip your go-between
And write your message on her back unseen.
Fresh milk's an ink that's safe and cheats the eye
(To read, a touch of charcoal-dust apply);
Or use as pen a stalk of moistened flax:
Letters can lurk beneath the virgin wax.
Close watched Acrisius lest his daughter err:
He failed, and found himself a grandfather. *

Poor escort! Theatres the city fill,
And chariot races she can watch at will,
At Isis' sacrifice with timbrel sit,
And go where male companions are not fit,
Where the Good Goddess' temple bans the sight
Of men—save those she chooses to invite.
Often the escort keeps her clothes outside
The bath, while she makes merry unespied.

---

* He immured his daughter Danaë, but could not prevent Jupiter from having access to her in the form of a shower of gold.

An artful friend will sickness feign at need
(She's not too sick her double-bed to cede).
Do master-keys not mistresses imply?*
Are doors the only way to reach you by?

Read by themselves, the *Ars* and *Remedia* may be accounted brilliant and entertaining works. Read after the *Amores* and *Heroides* they are apt to suffer, and not always undeservedly. Quite apart from the sameness of tone, there is too much *crambe repetita*. Surely we have heard before, and more than once, of lovers communicating by writing on the table in wine, exchanging glances and signs, drinking from the side of the cup where the other has drunk, and touching hands;[57] and how could the author of the brilliant monologue at the races in *Amores* III, 2 bring himself to introduce a garbled summary in didactic form at *Ars* I, 135–62? The trouble was that in his previous work Ovid had introduced themes which would have a rightful place in any *Ars Amatoria*, and whose omission might have made it seem incomplete. Had he known at the time that he was going to write the *Ars*, he would perhaps have avoided them. As it is, we feel before the end that his erotic vein is now worked out. Perhaps he felt the same. After all, he was now in his forty-fifth year; it was high time to leave such topics to *lasciva decentius aetas*.

---

* Literally 'Does not an *adultera clavis* (counterfeit key) teach us by its very name what to use it for?'

CHAPTER VII

THE 'METAMORPHOSES'

MOST CAPRICIOUS POET

Quaere novum vatem, tenerorum mater amorum. *

I<small>T</small> was natural that Ovid, now in the fullness of his powers, should aspire to create a *chef d'œuvre*. He might have essayed an epic of romantic adventure, like the lost *Argonautica* of Varro of Atax. Happily he did not; for Virgil had now set a new standard for epic, infusing it with philosophic import, and Ovid was no philosopher. What he did decide to do was more within his powers. He had already shown that he had a genius for imaginative story-telling:† he would retell a number of legends, many of them not well known,‡ after the manner of those Hellenistic poems which we call epyllia,§ following the tradition that went back to Hesiod and his collection of stories (*Eoeae*), but sustaining a more epic tone than the Hellenistic writers.

He might simply have recounted the stories in succession, without connexions or setting;‖ but instead, his ingenious mind, fascinated as ever by puzzles,¶ wove a continuous narrative in

---

* 'Seek a new poet, mother of the tender loves.'[1]

† Already in the *A.A.* he had treated legends that were to have a place in the *Metamorphoses*: II, 21–96, cf. *M.* VIII, 152–235 (Daedalus and Icarus); III, 687–746, cf. *M.* VII, 690–862 (Cephalus and Procris); I, 681–704, cf. *M.* XIII, 162–170 (Achilles and Deïdameia).

‡ *Vulgatos taceo* (sc. *amores*)...*animos dulci novitate tenebo*, IV, 276–84; *hoc placet, haec quoniam vulgaris fabula non est*, IV, 53. Cf. the practice of Callimachus.

§ This term is so bandied about nowadays that we are apt to forget that it is only once found in this sense in an ancient writer, in Athenaeus 65 A (*c.* A.D. 200).

‖ As Hesiod, Phanocles, Sosicrates and Nicaenetus did (see E. Martini, Ἐπιτύμβιον H. *Swoboda dargebracht*, pp. 169–75), or as Rex Warner has done in his adapted extracts from Ovid's *Metamorphoses* in English prose entitled *Men and Gods* (1950).   ¶ See p. 96.

which there are some fifty stories long enough to rank as epyllia and some two hundred others that are treated more cursorily or merely referred to.[2] Beginning with the Creation, he ends with the apotheosis of Julius Caesar and the amazing metamorphosis on which Augustan poets loved to dwell, that of Rome from a little village into the capital of the world.* The idea of linking such stories had already occurred to Callimachus and Nicander; but the idea of arranging them chronologically, though some have supposed he took it from a handbook, seems more likely to have been his own.

Why should he have restricted himself to stories of metamorphosis? The truth is, he did not. We have not far to read before we come to a major episode without such justification, that of Phaëthon, which is obviously introduced for its own sake, since we cannot suppose that its three hundred and fifty lines are simply a prologue to the briefly told transformation of his sisters, the Heliades, into poplars; and the same is true, for instance, of the picturesque story of Meleager, the Rape of Proserpine, the Rending of Pentheus and the Death of Achilles. But there were few legends that did not contain a metamorphosis at some point, which incidentally gave scope for the poet's penchant for the grotesque. Besides, others before him had produced collections of such stories in verse, among them his own friend Aemilius Macer, who had made a Latin version of the *Ornithogonia* of a shadowy Greek poet called Boeus,† a poem dealing with transformations into birds.

Into the labyrinthine question of Ovid's debt to his predecessors for material I do not propose to penetrate. Fifty years have done little to modify the necessarily tentative conclusions of

---

* Brooks Otis surely goes too far in seeing the *Metamorphoses* as a poem whose *conception* was due to the political atmosphere of Augustan Rome (*op. cit.*, summary, p. 229).

† Possibly of the third century. He apparently set out to discover why some birds are of good omen, others of bad. For Macer see *Tr.* IV, 10, 43:

> Saepe suas *volucres* legit mihi grandior aevo,
> quaeque nocet serpens, quae iuvat herba, Macer.

G. Lafaye* and L. Castiglioni† in their thorough examination of the subject. Besides unknown Hellenistic poets and Boeus and Macer there were the five books of Nicander's *Heteroeumena* from the (?) second century B.C., and the recent *Metamorphoses* in elegiacs of Parthenius, the friend of Cornelius Gallus who is reputed to have taught Virgil Greek. There was also a *Metamorphoses* by one Theodorus, which Ovid is stated to have used along with Nicander,[3] and no doubt there were already prose handbooks composed for the aid of schoolboys in their exercise called *ethopoeïa*.[4] Finally, there were epyllia‡ like the extant *Ciris*, and the lost *Alcyone* of Cicero, *Io* of Calvus, *Zmyrna* (=Myrrha) of Cinna and *Glaucus* of Cornificius, all dealing with stories treated in Ovid's work.[5] Since, however, it would seem that Ovid used various sources, sometimes even for the same story,§ and we have grounds for thinking that he did not hesitate to invent if it suited his purpose,[6] it really does not matter much where he found this or that detail or idea. In any case, the works whose titles would lead us to suppose that they might have been his chief sources have almost entirely perished;‖ and who knows what he may have taken from Euphorion, for example? Probably he relied on a good memory of wide reading as much as on source-books unrolled before him as he wrote, and he was nothing if not inventive himself. If we knew for certain where he was innovating, it would often be instructive: as it is, we must simply deal with the poem as we find it.

* *Les Métamorphoses d'Ovide et leurs modèles grecs* (Bibliothèque de la Faculté des Lettres XIX, Paris, 1904), an admirable work.

† *Studi intorno alle Metamorfosi d'Ovidio* (Annali della R. Scuola Normale Superiore di Pisa XX, 1907). He stresses the probable influence of lost Hellenistic poems.

‡ For Ovid's probable debt to these see Crump, *op. cit.* ch. X.

§ E.g. Euripides' *Cyclops*, Philoxenus' *Cyclops*, Theocritus VI and XI, and possibly Callimachus' Hymn III and his lost *Glaucus*, for the story of Polyphemus, *Met.* XIII, 750–897; Euripides' *Phaëthon*, Phanocles' *Erotes* and some Alexandrian narrative poem for the story of Phaëthon.

‖ Summaries of some of the legends told by Boeus and Nicander are to be found in the prose compilation of Antoninus Liberalis (2nd cent. A.D.).

The organization of this immense work (longer than the *Aeneid* or *Paradise Lost*) must have been a great labour, but we may be sure that it had a fascination for the author, solving his jigsaw puzzle, far greater than it can have for us, who merely survey the completed picture.* The ostensible basis is chronological—*ab origine mundi . . . ad mea tempora.*† But of course many of the legends have no place in time. Some of these are disposed of by letting them be told by some character in a gathering, of spinners or feasters or loungers or soldiers in a tent at evening;[7] a mother-in-law and daughter-in-law exchange stories,[8] and tales are woven into tapestries, or embossed on a bowl.[9] Some are associated antithetically, after the manner of contemporary wall-painting—the wicked Erysichthon and the pious Philemon, the accursed love of Byblis and the blessed love of Iphis.[10]

For some reason or other it was fashionable to insert in an epyllion a secondary tale which might have no bearing on the main theme. This may have been simply because Callimachus' *Hecale*, apparently the prototype of Hellenistic epyllia, had the story of Erichthonius inset.[11] We are familiar with Catullus' *Marriage of Peleus and Thetis* (LXIV), which consists largely of the inset story of Ariadne on Naxos, as embroidered on the bridal coverlet. Indeed, all extant epyllia dating from before Ovid except Theocritus' *Hylas* have such a digression. Of some fifty episodes in the *Metamorphoses* which are long enough to rank as epyllia about a third contain one.[12] It is apt to irritate us, like the ramblings in our early novels: we lose the thread, forget the situation or who is speaking to whom.

After the Introduction (the Creation and the Flood) the poem falls into three roughly equal parts, dealing respectively with Gods, Heroes and Heroines, and 'Historical' Personages, the whole being framed between a very brief personal Prologue and

* Cf. the elaborate chiastic symmetry of themes in Catullus LXVIII B, so pretty when set out in a diagram, so bewildering when we read the poem.

†This is an obvious enough scheme, but Ovid may have been influenced by the work of the Cyclic poets who filled in the tale of Troy round the *Iliad* and *Odyssey*.

Epilogue;* but there are many digressions that blur these classifica-
tions. From the Flood down to the end of Book XI the only basis
for chronological sequence is such as the ancient genealogies
might suggest, save that the legends in Part I are mainly primeval,
whereas those in Part II belong to an era which may be called that
of Hercules, conceived as being not much anterior to the Trojan
saga. For the rest, we have grouping round certain themes, places
or personalities, an arrangement found in the catalogue poems.†
In the course of Book XI we enter the twilight before history,
where there is a traditional sequence of events, from Priam's Troy
and Aeneas' wanderings to Romulus' Rome. Not until the last
book do we emerge into the full daylight of Roman history.

In his choice of legends Ovid was eclectic, though it is remarkable
how many he fitted in, losing no occasion to mention a metamorphosis.‡ Stories that were similar, and also different versions
of the same metamorphosis,§ were well spaced out. Where a well-
known poet had treated the same story, he tended to accept the
main outline and vary the details, passing over what had been
elaborated before, and *vice versa*. For instance, in the tale of
Orpheus he does not throw into relief his second loss of Eurydice,
the central theme in Virgil's treatment, but dwells on his death,

---

* Prologue, I, 1–4.
    Introduction: The Creation and Flood, I, 5–451.

        Part I. Gods, I, 452–VI, 420.
        Part II. Heroes and Heroines, VI, 421–XI, 193.
        Part III. 'Historical' Personages, XI, 194–XV, 870.
    Epilogue, XV, 871–9.

† E.g. Loves of the Gods, I, 452–II, 875.
        Thebes and Bacchus, III, 1–IV, 606.
        Revenges of the Gods, V, 250–VI, 420.
        Athens, VI, 421–IX, 100.
        Hercules, IX, 101–449.
        Loves of Heroes and Heroines, IX, 450–XI, 84.

I have here made use of the handy table of Dr Crump (*op. cit.* pp. 274–8).

‡ Of 26 stories from Nicander summarized by Antoninus Liberalis 21 were
used by Ovid.
  § E.g. Cycnus to a swan, II, 367–80, VII, 371–80 and XII, 63–145.

of which Virgil had told only briefly.*[13] It is also interesting to see how he modifies his treatment in the case of stories he has himself told elsewhere. Deïaneira's complaints are confined to eight lines, presumably because they had been fully vented in *Heroides* IX; similarly, the misfortunes of Medea, Dido, Laodameia and Ariadne are passed over in a few lines. Neither in the *Heroides* nor in the *Metamorphoses* does he deal with the events that formed the plot of Euripides' *Medea*, perhaps because he had done so in his tragedy of that name.

Quintilian remarks once: 'There is a frigid and puerile affectation in the rhetorical schools of making even a transition score a point and expecting applause for this conjuring trick; Ovid plays in this way in the *Metamorphoses*, but he has the excuse of being obliged to knit most diverse topics into the semblance of a whole.'[14] Transitions were, in fact, a large part of Ovid's game. Friendship or relationship between heroes was one link, identity of time or place another. Any chance association would serve; or an association could be invented, as at V, 489 ff., where he makes Arethusa (not the Sun, as at *F.* IV, 583–4) tell Ceres where Proserpina is, perhaps as a convenient way of introducing the story of her metamorphosis. The only occasion on which he shirks his self-imposed task is in the last book (XV, 622), when there are other indications that his zeal was flagging. The end of a story rarely coincides with the end of a book. He will even begin a new one within the last few lines. This is partly the time-honoured device of the serial writer to whet the reader's appetite for the next instalment; but it is also an indication of the continuity of the work, which should not have been divided into books at all were it not that its length necessitated a number of rolls.

For metre he chose the hexameter. It was the medium of the epyllia from which, perhaps more than from narrative elegy, the work seems to derive. Richard Heinze, in an important study, has maintained that the *Metamorphoses* differ in approach from the contemporary *Fasti*,[15] by comparing Ovid's treatment of legends

* Both Ovid and Virgil seem to be drawing on some Hellenistic poem.[16]

that appear in both.* In the *Metamorphoses*, he suggests, we have strong, active emotions, such as violent love or anger; the *power* of the gods is emphasized. In the *Fasti* the more tender emotions, such as grief and pity, predominate; the gods are humanized. The *Metamorphoses* are grandiose and objective: the high epic manner of the Rhapsodes, which characterizes the earlier Hellenistic epyllia as against the later and the Roman,† is sustained. The *Fasti* are idyllic, homely and more personal.

The epic manner demanded the use of the traditional heroic metre. But Ovid's hexameter is unlike Virgil's. The gravity, variety of rhythm and expressiveness of Virgil's verse were due largely to heavy elision, but also to variation of pauses in the line and to free use of spondees, whereas Ovid dispensed as much as possible with elision,‡ tended to pause at the caesura or at the end of the line, and in general was more dactylic, sacrificing everything to lightness and speed.§ His are the hexameters of an elegist. (In English therefore the effect is probably best rendered by retaining the couplet but allowing free enjambement, following the tradition of Chaucer rather than Dryden.) He also tightened up the rules for elision and caesuras, and denied himself exceptional licences. One must admit the justice of Dryden's criticism: 'Ovid, with all his sweetness, has as little variety of numbers and sound as [Claudian]: he is always, as it were, upon the hand-gallop, and his verse runs upon carpet-ground. He avoids all synaloephas [elision]...so that, minding only smoothness, he wants both variety and majesty'.|| Yet may not Ovid perhaps have been right, for the purpose in hand? The essential thing was that the reader

---

* E.g. the Rape of Proserpina, *M.* v, 341–661; *F.* IV, 417–620.

† Heinze, *op. cit.* p. 99 ff. For an attempt to differentiate between Hellenistic and Ovidian treatment of stories see H. Diller, 'Die Dichterische Eigenart Ovids Metamorphosen,' *Hum. Gym.* 1934, pp. 25–38.

‡ 15·6 on an average per 100 hexameters: Virgil has 50·5.[17]

§ 54·6 per cent of dactyls in the first four feet, to Virgil's 44·1 in the *Aeneid*.[18]

|| Preface to *Sylvae*. One must remember, however, that the majority of post-Augustan poets chose to conform to Ovid's practice, denying themselves the greater freedom of Virgil.[19]

should glide easily on without pausing to reflect. For his purpose in writing was clearly to entrance, ψυχαγωγεῖν, and nothing more. It was something in the post-Platonic world that a poet should have the courage to disregard the puritan critics. Instead of disparaging him for not displaying the intellectual passion of a Lucretius, the religious patriotism of a Virgil or the moral purpose of a Horace, we should be grateful that he realized his own limitations and chose a subject in which the qualities he did have could find scope. But both his merits and defects will come out more clearly if we consider various aspects of his work with illustrations.

(1) SPIRIT AND TREATMENT

When we take up a book, we usually have some idea of what pleasure or profit we may expect to derive from it. If it is a long poem, we soon discover its general tone, whether it be *The Faerie Queene* or *Paradise Lost* or *The Prelude*. But it is not so with the *Metamorphoses*. Sir Harold Nicolson has put clearly the dilemma of the ordinary reader:

'The difficulty in appreciating at its true value this compendium of *Myths, Ancient and Modern* is that we are unable to assess Ovid's own point of view. Was he poking covert fun at his gods and goddesses? Was he compiling merely a useful Companion to Literature? Was he collecting an anthology of these already fading fables? Or was he just using the stories as vehicles for his fluent narrative pen? It is hard to believe that a man so convivial, urban and disrespectful can have approached these myths with any reverence. It is as if some bright young man of the twenties had composed a long poem in fifteen books, in which he had interwoven such disparate themes as The Garden of Eden, the Ten Commandments, Samson and Delilah, King Alfred and the cakes, Drake's drum and the death of Nelson. We should be at a loss to decide whether he was writing ironically, allegorically, symbolically or simply with some perverted antiquarian purpose. We should be perplexed by our inability to define his state of mind.'[20]

Now here is a case where it certainly helps to know the ante-cedents of a poem. For it is safe to say that the *Metamorphoses* would not have been what they are but for the example of that perverse but brilliant Alexandrian whom most Roman poets admired so much, Callimachus. Like Ovid, he seems to have lacked 'depth', but his range was astonishing. We possess his baroque hexameter *Hymns*, the elegiac *Bath of Pallas* with its tense and beautiful narrative, and sixty-four exquisite epigrams, each perfect in its wit or grace or tenderness; and we also know from ruins or repute the elaborate and erudite *Aetia*, his most famous work, the grandiose dirge for Queen Arsinoë, the idyllic *Hecale*, the invective *Ibis*, lyrics whose fragments have a tantalizing grace, iambics whose vigour and variety pressage Lucilius, and various elegies and other works. Truly, as Crinagoras said of him, 'the man shook out every reef of the Muses'.*

When Callimachus set out to tell of the origins of obscure customs and names (*Aetia*), he apparently decided not only to make his poem a *carmen perpetuum*† by linking the stories with narrative, but to turn his great versatility to account, sustaining the interest by variations of mood and tone, and by every sort of trick and surprise. Even from the scanty fragments we can gather some idea of his method. We know that he began with his spirited and famous denunciation of the epic poets of his day, and apparently he continued with the Hesiodic fiction of a dream in which the Muses wafted him to Helicon. Here is an example, a chance survival, of the way he would manage a transition:[21]

'Nor did the morning of the Jar-broaching Day pass unheeded, nor that on which Orestes' pitchers bring a bright day for slaves. And when he kept the annual feast of Icarius' daughter, thy day, Erigone, most pitied by Attic women, he invited his boon-companions to a banquet, and among them a stranger who had recently come

* ὡνὴρ τοὺς Μουσέων πάντας ἔσεισε κάλως.[22]

† We now know that this does not apply to Books III and IV, which consist of disconnected pieces. The Διηγήσεις made this seem probable, and Oxyrhynchus Papyri 2170 and 2211 have since confirmed it for Books IV and III respectively.

to visit Egypt on some private business. He was an Ician by birth, and I shared a couch with him—not by arrangement, but Homer's proverb is not false, that God ever brings like to like; for he too hated to drink the wide-mouthed Thracian draught of wine, but rejoiced in a small goblet. To him I said as the cup went round the third time, when I had inquired his name and origin: "Surely it is a true saying that wine requires its portion not only of water but also of talk. So—since talk is not handed out in ladles nor do you have to ask for it by catching the haughty eye of the cup-bearer, in the hour when the free must fawn on the slave—let us, Theagenes, put talk in the cup to temper the liquor, and in answer to my questions do you tell me what my mind is longing to hear from you. Why is it traditional in your country to worship Peleus?"...'

Compare with this a transition from the *Metamorphoses*, VII, 670–81:

'Phocus led the Athenians into the inner court with its beautiful apartments and sat down among them himself. He noticed that Cephalus carried in his hand a javelin with a golden head, made of some strange wood. So after some talk he suddenly interposed, "I am an expert in forests and hunting, but for a long time I have been wondering what wood the weapon you hold is made of: if it were ash, it would be dark yellow; if cornel-wood, it would have knots. I cannot tell what it comes from, but I have never set eyes on a more beautiful weapon than that." Then one of the Athenian brothers replied...."*

We have from the *Aetia* considerable portions of a love story, that of Acontius and Cydippe.[23] Another fragment has a pastoral tone.[24] Another recalls the Callimachus of the more tender epigrams: 'That man finds old age lighter whom children love, and lead by the hand, like a father, to his own door.'[25] While the courtly, rococo Rape of the Lock, familiar from Catullus' version *Coma Berenices*, is now known to be also part of this work.[26]

I have cited these fragments to give some idea of the variety

---

* Five times in the *Metamorphoses* a meal is the setting for a tale, as in the passage from Callimachus here quoted.[27]

of mood and incident by which Callimachus sought to sustain interest in his compilation. But this was not merely an *ad hoc* device: it arose from his own nature, as we can see from the Hymns, which survive complete. Take No. III, to Artemis. We begin with her as a little child, sitting on the knee of her father Zeus and grotesquely asking of him already various attributes she is destined to possess—perpetual virginity, more names than her brother Phoebus, and so forth. She wants all mountains, but no city in particular—she will rarely be going to town except when summoned as goddess of childbirth. Zeus consents with a smile, adding that when goddesses bear him children like this it makes him care little how angry the jealous Hera may be. Artemis goes off to Oceanus to choose her attendant nymphs, and thence to the Cyclopes in Lipara, whose aspect terrifies them—no wonder, for when the gods' children are disobedient, they call in a Cyclops, or else Hermes comes and plays bogey till they fly and hide their faces in their mothers' lap. But Artemis boldly asks the Cyclopes to make her a bow and arrows. Then she goes to Pan in Arcady, who supplies her with hounds, and so to her first hunting. The burlesque tone has vanished now. Learned allusions mingle with apostrophes in splendid language. The places favoured by the goddess are enumerated, and the shrines built to her, and the poem closes with a sort of doxology.

This is not one of Callimachus' happier creations, though the sound and movement of the verse almost beguile one into thinking it so. But it does illustrate the way in which he will slip insensibly from burlesque or *genre* into romance, from romance and beauty into pedantry, all in what is ostensibly a Hymn to a goddess.

Now we know that Ovid studied Callimachus, as every elegiac poet did. He emulated the *Ibis*; his story of Philemon and Baucis in the *Metamorphoses* must owe much to the *Hecale*, as that of Erysichthon does to the sixth *Hymn*.[28] The *Fasti* purports to be a Roman *Aetia*, and the *Metamorphoses* is often aetiological also.*

---

* More than once he uses the word *causa* in the sense of αἴτιον: IV, 794; IX, 2. Nicander's *Heteroeumena* had also often been aetiological.[29]

It may well be that it was the example of the first two books of the *Aetia* which incited Ovid to make his a single poem with ingenious transitions;[30] and, like Callimachus, Ovid seeks to sustain interest by introducing every variety of literary form and mood. We have an Invocatory Hymn, a Homeric Hymn, a couple of Odes, a tragic *Agon* or debate, a Pastoral Idyll, a Heroine's Epistle, a Παρακλαυσίθυρον, and a couple of Epigrams,[31] not to mention the many epyllia. The difference was that Ovid chose to key up his whole poem to the loftier tone associated with epic objectivity, whereas Callimachus, with his more homely style, could appear in his own highly individual person. Ovid might qualify his

> Battiades semper toto cantabitur orbe

with

> quamvis ingenio non valet, arte valet[32]

> *Battus' son shall ever be sung throughout the world; though he has no power of genius, he has the power of art;*

but in any sense in which Ovid had *ingenium*, a quality he often claims, the son of Battus had it. To those who are familiar with Callimachus, there is nothing novel or unique about the spirit of the *Metamorphoses*.

Here, then, is a partial answer to Nicolson's question. We must approach the poem with no preconception about what we are to get out of it, taking each episode as we find it, letting 'the most capricious poet', as Touchstone called him,[33] lead us on through romance, burlesque, splendour, horror, pathos, macabre, rhetoric, genre-painting, debate, landscape-painting, antiquarian interest, patriotic pride—wherever his own fancy leads him. Of course we must know our Ovid first, but surely his other poems make him familiar enough. That done, if we clear our mind of water-tight compartments, we can at least hope to sense the chameleon variations of this masterpiece of Greco-Roman baroque art.

'Baroque' is not a word to use lightly in a metaphorical sense without some qualification. It has for some time been recognized

that there are affinities between Hellenistic and Baroque culture.[34]
In both periods an outburst of exuberance succeeded an age of
classic perfection, this having been the only immediate alternative
to fossilization and the dull repetition of formulae. Baroque art
tends to be grandiose, arresting, theatrical; full of restless and
exuberant vitality, it strives after variety, strangeness and contrast
—now fantastical, now playful, now picturesque. Indifferent to
truth, it claims the right to exaggerate or deceive for artistic ends.[35]

Is there not something baroque about the description of the
palace of the Sun with which Book II opens?*

> Regia Solis erat sublimibus alta columnis
> clara micante auro flammasque imitante pyropo,
> cuius ebur nitidum fastigia summa tegebat,
> argenti bifores radiabant lumine valvae.
> materiem superabat opus: nam Mulciber illic
> aequora celarat medias cingentia terras
> terrarumque orbem caelumque, quod imminet orbi.
> caeruleos habet unda deos, Tritona canorum
> Proteaque ambiguum ballaenarumque prementem
> Aegaeona suis immania terga lacertis,
> Doridaque et natas, quarum pars nare videtur,
> pars in mole sedens virides siccare capillos,
> pisce vehi quaedam: facies non omnibus una
> non diversa tamen, qualem decet esse sororum.
> terra viros urbesque gerit silvasque ferasque
> fluminaque et nymphas et cetera numina ruris.
> haec super imposita est caeli fulgentis imago
> signaque sex foribus dextris totidemque sinistris.

High-pillared rose the palace of the Sun;
With glittering gold and flaming bronze it shone;
The roof above was ivory gleaming white,
Silver the double doors' refulgent light.

* H. Bartholomé has suggested that this description of the universe has the
ulterior purpose of setting the scene for Phaëthon's annihilating disaster, *Ovid und
die antike Kunst* (1935), p. 75. The text used in this chapter is that of Ehwald,
unless otherwise stated.

More wondrous still its art, for Vulcan's hand
Had graved the Ocean coiled about the land,
The whole round earth, and sky o'erhanging all.
Sea-gods were in those waves, the musical
Triton, the changeful Proteus, Aegaeon,
His arms around huge-backed sea-monsters thrown,
And Doris' daughters—swimming some were seen,
Some perched on rocks to dry their tresses green,
Some riding fish, their faces not the same
Yet not unlike, as sisters true became.
The land had cities, forests, beasts and men,
Rivers and nymphs and gods of field and glen;
And crowning all was heaven's resplendent floor,
With signs of zodiac, six on either door.

And look at that Triton in Book 1, blowing the retreat for the waters of the Flood:[36]

Nec maris ira manet, positoque tricuspide telo
mulcet aquas rector pelagi, supraque profundum
exstantem atque umeros innato murice tectum
caeruleum Tritona vocat, conchaeque sonanti
inspirare iubet fluctusque et flumina signo
iam revocare dato: cava bucina sumitur illi,
tortilis in latum quae turbine crescit ab imo,
bucina, quae medio concepit ubi aëra ponto,
litora voce replet sub utroque iacentia Phoebo;
tunc quoque, ut ora dei madida rorantia barba
contigit et cecinit iussos inflata receptus,
omnibus audita est telluris et aequoris undis,
et, quibus est undis audita, coërcuit omnes.

Seas rage no more. The Lord of Ocean's tide,
To soothe the surge, his trident lays aside,
And calls the sea-green Triton, from the swell
Emerging, shoulders thick o'ergrown with shell,
To wind his echoing conch and sound retreat
To waves and rivers. He his trumpet great

With hollow spirals ever-widening takes,
Trumpet that, blown far in mid-ocean, wakes
Earth's utmost bounds from rise of sun to set.
So when those lips and beard all dripping wet
Touched it, and breathed, and gave the ordered sign,
'Twas heard by every water, fresh or brine,
And hearing each did straight his flood confine.

And what of Phaëthon's headlong career in Book II (195–328)? When he came face to face with the Scorpion's claws, in terror he dropped the reins. The horses plunged, and left the well-known path. The moon wondered to see her brother's chariot beneath her, and the clouds were singed and smoked. The higher regions of the earth caught fire and great cracks appeared. Vegetation first turned pale and was then burnt up; whole cities and nations perished. The mountains were on fire, even many-fountained Ida and Rhodope, bereft at last of her snows. Phaëthon gasped the stifling air and felt the chariot grow hot. Enveloped in smoke and falling ashes he could not see around him. Then was the Ethiopians' blood drawn to the surface of their bodies, and their skins went black. Then did Libya become a desert, and nymphs with dishevelled hair wandered looking for their springs and lakes. Rivers seethed, the gold in Tagus melted and the birds in Caÿster were boiled. The Nile fled and hid his head, which is hidden to this day, leaving seven dry valleys in his delta. Earth gaped, and light penetrated to the underworld, terrifying Pluto and Proserpine. Seas contracted and dried up, revealing the mountains they had covered. Fish sought the depths, the dolphins could not leap, and dead seals floated on the brine. Nereus with his daughters lurked in tepid caves, Neptune himself dared not emerge from the waves, and the Earth-mother, lifting her head and shielding her eyes with her hand, uttered an agonized protest to Jupiter.

The polychrome celature of the palace of the Sun suggests some fantastically ambitious design of Benvenuto Cellini; the Triton blowing his conch may be seen in Raphael's fresco of *Galatea* in the Villa Farnesina at Rome. It was from such works that the inspiration of baroque art was derived. As for the Earth shielding her face with her hand, one is reminded of the gigantic figure of the Nile on Bernini's Fountain of the Rivers in the Piazza Navona, shielding his eyes with his hand in order, it was said, that he might not see the rival Borromini's façade of Sant' Agnese in Agone.[37]

Yes, the *Metamorphoses* is 'baroque' in conception with its huge extent of ceaseless movement (like the Pergamene frieze of battling gods and giants), its variety, its fantasy, its conceits and shocks, its penchant for the grotesque and its blend of humour and grandiosity.* But one must not press the comparison too far. It is eminently classical in expression, with its clear and simple diction and versification; and for all its straining after variety, the bulk of the poem consists in straightforward narrative untrammelled with excess of detail.

Myths are apt to consist of a bare sequence of events, because they arise from a love of symbolism or aetiology, from something at any rate which is other than desire to tell a good tale. Ovid's method is to take the traditional story and 'play it straight', to imagine what would, as a matter of fact, have happened in the circumstances, human nature being what it is, and gods and demi-gods only human in their emotions. We are accustomed to this literalness in the treatment of the Bible stories by medieval artists. We are charmed and amused by the naiveté, for instance, of windows depicting the Ascension, with nothing but the soles of Christ's feet protruding from a very palpable cloud. Ovid is anything but naïve: he is pseudo-naïve, bent on exploiting the varied effects of literalness. Let us go ahead and see what happens, he seems to say. Some parts will prove pathetic, some grotesque, some stark, some comic—in fact, a great deal of the essential variety of tone will result automatically.

---

* "Strength at play", baroque has been called.[38]

(2) GROTESQUENESS, HUMOUR, WIT

The treatment of the act of metamorphosis itself claims first consideration. In Homer transformation takes place instantaneously, but in Hellenistic art as well as poetry we are invited to observe the process. Thus in Apollonius (III, 1381–98), and after him in Ovid (*M.* III, 106–10), we see the warriors springing from the dragon's teeth at various stages of emergence, like the rising dead in Signorelli's *Last Judgment* at Orvieto. On Pompeian wall-paintings of Hellenistic inspiration we see Actaeon with horns only, or with a stag's head only, not yet completely changed. We see laurel branches sprouting from the head and shoulders of Daphne. I doubt if Lafaye, who gives these examples, was right in detecting here a symptom of the analytical spirit of Alexandrian science, for he himself adduces also the example of the sailors half turned into dolphins by Dionysus on the Monument of Lysicrates at Athens, which dates from a generation before the founding of Alexandria.[39] It is rather a symptom of the rationalistic attitude deriving from the Sophists and Euripides.

Of course the effect is grotesque, but a taste for the grotesque was characteristic of the jaded palate of Hellenistic decadence.* Ovid usually describes the transformations in successive detail. This is how he treats the three which are depicted in the works of art mentioned above:

'No more Diana threatened, but on Actaeon's head which she had besprinkled she put the horns of a stag of many years, stretched out his neck, sharpened his ear-tips, changed his hands to feet and his arms to long legs and covered his body with a dappled hide. Quivering fear she gave him too: the hero son of Autonoë fled, marvelling to find himself so swift of foot.'[40]

'Scarcely had Daphne so prayed when a dragging numbness came over her limbs, thin bark grew round her tender breast, her

---

* Horace, by following this Hellenistic tradition, introduces an unfortunate grotesqueness into what is presumably meant to be a serious Ode, II, 20 (*Iam iam residunt* etc.); for which cf. Ovid's metamorphosis of Cycnus, II, 373–80.

hair was changed to leaves, her arms to branches; her foot, so swift of late, clung in retarding roots, and her face became a tree-top. There was left of her only her beauty's sheen.'[41]

'The men leapt overboard, goaded by madness or fear. And first Medon's body began to grow dark, and his back to be bent in a well-marked curve. To him Lycabas began, 'Into what strange creature are you turning?' But as he spoke his mouth spread wide, his nose grew curved, and his skin hardened with scales. While Libys, trying to ply the sluggish oars, saw his hands shrink and be no more hands but rather to be called fins. Another, seeking to stretch out his arms to a twisted rope, found he had no arms, and plunged with curved and limbless body into the waves: the end of his tail was rounded into the shape of a half-moon.'[42]

Is there some fascination, subtler than meets the eye, in the idea of metamorphosis which haunts the folklore of almost all nations? The lively imagination of primitive peoples invents a story to account for a natural feature which looks like something else, or for a name which sounds like something else. The resemblance between human character and that of various animals may also give rise to legends. But why should they appeal to sophisticated people? Whence the success of Garnett's *Lady into Fox*? Anything weird, of course, appeals to the part of us which enjoys fear that is unaccompanied by danger, the feelings we titillate by reading ghost stories. But Fränkel, who cites an imaginative experience of childhood recounted by André Gide,[43] may possibly be right in suggesting that there is ultimately something sexual about them. If so, however, the springs are deep in the well of the subconscious. With what modest restraint Ovid, so often referred to in tones that suggest he was salacious, describes the changing of Iphis from a girl into a boy![44]

We have seen that Daphne, even as a laurel, retained her beauty's sheen: Lycaon, turned to a wolf, has still his grey hair, his fierce look, his flashing eyes, his savage appearance.[45] The human race, sprung from stones thrown by Deucalion, shows its origin by its hardness and endurance, as Pindar and Virgil had already fancied.[46] The churlish rustics, changed by Latona into frogs for refusing to let her drink, 'even now exercise their ugly tongues in wrangling, and shamelessly even under water still try to curse, their voices hoarse, their throats swollen and their mouths distended with incessant quarrelling'.[47] Ovid likes to suggest thus the origin of the myths, as also the etymology of names—the bat (*vespertilio*) from his habit of flying at evening (*vespere*), the newt or lizard (*stellio*) from being spangled (*stellatus*) with spots.[48]

Nothing could be more grotesque than the metamorphosis of Scylla by Circe. 'She waded waist-deep into the water, when suddenly she saw her loins disfigured with barking monsters; and at first, not realizing they were part of her own body, she tried to flee and drive them off and feared the savage muzzles of the dogs; but as she fled she carried them with her, and feeling for her thighs and legs and feet she found only gaping jaws as of Cerberus in place of them.'[49]

On this side the grotesqueness of realism merges into horror. When Homer describes carnage we may not like it (after boyhood), but we recognize that this is something which belongs to his age; he is not self-conscious about it. Disgusting sights are inseparable from war; in this case it is not accurate to call unpleasant realism *false*.[50] But in the tender Virgil and the goodnatured Ovid of Augustan Rome such descriptions jar. Granted that in their Rome even the educated classes were familiar with the slaughter of the arena, if not also of war, the elaborate squalors described on occasion by these two poets (and Lucan is worse) strike one as conscientious attempts at Homeric realism. No doubt Ovid felt that his patchwork would be incomplete without a battle-piece or two, which would also give him an opportunity to include the emotion of shock among those with which he strove to vary the appeal of his poem, and there would be some at least among his audience whose jaded taste would respond to any novel sensation of gruesomeness he could inflict, like twentieth-century Parisians at the Grand Guignol. How these must have relished the flaying of Marsyas by Apollo![51] There are passages of ingenious gruesomeness in the fight between Perseus and the supporters of Phineus,[52] and still more in the battle of the Centaurs and Lapiths as described by Nestor.[53] We are shocked also (and should expect Ovid to be) at the mental brutality of Perseus as he turns to stone with the Gorgon's head the man whom he has succeeded as suitor for Andromeda: 'Nay, I will make you a monument to endure for all time, and you shall be ever on show in the house of my father-in-law, so that my wife may find solace in the statue of him who was once her betrothed.'[54]

On the other side grotesqueness merges into humour. The monstrous Cyclops, fallen in love with Galatea, begins to care about his personal appearance, combing his matted hair with a rake, trimming his beard with a pruning-hook, and using the reflexion of a pool for the purpose of composing and titivating his features.[*][55] A handsome Centaur is praised in detail, his man-half for its features, his horse-half for its points.[56] When the neighbouring rivers visit Peneüs after the transformation into a laurel of his daughter Daphne as a result of being loved by Apollo, they do not know whether to congratulate him or to condole.[57] Mercury, bent on putting the hundred-eyed Argus to sleep, sits down patiently, detains him in lengthy conversation, and then pipes to him till some of the eyes go to sleep; but the monster struggles to keep a quorum awake, until the god, having plunged into the story of Pan and Syrinx, sees the last eye finally close and forthwith cuts off his head.[58]

There is a kind of humour that evokes the response 'How charming!' rather than 'How funny!' English has no good word for describing it, but the Greeks used χάρις, recognizing that there is an element of neatness and grace involved.[†] Most of Ovid's humour is of this kind, and it pervades the *Metamorphoses*.[‡] Often

* Here Ovid is exaggerating the mild and sentimental burlesque of Theocritus VI and XI.

† εὔχαρις is the Greek equivalent of *facetus*, which has not the connotation of 'facetious'. For various kinds of χάρις in literature see Demetrius, περὶ ἑξέως 128 ff. γέλοιος was used for what we call 'funny'.

‡ It is strange by any definition that some critics, while allowing Ovid wit, should deny him humour; e.g. J. Wight Duff, *A Literary History of Rome in the Golden Age* (3rd edn., 1953), p. 439.

there is an element of burlesque. It is delightful to see Circe presiding, like any Roman matron, over her household. The busy scene is familiar, but with a difference. The girls in her service are Nymphs and Nereïds, and they are not employed in the usual task of carding and spinning wool: they are assistants in an efficient witch's botanical laboratory, sorting out flowers and herbs into baskets, while she superintends, well skilled in the use of each leaf and in blending them, and carefully weighs out the correct quantities.[59]

The story of Erysichthon, condemned to perpetual hunger for cutting down the grove of Ceres, gave ample scope for humour. Callimachus treats it in a spirit of broad farce in his Sixth Hymn. Twenty cooks were required for him, and twelve wine-drawers; his parents were hard put to it inventing excuses for declining invitations for him to dine out; he ate the draught mules, the race-horse, the war-horse, even the cat. Ovid chose instead to dwell, in a light and charming vein, on his final expedient, the selling of his daughter to buy food.† The spirited girl refused to gratify her new master; and as she fled before him she prayed to Neptune (who had ravished her once) to save her, whereupon he changed her on the spot into a fisherman:[60]

> Hanc dominus spectans, 'O qui pendentia parvo
> aera cibo celas, moderator harundinis,' inquit,
> 'sic mare compositum, sic sit tibi piscis in unda
> credulus, et nullos, nisi fixus, sentiat hamos:
> quae modo cum vili turbatis veste capillis
> litore in hoc steterat (nam stantem in litore vidi),
> dic ubi sit! neque enim vestigia longius extant.'
> illa dei munus sensit bene cedere, et a se
> se quaeri gaudens his est resecuta rogantem:
> 'quisquis es, ignoscas! in nullam lumina partem
> gurgite ab hoc flexi studioque operatus inhaesi,
> quoque minus dubites, sic has deus aequoris artes

† This episode does not occur in Callimachus, but is referred to by Antoninus Liberalis (17, 5) in connexion with a story from Nicander. Her name was Mestra.

adiuvet, ut nemo iamdudum litore in isto,
me tamen excepto, nec femina constitit ulla.'
credidit et verso dominus pede pressit harenam
elususque abiit: illi sua reddita forma est.
ast ubi habere suam transformia corpora sensit,
saepe pater dominis Triopeïda tradit, at illa
nunc equa, nunc ales, modo bos, modo cervus, abibat,
praebebatque avido non iusta alimenta parenti.

Spying her thus her master cried, 'Ho there!
Fisher with rod and line and baited snare,
So may your sea be calm, your fishes naught
Suspect nor sense the hidden hook till caught,
Say, where is she in rags with streaming hair
That trod this shore but now?—I saw her there
With my own eyes, and here the footprints cease.'
She, comprehending her divine release,
And smiling that he asked her, where was she,
Answered, 'Excuse me, sir, whoe'er you be:
Bent on their task my eyes have never stirred
From this same pool; but you may take my word
(So help me now the Sea-god!), but for me
No man has trod this foreshore recently,
Nor woman neither.' Turning in his track
The dupe retired. She changed to maiden back.
Perceiving then her mutability,
Her father sold her many a time, and she
As mare, or bird, or cow, or hind was freed,
Compounding fraud to gratify his greed.

Wit and pathos mingle in the story of Narcissus, who loved
only himself, and Echo, who pursued him but could speak only
to the extent of repeating the last words of others:[61]*

Ergo ubi Narcissum per devia rura vagantem
vidit et incaluit, sequitur vestigia furtim,

---

* Ariel uses echo in this way to tease Ferdinand in the Dryden-Davenant
version of *The Tempest.*

quoque magis sequitur, flamma propiore calescit,
non aliter quam cum summis circumlita taedis
admotas rapiunt vivacia sulphura flammas.
o quotiens voluit blandis accedere dictis
et molles adhibere preces! natura repugnat
nec sinit incipiat: sed, quod sinit, illa parata est
expectare sonos, ad quos sua verba remittat.
forte puer comitum seductus ab agmine fido
dixerat, 'ecquis adest?' et 'adest!' responderat Echo.
hic stupet, utque aciem partes dimittit in omnes
voce 'veni!' magna clamat: vocat illa vocantem.
respicit et rursus nullo veniente 'quid', inquit,
'me fugis?' et totidem quot dixit verba recepit.
perstat, et alternae deceptus imagine vocis
'huc coëamus!' ait, nullique libentius unquam
responsura sono 'coëamus!' rettulit Echo,
et verbis favet ipsa suis egressaque silva
ibat ut iniceret sperato bracchia collo.
ille fugit fugiensque 'manus complexibus aufer!
ante', ait, 'emoriar quam sit tibi copia nostri!'
rettulit illa nihil nisi 'sit tibi copia nostri!'

Narcissus roaming through the forests she
Beheld, and burning followed stealthily;
The closer he, the warmer her desire,
As on a torch quick sulphur will aspire
To anticipate and snatch the kindling fire.
How oft she yearned to approach and woo the lad
With soft, entreating words! Nature forbade:
Begin she may not, but this much she may—
Catch any sounds, and words thereto repay.
It chanced that, severed from his friends, he cried
'Anyone here?', and Echo 'Here!' replied.
Amazed he darted glances all about;
Then 'Come!' he shouted: she returned his shout.
He looked, and no one came, protested 'Why
Avoid me?', and received the self-same cry.

He stood, and by the answering voice deceived
Said, 'Here! I want you'.* Never more relieved
To answer any sound, Echo averred
'I want you!', and to implement her word
Forth from the wood she came and ran to throw
Her arms around that neck desirèd so.
He fleeing cried, 'Hands off and let me free:
I'll die before you have your will of me!'
She answered only, 'Have your will of me!'

Ovid's wit abounds in conceits of every kind. There is the reversal of literary cliché, as when the Bear, proverbial in Homer for not dipping in the Ocean like other constellations, seeks to plunge into the forbidden waves at the scorching of Phaëthon's chariot;[62] or when the Sun, who is supposed to be all-seeing (πανόπτης), has no eye for anything but his beloved Leucothoë.[63] (There are several examples of this kind of conceit in the Phaëthon passage already summarized.) Lines used symbolically of a flower by Catullus are adapted to Narcissus: he was so beautiful that

> multi illum iuvenes, multae cupiere puellae,
>
> *many youths, many maidens, desired him,*

but proved so cold and proud that

> nulli illum iuvenes, nullae tetigere puellae.[64]†
>
> *no youths, no maidens, touched him.*

Mercury looks down on Athens and the shrubs of the 'cultivated Lyceum' (*culti arbusta Lycei*), a pun on its future as the seat of Aristotle's school.[65]‡

---

* It seems impossible to render closely in English the *double entendre* of the Latin *coëamus*.

† Note that Ovid, to avoid the spondee and heavy elision, substitutes *tetigere* and *cupiere* for *optavere*.[66]

‡ By a similar anachronism Callimachus in the *Hecale* had allowed Theseus to see the Lyceum.

Then there are verbal conceits, especially where paradoxical characters are involved. Narcissus provides several:

> Spem sine corpore amat, corpus putat esse, quod umbra est;[67]

> Se cupit imprudens et, qui probat, ipse probatur,
> dumque petit, petitur, pariterque accendit et ardet.[68]

Circe undoes her spells in a line of suitable abracadabra,

> verbaque dicuntur dictis contraria verbis.[69]

Here we have the Ovid of the elegiac poems, *amator ingenii sui*.

More subtle are the conceits which presage the epigrams of Lucan. Earth prays to Jupiter that, if she must perish by fire, she may have the consoling honour of knowing that it is his fire, the lightning:

> liceat periturae viribus ignis
> igne perire tuo clademque auctore levare !'[70]

When he himself loved Ganymede, '*Something was found which Jupiter would rather be than what he was*',

> inventum est aliquid quod Iuppiter ipse,
> quam quod erat, mallet.[71]

Envy flies over Athens and almost weeps to see nothing there worthy of tears:

> vixque tenet lacrimas quia nil lacrimabile cernit;[72]

and Niobe would have been called happiest of mothers had she not seemed so to herself (for she challenged Latona):

> et felicissima matrum
> dicta foret Niobe, si non sibi visa fuisset.[73]

Finally, there is often wit in the ingenuity of Ovid's transitions. The shocking tale of Byblis concludes: 'The rumour of this unnatural passion might well have been the talk of the hundred towns of Crete (ἑκατόμπολις), had the island not lately produced a marvel nearer home, the transformation of Iphis' (whose story then follows).[74] Often some distant relationship forms the link. Ovid shows himself a Proust-like connoisseur of the Olympian Jesse-tree, with its endless ramifications. Ulysses' reply to Ajax is worthy of M. de Charlus:[75]

'Since Ajax claims to be great-grandson of Jupiter, let me say that Jupiter is the founder of my family also, and I am the same number of generations removed from him. For Laërtes is my father, Acrisius was his, and he was the son of Jupiter—and this line contains no exiled criminal.* I have also through my mother a further claim to noble birth, from Mercury: I have divine blood on both sides.'

(3) NARRATIVE AND DESCRIPTION

The bulk of the poem, however, consists of straight narrative. The acknowledged excellence of Ovid as a narrator depends in fact on economy and consequent swiftness, but more on his eye for significant detail, the quality we associate with 'good reportage'. 'If you look for Helice and Buris, once cities of Achaea, you will find them under the waves, and sailors will still show you the sloping towns with their walls engulfed.'[76] Here it is the word 'sloping' (*inclinata*) that makes the picture vivid; peering with the sailor into the depths, we see the shapes in refracted light. Aeacus describes a plague in Aegina: 'How often has a husband in the act of praying for a wife, or a father for a son, fallen dead before those implacable altars, *and in his hand has been found part of the incense still unconsumed.*'[77] How delightfully true to life is the description of young Icarus watching his father make the wings: 'The boy was standing by and, unaware that he was handling his own ruin, with smiling face now caught at feathers floating in the draught, now moulded the yellow wax with his thumb, and with his playing hindered his father's wondrous work.' And

---

* Peleus, who murdered his half-brother, Phocus, was Ajax's uncle. Ulysses conveniently ignores the later version, accepted of course by Ajax (l. 32), that his own father was really Sisyphus the damned, not Laërtes.

when later they soar, we see the whole scene: 'a man angling for fish with quivering rod, a shepherd leaning on his staff, a plough-man on his plough-shaft, beheld them and stood amazed, thinking they must be gods, that they could fly through the air.'*[78] Ovid prepares us for the naïveté of Scylla of Megara in her love-affair with Minos by a charming piece of description:

'There was a royal tower reared on the tuneful walls on which the son of Latona is said to have laid down his golden lyre, the music whereof still lingered in the stones. Thither Nisus' daughter, in the old days of peace, would often go up *and set the stones echoing with a pebble.* And now in war-time too she would often look out from there over the stern contests of the battle; and as the conflict dragged on she came to know the names of the captains, their arms and horses and apparel and Cydonian quivers.'[79]

Now here, now there, darts the eye of the poet's imagination. It does not always follow a story consecutively. For instance, when Triton blew retreat to the Flood, the result is described as follows: 'The rivers subside, and hills are seen to emerge; now the sea has a shore: the channels contain the swollen streams; the earth arises; as the waters decrease, places increase; and after all those days the woods show their uncovered tops again, with mud still clinging to the leaves.'[80] Lessing remarked that these events are not described in the order of their occurrence; the hills should appear first, and so forth.[81] In fact, the poet is showing us jumbled lantern-slides, not a film. But generally the slides are so well chosen that we can imagine the rest.

The freshness of Ovid's vision (or maybe his skill in exploiting the vision of predecessors) is particularly evident in his similes. These rarely extend beyond three lines, and are often shorter, for

---

* It has been suggested that this passage may have inspired the works of art at Pompeii depicting the scene.[82] P. Brueghel's well-known picture at Brussels, 'The Fall of Icarus', shows the fisher, shepherd and ploughman going on with their tasks again unheeding, as Icarus, a minute figure, strikes the water. It may well be that Ovid's description suggested to him this treatment.[83]

we must not be distracted for a moment from the story; but they are as apt as they are picturesque. Narcissus beats his breast till red patches show, like apples that are partly rosy and partly pale, or unripe grapes in a cluster beginning to purple; and Arachne flushes for a fleeting moment, as the sky grows crimson at dawn and anon pales again with the sunrise.[84] Apollo is inflamed by Daphne as stubble of the harvested corn, or as hedges burn with fire a traveller has brought too near, or left at daybreak unextinguished; and at sight of Coronis' pyre he groans as a cow groans when before her eyes the hammer, raised to the butcher's right ear, descends with resounding blow to dash out the brains of her suckling calf.[85] Aëtes' fiery bulls bellow and hiss like full furnaces, or hot limestones in a limekiln when water is sprinkled on them;[86] and Lichas hardens into stone in mid-air like drops of rain in a cold wind that turn first to snow and then to hail.[87] In the story of Hermaphroditus and the nymph Salmacis there are six comparisons in thirty lines.*[88]

Like Homer, Ovid does not hesitate to use similes taken from his own times. The Maenads attack Orpheus, flocking round him like birds in daylight mobbing an owl, or hounds harrying a stag to death some morning in the arena.[89] (Here again a single word, *matutina*, imparts reality to the scene.) Atalanta's body flushed as she ran, as when a crimson awning stretched over a white courtyard colours it with borrowed hues.[90] Mercury, winging over

---

* S. G. Owen, 'Ovid's Use of the Simile', *C.R.*, 1931, pp. 97–106, remarks (p. 105) that whereas Ovid piles up variant similes for their own sake, Homer, in the famous sequence *Il.* II, 455–76, makes each relevant to a different *aspect* of the Greek host in motion. He gives the following figures (p. 99):

	Lines	Similes
Iliad	15,600	202
Odyssey	10,912	50
Argonautica	5,835	77
Aeneid	9,896	105
Metamorphoses	12,015	252

Such figures are to be treated cautiously, since anything from two words to several lines is included; nevertheless the high proportion in the *Metamorphoses* is some indication of the richness of its texture.

Herse, was inflamed by her as a leaden bullet hurled from a Balearic sling grows hot as it flies, and finds beneath the clouds fire it had not before.[91] Particularly good is the likening of the warriors that arose from the dragon's teeth to figures embroidered on a theatre curtain rising (in Roman fashion) from the ground: 'Even so, as in the festive theatre the curtain is raised, figures of men emerge, showing first their faces, then little by little all the rest, till at last, drawn up with steady motion, their whole forms are revealed and they plant their feet on its lowest edge.'*[92]

It is easy to see how it came about that Ovid had such an immense influence on Renaissance art. There is a plastic quality about his work. He catches the significant moment or attitude or gesture and imprints it on our mind. Interesting attempts have been made to identify his own debt to particular works of art, or to distinguish their influence from that of literature or first-hand experience.[93] Guesswork though these must remain, we cannot doubt that works of art seen on his visit to Athens at an impressionable age, and those plundered or imported from Greece which adorned the colonnades, temples and palaces of the city which Augustus was turning under his eyes from brick to marble, coloured his whole imagination.† Thus he makes Acheloüs lean on his elbow,[94] just like those colossal statues of reclining river-gods, one of which, the celebrated 'Marforio' of the first century A.D., is to be seen in the *cortile* of the Capitoline Museum, and another, a Nile of the same period, in the Vatican.‡ An attitude of Venus well known in statues derived from the Cnidian Aphrodite of Praxiteles is described at *A.A.* II, 613-14.

Many of the best narrative episodes, such as the story of Alcyone and Ceÿx,[95] which attracted the Muse of the youthful

---

* Cf. Virgil's

Utque
purpurea intexti tollant aulaea Britanni[96]
(And how the embroidered Britons raise the crimson curtains).

† Ovid seems especially to have admired Apelles, particularly his Aphrodite.[97]

‡ To cite a possible example not mentioned by Bartholomé.

Cicero, are too long for quotation here in full; but Arethusa's account to Ceres of her pursuit by the river Alpheüs in human form, being fairly short, may serve as well as any to illustrate Ovid's genius at its best:[98]

Lassa revertebar (memini) Stymphalide silva;
aestus erat, magnumque labor geminaverat aestum;
invenio sine vertice aquas, sine murmure euntes,
perspicuas ad humum, per quas numerabilis alte
calculus omnis erat, quas tu vix ire putares.
cana salicta dabant nutritaque populus unda
sponte sua natas ripis declivibus umbras.
accessi primumque pedis vestigia tinxi,
poplite deinde tenus; neque eo contenta recingor
molliaque impono salici velamina curvae
nudaque mergor aquis; quas dum ferioque trahoque
mille modis labens excussaque bracchia iacto,
nescio quod medio sensi sub gurgite murmur
territaque insisto propioris margine fontis.
'quo properas, Arethusa?' suis Alpheüs ab undis,
'quo properas?' iterum rauco mihi dixerat ore.
sicut eram fugio sine vestibus (altera vestes
ripa meas habuit): tanto magis instat et ardet,
et, quia nuda fui, sum visa paratior illi.
sic ego currebam, sic me ferus ille premebat,
ut fugere accipitrem penna trepidante columbae,
ut solet accipiter trepidas urgere columbas.
usque sub Orchomenon Psophidaque Cyllenenque
Maenaliosque sinus gelidumque Erymanthon et Elim
currere sustinui, nec me velocior ille;
sed tolerare diu cursus ego viribus impar
non poteram, longi patiens erat ille laboris.
per tamen et campos, per opertos arbore montes,
saxa quoque et rupes et, qua via nulla, cucurri.
sol erat a tergo: vidi praecedere longam
ante pedes umbram, nisi si timor illa videbat;

sed certe sonitusque pedum terrebat et ingens
crinales vittas adflabat anhelitus oris.
fessa labore fugae, 'fer opem, deprendimur', inquam,
'armigerae, Dictynna, tuae, cui saepe dedisti
ferre tuos arcus inclusaque tela pharetra!'
mota dea est spissisque ferens e nubibus unam
me super iniecit: lustrat caligine tectam
amnis et ignarus circum cava nubila quaerit,
bisque locum, quo me dea texerat, inscius ambit,
et bis 'io Arethusa, io Arethusa!' vocavit.
quid mihi tunc animi miserae fuit? anne quod agnae est,
si qua lupos audit circum stabula alta frementes,
aut lepori, qui vepre latens hostilia cernit
ora canum nullosque audet dare corpore motus?
non tamen abscedit; neque enim vestigia cernit
longius ulla pedum; servat nubemque locumque.
occupat obsessos sudor mihi frigidus artus
caeruleaeque cadunt toto de corpore guttae,
quaque pedem movi manat locus, eque capillis
ros cadit, et citius quam nunc tibi facta renarro
in latices mutor. sed enim cognoscit amatas
amnis aquas positoque viri, quod sumpserat, ore
vertitur in proprias, ut se mihi misceat, undas.
Delia rupit humum, caecisque ego mersa cavernis
advehor Ortygiam, quae me cognomine divae
grata meae superas eduxit prima sub auras.

Returning tired from the Stymphalian chase—
And doubly hot with toil and sun I was—
I found a stream that smooth and silent ran,
Clear to the bottom, so that you could scan
Each pebble there; it hardly seemed to move.
Wild silvery willows shaded it above,
And poplars that by rivers nurtured grow.
I approached, I tried the water with my toe,
Then to the knee, nor yet content, undressed
And o'er a curving willow flung my vest,

And dived all naked in. I swam and plunged
And tossed my arms a thousand ways and lunged,
When suddenly beneath the pool I heard
A sound, and climbed the nearest bank afeared.
'Stay, Arethusa!' from his depths there cried
Alpheüs; 'stay!', again he did me chide.
I fled, just as I was and all unclad
(Ill chance, the other bank my clothing had).
Fired, he pursued my open nakedness:
The more I ran, more fiercely did he press.
As pigeons flee a hawk on fluttered wing
And hawk pursues the pigeons fluttering.
Right past Orchomenus, Psophis, Cyllene,
Maenalus, Erymanthus, did I flee,
And Elis' land, nor swifter yet was he.
Ill-matched, I could not long sustain that pace,
Accustomed he to endure a lengthy race;
Yet over fields and mountains forested,
O'er rocks and stones and pathless wastes I fled.
With sun behind I saw preceding me
A shadow huge—or terror made me see—;
I heard his dreaded footfall, that I swear,
And felt his breath beat on my braided hair,
Foredone, 'O help, or I am caught!' I cried,
'Dictynna,* help the maid who at thy side
Oft chosen bore thy bow and quiver's load!'
The goddess hearkened, and forthwith bestowed
A cloud for covering. In quest of me
The river roamed, groping bewilderedly.
Twice circled he my hiding-place about,
And 'Arethusa!' twice did loudly shout,
'Ho, Arethusa!' Ah, how felt I then?
As lamb that hears the wolves about the pen
Howling, or hare that, lurking in the brake,
Dread muzzles sees nor motion dares to make.

* Diana of the hunting-nets.

He moved not on, for further went no trace
Of footsteps—only watched the cloud and place.
Sweat from my leaguer'd limbs began to well,
And watery drops from all my body fell;
Each footstep left a pool, each tress a fount,
And sooner than I can the tale recount
I was a spring. But still the river knows
His love, and now his human shape foregoes,
To mingle with me turning back to waves.
Diana cleaves the ground, and through dark caves
To Ortygia, that bears her blessed name,
I pass, once more the daylight to acclaim.

Looking back, we can see what touches contribute to the success of this narrative. In the first place, it is told by the protagonist herself,* which gives it immediacy, and told in a fluent, limpid style. There is the delicious contrast of the heat of the day and the chase with the coolness and beauty of the river. Counting every pebble in its depths, we feel delight such as Ausonius was later to give us more abundantly in his description of peering into the Moselle.[99] Everything is lifelike, the nymph trying the water first with her toe, then going in up to the knee, and finally taking off all her clothes and hanging them on a tree. Eerily the hoarse murmur of the river-god rises from the depths. We feel the helpless plight of the maiden, cut off from her clothes (for all her terror she would think first of this). Then the breathless chase, first through recognized places that fly past, then through places without a name, and all the time that overhanging shadow which seems ever to be overtaking her and the inescapable breath that buffets her hair behind, an evocation of imaginative terror rivalling Coleridge's 'Like one that on a lonesome road...'. Then the contrasting terror of having to keep motionless, of hearing the pursuer searching round the cloak of mist, vividly conveyed

---

* Cf. the river Acheloüs' vivid description of his struggle with Hercules (ix, 4–88).

by the simile of the hare lurking in a brake, seeing the threatening muzzles of the hounds and not daring to stir.

However much at home Ovid may have felt in the sophisticated society of the Capital, he must sometimes have longed to escape, like Horace, to the hills and streams, far from

> fumem et opes strepitumque Romae.

The *Metamorphoses* is undoubtedly a poem of escape. It wafts the reader into a world where the geographical features may be familiar, but the actors, divine and human, move hither and thither with the swiftness of the wind, from Babylon and the Sun-god's palace beyond the Ethiopians to Sicily and the banks of Po, and look down on the earth as man could do only in imagination until eighteen centuries after Ovid wrote.* Naturally this primeval world is not urbanized: with rare exceptions we move among mountains, valleys, rivers, forests, seas.

To us it is a romantic world, quite apart from its inhabitants. Its very wildness makes it so. But are we importing modern sentiment if we attribute such feelings to Ovid? Let me put the point more concretely. J. H. Newman's words

> O'er moor and fen, o'er crag and torrent, till
> The night is gone,

though they are only a list of natural features, and indeed are ostensibly but symbols of the difficulties of our earthly journey, evoke strong romantic feelings in readers conditioned by Words-worth and his successors, for whom 'over the hills and far away' is the essence of poetry. When Ovid wished to describe some character traversing his world, he similarly used lists of natural features, as in

> per iuga, per valles, quo fors ducebat, euntem,
>
> *passing o'er hills, o'er dales, where chance led*

---

* Cf. *F.* IV, 561–72, and Chaucer's dream of being carried aloft by an eagle, *The Hous of Fame* II, 896 ff.

or

> per tamen et campos, per opertos arbore montes,
> saxa quoque et rupes et, qua via nulla, cucurri,

> *yet through fields, o'er forest-covered mountains, o'er rocks*
> *and stones and pathless places I ran,*

and here again romantic echoes are raised in our minds, though it is difficult to say how he could have expressed himself more plainly and realistically. An ancient poet has only to mention natural features of the countryside for modern critics to scent the poetry of romance.

Nevertheless, it is well known that after the urbanization of society in Hellenistic times both poetry and the visual arts began to view nature in a spirit not much different from ours; and I believe that when Catullus addressed Diana as born 'to be mistress of the mountains and the green forests and the hidden glades and the sounding rivers',

> montium domina ut fores
> silvarumque virentium
> saltuumque reconditorum
> amniumque sonantum,[100]

his feeling was indeed romantic; nor do I see any reason to doubt that Ovid had similar feelings. If he rarely indicates them expressly, it may be because of the nature of his genre; the early epyllion was objective; it did not dwell on the emotions expected of the reader, as the idyll and the later epyllion were apt to do. The very first word in Theocritus draws attention to the charm of the setting: 'Sweet is the whispered music of yon pine-tree by the springs, goatherd...'

> ἁδύ τι τὸ ψιθύρισμα καὶ ἁ πίτυς, αἰπόλε, τήνα,
> ἁ ποτὶ ταῖς παγαῖσι μελίσδεται....

and the goatherd replies 'Sweeter, shepherd, falls thy song than yon stream that tumbles plashing from the rocks above';

> ἅδιον, ὦ ποιμήν, τὸ τέον μέλος ἢ τὸ καταχές
> τῆν' ἀπὸ τᾶς πέτρας καταλείβεται ὑψόθεν ὕδωρ.

178

Ovid is sparing of comment, even the comment of epithets; he may suggest, but he does not exclaim.

Let us take a salient example. The miraculous beauty of the dawn has never ceased to challenge the descriptive powers of poets. One has only to think of Shakespeare:

> But look, the morn in russet mantle clad,
> Walks o'er the dew of yon high eastward hill.
>
> Night's candles are burnt out, and jocund day
> Stands tiptoe on the misty mountain-tops.
>
> Full many a glorious morning have I seen
> Flatter the mountain-tops with sovereign eye,
> Kissing with golden face the meadows green,
> Gilding pale streams with heavenly alchemy.
>
> I with the Morning's love have oft made sport,
> And, like a forester, the groves may tread
> Even till the eastern gate, all fiery red
> Opening on Neptune, with fair blessed beams
> Turns into yellow gold his salt green streams.

Roman poets were no less susceptible, as Seneca's burlesque testifies: 'The poets are not content to describe sunrise and sunset, and now they even disturb the noonday siesta.'[101]

The first dawn in the *Metamorphoses* is a colourful allegorical picture which is said to have inspired Guido Reni's once celebrated Aurora Pallavicini:[102]

'Lo, Aurora, waking from the ruddy east, opened the crimson doors and the halls full of roses: the stars fled away, marshalled by Lucifer, who last of all departs from his post in the sky. When the Sun-god saw him setting and the world growing red, while the slender horns of the moon seemed to vanish away, he bade the swift Hours yoke his steeds. Quickly the goddesses obeyed his command, led forth the steeds, filled with ambrosial nurture and breathing fire, from their lofty stalls, and fixed their jingling bridles.'

But after this, while we cannot doubt the poet's impressionability, his daybreaks are indicated in sparing language, for the narrative cannot wait:

>primo feriente cacumina sole[103]

>*as the first sunlight struck the peaks;*

or

>stellarum sublime coëgerat agmen
>Lucifer,[104]

>*Lucifer had marshalled the host of the stars on high*

or

>altera lucem
>cum croceis invecta rotis Aurora reducet,[105]

>*when next Dawn, borne on her saffron car, shall bring back the day;*

or at most,

>postera nocturnos Aurora removerat ignes
>solque pruinosas radiis siccaverat herbas,[106]

>*the next Dawn had banished the torches of night, and the sun's rays had dried the rimy grass.*

Nevertheless, the feeling for beauty is there; in the last example, as so often with him, one word, *pruinosas* (rimy), is enough to bring the picture to life.

It is the same with descriptions of scenery: Ovid rarely dwells on them in the idyllic manner. But there is one exception so striking that we may be justified in assuming that he is indulging an enthusiasm of his own. The reader cannot fail to have been struck by the lifelike beauty of the reach of the Alpheüs which tempted Arethusa to her fateful bathe. There are a dozen extended descriptions of natural scenery in the poem, and practically all of them centre round water, cool, calm and shaded. Mountain ridges and cliffs are not described; nor are valleys, forests or meadows, save as a setting for water; and the water is not generally cascading or hurrying, but gentle or calm and translucent, shaded by trees or overarching rocks.* Cool streams and fresh grass, we remember, are what Ovid in his mind's eye associated with the countryside of his boyhood home amid the Apennines.[107]

Here is a good example:

> Vallis erat piceis et acuta densa cupressu
> nomine Gargaphie, succinctae sacra Dianae,
> cuius in extremo est antrum nemorale recessu
> arte laboratum nulla: simulaverat artem
> ingenio natura suo; nam pumice vivo
> et levibus tofis nativum duxerat arcum;
> fons sonat a dextra tenui perlucidus unda
> margine gramineo patulos succinctus hiatus.
> hic dea silvarum venatu fessa solebat
> virgineos artus liquido perfundere rore.[108]

> *Thick set with pines and cypress-spires the glade*
> *Gargaphie lay—Diana loved its shade—*
> *And in its deepest nook a woodland grot,*
> *Not of man's art, but artfully begot*
> *By nature's genius, that from tufa soft*
> *And living pumice carved its arch aloft;*
> *Hence to the right a rivulet clear as glass*
> *Spread purling into pools begirt with grass.*
> *Oft would the Goddess, wearied in the hunt,*
> *Refresh her virgin limbs in that pure fount.*

In the same book (28–31) there is a copious spring in a low-arched cavern, thickly surrounded with bushes and saplings, in the depths of a primeval forest, and again (407–12) a clear pool of silvery-bright water, untouched by shepherds or by mountain-grazing goats or any other beast, undisturbed by bird or wild animal or falling branch, with fresh grass round the edge and

---

* See also *A.A.* III, 687-94. Grimal (*op. cit.* p. 151) finds rocks and forests to be Ovid's favourite components of landscape; but his more elaborate descriptions seem to centre on water. To some extent his sensibility to this may have been affected by bucolic poetry.[109]

a fringe of trees that fend off at all times the heat of the sun. Sometimes there are flowers too, like the crimson water-lotus on the shelving bank of the myrtle-crowned pool into which the nymph Lotis had been turned.[110] And of course they abound near the swan-lake of Enna whence Pluto seized Proserpina:[111]

> Haud procul Hennaeis lacus est a moenibus altae,
> nomine Pergus, aquae: non illo plura Caÿstros
> carmina cygnorum labentibus audit* in undis.
> silva coronat aquas cingens latus omne, suisque
> frondibus ut velo Phoebeos submovet ignes;
> frigora dant rami, varios humus umida flores:
> perpetuum ver est.

> *Not far from Enna's walls there is a mere,*
> *Deep Pergus: e'en Caÿster does not hear*
> *The singing of more swans upon its tide;*
> *A fringe of trees crowns it on every side*
> *With leafy awning to repel the heat,*
> *Branches o'erhead, rich flowers under feet—*
> *Eternal spring is there!*

Soft damp moss on the floor, and variegated shells on the roof, were the interior decoration of the dark cave of pumice and tufa where the river god Acheloüs dwelt.[112]

Sometimes it is sea water that makes the scene, like the favourite bow-shaped pool of Scylla on the Calabrian coast; or the height on the same coast on which she turned to face Glaucus, where the mountains gather to a wooded peak hanging far out over the deep; or the lonely shore of Euboea, its grass ungrazed by cattle, sheep or goats, its flowers unrifled by bees or human hands, its hay unmown, where Glaucus sat counting his fish before he ate the fatal herb that drove him into the sea.[113] And there is the lovely spot where Peleus found Thetis:[114]

> Est sinus Haemoniae curvos falcatus in arcus;
> bracchia procurrunt; ubi si foret altior unda,
> portus erat; summis inductum est aequor harenis;

* I slightly prefer this to the reading 'edit' accepted by Ehwald.

litus habet solidum, quod nec vestigia servet
nec remoretur iter nec opertum pendeat alga;
myrtea silva subest bicoloribus obsita bacis
et specus in medio, natura factus an arte,
ambiguum, magis arte tamen, quo saepe venire
frenato delphine sedens, Theti, nuda solebas.

On the Thessalian coast there curves a bay
With jutting arms; a haven, you would say,
Were but the water deeper; o'er the strand
Shallow it spreads; around, the solid sand
Records no footprint, checks no step, nor lies
With seaweed strewn. A myrtle-wood there is
With variegated berries hung, and close
A cave, by nature made or man—who knows?—
By man most like. Whereto, naked, astride
A harnessed dolphin, Thetis oft did ride.

One of the first landscapes we come upon in the poem is wilder
and still more romantic.[115] 'There is a glen in Thessaly shut in all
round by forest-clad steeps. Through it the river Peneus flows
with foaming waters from its source beneath Mount Pindus; its
heavy falls concentrate a mist that drives fine vapours up to scatter
spray on the tree-tops, and deafens the surroundings, near and far,
with its thunder.' Grimal may be equally right in suggesting that
Ovid had in mind the great gorge and falls of the Anio at Tivoli
and in detecting, here and elsewhere, the influence of landscape
painting.* For two centuries at least Romans had been familiar
with 'picturesque' landscapes in the Hellenistic manner painted
on the walls of rooms. From about 40 B.C. dates the romantic
series illustrating the *Odyssey* now in the Vatican, with its arched
or overhanging rocks.† Ovid's contemporary Vitruvius gives
instances of what such landscapes might represent, as painted in

---

* See pp. 104 n., 172.

† From a house on the Esquiline; illustrated, e.g. in K. Woermann, *Die antiken
Odysseelandschaften* (1875); B. Nogara, *Antichi Affreschi del Vaticano* (1907);
Rizzo, *op. cit.* tavv. clviii–clxiii.

colonnades—harbours, capes, shores, rivers, springs, straits, temples, groves, mountains, flocks, shepherds—adding that there are sometimes large pictures portraying the gods, or scenes from mythology unfolded in order (*fabularum dispositas explicationes*), likewise the Tale of Troy, or the Wanderings of Ulysses.*

Grimal draws attention to a passage in the *Metamorphoses*[116] which, he rightly claims, might be taken for a description of some landscape-painting at Pompeii:

'I had driven my weary herd down to the bay when the sun was high in the middle of his course. Some of the cattle had lain down on the yellow sand and were gazing out on the broad expanse of sea; some were slowly ambling up and down, while others were swimming out and standing with their heads reared above the surface. A temple stood by the sea, not resplendent with marble and gold, but made of heavy timbers and overshadowed by an ancient grove.'

Grimal also shows that Ovid freely varied traditional features, whether provided by literature or visual art.[117] We may fairly conclude that he was influenced by both of these, but that his own experience gave life to his pictures of traditional or conventional scenes.

Among the descriptive passages in the *Metamorphoses* are several that portray the surroundings of a personified abstraction in an allegorical way. We are shown Envy in her hideous abode, Famine in the waste land of Scythia, the House of Rumour and the Cave of Sleep.[118] These elaborate conceptions, none of them new, are forerunners of the medieval and renaissance allegories. The Cave of Sleep is perhaps the most worth quoting, and as it is the ancestor of one of the most famous passages in the *Faerie Queene*,[119] an attempt to translate it into Spenserian stanzas may at least bring out the affinity:

> Est prope Cimmerios longo spelunca recessu,
> mons cavus, ignavi domus et penetralia Somni,

---

* VII, 5, 2. For the development of landscape painting under Augustus see Schefold, *op. cit.* pp. 73–81.

quo numquam radiis oriens mediusve cadensve
Phoebus adire potest: nebulae caligine mixtae
exhalantur humo dubiaeque crepuscula lucis.
non vigil ales ibi cristati cantibus oris
evocat Auroram, nec voce silentia rumpunt
sollicitive canes canibusve sagacior anser;
non fera, non pecudes, non moti flamine rami
humanaeve sonum reddunt convicia linguae.

muta Quies habitat; saxo tamen exit ab imo
rivus aquae Lethes, per quem cum murmure labens
invitat somnos crepitantibus unda lapillis.
ante fores antri fecunda papavera florent
innumeraeque herbae, quarum de lacte soporem
Nox legit et spargit per opacas umida terras;
ianua, ne* verso stridores cardine reddat,
nulla domo tota, custos in limine nullus;
et medio torus est ebeno sublimis in antro,
plumeus, atricolor, pullo velamine tectus,
quo cubat ipse deus membris languore solutis.

> *Near the Cimmerians, in a mountain deep*
> *Hollowed, where morn nor noon nor evening pries,*
> *There lurks a cave, the abode of drowsy Sleep;*
> *Dark vapours from the ground and shadows rise*
> *Murky; nor there the wakeful cock with cries*
> *Summons the dawn, nor noisy vigil keep*
> *Watchdogs aroused, nor geese than dogs more wise;*
> *No rustling trees are heard, nor bleating sheep,*
> *Nor howling beasts, nor men that one another clepe.*

> *There Silence reigns, save that from nether floor*
> *Of rock up wells the river Lethe's spring,*
> *Whose whisper lulls to rest; and all before*
> *Poppies abound and herbs past numbering,*
> *Whose juices Night distils, and scattering*

---

* I prefer this reading to Ehwald's 'nec...reddit;...tota est'.

Puts the dark world to sleep. There is no door
  In all that house on creaking hinge to swing,
  No janitor; and in the midst doth soar
An ebon couch of down with dusky pall spread o'er.

Here lies the God himself, with limbs asprawl
  In slumber....

When Euripides brought the hero Telephus on to the stage disguised in rags and introduced 'familiar things such as we use and live among', he created a scandal in fifth-century Athens, but he also began a movement which had a profound influence on Hellenistic taste. Gods and mythological personages alike were brought down to human level and into the light of the present day; and further, both in the visual arts and in poetry there developed a love of depicting ordinary people realistically, not without affectionate sympathy, and also detailed scenes from everyday life.* In poetry we meet it, for instance, in the pseudo-Theocritean *Fisherman* (Idyll XXI).

Ovid shared this taste for 'genre' to some extent; at any rate, it could be one contributor to the variety of his patchwork. There is a trace of it in his description of Arachne, who, 'whether she was winding rough yarn into fresh balls, or fingering the stuff and reaching back for more wool, fleecy as a cloud, to draw out into long, soft strands, or plying the smooth spindle with deft thumb, or embroidering with her needle', brought such grace to her art that you could see she had been taught by Pallas.† But it comes in most appropriately in the story of Philemon and Baucis.

This tale of how an old peasant couple 'entertained angels unawares' is located in Phrygia, and was probably popular in Asia Minor, for, as Ehwald rightly notes, it may well have been a local tradition of this visit of Jupiter and Mercury to mortals which suggested to the people of Lystra that Barnabas and Paul were those

---

* For a study of this feature in epic poetry see G. Huber, *Lebensschilderung und Kleinmalerei im Hellenistischen Epos* (1926).

† VI, 18–23. He is probably thinking of a similar description in Catullus' epyllion, LXIV, 311 ff. See Ehwald's note.

gods come down in the likeness of men.[120] Wherever Ovid may have found it, he perceived that it had affinities with Callimachus' *Hecale*, the story of an old woman who entertained Theseus, and from that famous poem he borrowed both the idyllic colouring and the idea of painting a genre picture of peasant life, as well as several direct hints. The result is one of his happiest creations, and the description of the meal deserves quotation at some length:[121]

> Ergo ubi caelicolae parvos tetigere penates
> summissoque humiles intrarunt vertice postes,
> membra senex posito iussit relevare sedili;
> quo superiniecit textum rude sedula Baucis,
> inque foco tepidum cinerem dimovit, et ignes
> suscitat hesternos, foliisque et cortice sicco
> nutrit, et ad flammas anima producit anili,
> multifidasque faces ramaliaque arida tecto
> detulit et minuit parvoque admovit aëno,
> quodque suus coniunx riguo collegerat horto
> truncat holus foliis; furca levat ille bicorni
> sordida terga suis nigro pendentia tigno,
> servatoque diu resecat de tergore partem
> exiguam sectamque domat ferventibus undis.
> interea medias fallunt sermonibus horas. . . . *
>
> . . .torus de molli fluminis ulva
> impositus lecto sponda pedibusque salignis.
> vestibus hunc velant, quas non nisi tempore festo
> sternere consuerant, sed et haec vilisque vetusque
> vestis erat, lecto non indignanda saligno.
> adcubuere dei. mensam succincta tremensque
> ponit anus; mensae sed erat pes tertius impar:
> testa parem fecit, quae postquam subdita clivum
> sustulit, aequatam mentae tersere virentes.

---

* The manuscripts mostly have five verses here which are lacking however in the best and are for various reasons unsatisfactory; it seems best to presume a lacuna of some length.

ponitur hic bicolor sincerae baca Minervae
conditaque in liquida corna autumnalia faece
intibaque et radix et lactis massa coacti
ovaque non acri leviter versata favilla,
omnia fictilibus. post haec caelatus eodem
sistitur argento crater fabricataque fago
pocula, qua cava sunt, flaventibus illita ceris.
parva mora est, epulasque foci misere calentes,
nec longae rursus referuntur vina senectae
dantque locum mensis paulum seducta secundis:
hic nux, hic mixta est rugosis carica palmis,
prunaque et in patulis redolentia mora canistris
et de purpureis conlectae vitibus uvae;
candidus in medio favus est; super omnia vultus
accessere boni nec iners pauperque voluntas.

So when the gods came to this dwelling poor
And stooping entered through the lowly door,
Philemon brought a bench for them to sit,
And bustling Baucis spread a rug on it,
Stirred on the hearth the ashes scarce alive,
Yesterday's fire with bellows to revive,
Fed it with bark and puffed it into flame;
Chopped sticks, dry branches, from the roof the dame
Brought down, and broke, and placed beneath the pot,
And next the cabbage, from the garden-plot
Picked by her husband, stripped. He with a fork
Reached and unhooked a smoky side of pork
From a blackened beam, and from this treasured spoil
Cut a small piece and put it on to boil.
Meanwhile they both beguiled the time with talk...

...a mattress soft of river-sedge
Laid on a bed with willow legs and edge;
O'er this a quilt reserved for festal days
They drew, but cheap and old in truth it was
And no ill match for that old willow bed.

The gods lay down. Baucis the table laid,
Girt up and trembling. One leg of the three
Was short: a tile restored stability.
The top thus levelled she with mint did wipe,
Then set Minerva's olives clean and ripe,
Cherries of autumn-tide preserved in lees,
Endives and radishes and thick cream cheese,
And eggs cooked lightly on the gentle fire,
All served on earthenware. No metal higher
Than this the encrusted wine-bowl dignified
And beechwood beakers lined with wax inside.
Nor was it long before the hearth sent up
Its steaming dishes. Then they filled the cup
With wine of no great age. A little space
Was cleared, and these to nuts and plums gave place,
And wrinkled dates, and open baskets decked
With fragrant apples, purple grapes fresh-picked,
And last a honey-comb; but better still
Their kindly looks and bountiful goodwill.

Space forbids quotation of the rest of this charming story—how the gods performed with the wine-bowl the miracle of the widow's cruse; how the old couple were so impressed that they prepared to kill their only goose, but proved unable to catch it;* how the gods then sent them up a hill, so that they escaped from a flood which drowned their less hospitable neighbours; how their house was turned into a marble temple, and their prayer was granted that they should be priests in it for their lives and in death be not divided. In the end they were turned into trees on which the pious put wreaths, including Lelex, the narrator, who concludes,

cura deum di sunt, et qui coluere, colantur.

---

* This idea may have come from the similar story of the humble Molorchus who, entertaining Heracles before he slew the Nemean lion, was about to kill his only ram when the hero restrained him. It was told by Callimachus in the *Aetia* (see de Cola, *op. cit.* p. 66).

Whom the gods love are gods, and worshippers should have worship.

'I see Baucis and Philemon as perfectly before me', said Dryden, 'as if some ancient painter had drawn them.'[122]

(4) THE GODS

There is a story, apocryphal no doubt, of a certain lecturer on the *Metamorphoses* who exlaimed, 'What an extraordinary thing that such a sceptical man should have believed all this!' At least he was raising a question of fundamental importance for our understanding of the poem, but he could have found the answer in Ovid himself. In the *Tristia* he describes the transformations as 'not to be believed', and mentions Medusa, Scylla and the Chimaera as examples of patent impossibility.[123] In the *Amores* he speaks of the flights of Perseus and Triptolemus as fantasies:

Prodigiosa loquor veterum mendacia vatum:
    nec tulit haec unquam nec feret ulla dies;

these are the lying marvels of ancient bards I tell: no day ever did or shall produce such things;

and he attributes a number of the legends expressly to the invention of poets.[124]

But, it will be asked, may he not have had, towards the gods at least, a Virgilian attitude? Few educated Romans believed in the actual existence of the Olympian gods, but for some they were at least symbols or representatives of a divine power in which they believed, although for others they were simply traditional machinery without which epic poetry at least was unthinkable.* Here again Ovid has provided a clue. In a famous passage of the *Ars Amatoria* he gives a wholly irreverent defence of perjury in love:

Per Styga Junoni falsum iurare solebat
    Juppiter; exemplo nunc favet ille suo.

---

* Lucan did dispense with the divine machinery of Olympus, but it made an incongruous reappearance in the *Lusiad* of Camoëns.

Jove swore to Juno falsely by the Styx:
*Now he aids those who imitate his tricks.**

After which he proceeds to announce his *Credo*. This has been so often quoted in the first line only, and even misconceived by some who have quoted the rest, that we should make sure what he means:

Expedit esse deos et, ut expedit, esse putemus:
    dentur in antiquos tura merumque focos;
nec secura quies illos similisque sopori
    detinet; innocue vivite: numen adest.
reddite depositum; pietas sua foedera servet;
    fraus absit; vacuas caedis habete manus.

This may be paraphrased as follows:

It is expedient there should be gods, and this being so, let us suppose they exist. For the good of society we should keep up the traditional religious ceremonies, and use the gods to enforce the commandments: 'Thou shalt live innocently, for the gods are not remote or indifferent' (What use would the aloof Epicurean gods be as safeguards for society?); 'Thou shalt pay back what is entrusted to thee'; 'Honour thy father and thy mother'; 'Thou shalt not defraud'; 'Thou shalt do no murder'.

In other words, religion is a useful sanction for social morality. To take 'numen adest' as a statement of the poet's own view would be absurd: it is meant to be in inverted commas;† this is what we have got to tell people, he is saying. Fränkel reads too much sympathy with religion into Ovid's words when he paraphrases, 'let us rather continue to worship them with modest piety, in the

---

* I, 637–42. Nothing could be more irreverent than the passage in *Am.* II, I (17–20), where the poet tells Jupiter that his mistress' closing the door on him was a thunderbolt more to be feared than his.

† Ovid employs a similar technique at *F.* II, 35–46, giving instances of people who were purified (i.e. reputed to be) and then exclaiming on the folly of belief in purification.

    Amphiareïades Naupactoö Acheloö
    'solve nefas' dixit, *solvit et ille nefas.*
    a! nimium faciles, qui talia crimina caedis
        fluminea tolli posse putatis aqua!

fond, if forlorn, hope that they reward those who wrong no one';[125] he was not even 'faintly trusting the larger hope' at all. Lafaye goes so far as to say that he 'croit à l'existence des dieux et à la necessité du culte'.[126] But Ovid does not say that he really believes in their existence. However, his real convictions are not in any case involved here, for all are agreed that in most of the *Metamorphoses* he is dealing with the gods of mythology, which have very little to do with the religion of the Roman state. Heinze says rightly, 'The question how this mythical world of the gods should be represented by him in his poem was not one of belief, but of style, and he answered it differently for the *Metamorphoses* and for the *Fasti*'.[127] It would have put everything out of gear if he had not accepted the mythological gods along with the legends. He treats them very much in the manner of the epic tradition he was following, disregarding the higher criticism that began in the time of Xenophanes. He hardly ever suggests even surprise in this poem, as he does in the *Fasti*,*[128] and while he is not averse from retailing stories in which deities are worsted, he preserves his adopted attitude of orthodoxy by putting these into the mouth of their enemies.†

Nor are the gods of the *Metamorphoses* the factitious guardians of morality whose usefulness he proclaimed in the *Ars Amatoria*. Far from it. If they cannot frustrate Destiny, any more than Homer's gods can,[129] they are otherwise free to gratify their whims, which they do without scruple. Their chief motives are lust (especially in the males) and revenge for slights (especially in the females). Only on the rarest occasions is one divinity thwarted by another;‡ for the rest, their control is as complete as that of

---

* An exception is *M.* III, 311 (*si credere dignum est*) of Bacchus sewn in Jupiter's thigh.

† Thus the Pierid tells how the Olympians fled from the Giants to Egypt and concealed themselves by various metamorphoses, v, 318–31; Arachne weaves 'caelestia crimina' in her web, VI, 103–26; 131. On the other hand Ovid does not hesitate in the *Fasti* (II, 459) to tell *propria persona* a story about Venus in terror.

‡ Cupid thwarted Apollo by shooting Daphne with a blunt arrow bringing indifference, and the river-god Peneüs thwarted him by turning his daughter into a laurel.[130]

Dionysus in Euripides' *Bacchae*. Their only sign of compunction is in the grief they display for the loss of those they have loved. It would have been out of keeping if Ovid had raised the question which Virgil himself raised only to drop—*tantaene animis caelestibus irae?* 'Can there be such anger in celestial hearts?'

The Creator with whom the poem opens belongs to a different category. He is the Zeus of the philosophers, and has nothing to do with the mythological line which culminated in Jupiter. We will deal with him in a different context. Jupiter himself, however, is sometimes impressive, as Zeus often is in Homer. There is a scene of Wagnerian magnificence in heaven when his son Hercules, in the throes of death, builds himself a huge pyre on Mount Octa, spreads on it his Nemean lion's skin, and putting his club for pillow, lies down on it with the demeanour of one reclining on a banquet-couch, bidding Philoctetes kindle the fire beneath:[131]

> Iamque valens et in omne latus diffusa sonabat
> securosque artus contemptoremque petebat
> flamma suum. timuere dei pro vindice terrae.
> quos ita, sensit enim, laeto Saturnius ore
> Iuppiter adloquitur: 'nostra est timor iste voluptas,
> o superi, totoque libens mihi pectore grator,
> quod memoris populi dicor rectorque paterque
> et mea progenies vestro quoque tuta favore est.
> nam quamquam ipsius datis hoc immanibus actis,
> obligor ipse tamen. sed enim nec pectora vano
> fida metu paveant, istas nec spernite flammas.
> omnia qui vicit, vincet, quos cernitis, ignes;
> nec nisi materna Vulcanum parte potentem
> sentiet. aeternum est, a me quod traxit, et expers
> atque immune necis, nullaque domabile flamma.
> idque ego defunctum terra caelestibus oris
> accipiam, cunctisque meum laetabile factum
> dis fore confido. siquis tamen Hercule, siquis

forte, deo doliturus erit, data praemia nolet,
sed meruisse dari sciet invitusque probabit.'

Now roared the flames and spread to every side,
And sought the limbs of that unterrified
Defiant hero. E'en the gods above
Feared for earth's champion. This perceiving, Jove
Gladly addressed them: 'Heavenly ones, to me
Your fear is joy, for proud am I to be
Called Lord and Father of a grateful race;
My son is shielded also by your grace.
This tribute as to his own prowess due
You pay, yet I beholden am to you.
But fear not, friends, nor take these flames amiss,
For he who vanquished all shall vanquish this;
His mother's part alone shall feel the power
Of Vulcan, for eternal was the dower
I gave him, deathless, spurning fire's assault;
Which after earthly life I will exalt
To heavenly habitations, and it is
My faith that all the gods will welcome this.
Or if some one of you should take it ill,
This prize of godhead, he must grudge it still,
But knowing it deserved consent against his will.'

Homer sometimes treated the gods with irreverent humour,
but never to the extent of precluding them from being impressive
when he wanted them to be. Ovid consciously follows the epic
tradition, but he goes further in the direction of irreverence,
influenced no doubt by Alexandria, and by Callimachus in
particular. The Alexandrians, as we saw in the case of the *Hymn to
Artemis*, took particular pleasure in making gods and heroes
behave just like ordinary people of the day.* The sophisticated no
longer believed in their literal existence, and we cannot doubt
that they were amused at the aroma of burlesque which anthropo-

* Cf. Amphitryon and Alcmena in Theocritus' *Heracliscus* (XXIV, 34–63).

morphism produced when pushed to extremes. And sometimes they went further. Pindar, in the age of faith, had stood aloof when faced with the story that the gods had carved up the limbs of Pelops, because his piety would not allow him to say any such thing of them:[132] Callimachus, in the age of sophistication, checks himself apparently out of sheer mischief, to allow the reader to imagine the worst:[133]

'And already the maid had been bedded with the boy, even as ritual ordained that the bride should sleep the night before her wedding with a male child that had both parents living. For Hera once, they say—down, you dog, down, my shameless soul! You are going to sing what it is impious to reveal! It is a good thing you have not witnessed the rites of the Dread Goddess, else you would be blurting them out also.'

Ovid's Jupiter, even in the Hercules scene, lacks something of the remoteness that makes the Homeric gods impressive for all their escapades. He behaves rather like the Emperor seeking Senatorial approval for something he intends to do in any case, as the conferring of some signal honour on a member of his own family, relieved to find that there is general support, and confident that Pollio and the die-hards will swallow it with as good a grace as possible.* Indeed, the very first appearance of the Olympians in the *Metamorphoses* is at a council summoned to what the poet ventures to call *magni Palatia caeli*. This is approached by the Milky Way, a *clivus Palatinus* off which open the mansions of the *dei nobiles*, their doors wide open and their halls thronged. The plebeian gods live elsewhere; in this quarter the right honourable (*clari*) and influential deities have set up their *Penates* (aristocratic gods revering household gods of their own!).† This passage in

---

* There was almost a riot when Hebe was allowed to restore Iolaüs to youth: each deity clamoured for her favourite to be rejuvenated, Aurora for Tithonus, Ceres for Iasion, Vulcan for Erichthonius, and Venus (with an eye to her *future* amour) for Anchises.[134]

† I, 168–76. In IV, 444 the dead have their Forum.

itself is sufficient intimation that we need not hesitate to accept as burlesque any future treatment of the gods that appears to be such.

The myths being what they were, the gods had frequently to be represented as loving nymphs or mortals, nor would this be uncongenial to the poet of the *Amores*. The aristocrats among them were generally irresistible. What chance had Proserpine?

> paene simul visa est dilectaque raptaque Diti.*
>
> *within a trice seen, loved, and raped by Dis.*

But the circumstances were seldom dignified; for

> non bene conveniunt nec in una sede morantur
> maiestas et amor.[135]
>
> *There's no concordance or companionship*
> *Twixt majesty and love.*

At the outset we have Apollo, hybristic in his triumph over the Python, jealously reproving Cupid for usurping his weapon, the bow; whereupon Cupid asserts his supremacy by wounding him with a shaft of love for Daphne.[136] Thereafter we are shown the gods, one after another, in amorous situations which can only be called comic. Heinze, in his desire to emphasize the higher tone of the *Metamorphoses* compared with the *Fasti*, belittles this element. He represents it as an awkward thing for Ovid to have to deal with these love affairs which can only seem undignified when pursued in detail, and maintains that 'Ovid is clearly striving to sacrifice as little as possible of the divine sublimity'.[137] In view of the gusto with which he describes these scenes it is hard to accept such a conclusion. The domestic life of Jupiter and Juno was food for amusement already in Homer. Ovid loses no time in introducing it. In the first book we find Jupiter enticing Io into the woods with disingenuous offers of protection from wild beasts,

* v, 395. Cf. *F.* III, 21 of Rhea Silvia:
  Mars videt hanc visamque cupit potiturque cupita.

and then, when she tries to flee, impeding her with a thick mist and so ravishing her. Juno, perceiving this preternatural darkness, instinctively looks round to see where her husband has got to, suspicious from bitter experience. Not finding him, with a hasty 'aut ego fallor aut ego laedor', she glides down to earth and dissipates the fog. But already Jupiter has foreseen this and changed Io into a cow. Even in this form she is still beautiful, and Juno, regarding her with grudging admiration, inquires with feigned innocence who is her owner and what her herd. Jupiter, to stop her awkward questions about ownership, answers that she is sprung from the earth itself, whereupon Juno promptly asks for her as a gift. Caught in a cleft stick, Jupiter can only comply. But Juno, still suspicious, sets the hundred-eyed Argus to watch her, and when Mercury kills him at Jupiter's instigation, sends a Fury to drive her across the world, till she prays to Jupiter for release, whereupon he throws his arms round Juno's neck and begs her—successfully—to relent.[138]

The episode of Phaëthon follows, but no sooner is that over than Jupiter, touring Arcadia to inspect the damage, spies the nymph Callisto, lying weary and all unguarded in the depths of a forest. 'Surely here is an intrigue my wife will never find out', he says; 'or if she does—this, oh this, is well worth any railing ! (sunt, o, sunt iurgia tanti!).' Straightway he puts on the guise of Callisto's mistress Diana, rouses her, and not put off by her response, 'Hail, deity, greater in my judgment than Jupiter, as I would say to his face', ravishes her and so betrays himself. Full of shame, she rejoins the train of Diana (after making sure the goddess is not Jupiter in disguise again). The other nymphs (sophisticated after much experience of Satyrs) perceive by a thousand signs that something has happened, but the virgin goddess remains innocently unaware until on one occasion, now nine months gone with child, the blushing victim is constrained by her companions to join them in a bathe.[139]

Surely all this is sheer comedy, in the spirit of the Amores: lascivus quidem in herois quoque Ovidius, as Quintilian said.[140]

Before the book is out Jupiter has gone off after Europa, changing himself into a bull of immaculate beauty, whose points are described in detail. When the princess holds out flowers to him he takes the opportunity to kiss her hands—*vix iam, vix cetera differt*—and leaps sportively about in the grass; and so little by little entices her to the famous sea voyage.[141]

Things reach such a pitch that poor Juno falters pathetically in the proud threat she has always made when angry:

> Si sum regina Iovisque
> et soror et coniunx—certe soror,[142]

> *if I am queen to Jupiter, and both his sister and wife—sister at least for sure.*

When she was succeeding by 'sympathetic' magic in preventing Alcmena from bearing her son to Jupiter, the lie of a servant-girl trapped her into breaking the spell.[143] Her bitterness was tersely colloquial when she heard about Semele: *concipit: id deerat!* 'and to crown it all, she's with child!'[144] It was the last straw when she found that, just as she was about to catch her husband with nymphs on the mountain-sides, Echo had been in the habit of detaining her in idle conversation till they got away.[145]

Yet there were moments of conjugal truce. On one such occasion Jupiter, mellowed with nectar, put cares aside and bandied good-humoured badinage with her, saying: 'I maintain that you females get more pleasure than we males do.' Juno denied this, and the only way of reaching a conclusion was to summon Tiresias, who had been both in his day: *Venus huic erat utraque nota.* Needless to say, Tiresias supported Jupiter, and Juno (how feminine!), taking too seriously a matter of no consequence, blinded him for life, a penalty which Jupiter could only mitigate by giving him the gift of prophecy.*[146]

How could anyone assert that Ovid sacrifices as little as possible of divine sublimity? Much of this by-play is not necessitated by

---

* T. S. Eliot quotes this passage in his notes to *The Waste Land*.

the stories at all. Nor is it only Jupiter and Juno who are affected: most of the major deities contribute to the comedy. We have already encountered the virgin unawareness of Diana. Her brother Apollo, victim of Cupid's nemesis, is ludicrous enough as he pants out a long speech while vainly pursuing Daphne. He is terrified that she will hurt herself, and offers to run more slowly if she will too !* That failing, he launches into fifteen lines of self-recommendation, qualified by regrets that his arrow is not after all the most potent and his art of healing cannot cure love.[147] Mercury, desiring to seduce Herse, does not seek to disguise himself; such is his confidence in his looks. Nevertheless, he thinks it prudent to smooth his hair, arrange his cloak to hang neatly, with all the border and gold embroidery showing, hold his wand gracefully and see that his feet are clean and his winged sandals polished—for all the world like a Greek dandy.[148] Just as Jupiter examines Arcadia for damage after the Phaëthontic conflagration, so Dis tours Sicily to inspect the foundations after an eruption of Typhoeus, the giant pinned underneath it. Venus sees her chance, and exhorts Cupid to take this opportunity of asserting supremacy over the underworld, for her prestige in heaven is waning since Pallas and Diana decided for virginity, and Proserpine looks like following them.[149] Venus herself is not spared, and the divine comedy sung by Demodocus in the *Odyssey* is retold in brief, how Vulcan was informed of his wife's adultery with Mars, trapped them in the act with invisible nets and ropes, and invited all the gods to come and see the spectacle.[150] In the contest of weaving between Arachne and Pallas we expect the goddess to win; but in the event neither she nor Envy can find any fault in Arachne's work, and out of sheer pique and jealousy she tears the web and beats her rival over the head with her shuttle till she takes refuge in hanging herself. Only then does the goddess relent, so far as to let her hang on alive in the form of a spider.[151]

* I, 510–1; like the Cambridge Proctor's 'bulldog' who protested, 'If you don't run faster, sir, I shall have to catch you.'

Sometimes the anthropomorphism produces charming effects, as when Pallas calls on the Muses on Helicon in order to inspect the miraculous new spring of Hippocrene.[152] She admires their home and says they must be happy in their surroundings and their pursuits. In reply one of them, after modestly remarking that the goddess would be a welcome member of their band if her valour had not marked her out for more important work, agrees that they should be happy, if only they could feel secure; but lately, for instance, being caught in a storm while on their way to Parnassus, they had been invited to shelter in his house by the usurping king Pyreneus, only to find when the rain stopped that he would not let them go, so that they had had to put on their wings and fly for it. Further, they had been challenged to song by the Pierides, and had felt bound to accept. The nymphs were appointed judges, took the oath by their own streams, and seated themselves on benches of living rock; whereupon instead of drawing lots for first innings, the eldest Pierid rudely began. After summarizing her offensive song the Muse begins to recount their own reply, then politely breaks off—'But perhaps you are in a hurry and have no time to hear what we sang?' 'Not at all', replies Pallas, sitting down in the shade; 'Please tell me in order everything you sang.' The modesty of the Muses is as delightful as the graciousness of the *grande dame*.

What the Muses' representative, Calliope, had sung was a Hymn to Ceres on the lines of a Homeric Hymn, telling the story of the goddess' search for Proserpine, with the story of Arethusa interwoven.[153] This extends to 320 lines, and has considerable beauty besides being more serious than the tales of the gods' amours. (The same applies to the invocation of the Theban women to Bacchus, which follows the regular form of the cletic hymn.[154])

Some of the stories have more in common with folklore than with the Olympian mythology.[155] To this category belongs the story of Midas, with the delightful incident of his slave who, in his capacity of barber, could not help knowing the secret of those ass's ears concealed beneath the royal turban. Bursting to tell it but fearing the consequences, he dug a hole, muttered the story into it, and filled it in. But whispering reeds sprang up there, which in due course betrayed the secret when rustled by the breeze.[156] In the story of Phaëthon the Sun, though called Phoebus, is the all-seeing god of folklore, having his palace not at Delos or Delphi but in the mystic realms beyond the Ethiopians.[157]

As for the lesser divinities, rivers, mountains, nymphs and so forth, they are generally innocent and attractive. Ovid plays characteristically with their ambiguous form—natural object and personification at the same time. Tmolus, where Pan was singing to the nymphs and daring to challenge Apollo, is presented as a mountain towering and steep, looking far out to sea, with one slope running down to Sardis and the other to Hypaepae. A few lines later he has been chosen to judge the contest: 'The aged judge took his seat on his own mountain-top and shook his ears free of trees.'[158] Again, Acheloüs invites Theseus to stay at his house for a while, as his waters are in spate and impassable, and entertains him with reminiscences: how when the nymphs were sacrificing once they forgot to invite him; he swelled with rage (*intumui*)— and in what followed there is no doubt that he was the river itself, not merely its hospitable personification who is telling the tale.[159] In his spirited account of his struggle with Hercules he is in human form again, though his green cloak suggests his other nature, and he has the horns with which rivers were popularly credited.[160]

The nymph Cyane originally lived in the pool in Sicily to which she gave her name. Rising from this she protested to Dis as he passed against the rape of Proserpine. He thereupon smote her pool with his sceptre and opened a path to Hades. In grief at this she melted into her own pool; hence she had no voice to tell Ceres, when she came, where Proserpine had gone, but she could give a clue by showing on her surface the girdle the latter had dropped.[161] It all depends on what the poet finds effective for the moment; for a few lines later Arethusa, though she is a spring, has green locks which she brushes back from her brow, and her waters keep silence while she speaks.[162] What she tells Ceres,

indeed, must rank among Ovid's most beautiful imaginings,
culminating in two unforgettable lines:[163]

> O toto quaesitae virginis orbe
> et frugum genetrix, immensos siste labores,
> neve tibi fidae violenta irascere terrae!
> terra nihil meruit patuitque invita rapinae.
> nec sum pro patria supplex: huc hospita veni.
> Pisa mihi patria est et ab Elide ducimus ortus,
> Sicaniam peregrina colo, sed gratior omni
> haec mihi terra solo est: hos nunc Arethusa penates,
> hanc habeo sedem. quam tu, mitissima, serva!
> mota loco cur sim tantique per aequoris undas
> advehar Ortygiam, veniet narratibus hora
> tempestiva meis, cum tu curaque levata
> et vultus melioris eris. mihi pervia tellus
> praebet iter, subterque imas ablata cavernas
> hic caput attollo desuetaque sidera cerno.
> ergo dum Stygio sub terris gurgite labor,
> visa tua est oculis illic Proserpina nostris:
> illa quidem tristis neque adhuc interrita visu,
> sed regina tamen, sed opaci maxima mundi,
> sed tamen inferni pollens matrona tyranni.

> *O thou distraught*
> *Mother of fruits and of that maiden sought*
> *The wide world over, rest, nor angry be*
> *With faithful, innocent earth. Unwillingly*
> *She opened for that rape. 'Tis not my land*
> *I plead for, brought from Elis to this strand,*
> *From Pisan home; yet Sicily I love,*
> *Though foreign-born, all other lands above;*
> *Here have I, Arethusa, made my home.*
> *Spare it, most merciful. Why I did come*
> *Displaced beyond such wide expanse of sea*
> *To Ortygia, that will I presently*
> *Tell thee in timely hour of better cheer.*

Earth gave me way through cavernous depths, till here
Emerging I beheld the stars again.
On Hades' Stygian flood as I was then
Passing, these eyes your Proserpine espied,
Still sad indeed nor yet unterrified;
Aye, but a queen, supreme in that dark land,
Dowered with the might of Pluto's royal hand.

(5) MORTALS

The world of the *Metamorphoses* has something of the quality of
A Midsummer Night's Dream. It conveys an impression of freedom
and clarity combined with a sense that we are temporarily detached
from the realms of ultimate seriousness, of normal logic and moral
values:

Al was this land fulfild of fayerye.

The distresses of the actors, more frequent than their joys, are
often made less real by the pervading atmosphere of miracle. They
are pathetic for the moment, but not tragic; and in any case we
witness them for too short a time for our sympathies to be more
than superficially engaged. Who weeps for the divine Calypso
deserted by Homer's Odysseus?

It is in keeping with the tradition from the Hesiodic *Eoeae*, but
also with what we know of Ovid's character, that interest is
concentrated on the women more than the men, as in the story of
Pyramus and Thisbe, one of the most delightful in the whole
work.[164] No one knows where Ovid found this romance. The
setting is in Babylon, and its ultimate origin may have been in
some ancestor of the *Arabian Nights*. The daughter of Minyas who
tells it to her companions over the wool hesitates between choosing
it and other tales of the East, that of Dercetis of Babylon, or of
her daughter Semiramis, or of a Naiad of the Indian Ocean,
doubtless from the same source.*[165] The story of the wall with

* The tale of Leucothoë (IV, 190–233) is apparently of Persian origin. It looks
as though Book IV is particularly oriental in origin. The tale of Myrrha also has

a crack through which they had perforce to make love, of their tryst at Ninus' tomb forestalled by a lioness, and of the tragic misunderstanding that brought both to suicide, is familiar from Shakespeare. Ovid is here at his best. In short, staccato sentences he tells the exciting story, with romantic touches to set the scene and frequent soliloquy to keep it alive. It is a purely human story: the aetiological motive, the changing of the mulberry into a blood-red fruit in memory of their death, is merely incidental. There are many vivid touches: the chink in the wall wide enough for them to converse, but not to join kisses; Thisbe stealing out *versato cardine*—terrified the hinge will creak; the lioness seen by her far off in the moonlight, as she waits under the mulberry tree by the tomb. But it is a pure romance of incident: the feelings of the lovers are as simple as they are strong, and they are taken for granted.

The companion piece of Cephalus and Procris[166] is equally good, but more complicated psychologically—a tragedy of jealousy and misunderstanding which leads to the death of Procris. Unlike Pyramus and Romeo, Cephalus did not himself commit suicide, and the story is made more poignant through being recounted by him. The experience of being ravished by Aurora against his will begot in him suspicions of the faithfulness of his newly married wife; he disguised himself and laid siege to her chastity, only to find misery when she began to yield, and to lose her when he revealed himself. He begged and won her back, there was a blissful period of married love, and then another tragedy of misunderstanding, all the more bitter because now it was Procris who lost faith.

The story of Ceÿx and Alcyone,[167] one of the best in the *Metamorphoses*, is moving in the same way as that of Cephalus

an oriental setting, Araby being the proverbial land of myrrh (x, 478; cf. 308–10; 315–17). See further P. Perdrizet, 'Légendes babyloniennes dans les Métamorphoses d'Ovide', *Rev. Hist. Relig.* cv (1932), pp. 192–228. He suggests (p. 227) that the Hellenistic writers of Seleucid Antioch may have been one medium through which these stories reached Ovid. For the Naiad see Arrian, *Ind.* xxxi, drawing on Alexander's admiral Nearchus.

and Procris or Protesilaüs and Laodamia, because it deals with deep conjugal affection, which Ovid does not hesitate to call *ignis*.[168] Here is a sequence of events only too real to us, the wife left at home while her husband goes overseas, the ship gradually passing out of sight, the counting of the nights, the preparations for his welcome home and prayers for his safety and fidelity; and then the vivid dream bringing conviction that he is dead, and the grim reality of finding his corpse washed up on the self-same beach on which he had said good-bye. The story is long enough for us to enter into Alcyone's feelings, though much of it—too much— is occupied with the brilliantly vivid picture of the rise and fury of the storm at sea.

Here again the miraculous element, the metamorphosis of the pair into halcyons, only intrudes incidentally, at the end. But there is also a peculiar, wistful pathos in some of the stories in which it plays an integral part; in Io, for instance (here the pathos is tinged with humour), starting in terror at the sound of her own lowing, or at the sight of her bovine face reflected in the familiar pool, and following her sisters and father in the hope of caresses; then later, when restored to human form again, afraid to speak lest she moo, and hesitatingly trying out words so long unused;[169] or in Callisto, changed to a bear, when she comes face to face with her hunter son Arcas, fixing on him eyes that seemed to recognize him, so that he shrank back full of uncanny fear and poised his spear when she tried to approach him.[170]

Ovid's interest in psychology comes out especially in the five soliloquies expressing a conflict in the soul of a woman about to commit a crime.* In the days when Socrates was teaching that virtue was a matter of knowledge Euripides had made his Phaedra say,

τὰ χρήστ᾽ ἐπιστάμεσθα καὶ γιγνώσκομεν
οὐκ ἐκπονοῦμεν δ᾽.[171]

---

* Medea betraying her father (VII, 11–71); Scylla betraying her father (VIII, 44–80); Byblis committing incest with her brother (IX, 487–516); Myrrha committing incest with her father (X, 320–55); Althaea murdering her son (VIII, 481–511). Heinze has a useful appendix on these monologues, *op. cit.* pp. 110–27.

These words Ovid Latinized and put into the mouth of the young Medea as

> Video meliora proboque,
> deteriora sequor;[172]

I see and approve the better course, yet choose the worse.

Indeed, the chief ancestor of his soliloquies of this kind is probably the famous speech in which Euripides' Medea deliberates whether to kill her children,[173] though in this particular case the Medea of Apollonius stands nearer. This barbaric woman, with her power of magic and her intolerable grievance, who twice had to make a terrible decision, obviously fascinated Ovid. Having envisaged her in the *Heroides* and in his lost tragedy, he devotes more than half of *Metamorphoses* VII to her. There is a piquant touch of irony when Jason begs her use her magic to transfer part of his life to his father Aeson: his filial devotion suddenly makes her ashamed of her own disloyalty to her father Aeëtes, which had nevertheless saved Jason's life:

> Mota est pietate rogantis,
> dissimilemque animum subiit Aeëta relictus.[174]

she was moved by the devotion of the pleader, and the thought of Aeëtes abandoned stole into her heart, how different from his!

Love is the chief theme of the *Metamorphoses*, and in most cases it is quite normal; but on occasion Ovid deals with a story of abnormality such as fascinated the Alexandrians and figures largely in the summaries of Parthenius and Antoninus. Here alone does he abandon his attitude of objectivity and adopt, or affect, a moral standpoint:

> Byblis in exemplo est ut ament concessa puellae.[175]

Byblis is a warning that girls should be lawful in their loves.

This much said, he tells with unmistakable gusto the story of the girl who loved her twin brother, Caunus. It gives him every opportunity for conceits and for psychological imagination. At first she fancied her kisses and embraces were only those of a sister; then she began to dress for him, and to envy more beautiful girls who came into their presence. Even so there seemed nothing physical yet in her desire, but she found herself preferring him to call her 'Byblis' rather than 'sister'. It was dreams that first revealed to her the physical nature of her passion. She began to hope that such dreams would come again, provided she could control herself when awake; after all, the pleasure was only imaginary, as well as being safe—and what pleasure it was!

So far this is excellent psychology; but now Ovid is overcome by the opportunity for conceits inherent in the situation. If only she were someone else, she regrets, and could marry Caunus, she would be a model daughter-in-law, as he would be son-in-law. They would have everything in common except grandfathers. She would prefer him to be better born than herself. 'Have dreams any weight? The gods forbid!—The gods! Have not they loved their sisters?' And so it goes on, while she wavers and finally decides to write him a letter. This is easier said than done, and there are a number of false starts before she is satisfied. The final draft is reminiscent of Phaedra's in the *Heroides*; after an apologetic start it comes out into the open: 'Let us leave it to old men to know the moral code and investigate what is right and wrong and observe the niceties of law;* reckless love befits our years; we are too young to know what is lawful, and believe everything is, and follow the example of the mighty gods.' (The rest can be quickly told. Caunus in horror flees from the country; Byblis follows him distracted and is finally turned into a fountain.)

Ovid keeps 'on the right side of the law', but one may doubt whether he is in fact much concerned about propriety, as can be seen from the jaunty tone of the warning he prefixes to the still more scandalous story of Myrrha, who loved her father:† 'This is a dreadful tale; keep far off now, daughters and fathers; or if

---

* Cf. p. 10, 'senes sic amant', in his own *Controversia*.
† x, 298–518; cf. his safeguarding disclaimers in the *Ars Amatoria*.

my songs charm you, do not believe this one; or if you must believe it, believe also in the punishment of the deed.' On the other hand, anyone familiar with Alexandrian literature must be struck by the infrequency and restraint with which Ovid deals with homosexual love. He mentions the tradition that such practices were introduced into Thrace by Orpheus, touches on Jupiter's rape of Ganymede, and tells at no great length of the passion of Apollo for Cyparissus, who became a cypress tree, and Hyacinthus, who became a flower.¹⁷⁶ But these last two episodes, involving as they do well-known instances of metamorphosis, are the only ones he chose out of a large number such as he could find in his probable source, the Ἔρωτες ἢ Καλοί of Phanocles, a whole volume of elegiac poems on the subject. In passing from Phaëthon to Cycnus in Book II he says they were linked by kinship and still more by like-mindedness (*mente*), avoiding reference to their love, which seems to have been known to Virgil.*¹⁷⁷ All this is consonant with Ovid's own disposition, as we have already noted in the case of the elegiac poems;† in view of Greco-Roman tradition and practice it suggests a positive attitude rather than mere indifference.

Two of the most haunting episodes of the whole poem deal with abnormal sexuality of a slightly different kind, those of Narcissus and Hermaphroditus.¹⁷⁸ As to the former, we have already glanced at his rejection of the pathetic Echo, the beauty of the pool in which he gazed, and the conceits for which his nature gave Ovid such good opportunities.‡ The story of the latter is said by its narrator to be unfamiliar; it is an *aetion* for the reputedly enervating quality of the spring of Salmacis in Caria. The son of Hermes and Aphrodite is a beautiful boy who roams the world for the sheer joy of seeing new country. Wandering from his birthplace on Mount Ida through Asia Minor he came upon one of those beautiful pools that Ovid loves to describe. 'The spring was clear right to the bottom. No marsh-reeds grew there nor

---

* The date of Phanocles is unknown but, probably third century B.C.
† See p. 25.   ‡ Pp. 165–8.

clogging sedge nor spiky rushes; the water was translucent; but the margins were fringed with fresh turf and evergreen grasses.' Here dwelt the naiad Salmacis, the only one who never followed the train of Diana the huntress. At most she bathed from time to time and did her hair in the mirror of her own pool before lying down in a shimmering dress on the grass, or picked flowers, as she was doing when she saw and fell in love with Hermaphroditus. Eager as she was to approach him, she collected herself first, tidied her clothes, composed her features, and 'deserved to seem beautiful'. Then she boldly accosted him with expressions of admiration and prayed to be his wife or paramour. The passage that follows is remarkable for its succession of vivid similes:[179]

> Naïs ab his tacuit. pueri rubor ora notavit,
> nescit enim, quid amor; sed et erubuisse decebat;
> hic color aprica pendentibus arbore pomis,
> aut ebori tincto est, aut sub candore rubenti,
> cum frustra resonant aera auxiliaria, lunae.
> poscenti nymphae sine fine sororia saltem
> oscula iamque manus ad eburnia colla ferenti
> 'desinis? aut fugio tecumque' ait 'ista relinquo!'
> Salmacis extimuit 'loca' que 'haec tibi libera trado,
> hospes', ait, simulatque gradu discedere verso.
> tum quoque respiciens fruticumque recondita silva
> delituit flexuque genu submisit; at ille,
> scilicet ut vacuis et inobservatus in herbis,
> huc it et hinc illuc et in adludentibus undis
> summa pedum taloque tenus vestigia tingit;
> nec mora, temperie blandarum captus aquarum
> mollia de tenero velamina corpore ponit.
> tum vero obstupuit* nudaeque cupidine formae
> Salmacis exarsit, flagrant quoque lumina nymphae,
> non aliter quam cum puro nitidissimus orbe
> opposita speculi referitur imagine Phoebus;
> vixque moram patitur, vix iam sua gaudia differt,

* Heinsius; MS 'placuit'.

iam cupit amplecti, iam se male continet amens.
ille cavis velox adplauso corpore palmis
desilit in latices alternaque bracchia ducens
in liquidis translucet aquis, ut eburnea siquis
signa tegat claro vel candida lilia vitro.
'vicimus et meus est!' exclamat Naïs, et omni
veste procul iacta mediis immittitur undis,
pugnantemque tenet, luctantiaque oscula carpit,
subiectatque manus, invitaque pectora tangit,
et nunc hac iuveni, nunc circumfunditur illac;
denique nitentem contra elabique volentem
implicat ut serpens, quam regia sustinet ales
sublimemque rapit: pendens caput illa pedesque
alligat et cauda spatiantes implicat alas;
utve solent hederae longos innexere truncos
utque sub aequoribus deprensum polypus hostem
continet ex omni dimissis parte flagellis.

She said no more. He blushed, too young to tell
What love is, and the blush became him well;
So apples redden in the sun, and so
Stained ivory, and neath her pallid glow
*The moon, when bronzes clash their aid in vain.**
As the nymph begged again and yet again
If but a sister's kiss, and sought to embrace
His ivory neck, 'Hold, or I leave this place—
And you!' he cried. Trembling Salmacis said,
'I leave the place to you, young sir', and made
As if to go, yet oft looked back, and mid
Some neighbouring bushes closely crouched and hid.
The boy, alone, unwatched, as he did deem,
Paced in the grass, and in the lapping stream
His toes at first and then his ankles dipped;
Lured by the water's coolness, swift he stripped
His delicate garments from his body's grace.

* The clashing of bronze was supposed by the superstitious to aid the moon in struggling against eclipse.

Then did Salmacis burn and in amaze
Long for his naked form, her eyes alight,
As when the sun's clear orb exceeding bright
Shines from a mirror with reflected ray;
Scarce can she wait and scarce her joys delay,
Mad with desire his dear embrace to essay.
He clapped his body with his hollow palms,
Swiftly dived in and with alternate arms
Swam: like an ivory through the water clear
Or lilies cased in glass he did appear.
'I have won and he is mine!' the Naiad cried,
Flung off her clothes and plunged into the tide,
Clasped as he struggled, as he fought caressed,
Slipped her hands under him to feel his breast,
This side and that the unwilling boy confined
And, as he strove to free himself, entwined;
Even as a snake, caught up into the air
By an eagle, writhes its tail and hanging there
Tangles the head, the feet, the flapping wings;
Or as the ivy to the tree-trunk clings,
Or octopus its prey beneath the tide
Grapples with tentacles on every side.

Hermaphroditus struggled, but Salmacis prayed that no day might ever separate them and her prayer was granted, for they became merged in one ambiguous body; whereupon he in turn prayed that whoever entered the pool as a man should emerge but half a man.

Somewhat similar is the story of Iphis,[180] whose father told his expecting wife he would put her child to death if it proved to be a girl. (It is startling to remember that this was quite common practice in the Greco-Roman world.)[181] Isis appeared to her in a dream and told her to preserve the child whatever its sex; so when it was born a girl she gave out that it was a boy, and called it by the equivocal name of Iphis. Trouble came when Iphis, now thirteen, was betrothed to Ianthe and fell in love with her; in a long soliloquy Iphis enlarges on her plight; till her mother takes her to Isis' temple to pray, whence she emerges as a boy, and duly marrying Ianthe, lives happily ever after.

Finally, there is the famous story of Pygmalion, who could only love the ivory statue of a woman which he had made.[182] It is tempting, especially to the Teutonic mentality, to intellectualize these myths; to see in Pygmalion, for instance, the eternal seeker after ideal perfection, dissatisfied with the world around him; but we must not force such interpretations on stories which, whatever their mythological origin, are surely told by Ovid for their own sake, and for the psychological paradoxes which intrigued him. He was certainly conscious of the protagonists as types of sexual abnormality, as he shows, for instance, by emphasizing the vanity of Salmacis, which would emerge as a trait of the fused Hermaphrodite; but they are only that, not symbols of something wider. Ovid's Narcissus may be the *Urnarzissist*, but he is not presented as a symbol of self-love in general. *

Had Ovid pity for these psychological misfits? He could in any case hardly express it directly, having adopted the role of detached spectator, though once he makes dramatic use of a familiar rhetorical figure of speech, when, as though unable to stand aloof any longer, he breaks in to warn Narcissus against his reflexion: *credule, quid frustra...?*

> Nil habet ista sui; tecum venitque manetque
> tecum discedet—si tu discedere possis.[183]
>
> *Naught in itself, with you it came, it stays:*
> *With you 'twill leave—can you but go your ways!*

This show of sympathy makes one wonder how Ovid felt towards the counterparts of these psychological misfits in the world around him. At least, as their soliloquies show, he was capable of imaginative understanding of how they would feel.

---

* It is here that Fränkel's interpretations seem most hazardous, interesting though they are. He himself says justly (*op. cit.* p. 83), 'The Ovid of the *Metamorphoses* is far from composing parables or preaching sermons; he merely tells fascinating stories, and yet, in so doing, he furnishes material for many a sermon.'

One word more. Ovid shows a sympathetic understanding of young people. It is no mere conceit when he makes Proserpine, in the moment of her abduction, distressed also for the loss of the flowers she has been gathering.[184] And when young Phaëthon, having boasted of being the son of Apollo, is told by his companion Epaphus that he should not believe all his mother tells him, his reaction is as charming as it is probable:

'He blushed, shame choking down his anger, and took Epaphus' words to his mother: "and what will hurt you more, mother, I who am always so quick-tempered and free of speech said nothing (*ille ego liber, ille ferox tacui*). I am ashamed that any one could have so insulted us and that I could not refute him. But if indeed I am sprung from heavenly parentage, give me some proof of my noble birth to assert my divinity."'[185]

(6) PHILOSOPHY

If it is a mistake to philosophize the legends of love and metamorphosis, what are we to make of the two openly speculative portions of the poem, the exordium recounting the Creation and the exposition of Pythagorean doctrine near the end?[186] It cannot be said that Ovid ever gives the impression of being a philosopher; indeed, he sometimes displays an indifference to truth which is characteristic of the average Roman. But it would obviously suit the artistic form of his poem if he could begin with an account of how the world began and rise at the end to a plane of thought which had something in it of the 'sublime'. He would choose the accounts which seemed to him most suitable and poetic. He had obviously studied at least the less technical parts of Lucretius,[187] and may have wished to emulate him here, while lacking his intellectual passion and integrity.

The precise pedigree of his eclectic cosmology cannot now be determined, but it smacks most of Posidonian Stoicism. His

hanc deus et melior litem natura diremit

this strife God and kindlier Nature dissolved

seems to identify God and Nature in Stoic fashion, while later he contents himself with a non-committal *quisquis fuit ille deorum*.[188] Lafaye is surely right in his comment, 'On dirait qu'Ovide est surtout jaloux de mettre tout le monde d'accord.'[189] Why quarrel about metaphysics? The Creator is assumed to be benevolent:

> ille opifex rerum, mundi melioris origo;
>
> *that demiurge, source of a better world;*

and his supreme work is man, made from divine seed to be lord of creation; or was it Prometheus who moulded man out of clay which still retained something of its heavenly origin? Ovid, like the Book of Genesis, presents us with alternative versions and leaves it at that. Prometheus moulded man in the image of the almighty gods and made him stand erect by contrast with the beasts:

> Os homini sublime dedit caelumque videre
> iussit et erectos ad sidera tollere vultus.
>
> *To man he gave to hold his forehead high,*
> *Bade him look up and view the starry sky.*

So Ovid expresses an old Socratic fancy already Latinized by Cicero.[190] It is his mastery of verse and language that gives value to this second-hand exordium, which all the time was leading him on, through the Fall of Man, to two great events which would give full scope to his powers of grandiose description, the Deluge and the Conflagration.

But he gives us even before the Deluge one foretaste of what was to come, a story of metamorphosis due to divine vengeance (Lycaon turned to a wolf); and before the Conflagration two stories of metamorphosis due to divine lust (Daphne and Io); and thereafter we are in the main stream of the poem. Not until the last book do we come into touch with philosophic speculation again. There, by what Ovid must have known to be a glaring anachronism, Numa is made, in accordance with tradition, to imbibe from Pythagoras at Croton his doctrines, which are expounded for the space of four hundred lines.

Was Ovid a neo-Pythagorean? Surely not. It is true that for two generations the sect had been in vogue at Rome, but it was characterized on one side by a mysticism, not untinged with quackery, alien to his rational temperament. It is easy to see why he should choose nevertheless to expound it here: its doctrine of the transmigration of souls, which made no distinction between human and animal forms, provided an imposing climax to the stories of metamorphosis.* Indeed, it is hard to think of any other philosophy which could have been brought in here without disrupting the thread of the whole poem. Besides, Ennius had introduced it into his *Annals*,[191] at a time before Lucretius had set a new standard in poetic exposition, a fact which in itself may have spurred Ovid to emulation.†

We need not discuss here the theories about what secondary sources he may have used. His Pythagoras begins (xv, 75) with the injunction against eating meat, a straightforward topic which at once allowed the poet to indulge in conceits after his own heart:

> Heu quantum scelus est in viscera viscera condi,
> congestoque avidum pinguescere corpore corpus,
> alteriusque animantem animantis vivere leto !‡[192]

> *To bury flesh in flesh! O dreadful deed!*
> *With body's meat to fatten body's greed,*
> *And life by theft of other's life to feed!*

Then he launches into an impassioned plea based in the first instance not on the doctrine of transmigration but simply on the

---

* Dryden thought this part the masterpiece of the *Metamorphoses*; Preface to the *Fables* (1700).

† Dr Crump seems right in scouting the idea of D. A. Slater (*Ovid in the Metamorphoses*) that the whole poem has a Pythagorean background (*op. cit.* p. 211 n.). On the other hand her suggestion that the speech may be a *parody* of didactic poetry and a *burlesque* of Pythagoreanism is not consonant with its tone.

‡ The first line harks back to Lucretius' terrifying vision of primitive man in the jaws of a wild beast (v, 991),

viva videns vivo sepeliri viscera busto.

sentiment of kinship between men and animals, such as we find in Virgil's *Georgics*. There is nothing here which might not come naturally from a modern vegetarian. Ovid's capacity for putting himself in the position of others, already seen in his soliloquies, is here extended with moving effect to the ox. He may not have been a vegetarian himself, but he was a born advocate who in this case had at least a strong sympathy with his brief:[193]

> Quid meruistis, oves, placidum pecus inque tuendos
> natum homines, pleno quae fertis in ubere nectar,
> mollia quae nobis vestras velamina lanas
> praebetis vitaque magis quam morte iuvatis?
> quid meruere boves, animal sine fraude dolisque,
> innocuum, simplex, natum tolerare labores?
> immemor est demum nec frugum munere dignus
> qui potuit curvi dempto modo pondere aratri
> ruricolam mactare suum, qui trita labore
> illa, quibus totiens durum renovaverat arvum,
> tot dederat messes, percussit colla securi.
> nec satis est, quod tale nefas committitur: ipsos
> inscripsere deos sceleri numenque supernum
> caede laboriferi credit gaudere iuvenci!
> victima labe carens et praestantissima forma
> (nam placuisse nocet) vittis insignis et auro
> sistitur ante aras auditque ignara precantem
> imponique suas videt inter cornua fronti
> quas coluit fruges, percussaque sanguine cultros
> inficit in liquida praevisos forsitan unda.
> protinus ereptas viventi pectore fibras
> inspiciunt mentesque deum scrutantur in illis.
> unde (fames homini vetitorum tanta ciborum est!)
> audetis vesci, genus o mortale! quod, oro,
> ne facite, et monitis animos advertite nostris;
> cumque boum dabitis caesorum membra palato
> mandere vos vestros scite et sentite colonos![194]

Poor sheep, what harm do you, a placid tribe,
Born to serve man, whose nectar we imbibe
From udders full, who wool for clothing give,
Less useful if you die than if you live?
Oxen, what harm do you, beasts without guile,
Innocent, simple, born for honest toil?
Thoughtless, nor worth the bounty of the plough,
He who his partner of the fields, but now
Unyoked, can bear to slay, with axe to rive
That toil-worn neck that often did revive
His stubborn fields and make his harvests thrive!
Nor is this crime enough: they implicate
The gods themselves, and fancy that the great
Immortals joy in patient bullock slain.
A noble victim, perfect without stain,
('Tis death to please) stands at the altar there
With gold and fillets decked, and unaware
Hears the priest pray, sees sprinkled on his brow
The barley-meal he laboured for. And now
Those knives, perchance glimpsed in the pool, descend
And redden with his blood. Forthwith they rend
His entrails from his living breast, to scan
In them, forsooth, the gods' intent for man.
Next, mortals (so you crave unhallowed meat!)
You dare to feed. Ah, do not, I entreat.
Tasting bull's flesh, reflect that you devour
Your own familiar country-labourer.

The incidental rejection of augury here prepares us for the transition to the second part, an eloquent passage in the high Lucretian manner[195] on the delight and novelty of the doctrine about to be expounded. Indeed, the opening words of the exposition might have been written by Lucretius himself:

O genus attonitum gelidae formidine mortis,
quid Styga, quid tenebras et nomina vana timetis,
materiem vatum falsique pericula mundi?

Ah, race whom fears of chilly death appal,
Why dread ye Stygian shades, mere fables all,
Perils by poets feigned fantastical?

But then comes the surprise: it is the certainty, not of the dissolution but of the immortality of the soul, through transmigration, that is to banish fear of death. Lucretius had said of corporeal things, *omnia mutantur, nihil interit*; Pythagoras says it of the soul.

From transmigration the theme widens to embrace the doctrine that all things are in flux. Even here there is still a superficial connexion at least with the main theme of the poem, since the metamorphoses as described take place so fluently as to suggest that the identity of species is less hard and fast than we think; but it is tenuous enough, and in essence literary rather than philosophic.[196] There is still no effort of thought involved, as there is in Lucretius; the poet simply does what other Roman poets had done: he takes a Greek generalization and enlarges on concrete illustrations of it. It was not hard to marshal a series of natural phenomena, inorganic and organic, up and down the world, which involved change, such as springs that are alternately hot and cold, and the recital of them would be picturesque. *Vidi ego,* says Ovid, using the formula which so often introduces a tall story: the ancients no doubt found sea-shells far inland, but did they ever really find an old anchor on a mountain-top?[197] The recital finally modulates into a higher key with the thought of the rise and fall of famous cities.

From time to time in the course of the poem there have been passing reminders that the poet is a citizen of no mean city: the amber into which the tears of Phaëthon's sisters are changed is 'destined to be worn by Latin women'; Apollo, still in love with Daphne when she has become a laurel, foretells among her honours that she will be the pride of Roman generals proceeding in triumph to the Capitol, and guard on either side the civic crown of oak-leaves before the door of Augustus; and the long roll of the rivers affected by Phaëthon's fires is made to culminate in the

Tiber, 'to whom dominion over the world had been promised'.[198] Pythagoras now prophesies the future greatness of Rome: 'Even so in these days fame has it that Trojan Rome is rising, which beside the waters of Apennine-born Tiber is laying its foundations under a weighty charge: so is she by growth being transformed, and shall one day be the head of the whole wide world.' This, he adds, is no new prophecy, for Helenus foretold to Aeneas at the fall of Troy that a better Troy would arise

> quanta nec est nec erit nec visa prioribus annis.[199]

> *greater than any is, or shall be, or has been seen in former years.*

(7) ITALY AND ROME

We have anticipated, however, for much has been heard of the Romans before we come to Pythagoras. Towards the end of Book XIII (ll. 665 ff.) Aeneas leaves Troy on his fateful journey. From now onwards Ovid would be dealing not only with Greek legends which might or might not be familiar to his Roman audience (those in his Greek sources, Nicander at least, and probably Parthenius, covered Sicily and south Italy—*Magna Graecia*), but also with events which were believed to be semi-historical and which had been dealt with by Latin writers of towering genius and repute, Ennius, Virgil and Livy, not to mention Propertius and antiquarians such as Cato, Varro, Verrius Flaccus and his own friend Hyginus. He interweaves Greek and Roman legends cunningly, so that we never feel there is a complete break in the texture and continuity of the poem; even in the latter part of the last book he contrives to introduce the Greek Hippolytus, restored to life as the Italian Virbius, telling of his death on the shore at Troezen.

The passages which are a mere summary of the *Aeneid* must have been irksome to Ovid as they are to us, but how else could he cross over from Greece to Italy? Aeneas' arrival at the Straits of Messina gives occasion for two famous stories: Galatea tells Scylla how she was wooed by the Cyclops Polyphemus, and Scylla herself, for rejecting the advances of the marine deity Glaucus (who also tells her his story), is transformed by Circe into a monster. Thirty lines suffice to cover the diversion to Carthage, and the journey on again as far as the coasts above Naples. Here there is another interlude, while two sailors left behind by Ulysses tell each other what has happened to them since; Achaemenides enlarges on his terror-stricken life among the Cyclopes before Aeneas rescued him to Macareus, who in turn recounts the story of Circe.

Circe brings us very near to Rome; her island, now a rugged mountain-peak joined to the mainland by the drained Pontine Marshes, is visible from the neighbourhood of the Campagna; and while she was dallying with Ulysses, Macareus had heard from one of her nymphs the story of Picus, the mythical king of Italy, who loved the nymph Canens, born on the Palatine to Janus and Venilia, and was changed by her rival Circe into a woodpecker. By such easy stages does the Greek world melt into the Italian. We are borne as on a tide which, as its waves advance and recede, yet almost insensibly gains ground. The events of the second half of the *Aeneid* are briefly told, and then, with the interlude of two stories, one Latin (Vertumnus and Pomona) and one Greek (Iphis and Anaxarete), which Vertumnus in the guise of an old woman tells Pomona as a cautionary tale, we pass to those of the *Annals* of Ennius, and his famous scene of the council of the gods at which Mars claimed the apotheosis of his son Romulus, reminding Jupiter how once he had promised him:

> unus erit quem tu tolles in caerula caeli.

> *one there shall be whom thou shalt raise to the azure heavens.*

Like Hercules', Romulus' mortal part was dissolved, and he received a new form worthier of his heavenly home.[200]

The first half of the last book is taken up with Pythagoras' speech, the teaching imbibed by Numa. This is followed by the legend of Hippolytus-Virbius, and the Roman story of Cipus. Roman indeed this is, for here first in the poem is sounded the true note of patriotism which we hear in Livy. Cipus was a praetor who suddenly grew horns, and on being told by an Etruscan augur that this portended that he should be king if he returned within the walls, went into voluntary exile rather than subject the city to a monarchy. It is a far cry from the *Naturkinder* of the dawn of the Greek world to this stoical Roman, *egregius exsul*, the forerunner of Regulus.

Cipus takes us at one bound into Republican times, more than a century beyond Numa. Ovid does not even try to carry us over the next bound to the year 292 B.C., when we assist at the migration of Aesculapius to Rome; and there is only the connexion of contrast to bridge the next two hundred and fifty years and bring us to Julius Caesar. It looks very much as if his delight in invention was flagging, as well it might by now, so that he made haste to his designed conclusion. Roman legends were more stereotyped than Greek, and they tended to be moral rather than imaginative; and he himself was treating them simultaneously in the *Fasti*, a very good reason for skating over them here. But this decline really began with Book XII, in which we are aware of a conscious effort to raise the poem into a 'higher' strain. One is reminded of Virgil, straight from the triumph of *Aeneid* VI, vainly flogging the horses of his Muse to a greater effort which they could not be expected to produce:[201]

> Maior rerum mihi nascitur ordo,
> maius opus moveo.

> *a greater sequence of events I am bringing to birth, a greater work I am assaying.*

The conventional view was that war was the highest of themes, but after the *Iliad* it rarely produced the best poetry.

There are fine things in the last four books, such as the contest of Ajax and Ulysses, and parts of the speech of Pythagoras, itself hardly justified save as part of an attempt to give the poem a serious climax. Only occasionally, as in the idyll of Polyphemus and Galatea and the tale of Vertumnus and Pomona, is there a touch of the old whimsical humour. Aesculapius is brought all the way from Epidaurus to Rome in the form of a snake with complete solemnity (so it seems to me); to have exploited the ample opportunities for burlesque would no doubt have been too near the knuckle. We have passed insensibly from the mythology of Greece to the religion of the Roman state for which the Emperor was concerned to restore respect. The Island of Aesculapius in the Tiber was a sacred place, and many readers would resent any aspersions on its sanctity.

Ovid's Polyphemus idyll, based on Theocritus VI and XI, is obviously written with one eye on Virgil's *Eclogue* VII. Theocritus' Cyclops addresses his love with four complimentary comparisons; Virgil's (l. 37) deems four one too many; but Ovid's launches into no less than fifteen, and before we can recover, adds fifteen uncomplimentary ones. This is obviously burlesque, not a case of *nescit quod bene cessit relinquere*; but it is not critical burlesque. Here, as elsewhere, there are many instances of his openly borrowing from Virgil, *palam imitatus hoc animo ut vellet agnosci* ('openly imitating with intent that it should be recognized'), in the words of Gallio.[202] In dealing with the events covered by the *Aeneid* he shows dexterity in avoiding competition, enlarging where Virgil only hints or sketches, and *vice versa*. Nevertheless, it was inevitable that his style should be cramped, his genius rebuked, by his greater predecessor.

We must remember, however, that while our interest may flag the nearer he gets to Rome, that of his Italian readers would become more intense. To hear legends told of familiar places, and told in literature that has the stamp of immortality, is an inspiring thing. The 'Gathering of the Clans' in *Aeneid* VII would not be such an anticlimax after the Descent into Hades to the Italians of Virgil's day as it may seem to us; it was their Magna Carta, the seal of their right to a share in the glory of Rome. With something of the same feelings they would hear how Aesculapius

'won through the Sicilian Sea and the Straits of Pelorus, sailed by the islands of King Aeolus and the copper-mines of Temesa and made for Leucosia and the rose-gardens of mild Paestum. Thence he skirted Capri and Minerva's promontory and the vine-clad hills of Surrentum, Herculaneum and Stabiae and Parthenope made for leisure, and on to the temple of the Cumaean Sibyl. Then he came to the warm springs and Liternum with its mastic trees, the Volturnus rolling much sand beneath its stream, Sinuessa thronged with white doves, sultry Minturnae and her whom her foster-son buried (Caieta); and on to the home of Antiphates, and Trachas beset by marshes, Circe's land and the hard sands of Antium.'*[203]

It is said that as Mommsen passed through Italian villages a local patriot here and there might be heard boasting, 'Ha parlato bene del nostro paese'—'he spoke well of our village'.[204]

And now Ovid gathers up the threads of his poem. In the first book, when Jupiter revealed the treason of Lycaon, the gods 'all clamoured and with eager loyalty demanded the man who had dared such a plot; even so, when an impious band was mad to quench the name of Rome in Caesar's blood, the human race was stunned by the terror of such a catastrophe and the whole world trembled; nor is the devotion of your people, Augustus, less comforting to you than the gods' was then to Jupiter'.[205] And as the end was approaching Pythagoras had prophesied:[206]

Urbem etiam cerno Phrygios debere nepotes
quanta nec est nec erit nec visa prioribus annis.
hanc alii proceres per saecula longa potentem,
sed dominam rerum de sanguine natus Iuli
efficiet; quo cum tellus erit usa, fruentur
aetheriae sedes, caelumque erit exitus illi.

* Aeolus' Island may be Lipari; Surrentum=Sorrento, Parthenope=Naples, Caieta=Gaeta, Antiphates' home=Formiae, Trachas=Tarracina, Antium=Anzio.

I see Troy's offspring found a city home
Greater than was, or is, or is to come;
Leaders from age to age shall build her might,
Only a Julius raise her to the height
Of world-dominion; him, when earth has known
His bounty, heaven shall claim and call her own.

At last the climax has come:

Caesar in urbe sua deus est.

The idea that mortals might be transformed into stars or constellations was inherent in the very names of many of these, and in the third century the celebrated Eratosthenes had made a collection of aetiological stories about them, a source-book for many writers.[207] Several such metamorphoses have occurred in Ovid's poem, as that of Callisto and Arcas, and now comes the greatest of all, an event fresh in the memory of men. Suetonius describes it as follows:

'Julius Caesar died in his fifty-sixth year and was received into the company of the gods, not only by the decree of the Senate, but also in the conviction of the populace. For at the first games which his heir Augustus was giving in his memory a comet shone for seven nights continually, and this was believed to be the soul of Caesar translated to heaven; for which reason a star is placed over his forehead on his statue.'*[208]

But Julius must not outshine Augustus; so Ovid hastens to say that his chief title to divinity was neither his military nor his civil triumphs, great though they were, but his offspring. He does not hesitate to use words of real paternity, *progenies, pater huius, genuisse,* culminating in a conceit worthy of Lucan,

Ne foret hic igitur mortali semine cretus,
ille deus faciendus erat,[209]

that Augustus might not be sprung from mortal seed, it was
right that Julius should be made a god,

---

* Virgil's Fifth Eclogue (Daphnis) may refer to this. The effect of the co-incidence on popular credulity can readily be imagined.

though all the world knew that Augustus' father was Gaius Octavius, and Julius only his adoptive father! Flattery could hardly go further, and when all allowance is made for differences of convention, we cannot help being alienated. There is nothing in Virgil or Horace, especially after the settlement of 28 B.C., that affects us quite as this does.

It is also unfortunate that he should have followed this with a description of the portents that preceded the murder of Julius; for eloquent though the passage is, it challenges comparison with one of the greatest in Virgil, the close of the first *Georgic*, and cannot stand it.[210] In reply to Venus' appeals to avert the tragedy Jupiter reveals to her the decrees of fate, engraved on everlasting adamant, the deification of Julius, the conquests of Augustus and his domestic reforms. It is strange to find Ovid writing in the serious vein of the Augustans: 'When he has given peace to the world, he shall turn his mind to civic justice and be a most righteous author of laws, and shall guide morality by his own example; and looking to the age of posterity and the generations to come shall bid the son of his revered wife to bear his name and his burdens alike.'*[211] When Jupiter ends, Venus at his bidding enters the Senate-house unseen, snatches the soul of Julius from his body as he is stabbed and translates it as a comet to heaven, whence he looks down and agrees with fame in setting Augustus' deeds above his own.

Once more Ovid challenges Virgil, with a variation of the great prayer to the *Di patrii* that closes the First *Georgic*, and adds his own *Serus in caelum redeas*.[212] When Virgil uttered that appeal and Horace composed his second Ode the whole future was at stake; it was uncertain whether the young Octavian would be allowed to heal the wounds of the civil war; there was a motive of desperate urgency which was lacking when Ovid wrote under the ageing Emperor, and we feel this, as well as discomfort at the garbling of a great and familiar passage, as we read what Ovid intended to be his grand finale. The last hundred and thirty lines

* The son of Livia is Tiberius.

of the *Metamorphoses* are as eloquent as a master of language could make them; but the sap of the Augustan spring, like the dew of the Hellenic dawn, has dried up, and the autumn leaves are falling, gorgeous still in their way and reminiscent of past glories, but faded and tarnished and rather melancholy.

(8) DRAMA, RHETORIC, WORDS

Dryden, discussing the wit of the Ancients in his *Essay of Dramatic Poesy*, gives his opinion that 'he of them who had a genius most proper for the stage was Ovid; he had a way of writing so fit to stir up a pleasing admiration and concernment, which are the objects of a tragedy, and to show the various movements of a soul combating betwixt two different passions, that, had he lived in our age, or in his own could have writ with our advantages, no man but must have yielded to him'. He cannot believe that 'he who in the epic way wrote things so near to drama as the story of Myrrha, of Caunus and Byblis and the rest,* should stir up no more concernment where he most endeavoured it' (than is aroused by Seneca's *Medea* falsely attributed to Ovid). We may grant that the author of *Aurungzebe* may not be an infallible critic of drama, but his opinion is at least interesting. Had there been a healthy stage and a judicious audience in Augustan Rome, Horace might have written for it successful Terentian comedy, and Ovid successful Euripidean psychological melodrama. In monologue and messenger speech at least he would have excelled, as abundant passages in the *Metamorphoses* testify, and perhaps also in dialogue.† (One of the things which keeps the poem alive is the abundance of directly reported speech.)

Some critics may reply that he is rhetorical, thereby betraying

---

* Note that Dryden is most moved by the episodes which Dr Crump (*op. cit.* p. 232, cf. 230) finds 'entirely repulsive'. Ovid himself said of tragedy, 'huic operi...aptus eram' (*Am.* II, 18, 14).

† There is plenty of dialogue embedded in the story told to Pentheus by the disguised Dionysus (III, 579–691).

lack of sincerity, and that this is fatal. But is not sincerity an equivocal term to use of a dramatist? His business is, not to express his own emotions, but to imagine other people's; and surely in this Ovid excels. If his characters sometimes speak rhetorically, this may be because rhetoric was ingrained in the Romans, making them speak, even in moments of passion, in a way more likely to sound artificial to an Englishman than to an Italian or to a Frenchman nurtured on Corneille and Racine. Even in Euripides the influence of the new art can already be felt.

For a century or so it has been axiomatic in England that Ovid has no genuine feeling. Here is Sellar, whose account of him is in general admirably just and perceptive: 'He has little power over the springs of pathos.... A great sorrow, a great affection, a great cause or a great crisis, awakens in him little corresponding emotion.'²¹³ This may possibly be true of the cause or crisis, but is it so of the sorrow or affection? The sorrow of Cephalus, or the affection of Alcyone? Dr Crump is very severe on the deliberative monologues: 'None of these speeches has any real note of passion. The heroines state that they are the victims of emotions which they cannot control, and the reader accepts the statement as necessary to the story; but the emotion is not felt.' 'All, though voicing a real mental process, are incapable of rousing the sympathy of the reader.'²¹⁴ It was not ever thus, and one wonders whether we are now reading Ovid without prejudice. The opinion of Dryden may come as a shock:

'Though [Virgil] describes his Dido well and naturally, in the violence of her passions, yet he must yield in that to the Myrrha, the Byblis, the Althaea, of Ovid; for, as great an admirer of him as I am, I must acknowledge that if I see not more of their souls than I see of Dido's, at least I have greater concernment for them: and that convinces me that Ovid has touched those tender strokes more delicately than Virgil could.'²¹⁵

I would agree with this up to a certain point: I find Dido's outburst as 'rhetorical' as anything in Ovid—until the supreme moment when her pride breaks down and with it all her fine rhetoric,

> Si quis mihi parvulus aula
> luderet Aeneas, qui te tamen ore referret,
> non equidem omnino capta ac deserta viderer;[216]

and I do find myself 'concerned' for Myrrha and Byblis and Althaea, despite their occasional conceits. As for the 'rhetoric', Heinze is surely right when he says that 'not a slightest track leads us to the supposition that Ovid for his pathetic monologues of deliberation can have learnt anything from the rhetorical schools more than the art of speech in general, the sharpening of thought into effective words'.[*217]

This is not to deny that there are passages in the *Metamorphoses* in which the influence of those schools is to be detected. There are speeches on what were probably already stock subjects for *Suasoriae*; there are conceits or epigrams which are known to be borrowed from his admired Porcius Latro;[218] and Cepheus' speech to Phineus, who is about to attack Perseus, the rescuer of his betrothed Andromeda, suggests at least a typical theme for *Controversia*: 'A man rescues a girl from imminent death, and on being offered the reward of his choice, requests to marry her. Should her betrothed give way, on the ground that but for the rescuer she would not be alive?'

The thirteenth Book opens with a grand debate on a time-honoured subject, the contest between Ajax and Ulysses for the arms of the dead Achilles, which were awarded to the latter.† The story is assumed as known in the *Odyssey*,[219] where Ajax, called up from Hades, refuses to speak to the victor, and it had its place in the Epic Cycle. What gave the event its lasting interest was the contrast between two types of character. In Homer Ajax is the tower of strength in battle, the man of stolid, unquestioning

---

* As we have seen, these speeches have an independent descent from Greek tragedy; p. 206.

† In the account that follows I am much indebted to Prof. W. B. Stanford's 'Studies in the Characterization of Ulysses' I–III in *Hermathena*, LXXIII–LXXV (1949–50).

courage and huge physique, less skilful and nimble than Achilles as he was less temperamental (until his breakdown). Odysseus is the man of many wiles who is at the same time a courageous hero. He has a *reputation* for cunning, but does nothing seriously deceitful either in the *Iliad* or *Odyssey*. He is an accomplished, but not malicious, liar.[220] One cannot imagine him cheating his brother of his birthright, like his Jewish counterpart, Jacob.

The denigration of Odysseus-Ulysses began with the Cyclic epic. Pindar furthered it in the seventh and eighth *Nemeans*;[221] he was writing for Aeacid Aegina, so it was natural that he should exalt the Aeacid Ajax; but it is also probable that he himself preferred Dorian bluntness, of which he saw a prototype in Ajax, to Ionian suppleness, presaged in Odysseus. As for tragedy, Odysseus comes very well out of the second half of Sophocles' *Ajax*, but a generation later, in the same dramatist's *Philoctetes*, as in Euripides' *Philoctetes, Troades, Hecuba* and *Iphigeneia in Aulis*, he has become a villain, whether before or behind the scenes, 'cruel, corrupt, chauvinistic, jesuitical, ambitious, demagogic, *capable de tout*'.[222] He has, in fact, become the prototype of the post-Periclean politicians, Cleon and the rest, consumed with φιλοτιμία, fascinated by τὸ σόφον.[223] One might have expected Euripides to idealize so clever and resourceful a hero, but there was another man of wits in the Epic Cycle, Palamedes, whose death Odysseus compassed. So Palamedes becomes the good clever man and Odysseus the evil.

Meanwhile the Sophists were busy, Gorgias' *Defence of Palamedes* disparaging Odysseus, and his pupil Antisthenes' *Ajax and Odysseus* coming to his defence. Ajax calls him a common criminal, a temple-robber (of the Palladium) and a reluctant conscript. Odysseus replies that he shared the common dangers at Troy as much as Ajax; that he volunteered for lonely enterprises in which detection would mean an inconspicuous death, which needed more courage than fighting in heavy armour; and that the object of the war being to take Troy and recover Helen, not to kill Trojans, ruses and diplomacy were more valuable; Ajax is a stupid, jealous blockhead, ignorant of strategy and tactics, fighting blindly like a wild boar. (But Antisthenes' defence was a paradoxical exception amid the general condemnation.)

The rhetoricians of Rome did not overlook so promising a subject for debate; a declamation by Porcius Latro upon it gave Ovid the idea for his line 121.[224] One can guess where Roman sympathies would lie—not with the know-all *Graeculus esuriens*. In this they had on their side the dominant tradition, echoes of which we find in Virgil.*[225] We can say with some confidence that when Ovid saw to it that Ulysses won heavily on points, he was taking a positive stand against the tide.† His 'blockish' (*stolidus*) Ajax is the dull-witted soldier little respected by the bright elegiac poets of love, while Ulysses is the man of *ingenium*, the clever, subtle thinker and speaker. This revelation of his sympathies is important for our estimate of his character.

The debate cannot be classed as a *Controversia*, for no general principle is in dispute; it is rather a tragic *agon* extended till it resembles a pair of opposing *Suasoriae*. Let us see what the protagonists had to say, when the chiefs had taken their seats and the commons stood round in a ring. The impatient Ajax spoke first (unwisely, like Shakespeare's Brutus).[226] Taunting Ulysses with cowardice he made some abusive points: 'I need not detail my exploits, you have seen them. Ulysses is obliged to tell of his, since night was their only witness.' 'The fact that Ulysses has aspired to this prize diminishes its value.' 'Even if I were inferior in valour, I should still be his superior in birth; and Achilles was my cousin.' 'It needed no informing Palamedes to bring me to fight against Troy:‡ is he to take the best arms now because then

---

* It is true that Sinon tells the tale, and his story that Ulysses slandered him proves to be a lie; but he was obviously inventing a tale calculated to ring true, and he refers to the treacherous murder of Palamedes as an event likely to be accepted as such by his hearers.

† Here again I am indebted to Professor Stanford, for letting me see some unpublished pages on Ovid's Contest. Ulysses did have his supporters, the Stoics.

‡ Palamedes exposed the feigned madness by which Ulysses had sought to avoid service.

he tried to take none? But it has proved a pity that his madness was ever detected as false; else would Philoctetes never have been treacherously put ashore at Lemnos, whose arrows we need now. Still, he was luckier than Palamedes, who stayed with Ulysses and was brought to death by him.' 'Ulysses deserted the aged Nestor in battle; he hid behind my shield, pretending to be heavily wounded, but he was not too badly wounded to run away after that.' 'I withstood Hector and saved the ships alone. Where were you? All your deeds were done at night, and you needed Diomede to help you.' 'The arms would be worse than useless to him: their glint would betray him lurking in his ambushes; and in any case they are too heavy for him, and would impede his flights. Also his own arms are as good as new from under-use.' 'But what good are words? Let us make trial by putting the arms in the midst of the enemy and awarding them to whichever recovers them.'

Ovid was too good an artist, and too keen a rhetorician, to give Ajax an ineffective speech. No hint in the *Iliad* is unexploited. The points are commonplace enough, but they are neatly made—so much so as to be out of character:

> Sed nec mihi dicere promptum est,
> nec facere est illi.
>
> frater erat, fraterna peto.
>
> optima num sumat, quia sumere noluit ulla?
>
> luce nihil gestum, nihil est Diomede remoto.

There was some applause from the crowd when he finished.

But Ulysses is the true orator, up to all the tricks of the trade. Whereas Ajax had begun uncontrolledly, with an outburst, he kept his eyes fixed on the ground for a few moments before he replied, and having thus relaxed the tension began quietly, 'nor was his eloquence unaccompanied by charm'.[227] With more tact than his opponent he paid a graceful tribute to the deceased, regretted that he was not still alive to use the arms, and wiped his eyes as though they were weeping before going on to submit his own claim. 'Let it not tell in this man's favour that he seems (and indeed is) dull-witted, nor against me that I have wits which have often been used to your public advantage; and let not my gift of speech, such as it is, arouse prejudice, if now it speaks for its owner as often it has spoken for you.' (*Meaque haec facundia, siqua est*: there speaks the Roman orator making his *captatio benevolentiae*, just like Cicero in the well-known exordium of the *Pro Archia*.) To continue with our *précis*:

'As to nobility of birth, in point of fact I surpass Ajax (and *my* father did not kill his brother), but I submit that the contest should be decided by merit, not birth. Nor should his kinship count, otherwise Achilles' father Peleus or his son Neoptolemus have clearly a prior claim. Let us turn then to merits. It was I who by putting arms in his hands penetrated Achilles' disguise,* and so brought him to Troy. In all his deeds I thus have some credit; in this sense *I* overcame Telephus, and can claim the capture of Thebe, Lesbos, Chryse, Cilla; *I* sacked Lyrnesus; and finally, Hector fell to the man *I* brought:

> Illis haec armis, quibus est inventus Achilles,
> arma peto: vivo dederam, post fata reposco.
>
> *Arms found him out: those arms I seek once more:*
> *In life he took, in death let him restore.*

At Aulis, for the public good, I stifled my natural pity and persuaded Agamemnon to sacrifice Iphigeneia, else the expedition could never have proceeded. It is a good thing they sent me, and not Ajax, to obtain the princess by cunning from Clytemnestra. I entered hostile Troy as ambassador, at peril of my life, and nearly persuaded the Trojans to give up Helen. What use was Ajax all those nine years before the assault began, while I was laying traps for the enemy, devising fortifications, keeping up the allies' morale, working at logistics, going on missions? When Agamemnon, warned by Jupiter in a dream, was for withdrawing from Troy,

---

* When Achilles was hiding in Scyros, disguised as a girl in order to escape service, Odysseus put arms in his hands, and the way he handled them betrayed him.

Ajax began to pack up like the rest: it was I who persuaded him to reverse his decision, but I too who then punished Thersites for railing at the kings. Finally, what Greek will partner you, as Diomede came with me, when we killed Dolon after extracting from him the Trojan plans, and Rhesus too? I slew many Trojans and have many wounds (here, in true orator's style, he bared his breast), whereas Ajax has none. I will not be churlish and deny that he stood in defence of the fleet; but why does he claim all the credit and refuse you your share? The late Patroclus did as much as anyone. Ajax's single combat with Hector fell to him by lot only, and he failed to give him a scratch. When Achilles was killed, it was I who carried him, armour and all, from the field. And would Thetis want an insensitive soldier to have that wonderful shield, whose artistic workmanship he would be incapable of appreciating?

Ajax reproaches me with coming late to the expedition: in so doing he must reproach Achilles himself. A loving wife detained me, a loving mother Achilles: our first time was given to them, the rest to you. No shame to share a reproach with such a hero. But while I found him out by wit, it was not Ajax' wit that found out me.

> Deprensus Ulixis
> ingenio tamen ille, at non Aiacis Ulixes.

And if my charges against Palamedes were false, as he suggests, then you are to be blamed for condemning him; but the evidence was there for all to see.* Again, you consented to Philoctetes' being left at Lemnos, on my advice, to heal his wound; if he had not been so, he might now be dead. Now that the gods say his presence is necessary for the fall of Troy, is it Ajax you will send rather than me to persuade or trick him into coming? No, it is I who will obtain you both him and his arrows, as I obtained Helenus and Palladium. That was a most perilous enterprise, and

---

* Gold found in Palamedes' tent was maintained by Ulysses to be a bribe from Priam for treachery. Ajax insinuated that Ulysses planted it there, in order to take vengeance on Palamedes for penetrating his disguise when he was evading service.

without it all Ajax' efforts would have been doomed to failure.
On that night I conquered Troy. And do not keep reminding
me that Diomede was my partner: he has his share of praise. But
if he did not know that a thinker was worth more than a fighter,
would not he be claiming the arms himself, and others too? It all
comes to this:[228]

> Tibi dextera bello
> utilis, ingenium est quod eget moderamine nostro;
> tu vires sine mente geris, mihi cura futuri;
> tu pugnare potes, pugnandi tempora mecum
> eligit Atrides; tu tantum corpore prodes,
> nos animo; quantoque ratem qui temperat anteit
> remigis officium, quanto dux milite maior,
> tantum ego te supero! nec non in corpore nostro
> pectora sunt potiora manu: vigor omnis in illis.

> *Your arm for martial deeds*
> *Is apt, your mind my cleverer guidance needs;*
> *Brawn without brain is yours, forethought is mine;*
> *You fight, but I with Atreus' son divine*
> *The moment; you by sinews play your part,*
> *By counsel I; and as the helmsman's art*
> *Excels the rower's, or the chief of staff*
> *The private, so I thee! The better half*
> *Of us is head, not hand: there's the true man.'*

This concludes his argument, and only the eloquent peroration
remains. He repeats that by stealing the Palladium he has opened
the way for the fall of Troy, and ends with a dramatic gesture
'—if you do not give the arms to me, give them to her!', pointing
to the fateful image of Pallas he had stolen from the city. No
wonder 'the company of the chiefs was moved, and the power of
speech was proved indeed, for the eloquent man carried off the
arms of the brave'.

Even a bare summary may have conveyed the masterly use
Ovid's Ulysses makes of the data provided by the saga. As the

poet warms to his task he leaves no doubt where his sympathies lie. He is hitting back at 'gnawing Envy', which reproached him in his youth,

> Non me more patrum, dum strenua sustinet aetas,
> praemia militiae pulverulenta sequi.

The idea of making Ulysses say that Ajax would in any case not appreciate the marvellous engravings on the shield described by Homer must have given him particular pleasure.

Erudition plays a lesser part than rhetoric in the *Metamorphoses*. Ovid does not speak in riddles, as the Alexandrians often did, though he sometimes throws out hints that he knows many more stories than he tells.* Sometimes also, to add yet one more ingredient to his hotch-potch, he will rehearse a catalogue in the Hesiodic manner revived by the Alexandrians.[229] We have noted already his unfortunate passion for being exhaustive:† he destroys credibility in his description of Hercules' end by making the hero in the midst of his agony recall each one of his twelve labours; Sophocles knew better, and achieved twice the effect by making him mention only half of them.[230] Ovid has not indeed the face to recite the names of all Actaeon's hounds (Hyginus knew eighty-five), but he does go so far as thirty-three (Aeschylus thought four enough) before relenting with a *quosque referre mora est*, and is careful a few lines later that the three mentioned as first leaping on the victim should not be from among those already named.‡[231]

No one who appreciates Milton will maintain that catalogues of names cannot be poetic, provided at least that they are not unduly prolonged. The panorama of peaks that burned in Phaëthon's conflagration is magnificent in sound as well as imagination, especially the culminating line, which Virgil himself might have envied:

> Ardet Athos Taurusque Cilix et Tmolus et Oete
> et tum sicca, prius creberrima fontibus, Ide

---

* E.g. XIII, 717; and esp. VII, 350–90, when detailing the places over which Medea flew in her dragon-chariot.　　　　　† See p. 96.

‡ The list of trees attracted by Orpheus (X, 90–105) is also much too long.

virgineusque Helicon et nondum Oeagrius Haemus:
ardet in immensum geminatis ignibus Aetna
Parnassusque biceps et Eryx et Cynthus et Othrys
et tandem nivibus Rhodope caritura Mimasque
Dindymaque et Mycale natusque ad sacra Cithaeron
nec prosunt Scythiae sua frigora: Caucasus ardet,
Ossaque cum Pindo maiorque ambobus Olympus,
aeriaeque Alpes et nubifer Apenninus.*

Here the epithets and touches of literary allusion are just sufficient
to relieve monotony; and the same applies to the catalogue of
rivers which follows shortly after. (The mention of so many
geographical names should not, however, lead us to suppose that
Ovid worried about geographical accuracy.[232]) Cicero, quoting
an old line,

qua pontus Helles, supera Tmolum ac Tauricos

remarked that it was lit up by the splendid place-names, and
Quintilian noted that Latin poets, when they wanted to make their
verse delightful, were apt to embellish it with Greek names.[233]

It might be expected that a poem so pictorial as the *Metamorphoses* would abound in onomatopoeia. This is notoriously an
effect to which some are far more sensitive than others, and there
is a strong element of subjectivity involved. I can only say that
I find surprisingly little in this poem compared, for instance, with
the work of Virgil, who is admittedly one of the great masters of
the art.† The croaking of the frogs at VI, 376 is admirable,

quamvis sint *sub aqua, sub aqua* maledicere temptant;

but this is one of the few examples that I should admit, though

---

* II, 217–26; cf. 241–60. The list of Cyclads at VII, 461–74 is also effective.

† Here I must disagree with Martini, *op. cit.* p. 34. Of the instances listed in
Lüdke, *Ueber Lautmalerei in Ovid's Metamorphosen* (1871), *Ueber rhythmische
Malerei in O.M.* (1878–9), many would occur only to a seeker determined to
find.

I have read through the poem on the look-out for it.* The fact is that poets vary as readers do in the value they attach to ono-matopoeia. Those who, like Virgil or Wordsworth or Tennyson, concentrate on the object and try to convey it as vividly as possible to the reader, will naturally pay great attention to so helpful a device; while those who are chiefly concerned to create beauty or convey thought will care less about it.[234] The fact that Ovid sacrificed the expressive flexibility of Virgil's hexameter for a more regular rhythm of lightness and speed in itself suggests that he did not regard it as of prime importance.

The general style of the writing has been sufficiently illustrated in the passages quoted. There is no trace in the diction of rare and mysterious words such as the Alexandrians favoured. The Italian dialects, unlike the Greek, were too different for blending, and Latin was always Latin. But whereas Virgil and Propertius, for instance, had contrived to make even this clean-cut language suggestive, Ovid preferred to keep it neat and precise. It cannot be denied that the *Metamorphoses* seem monotonous if read for long on end, but this is the fault of the versification rather than the language.

(9) CONCLUSION

To the Romans, who had as yet no novels, these stories must have given a delight beyond what we can recapture. (The story of Tereus, Procne and Philomela,[235] for instance, has many of the elements of a modern 'thriller'.) They had mostly been told in Greek, but the time had come when only a new language and the fresh outlook of a different race could bring them to life again. They continued to give this delight in the Middle Ages and well after the Renaissance. The first eleven books are the best, when Ovid's fancy is freer. As soon as he begins to aspire to epic

---

* Mr T. F. Higham has drawn my attention to *M.* II, 684,

> incustoditae Pylios memorantur in agros
> processisse boves,

comparing the use of long *o*-sounds in the opening of Gray's *Elegy*.

seriousness, he comes into competition with poets who surpass him in this vein; one feels one is passing from carefree youth to careful middle age. But taken as a whole the poem gives an effect of completeness. On his way to exile Ovid, charging a friend with its publication, insists that he would have emended it if he had had the opportunity:[236]

> emendaturus, si licuisset, eram.

He says that on his departure for exile he burnt the manuscript with his own hand—a gesture doubtless challenging comparison with Virgil's dying request to his executors to burn the *Aeneid*, but a 'rhetorical' one in any case, since friends had copies, and he must surely have known it at the time.* Even supposing that the poem lacks the *summa manus*, the *ultima lima* (though it is hard to say where, given its general nature), it bears no such traces of incompleteness as the *Aeneid*. There are no apparent faults of construction, and, for Ovid, remarkably few faults of taste; and, indeed, if he had recognized any later, he might still have kept them in, for did he not say that a poem, like a face, was the more attractive for having a mole somewhere?[237] It is surely inconceivable that he intended to recast the whole of the last four books —the change we might most desire to see. One cannot but suspect that he is seeking to safeguard himself against criticisms, or simply to enhance his reputation, in a way reminiscent of Pope, by suggesting that even a masterpiece was not his best. There are some who hold that the version we have was in fact revised by Ovid. It is true that our manuscripts sometimes give alternative drafts, which some would attribute to the poet himself;[238] but we cannot deny the possibility that these existed in copies made before his exile. The chief piece of evidence cited, however, is the lines on Actaeon's being blinded for seeing Diana bathing:

> At bene si quaeras, Fortunae crimen in illo,
> non scelus invenies, quod enim scelus error habebat?[239]

---

* Early in his exile he invites the Emperor to look into the *Metamorphoses* and see the evidence of his loyalty.[240]

> *But to right thinking, Chance was here to blame,*
> *Not shameful guilt: in error is no shame.*

This passage certainly sounds like the direct appeal of a man who
thinks he has been unjustly punished for an accidental fault; and
it seems to link up with his own words about the cause of his
exile:

> Cur aliquid vidi? cur noxia lumina feci?
>   cur imprudenti cognita culpa mihi?
> inscius Actaeon vidit sine veste Dianam:
>   praeda fuit canibus non minus ille suis.[241]

> *Why did I see it, implicate my eyes?*
> *Why did this guilty secret me surprise?*
> *Actaeon saw Diana's nakedness*
> *By chance: his hounds devoured him none the less.*

Yet it would not be out of keeping with Ovid's rational and
sympathetic mind to make the comment in the *Metamorphoses*
when it had no reference to himself, and natural that he should
recall it in the *Tristia* when by now it had.

This theory must remain unproven. But at all events there is
no sign of dissatisfaction in the epilogue as we have it, in which
the poet proclaims his *non omnis moriar*, arrogating in a literary
sense* to his own *pars melior* the immortality he had claimed for
that of Hercules and Julius Caesar:

> Iamque opus exegi quod non Iovis ira nec ignis
> nec poterit ferrum nec edax abolere vetustas.
> cum volet, illa dies, quae non nisi corporis huius
> ius habet, incerti spatium mihi finiat aevi;
> parte tamen meliore mei super alta perennis
> astra ferar, nomenque erit indelebile nostrum,
> quaque patet domitis Romana potentia terris
> ore legar populi, perque omnia saecula fama,
> siquid habent veri vatum praesagia, vivam!

---

* Cf. Horace, *Odes* IV, 8, for the working out of this idea. Ovid calls the
Metamorphoses a better picture of himself than any portrait.[242]

So ends my work, that not Jove's wrath, nor flame,
Nor steel can vanquish, nor devouring age.
Let come that day, which o'er this mortal frame
Alone has power, to end my pilgrimage,
Yet shall my better part have heritage
Among the stars, indelible my name.
Wherever Rome extends her sway my page
Shall there be read; and if what bards proclaim
Has truth, throughout all time I shall survive in fame!

How amply this prophecy was fulfilled shall be told in due course.

CHAPTER VIII

THE 'FASTI'

TEMPORA CUM CAUSIS

THE last two books of the *Metamorphoses*, as we have seen, dealt in part with legends of Rome, a subject which was occupying Ovid at the same time in a major work in elegiac couplets. It was like him to engage simultaneously on works belonging to two genres over which the literary world of Callimachus' day had been split, the continuous epic and the 'collective' poem of disconnected stories.[1]   In composing these two works, as Martini has demonstrated,[2] he was the consummator of the Neoteric movement which transplanted Hellenistic poetry to Rome. We do not know when he began the *Fasti*,* but he had composed six books by the time of his exile, half of a poem which, if completed, would have run to about ten thousand lines. Each month has a book to itself, beginning with a discussion of the significance of its name and then following the almanack of the Julian year:

Tempora cum causis Latium digesta per annum
lapsaque sub terras ortaque signa cano.

I sing of occasions, with their origins, spread throughout the Latin year, and of the rising and setting of constellations.

So Ovid introduces his poem, a jumble of astronomy, history, legend, religion, superstition, scholarship, guesswork and anti-

* The Prolegomena to R. Merkel's ed. (1841) are fundamental. The commentary of H. Peter (1874) is most useful. Sir James Frazer's great edition (1929) used in this chapter for the text, is outstanding for its commentary on Roman religion and folk-lore. (The translation inclines unfortunately to the traditional false-antique style). The first eighty-seven pages of F. Peeters' *Les Fastes d'Ovide* (1939) form a valuable introduction, with full references to the literature. He gives such evidence as there is for dating the various books, pp. 29–31.

quarian lore. The ingenious transitions of the *Metamorphoses* are not attempted, but the right to pass over one item and elaborate another at whim is maintained. Roman legends connected with the festivals are interwoven with Greek. Why do the Luperci run naked? We are told first that Faunus, the deity concerned, is the naked Pan of primitive Arcadia, where men lived naked as the beasts (besides, it is easier to run naked). Then follows a Greek legend of how he was deceived by a change of clothing, and a Latin one of how Romulus and Remus, when the alarm was raised that thieves were stealing their cattle, ran naked as they were to intercept them.[3] The myths of the origin of the stars are Greek.

The choice of such a subject would be easily accounted for by reading, and no less easily by environment. The literary grand-parents of the *Fasti* are, on the aetiological side, the *Aetia* of Callimachus, admired of all Roman elegists, and on the astro-nomical side the no less admired *Phaenomena* of Aratus.* A Hellen-istic great-uncle may perhaps be discerned in the lost elegiac poem of Simias of Rhodes on the months and the origin of their names. The first man whom we know to have treated Roman legends of origins in verse was a Greek elegiac poet called Butas, probably a freedman of the younger Cato.† There is a charming elegy of Tibullus[4] introducing us in the dramatic manner of Callimachus' *Hymns* to a rural festival; but the true father of the *Fasti* is clearly the last book of Propertius. In it the self-styled Roman Callimachus claims to have set out to emulate his hero,

> sacra diesque canam et cognomina prisca locorum.[5]

> *I sing of sacred rites, and days, and the ancient names of places.*

It looks as though he intended to write a separate elegy on each topic, like that on the constellation Coma Berenices in Callimachus'

---

* Ovid himself wrote a hexameter *Phaenomena* at some time, of which two small fragments survive (VI and VII in Owen's Oxford Classical Text).

† Plutarch, *Romulus* 21, 6, quotes a couplet about the Lupercalia.

Aetia, but he completed only four,[6] and the introductory poem of his last, miscellaneous collection that contains them is a whimsical apology for not having persevered.

There were other reasons besides poetic emulation why Ovid should have taken up the task that Propertius, and possibly also his own friend Sabinus,* had abandoned. The Romans had long been interested in the origins of their customs and the early legends of their people, witness the *Annals* of Ennius and the *Origins* of the elder Cato. More learned writers had recently entered the field, and finally Augustus, in his efforts to restore the old Roman virtues, was attempting not only to revive the old religion but also to kindle an admiration for the old worthies of Rome, whose statues he set up round his new forum. We know how Virgil, and eventually Horace and Propertius also, wrote poetry in sympathy with this movement.

The idea once conceived, Ovid set to work. He chose as metre the elegiacs of the *Aetia* rather than the hexameters of the *Phaenomena*, probably because he felt most at ease in them. He does apologize for making the vehicle of his lighter poems bear more serious themes,[7] though in fact Propertius had shown the way. The basis of the poem was to be the calendar as reformed by Julius Caesar and inaugurated on January 1, 45 B.C.† This reform had led to a widespread setting up of Fasti on tablets in public and private places all over Italy, and it is from remains of these that we are able to reconstruct the Roman calendar.‡ (That of Praeneste is of particular interest because we know that it was sponsored by the great antiquarian Verrius Flaccus, and the comments included

* *P.* IV, 16, 15–16 says he was engaged on a work on '*dies*' at the time of his death.

† Augustus had made a further adjustment in 8 B.C., rendered necessary by pontifical incompetence in carrying out Julius' instructions. For the Roman calendar see Warde Fowler, *The Roman Festivals* (1925), Introd. It is noteworthy that Callimachus wrote a prose work on the Greek calendar.

‡ Edited by Mommsen in *C.I.L.* vol. I; the Fasti Maffeiani, written on marble and discovered in a Roman palace in 1547, are almost complete; they can be supplemented from some thirty others.

are presumably due to him.)* This skeleton Ovid proceeded to clothe with flesh. Of his Greek fables, that of Arion and the dolphin comes from Herodotus,[8] but the majority were no doubt derived from Hellenistic sources, notably the work of Eratosthenes on the origins and names of constellations. The Roman material was much of it common property by now. The 'ancient annals' he claims to have consulted might include the pontifical *Annales*, the *Fasti Triumphales* and other official records besides literary works such as those of Ennius, Fabius Pictor and Cato; but there can be little doubt that his chief debt was to more recent scholarship, to Varro above all in his *Antiquitates Rerum Humanarum et Divinarum* and his *Aetia*, to a handbook by Verrius Flaccus, and finally to his own antiquarian friend and mentor Hyginus.†
One source of material as well as inspiration must have been Livy's new history, as we can detect from verbal similarities in the versions of the stories of the Fabii and Lucretia.[9]

Since the chief authorities he is likely to have consulted have survived at best only in fragments, there is little to be gained from trying to deduce his debt to each. More interesting, and more vivid, are the passages in which he claims, in Callimachean style, to be drawing on his own experience. Already in the *Amores*[10] he showed his enthusiasm for old ceremonies by describing the festival of Juno which he chanced to witness at his wife's home town of Falerii. In the *Fasti* he mentions that he himself has taken part in the rites of the Parilia on April 21, carrying the means of expiation, bean-straws and the ashes of a burnt calf, jumping over the three fires arranged in a row, and letting himself be aspersed with water from a laurel branch.[11] He had drunk, too, of the spring in the awesome shrine of Diana beside Lake Nemi, and perhaps caught a glimpse of its priest, the prowling 'King of the Grove', who, having slain his predecessor in single combat,

---

* Suetonius, *De Gram.* 19. It is significant that Augustus chose this man to be tutor to his grandsons (*ibid.* 17).

† Frazer, Preface, p. xii. Merkel labours valiantly in his Prolegomena to sort out the various sources. For a recent and useful survey see Peeters, *op. cit.* pp. 49–63.

reigned till another appeared and slew him in turn.[12] (Readers of the *Golden Bough* will remember that it is from this grove, whose Latin inmate Virbius was identified with the Greek Hippolytus, that Frazer began his world-wide pilgrimage.)

Vallis Aricinae silva praecinctus opaca
    est lacus, antiqua religione sacer.
hic latet Hippolytus loris direptus equorum,
    unde nemus nullis illud aditur equis.
licia dependent longas velantia saepes,
    et posita est meritae multa tabella deae.
saepe potens voti, frontem redimita coronis,
    femina lucentes portat ab urbe faces.
regna tenent fortes manibus pedibusque fugaces,
    et perit exemplo postmodo quisque suo.
defluit incerto lapidosus murmure rivus:
    saepe, sed exiguis haustibus, inde bibi.
Egeria est quae praebet aquas, dea grata Camenis:
    illa Numae coniunx consiliumque fuit.

Ringed with dark woods under Aricia's lee
There lies a lake of age-old sanctity.
Here lurks Hippolytus by horses rent
(Hence to that grove no horse may e'er be sent).
Tablets on threads the long-drawn fences crowd,
Thank-offerings for the goddess' favour vowed;
And many a woman brings, for answered prayer,
Torches from Rome, with garlands on her hair.
The strong of arm and fleet of foot there reign,
And as he slew each slayer will be slain.
A pebbly brook flows fitfully murmuring nigh;
Oft have I drunk of it, but sparingly;
Egeria, Numa's wife and counsellor,
Loved of the Muses, doth that water pour.

Other stories that are vivid he claims to have picked up in talk. On April 19, it appears, foxes were let loose in the Circus Maximus with burning torches tied to their tails, as part of the shows in honour of Ceres, and Ovid tells a myth to account for this.*[13]

> Frigida Carseolis nec olivis apta ferendis
>   terra, sed ad segetes ingeniosus ager;
> hac ego Pelignos, natalia rura, petebam,
>   parva, sed assiduis uvida semper aquis.
> hospitis antiqui solitas intravimus aedes;
>   dempserat emeritis iam iuga Phoebus equis.
> is mihi multa quidem sed et haec narrare solebat,
>   unde meum praesens instrueretur opus:
> 'hoc' ait 'in campo' (campumque ostendit) 'habebat
>   rus breve cum duro parca colona viro.
> ille suam peragebat humum, sive usus aratri
>   seu curvae falcis sive bidentis erat.
> haec modo verrebat stantem tibicine villam,
>   nunc matris plumis ova fovenda dabat,
> aut virides malvas aut fungos colligit albos,
>   aut humilem grato calfacit igne focum.
> et tamen assiduis exercet bracchia telis
>   adversusque minas frigoris arma parat.
> filius huius erat primo lascivus in aevo
>   addideratque annos ad duo lustra duos.
> is capit extremi vulpem convalle salicti:
>   abstulerat multas illa cohortis aves.
> captivam stipula faenoque involvit et ignes
>   admovet: urentes effugit illa manus:
> qua fugit incendit vestitos messibus agros;
>   damnosis vires ignibus aura dabat.
> factum abiit, monumenta manent; nam dicere certa
>   nunc quoque lex vulpem Carseolana vetat,
> utque luat poenas gens haec Cerealibus ardet,
>   quoque modo segetes perdidit, ipsa perit.'

> *At Carseoli the land is cold, unfit*
> *For oliveyards, but corncrops thrive in it.*

* Frazer (*ad loc.*) thinks that a fox bound up in straw was burnt on April 19 simply as a warning to foxes to leave the fields alone.

Passing that way to my Pelignian dale,
My little home whose waters never fail,
A friendly house I entered, oft a guest,
When now the Sun had loosed his steeds for rest.
My host was wont to furnish for my pen
Many a tale, and this he told me then:
'Once on the plain out here'—he waved his hand—
'A frugal wife and husband had some land.
He with the plough his little plot would work,
Now use a sickle, or again a fork;
While she would sweep their humble, wood-propped farm,
Anon put eggs under a hen to warm,
Or gather mallows green or mushrooms white
Or keep the hearthstone's cheerful blaze alight,
And tireless yet find time to ply her loom,
Weaving defences 'gainst the cold to come.
A son she had, mischievous as his age—
Twelve years he'd run of earthly pilgrimage—
Who caught a fox beyond the willow-den
That from the coop had stolen many a hen;
He wrapped the wretch in straw and hay, and gan
Set fire to him: he felt the fire and ran;
Where'er he ran he set the crops alight
And breezes fanned the flames' destructive might.
The event, forgot, has left memorial,
For here to name a fox is criminal;
And penance still is done at Ceres' feast,
When, as he burnt the crops, so burns that beast.'

This glimpse of the eager listener is followed shortly by one of the eager inquirer.[14] Returning one evening from Nomentum to Rome—the date was April 25—Ovid fell in with a crowd clothed in white for ceremonial purity which was escorting a priest to the grove of a typically Roman deity—Mildew (*Robigo*). (The procession of the Robigalia was long continued on this day by the Church, still as a protection for the crops against mildew but now

under the patronage of St Mark.)[15] He immediately approached
the officiating Flamen Quirinalis, to find out why he was going to
burn the entrails of a dog and a sheep at the grove, and overheard
his prayer, which was designed not only to protect crops but to
divert the deity, in his cognate capacity as rust, from agricultural
to warlike implements. Having put on the flames the entrails,
which apparently caused a shudder to the sensitive poet, used
though he must have been to such sights—

> turpiaque obsceni (vidimus) exta canis—

the Flamen answered his question, at least as regards the dog: it
was a substitute for the parching Dog-star.*

The personal approach that we find everywhere in the *Fasti* is
a happy legacy from the *Aetia* of Callimachus. One might be
tempted to suppose that Ovid was merely enlivening his work
with the fiction of autopsy, but the thought is banished by a
passage such as this:[16]

> Est mihi (sitque, precor, nostris diuturnior annis)
>   filia, qua felix sospite semper ero.
> hanc ego cum vellem genero dare, tempora taedis
>   apta requirebam, quaeque cavenda forent:
> tum mihi post sacras monstratur Iunius Idus
>   utilis et nuptis, utilis esse viris,
> primaque pars huius thalamis aliena reperta est;
>   nam mihi sic coniunx sancta Dialis ait:
> 'donec ab Iliaca placidus purgamina Vesta
>   detulerit flavis in mare Thybris aquis,
> non mihi dentosa crinem depexere buxo,
>   non ungues ferro subsecuisse licet,
> non tetigisse virum, quamvis Iovis ille sacerdos,
>   quamvis perpetua sit mihi lege datus.
> tu quoque ne propera. melius tua filia nubet,
>   ignea cum pura Vesta nitebit humo.'

> *I have a daughter (may she me survive,*
> *For while she lives 'tis joy to be alive).*

---

* Ovid seems to have confused its evening setting with its rising (904).

When I would fix her wedding-day, I sought
To know which times were lucky, which were not.
After the sacred Ides of June, 'twas said,
Was most auspicious both for man and maid:
June's earlier half ill sped the marriage yoke.
For thus the holy Flaminica spoke:
'Till yellow Tiber to the sea consign
All that is purged from Ilian Vesta's shrine,
I may not cut, I may not groom my hair
With boxwood comb, my nails I may not pare,
Nor touch a man, though priest of Jove he be
And mine by law in perpetuity.
So haste not thou, nor make thy girl a bride
Till fiery Vesta's floor be purified.'

There is something quaint and very Roman about this incident
of the sceptical poet consulting the grave lady with her elaborate
taboos, whom on another festival he had seen begging ceremonially
for the *februa* (means of purification) and being given, for some
reason, a sprig of pine;[17] but whatever he may have thought himself, he was not the one to disregard the feelings of his daughter,
and anyway many hardened rationalists have their superstitions.
The idea that the whole of May as well as the first half of June
was unlucky for marriage was deep-rooted, though Ovid ascribes
it only to the *vulgus*;*[18] Frazer says that it persists in England,
and Ripert claims to have seen a throng of wedding parties in their
best besieging the *mairie* of Marseilles on April 30.[19] On another
occasion Ovid, returning down the *Via Nova* at the time of Vesta's
festival, was astonished to see a lady descending barefoot, till an
old woman who lived near by invited him to sit down beside her
and explained that this custom was a survival of the distant days
before the *Cloaca Maxima* and other sewers drained the Forum,
when the *Lacus Curtius* was indeed a lake.[20]

Now and then he gives us what purports at least to be a glimpse

* One of Plutarch's suggestions, 'Is it because in that month many of the Latins
sacrifice to the dead?' is probably correct.[21]

249

of his work in progress: 'For a long time I fondly imagined there were images of Vesta, but then I discovered there are none under her dome';[22] or again, 'Three or four times I went all through the calendar, but could find nowhere the Day of Sowing, till the Muse, observing me, interposed, "That day is appointed each year: why look for a movable feast in the calendar?"'*[23] This co-operation of the Muses and other deities, a feature of the *Aetia* of Callimachus, is the commonest piece of 'stage business' with which Ovid seeks to enliven his poem.[24]   As the weird, impressive train of Cybele passes, the poet takes courage, in spite of the awe-inspiring din of flutes and cymbals, to ask the goddess of whom he may inquire their purpose, and is referred to her granddaughters, the Muses.[25]   Indeed, various deities themselves are freely summoned for cross-examination. When he questions Minerva about the Lesser Quinquatrus, the learned goddess answers him after laying aside her spear—though the poet cannot be sure that he is quoting her *ipsissima verba*.[26] For information about the Lemuria, or festival of the dead, he naturally summons by prayer the conductor of the dead to Hades, Mercury.[27]   As he muses, tablet in hand like Callimachus premeditating the *Aetia*, on the identity of Janus, the house grows brighter and suddenly the god himself appears, with his two faces, his staff and key; the poet is duly terrified, his heart frozen and hair standing on end.[28] But elsewhere, by way of variety, he turns to account his *not* having seen Vesta, whose temple no man might enter:[29]

> Non equidem vidi (valeant mendacia vatum)
>   te, dea, nec fueras aspicienda viro.
>
> *I saw thee not (begone, poetic lies!),*
> *Goddess on whom no man should e'er set eyes.*

Rapt in prayer he *felt* the presence of divinity, and a glory shone around; and with no apparent instructor he felt his ignorance enlightened and his errors banished.

---

* I.e. the *permanent* calendar.

In arranging his work Ovid seems to have sought to keep his books roughly equal in length; thus, Book IV having reached 950 lines, he postpones treatment of the rites of Flora, which began on April 28, until the book on May, since they conveniently extended into that month.[30] In spite of the licence he took of ἀσυμμετρία—expatiating on one topic, merely referring to another —he seems to have felt constrained to devote two hundred lines to so well known a story as that of Ceres and Proserpine, even though he was telling it elsewhere at still greater length,[*][31] introducing it with a not very reassuring apology:

> Exigit ipse locus raptus ut virginis edam:
> plura recognosces, pauca docendus eris.

> *The Virgin's rape must here perforce be told:*
> *Some may be new to you, though most be old.*

How did it come about that the *Fasti* were never completed? Four lines in the *Tristia* tell us the beginning of the story:[32]

> Sex ego Fastorum scripsi totidemque libellos,
> cumque suo finem mense libellus habet;
> idque tuo nuper scriptum sub nomine, Caesar,
> et tibi sacratum sors mea rupit opus.

Efforts have been made to twist the obvious meaning of these words, but they are futile. The first line says (as well as a poet can say it in a metre which does not admit of the word *dŭŏdĕcim*[†]) that the *Fasti* comprised twelve books, and the second line merely adds that each book covered one month; the third tells us that it was written recently, and inscribed and dedicated to Caesar, who must be Augustus, and the fourth that the poet's exile interrupted the work. We know in any case, even if we could not have guessed, that twelve books were planned, since he thrice postpones a topic with a promise to treat it in its proper place in one of the last six

---

* For a possible explanation see pp. 149–50.
† Cf. *F.* VI, 725: *sex et totidem luces* for 'twelve'.

months,[33] and presumably *scripsi* indicates that the last six books
were indeed to some extent drafted.

Six books, then, were reasonably complete, but the remaining
six only in a rough form. If Catullus found it hard to write poetry
at Verona, separated from his library at Rome,[34] how much
harder would it be for Ovid to continue the *Fasti* on the confines
of barbary. He says as much in the *Tristia*:[35]

> non hic librorum, per quos inviter alerque
> copia.

I have here no supply of books, to stimulate and sustain me.

Even if he took a modicum of source-books with him, he would
lack the help and stimulus of daily observation and discussion, and,
indeed, the minute recollection of what went on in Rome might
be painful to him. He put the *Fasti* aside, and turned his energies
to poems designed to compass his recall. That was his prime
objective, and while he nursed a spark of hope that he would
succeed there was every reason why the torso of the *Fasti* should
remain on the shelf. A few odd passages in later authors which
might seem to show knowledge of the last six books are easily
explained away, and are as nothing compared with the fact that
writers such as Lactantius, who quote freely from Books I–VI,
quote nothing as coming from the remainder.

The rest of the story is guess-work, but reasonably certain. In
A.D. 14, six years later, Augustus died. Tiberius, his successor,
presented little hope of a relaxation, but his nephew and adoptive
son Germanicus might be sympathetic. He was a charming and
popular prince with an interest in literature, who had himself, like
Cicero, made a verse translation of Aratus' *Phaenomena*.[36] He had
at some time for Quaestor Ovid's stepson-in-law Suillius, whom
the exiled poet implored to intercede with his adored master and
act as intermediary.* And when, after establishing peace by his

---

* Tacitus, *Ann.* IV, 31; Ovid, *P.* IV, 8. See esp. l. 67,

> non potes officium *vatis* contemnere *vates*,

where Ovid has turned from Suillius to address Germanicus directly, and ll. 33ff.,
which seem to promise the dedication of a poem to him.

operations in Germany,* he was appointed in the autumn of 16 to go on a mission to the East next year, Ovid's hopes must have soared. He did eventually visit the Sea of Marmora and look on the Black Sea; and though by then the poet was dead, the rumour of his plans may have long preceded him.

This would amply account for the fact that the *Fasti* as we have them are dedicated, not to Augustus, as stated in *Tr.* II, 551, but to Germanicus. The death of Augustus had in any case made some changes in the *Fasti* necessary; and besides, the ageing poet, now close on sixty, could scarcely hope to conceive and complete against time a new poem of any weight: what he could perhaps do was re-dress the abandoned *Fasti*. But our text shows clearly that he only succeeded in treating Book I before death overtook him about the end of 17.† An executor presumably gave to the world Books I–VI much as he found them,‡ and if he came upon any draft of Books VII–XII, decided that it was too rough to publish.§

Thomas Keightley, in the Preface to his edition of the *Fasti* (1848), commented on the variety of their appeal and exclaimed: 'There is not, perhaps, in the whole compasss of classical literature a work better calculated to be put into the hands of students.' That begs many questions, and in assessing the poem we must distinguish at least three main aspects—its relation to the Roman public for which it was written, its contribution to our knowledge of religious history and cognate subjects, and its merits for us as literature. Let us deal with these in turn.

The close of the *Metamorphoses*, as we have seen, was a highly

---

* Ovid refers, perhaps by anticipation, to his triumph, I, 285 ff.

† This has long been recognized. A dozen passages in Book I belong clearly to the revised version. There is indeed one passage in a later book, IV, 81–2, addressed to Germanicus from exile, which presumably dates from this period; but with the exception of this, and perhaps of VI, 666, all the other passages in the *Fasti* which refer to the exile or to events subsequent to it occur in Book I.[37]

‡ It is hardly conceivable that Ovid intended to retain at VI, 318–48 the story of Priapus and Vesta which is a doublet of that of Priapus and Lotis at I, 393–440.

§ Peter's view that II, 3–18, addressed to Augustus, may be the original prologue to Book I, inserted here by Ovid's executor, has found widespread acceptance, and may well be right. See however Fränkel, *op. cit.* p. 239, n. 8.

rhetorical eulogy of Julius Caesar, extolling his conquests and deploring his murder, and of Augustus, as his still greater successor.* The contemporary *Fasti*, with more frequent opportunities, display the same spirit of unbridled adulation, which goes beyond anything in the later work of Propertius and Horace, let alone Virgil, and presages the excesses of the Silver Age poets.† Julius Caesar deserved his place in the story for his reform of the calendar, but Ovid must needs inflate by suggesting that the interest of 'that god' in the stars was prompted by a desire to have foreknowledge of the heavenly mansions to which he was destined.[38] If a compliment is paid in passing to Pompey,

> Magne, tuum nomen rerum est mensura tuarum,
>
> *Magnus, your name is the measure of your exploits,*

it is only to make the point that his conqueror had an even greater name;[39] there is nothing of the republican sympathy of a Livy or a Lucan. The tyrannicides were sacrilegious murderers (but Vesta foiled them, for it was only a wraith of Caesar they stabbed), and the revenge taken at Philippi had been the first duty of his successor.[40]

It was, however, in token not only of this but of his recovery of the standards lost over thirty years before by Crassus at Carrhae that Augustus erected in his own new forum the great temple of Mars the Avenger.[41] The fact that such a signal and symbolic diplomatic victory could be won without bloodshed made a great impression at Rome and gave peace-loving poets their chance. The *Fasti* dwell singularly little on fighting.‡ It is as peacemaker that Augustus is chiefly hailed by Ovid:

> Caesaris arma canant alii: nos Caesaris aras...[42]
>
> *let others sing of Caesar's arms: I Caesar's altars—*

---

* xv, 745–870. The references to passages in the *Fasti* bearing on Augustanism are conveniently collected by K. Allen, 'The Fasti of Ovid and the Augustan Propaganda', *A.J.P.* 1922, pp. 250–66.

† Ovid seeks to claim credit for this (*Tr.* II, 53–76).

‡ Heinze suggests that one of the few exceptions, the story of the Fabii at II, 195–242, may have been introduced as a compliment to the poet's exalted friend Paullus Fabius Maximus; its epic style contrasts with that of the rest of the poem (*op. cit.* pp. 43 ff.).

and greatest among these altars was the Ara Pacis, voted in 13 B.C. when he returned from pacifying Spain and Gaul, and dedicated four years later.* Ovid rises to the occasion:[43]

> Frondibus Actiacis comptos redimita capillos,
>   Pax, ades et toto mitis in orbe mane.
> dum desint hostes, desit quoque causa triumphi:
>   tu ducibus bello gloria maior eris.
> sola gerat miles, quibus arma coerceat, arma,
>   canteturque fera nil nisi pompa tuba;
> horreat Aeneadas et primus et ultimus orbis:
>   si qua parum Romam terra timebat, amet.
> tura, sacerdotes, pacalibus addite flammis,
>   albaque percussa victima fronte cadat,
> utque domus quae praestat eam cum pace perennet,
>   ad pia propensos vota rogate deos.

> *Thy braided tresses wreathed with Actian bay*
> *Come, gentle Peace, in all the world to stay.*
> *If but our foes be gone, let triumphs go:*
> *Thou on our chiefs more glory shalt bestow.*
> *Save to quell arms, no arms let any take,*
> *Nor trumpet sound save in religion's wake,*
> *Lands near and far Aenead valour prove,*
> *And who feared Rome too little, learn to love.*
> *Burn incense, priests, at Peace's festival;*
> *Anointed let the snow-white victim fall;*
> *And pray the gods, disposed such prayers to hear,*
> *The House that brought may have her all the year.*

The striking and well-contrived surprise of *amet* for the metrical equivalent of *timeat* at the end of the line

> si qua parum Romam terra timebat, amet,

---

* Impressive reliefs from this that survived have now been embodied in a reconstruction on the Tiber bank in what was the Campus Martius.

is an indication of how the Augustan attitude to empire had progressed even beyond Virgil's

> parcere subiectis et debellare superbos.
>
> *to spare the yielded and subdue the proud.*

Julius Caesar's experiments in clemency had become an ideal for imperialists.* No praise could be too high for the man who had secured peace and was yet content to be *princeps*, not *dominus*, whose door by Senatorial decree was decorated not only with the laurels of victory but with the crown of civic oak for preserving his fellow-citizens (*ob cives servatos*);[44] he is already *aeternus*, and the poet does not hesitate to compare him with Jupiter.[45] Opportunities would occur for other gods of the *Fasti* also to be ranged on the side of peace, and not merely Ceres or Janus, but Mars himself.[46]

Rome was now at the height of her power and properity, and her citizens realized, with wonder as well as pride, that what they were already calling 'The Eternal City'† had become in a sense the whole world. The poet who composed four centuries later the much-quoted line

> urbem fecisti quod prius orbis erat
>
> *thou hast made the City what was once the world*

was merely rewriting a line from the *Fasti*,

> Romanae spatium est urbis et orbis idem.[47]
>
> *the domains of Rome's city and the world are one.*

Events were moving fast: Ovid remarks that by the time the Senate, Knights and People decreed for Augustus the title of *Pater Patriae* (2 B.C.) history had already conferred it; and now

---

* Ovid expressly credits Augustus with it (*Tr.* II, 39–50).

† III, 72. The phrase occurs first in Tibullus II, 5, 23. Cf. Virgil, *Aen.* I, 276–9; Livy IV, 4, 4; VI, 23, 7.

also, though even that is too late, it is giving him the true title he has long in fact earned of *Pater Orbis*.*

Their wonder was chiefly expressed by contrasting in imagination the rural simplicity of the site which Evander and then Romulus chose with its eventual destiny. This theme, familiar from *Aeneid* VIII and beloved of Augustan poets, occurs time and again in the *Fasti*; a single instance may be quoted, where Evander, guided from Arcadia by his prophetess mother Carmentis, comes upon the spot:[48]

> Iamque ratem doctae monitu Carmentis in amnem
>   egerat et Tuscis obvius ibat aquis:
> fluminis illa latus cui sunt vada iuncta Tarenti
>   aspicit, et sparsas per loca sola casas;
> utque erat, immissis puppem stetit ante capillis,
>   continuitque manum torva regentis iter,
> et procul in dextram tendens sua bracchia ripam
>   pinea non sano ter pede texta ferit;
> neve daret saltum properans insistere terrae
>   vix est Evandri vixque retenta manu;
> 'di' que 'petitorum' dixit 'salvete locorum,
>   tuque novos caelo terra datura deos,
> fluminaque et fontes, quibus utitur hospita tellus,
>   et nemorum nymphae naïadumque chori,
> este bonis avibus visi natoque mihique
>   ripaque felici tacta sit ista pede!
> fallor, an hi fient ingentia moenia colles
>   iuraque ab hac terra cetera terra petet?
> montibus his olim totus promittitur orbis.
>   quis tantum fati credat habere locum?'

> *And now, at sage Carmentis' word, he neared*
> *A river-mouth, and up the Tiber steered;*
> *Till she the bank Tarentum's pool beside,*
> *A lonely spot with scattered huts, espied;*

---

* This I take to be the meaning of II, 127–30.

Then straight before the poop, with streaming hair,
Wildly she stood and checked the steersman there,
And, arm outstretched towards the right-hand shore,
With frenzied foot thrice smote the pinewood floor.
Scarce, in the nick of time, Evander's hand
Saved her from leaping, fain to reach that land.
'All hail!' she cried, 'Gods of this long-sought place,
Thou land that shalt increase the heavenly race,
Rivers and springs this hospitable ground
Enjoys, and groves where naiads dance their round!
Greet with good omen me and this my son,
And bless the foot that steps your bank upon.
Shall not these slopes give place to walls immense
And every nation justice seek from thence?
These hills, 'tis promised, shall possess the earth.
Wondrous such destiny should here have birth!'

In the same way the Augustans loved to contrast the simplicity of the first Roman buildings with the splendour of those they now saw, to think of the wattle huts of King Numa's day with roofs of thatch where now stood great buildings roofed with bronze, and of his palace on whose foundations the small round temple of Vesta was said to stand,[49] or contemplate the rude shack on the edge of the Palatine still shown as the dwelling of Romulus.[50] Jupiter in those days could scarcely stand upright in his little temple, and the thunderbolt he held was of clay; and men carried foliage to the Capitol where now they carry jewels.[51] (Here pride had to yield to that deprecation of modern luxury, which in theory was good form for every Augustan writer, and in practice was embodied in sumptuary laws.)

Such thoughts stir feelings that spring from deep in the human heart. Ovid was struck by the contrast of Romulus, son of Mars and destined for heaven, asleep on his humble pallet:

In stipula placidi capiebat munera somni,
    sed tamen ex illo venit in astra toro.[52]

How sound he slept, content on straw to lie,
Yet from that couch ascended to the sky!

In that couplet lies half the appeal of what was to become the Christmas legend.

The *Aeneid* is the inspiration of the fine rhetorical passage with which Carmentis concluded her prophecy.[53] Particularly moving is the apostrophe to Pallas, the young son of Evander whose death in Book x so roused Aeneas against Turnus: her first thought is to save him, but instantly she checks herself from seeking to frustrate in the interest of her own personal feelings the great purposes of destiny:

Et iam Dardaniae tangent haec litora pinus:
   hic quoque causa novi femina Martis erit.
care nepos, Palla, funesta quid induis arma?
   indue! non humili vindice caesus eris.
victa tamen vinces eversaque, Troia, resurges:
   obruet hostiles ista ruina domos.
urite victrices Neptunia Pergama flammae!
   num minus hic toto est altior orbe cinis?
iam pius Aeneas sacra et, sacra altera, patrem
   adferet: Iliacos accipe, Vesta, deos!
tempus erit cum vos orbemque tuebitur idem,
   et fient ipso sacra colente deo,
et penes Augustos patriae tutela manebit:
   hanc fas imperii frena tenere domum.
inde nepos natusque dei, licet ipse recuset,
   pondera caelesti mente paterna feret;
utque ego perpetuis olim sacrabor in aris,
   sic Augusta novum Iulia numen erit.

Soon shall Dardanian vessels touch these shores;
Once more a woman shall give rise to wars.*
Pallas, dear grandson, why gird on thy bane?—
Gird it! a hero shall avenge thee slain.

* Lavinia, daughter of Latinus, betrothed to Turnus, whom Aeneas married.

Thou, conquered Troy, shalt conquer, overthrown
Shalt rise: that ruin shall thy foes cast down.
Triumph, ye flames, o'er Neptune's Ilium hurled:
Yet shall its ashes overtop the world;
Aeneas shall his gods and sire convoy,
Both sacred: Vesta, welcome gods of Troy!
Some day shalt thou and earth one guardian share:
A god himself shall for thy service care;*
The Augustan line shall keep the fatherland,
The reins of empire destined to their hand.
The third, though fain the burden to decline,
God-born, shall handsel it with mind divine;
And, e'en as altars shall be raised to me,
Julia Augusta shall a goddess be.†

The *Aeneid* and the history of Livy are the greatest monuments to the Augustan desire to reawaken in the Roman people a pride in their past, but the *Fasti* too could play its part. In a long passage Ovid traces the descent of Romulus through his mother Ilia back to the Trojan dynasty and to Jupiter himself, not omitting to mention Solymus, a companion of Aeneas, who was the mythical founder of Sulmo;[54] in another he speaks of the proud titles, derived from the conquest of this land or that, which were engraved under the ancestral masks displayed round their halls by Roman aristocrats entitled to the *ius imaginum*; of Scipio *Africanus*, of Servilius *Isauricus*, of Metellus *Creticus* and Metellus *Numidicus*, of that Valerius who took Messana in the second Punic War and became the first *Messalla*, of Scipio *Numanticus*, and finally of the ill-fated Drusus *Germanicus*, whose son he was now addressing; and then of honourable titles other than territorial, Manlius *Torquatus*, Pompeius *Magnus*, and the proud name of a family with which he was brought in contact by his third marriage, Fabius

---

* Augustus transferred the sacred fire of Vesta to his own house on the Palatine; cf. IV, 949.

† The last four lines belong, of course, to the second draft. For Tiberius' reluctance see Tacitus, *Ann.* I, 11. Livia became Iulia Augusta after Augustus' death, by his will; she did not in fact become a goddess until Claudius' reign.

Maximus.[55] True, Ovid only rehearses these in order to lead up to
the glory of the Emperor, who would be entitled to a *cognomen*
drawn from every race in the world, and whose surname of
Augustus is distinguished from those above by its associations with
the divine; yet nevertheless the very roll of names awakens echoes
of the Sixth *Aeneid.*

As for Augustus' *cura morum et legum,* the author of the *Ars
Amatoria* makes a couple of references in the *Fasti* to the Emperor's
zeal for chastity,*[56] and one, more interesting, to his gesture
against luxury in destroying the huge palace of the infamous Vedius
Pollio, though he had himself inherited it.†[57] But the main
emphasis is naturally on the religious revival, which he inaugurated
as early as 28 B.C. with a great programme for the restoration of
temples, amplified with the Ludi Saeculares in 17, and furthered
by succeeding Lepidus as Pontifex Maximus in 12. Addressing
him, in a phrase reminiscent of Livy,[58] as

templorum positor, templorum sancte repostor,

founder of temples, holy restorer of temples,

Ovid praises him for restoring the temple of Juno Sospita, as else-
where for that of the Great Mother, and through Livia, that of the
Good Goddess.‡[59] Besides founding new temples for Divus Julius
and Mars Ultor, and the Ara Pacis, he established the Lares
Compitales in his 265 parishes (*vici*) throughout the City, his own
Genius being set among them; and when he became Pontifex
Maximus, instead of going to live in the old official residence (the
Regia) between the Forum and the House of the Vestals, he
dedicated to Vesta a chapel and altar in his own palace. All these
actions are recorded by Ovid with approval.[60]

---

* II, 139; VI, 457. Fränkel rightly points the contrast between II, 139 and
A.A. I, 131–4 (*op. cit.* p. 239, n. 7).

† The Portico of Livia was built on the site of Vedius' palace.

‡ The reference to the dedication, in 10 B.C., of the Temple of Concord is one
of the insertions made in the second draft of Book 1 (637 ff.) during the poet's
exile.

In fact he could hardly have put his pen more completely at the service of the regime. The trouble is that, while no doubt it did not go against the grain for him to do so (since in any case he does not seem to have been a man of strong principles), he cannot in his heart have cared genuinely about such propaganda. With Virgil, and to a less extent Horace, one feels that there was an important side of their character which deeply sympathized with what Augustus was trying to do—indeed, these two probably helped to determine his policy to some extent; but nothing that we know about Ovid from his previous works would suggest an enthusiasm for moral regeneration; while as for the religious revival, we may reasonably suppose that Augustus himself merely took the view that, irrespective of belief, it is the greatest security for a decent degree of social order, and are we to suppose that Ovid was more religious than the Emperor?* Roman religion was a formalistic affair, deserving for the most part to be called rather superstition; deities like Cardea, goddess of hinges, Limentinus, god of thresholds, are the barest of abstractions, well deserving St Augustine's mockery.[61] It would perhaps be better to call it *Latin* religion, for it goes back to the animism of the agricultural community that preceded the miraculous growth of the city. At first everything around a man seemed somehow alive and part of a universe where magic ruled. Next came a vague belief in spirits that had to be propitiated, leading in turn to the idea that certain places were particularly holy, which the Romans expressed by saying that there must be a divinity there—*numen inest*.† Many *numina* acquired names and special functions. Out of such beginnings, overlaid with the highly developed structure of Greek religion and mythology, grew the complicated round of ceremonies that marked the Roman year. Among the educated that

---

* For his attitude see pp. 190–2.

† E.g. *F.* III, 296, of a grove on the Aventine. For Ovid's realization of underlying animism see his remark at VI, 291, on Vesta as the living flame,

nec tu aliud Vestam quam vivam intellige flammam.

C. Bailey, Introd. to edn. of Book III (1921), p. 23. He gives a good account of the growth of Roman religious ideas.

godfearing habit of mind (δεισιδαιμονία), to which Polybius attributed this people's rise to world-power, faded with the influx of Greek philosophy and rationalism in the second century; but the other great national characteristic of conservatism ensured the survival of the rites themselves.

In general, Ovid treats this religion with an affectation of naïve faith: it would have been out of place to indulge either in theological speculation or in open irony. But once or twice the old Ovid peeps through the mask. Saturn, warned by an oracle that his son would overthrow him, devoured his offspring as soon as they were born; fretting at this, his wife Rhea swaddled a stone, and he swallowed it instead of the new-born Jupiter. In telling this grotesque Hesiodic tale the poet cannot help interjecting, surely not without irony, 'antiquity is believed in default of good witness: do not shake established belief'.[62] His Flora, about to recount how she contrived the virgin birth of Mars out of Juno, expresses a hope that Jupiter may never find out, which makes him comically anthropomorphic,[63] and Mars in turn is grotesquely fooled by Anna Perenna.[64] Again, the rationalistic outburst against the efficacy of water to purify from murder might well suggest insidious doubts about the efficacy of any ritual purification.[65] Ovid's Claudia Quinta, the Vestal falsely rumoured to be unchaste, is not, as others might have made her, 'of a holy, cold and still conversation', but a gay and high-spirited girl:[66]

> Cultus et ornatis varie prodire capillis
>   obfuit, ad rigidos promptaque lingua senes;

> *Her style, her varied coiffure, and a tongue*
> *That answered back old carpers did her wrong.*

The Augustan ideas were at least new when Virgil and Horace proclaimed them, but it is hard to believe that where they seem to us trite and mechanical in Ovid they did not seem trite and mechanical to his contemporaries also. No brilliance of expression could refresh them. A whole generation had had them dinned into its ears. However, a large part of the *Fasti* comprises legends or descriptions of old customs. It is true that, even when treating of these, Ovid remained a man of his times:

laudamus veteres, sed nostris utimur annis.[67]

we praise the ancients, but act according to our own times.

He was not like Livy, who said that when he told of ancient times he became an ancient in soul: in the words of Gaston Boissier, 'il ramène à lui l'antiquité au lieu d'aller vers elle'.[68] But in a literary or antiquarian way he does seem to have relished them, so that from time to time his verse-almanack does come to life.

This brings us to our second question—what profit can antiquarians, astronomers or students of comparative religion derive from the *Fasti*? Sir James Frazer thought it worth a monumental edition in five volumes, and Warde Fowler in his *Preface* to *The Roman Festivals* asserted that the only sound method of exhibiting the religious side of the Roman character was to follow the Roman Calendar, testimonies which sufficiently indicate that at lowest the work forms a convenient text or basis for discussion of the topics it deals with.

First of all, let us clear away the astronomical portions. Cicero remarked that Aratus 'homo ignarus astrologiae', had written an excellent poem on astronomy,[69] and ignorance of astronomy would not deter Ovid or seem to his readers a *prima facie* disqualification. He himself, like Cicero and Germanicus, at some period wrote a hexameter *Phaenomena* after Aratus.[70] But he was indeed as ignorant as most of us are, and these portions are full of blunders, exposed in detail by Ideler more than a century ago.[71] Admittedly some of his mistakes are traceable to the Julian calendar itself, for Caesar's astronomer Sosigenes came from Alexandria and sometimes followed works based on observations made in that latitude; while others, un-Julian but common to Ovid and Columella, were presumably derived from another source used by both, which in turn drew partly on observations made in more southerly latitudes.[72] But he had clearly no understanding of the

264

principles of the subject, being a townsman writing a work of literature for townsmen who had long since regulated their lives by looking at calendars instead of stars.* They had recently acquired a reliable one, and Ovid's astronomy could have no practical value except as an advertisement for it; nor can it have much practical value for us, since it gives a distorted version of contemporary knowledge, let alone of scientific truth.

As for the rest of his material, there is no good reason to doubt that he consulted many authorities, though unlike Callimachus he names none. His other works suggest that he was a voracious reader. (On the literary side we are reminded of this by his incidental rendering of a Greek epigram by Evenus.)[73] He twice bids his reader inspect a number of calendars of Latin and Sabine towns, reporting what will be found in each with the implication at least that he himself has had access to them, though some of his statements about them conflict with other authorities, and of course he may be relying on some previous collator.[74] What he professes himself to have witnessed we have no reason to suspect.

What we may suspect is that he did not think deeply about what he read. He will give us five possible derivations of the *Agonalia*, or four possible reasons for Romulus having divided the year into ten months, or seven possible origins of the custom of fumigation, and leave the matter there.[75] His ideas about the derivation of words strike us aghast—*Janus* from *Chaos*, *carpenta* from *Carmentis*, *Latium* from *latere* (because Saturn hid there from Jupiter), *Vesta* from *vi stare*†[76]—though these are no more absurd than etymologies found in Varro and other more scholarly ancients. More reprehensible, he will support one version in one place, and another in another, from sheer literary opportunism. In I, 123–4 the gates of Janus are shut to keep War inside, whereas in I, 281 it is Peace who is to be confined there for safety. Where

---

* It is hardly likely that the countrymen and sailors who did still live by the stars were readers of Ovid.

† Fränkel reminds us that scientific etymology, long practised in India, did not reach the West till the nineteenth century.[77]

Romulus is to be glorified, the murder of Remus is ascribed to Celer, and his brother's grief is emphasized; but where Augustus is to be glorified by comparison with Romulus, then it is implied that Romulus is the murderer.[78] The origin of the name of May is in dispute. The Muse Polyhymnia derives it from *maiestas*, Urania from *maiores*, Calliope from *Maia*, and Ovid, observing that three Muses vote for each, declines to decide between them; yet in the same book he can remark casually,

mensis erat Maius, *maiorum* nomine dictus,[79]

and in the next he can make Juno presume *Maia* and Hebe *maiores*, according as it suits the present argument of each.[80] Let us accept the fact: Ovid was interested primarily in rhetorical or literary effect, and only secondarily in truth.

In an important passage Wissowa gave a warning against unwary use of Ovid as a source for scientific deductions.* He characterizes him justly as 'a poet equipped with neither very extensive nor deep knowledge, and very little understanding for the peculiar characteristics of Roman religion, but compensated for this with a rich imagination and an outstanding gift for painting'. A most revealing passage is I, 89, where Ovid says, 'But what god am I to say you are, Janus of double shape? For Greece has no divinity like you.' Whenever he could, he equated a Latin with a Greek deity, and was at once supplied with material; for Latin mythology in itself was jejune. Faunus, equated with Pan, becomes *semicaper* and *biformis*, Virbius is the Greek Hippolytus, Stimula is Semele, Mater Matuta is Ino, Libera is Ariadne. Not that Ovid was necessarily the first to make the identification: thus Faunus in Horace inhabits Pan's Mount Lycaeus, and the story of Menelaus and Proteus in the *Odyssey* had probably already been adapted to Numa and Picus.[81]

There is a common idea that the *Fasti* are a source of unique

---

* *Ges. Abh. zur röm. Religions- und Stadtgeschichte* (1904), pp. 136 ff. For a good summary of how the *Fasti* should be used see C. Bailey, *op. cit.* p. 24.

importance for knowledge of Roman religion.* Let us take a sample, and see how much information Ovid adds to what we know in any case from other sources (irrespective of whether those sources may have drawn from him). Book 1 will do as well as any other. Let us isolate each piece of information it gives, and check it against Frazer's notes, which supply references for other ancient sources in each case. The residue is remarkably meagre. We have no other authority for the sacrifice of a cock to Night (455). In some cases we have heard of a general practice and Ovid gives us a specific instance. Thus we know from Columella that, while farmers did no work from January 1 to 12, they did a token job, *auspicandi causa*, on New Year's Day; Ovid indicates that the same was true of lawyers.[82] We know from Varro that the Rex Sacrorum sacrificed a ram on the *Agonalia*; Ovid specifies that it was to Janus.[83] We know from Varro again that there were shrines into which leather might not be brought because of its connexion with the slaughter of animals; Ovid tells us that that of Carmentis was one.[84] For what it is worth, he tells us that on the Ides of February the sacrifice to Jupiter was a wether, whereas he and Macrobius specify a ewe-lamb for Ides in general.[85] We know from several sources that dogs were sacrificed to Hecate; Ovid professes to have seen the Thracian tribe of the Sapaeans do this (presumably when on his way to Tomis).[86] In some cases he not only gives an instance but adds what is probably the correct explanation. Martial tells us that a gilded date was often a poor man's New Year present; Ovid adds figs and honey, and explains that the intention is an omen to sweeten the year.[87] The statement (381–2) that sheep were first sacrificed because they cropped holy herbs which an old woman used to offer to the gods refers to a story otherwise unknown; can it be that Ovid invented it, having aetiological stories at hand for the other animals? He was probably right in guessing that cash was given as a present

* E.g. 'Un document de science érudite sur lequel les meilleurs esprits de ce temps n'ont pas craint de s'appuyer pour esquisser un tableau de la religion païenne' (Peeters, *op. cit.* p. 18).

on New Year's Day as an omen (221–2). That, it seems, is the sum total for Book I.*

No, it is as literature rather than a work of scholarship that the *Fasti* must be judged, as a popular introduction to Roman religion; and Warde Fowler, who undertook to expound the Roman Festivals month by month, has as much right as any to sum up. After frankly acknowledging Ovid's shortcomings as an authority he concludes with his own experience, that 'When after the month of June we lose him as a companion, we may feel that the subject not only loses with him what little literary interest it can boast of, but becomes for the most part a mere investigation of fossil rites, from which all life and meaning have departed for ever.'†

We come, then, to the final task of estimating the value of the *Fasti* as literature. Peeters, seeking to exalt it above the *Metamorphoses*, alleges among other things the superiority of its scheme of arrangement.[88] I cannot accept either his judgment or this ground for it. The scheme of the *Metamorphoses* is an ingenious, imaginative *jeu d'esprit*; that of the *Fasti* is a convenient but prosaic rule of thumb. It is true that Roman mythology lacked the coherence which Greek had acquired, while Roman religion largely consisted in scrupulously doing the traditional thing on the traditional day, so that Ovid had less opportunity here to attempt an artistic whole; but we have had occasion before to note his passion for being exhaustive, for bringing everything in;‡ *exigit ipse locus*...having once chosen to follow the calendar, he can leave nothing out. Moreover, the superficial order of the *Fasti* makes things, in some ways, more chaotic. Thus the beginning of Hippolytus' story is told at VI, 737–56 *à propos* the rising of the constellation Anguitenens (identified with Aesculapius, who

---

* Book I does, in addition, contain one contribution to aetiological literature which we find in no other author, the story of Priapus and Lotis (391–440), told to account for the sacrifice of an ass to the obscene god.

† *Op. cit.* p. 14. It is fair to say that Frazer rated the *Fasti* higher as a source for students of comparative religion (Loeb edn., pp. xxi ff.).

‡ Pp. 96, 235.

restored him to life); its natural sequel has already occurred at III, 263–76, in connexion with Egeria. The legends Ovid tells from early Roman history, when marshalled by Frazer in chronological order in his Preface (VII–IX), might lead one to expect a continuous pageant corresponding to the early books of Livy, whereas in fact, of course, the stories are told haphazard wherever opportunity offers. As for the risings and settings of the constellations, their bare intrusion is most inartistic when no story is told in connexion with them.

I have already spoken of an element of triteness, and perhaps also of underlying insincerity, in the sections which can specifically be classed as Augustan propaganda, and there is a certain rhetorical conventionality about other passages. The *nequitia* of youth, out-rageous but alive, has faded into the respectability of middle age, a development which, however gratifying to the moralist, has taken some of the edge off Ovid's writing. We have the conven-tional praise of old, rugged, military Rome uncorrupted by the arts of Greece. Contrast this Philistine couplet,

> Nondum tradiderat victas victoribus artes
> Graecia, facundum sed male forte genus,

> *not yet had the conquered arts been handed over to the*
> *conquerors by Greece, an eloquent but weakling race,*

with Horace's generous enthusiasm,

> Graecia capta ferum victorem cepit, et artes
> intulit agresti Latio;

> *Captured Greece took captive her uncivilized conqueror, and*
> *introduced the arts into rustic Latium;*

who would ever have thought to hear the gruff voice of old Cato grumbling on through Ovid's mouth?*[89] Janus' condemnation

---

* Of course Ovid can turn a pointed couplet on this, as on any theme:
> Qui bene pugnabat, Romanam noverat artem:
> mittere qui poterat pila, disertus erat;
> *He who fought well had learnt the Roman art: he who could aim his javelins*
> *was eloquent;*

of the modern scramble for wealth is eloquent and pointed enough —*in pretio pretium nunc est*—but it is a rhetorical school-piece, and how often we have heard it before! Even that mystic-sounding eulogy of astronomers as being above worldly thoughts strikes one in Ovid as having become by now a conventional *locus*, a stock purple-patch of Pythagorean-style 'sublimity'.* And who can read with much enthusiasm the story of Aristaeus and the bees as told in a few neat couplets when Virgil has told it at length in one of the loveliest passages in all Latin poetry?⁹⁰ One feels continually that Ovid has come into the field too late.

This much said, we can turn to the less invidious task of selecting from the five thousand lines of the poem some examples of what can give pleasure. To begin with there are passages which stand out as interesting for their subject-matter, though of course what seems interesting varies from age to age, and even from person to person. I have already quoted passages which are alive because Ovid is reporting scenes he actually saw, or local tales he heard. Even in bare prose the account of what happened at the festival of Venus on April 1st must intrigue us, if only for its curious details and its difference from anything thinkable to-day:⁹¹

'Duly do you worship the goddess, Latin mothers and brides, and you too who wear not the fillet and long dress [prostitutes]. Take from her marble neck the golden necklaces, take off her rich adornments: the goddess must be bathed entire.† Now dry her neck and restore its golden necklaces; then give her other flowers and fresh roses. Yourselves too she bids to bathe wearing wreaths of green myrtle, and for a certain reason which I will

and again (playing on the double meaning of signum—'constellation' and 'military standard')

> Non illi caelo labentia signa tenebant
> sed sua, quae magnum perdere crimen erat.

* I, 297–310. The thought is best expressed by Ptolemy in the well-known epigram, οἶδ' ὅτι θνατὸς ἐγώ (*A.P.* IX, 577); for its occurrence as a *locus* in Latin, see Manilius I, 40–52 and II, 105–25, referred to by Frazer, *ad loc.*

† The images of gods were often ritually bathed in antiquity. For a good description see Callimachus' elegiac Hymn on the Bath of Pallas (v).

reveal. Once naked on the shore she was drying her oozy locks, when a wanton crew of satyrs espied her. She screened her body with myrtle: thus she was protected, and she bids you do likewise. And now learn why you should offer incense to Fortuna Virilis [Success with Men] in the place that reeks with warm water.* All of you strip when you enter there and every blemish in your body is exposed; Fortuna Virilis enables you to hide this and conceal it from men, if supplicated with a little incense. Nor disdain to take pounded poppy in white milk and liquid honey squeezed from the comb: Venus drank that when first she was escorted to her husband; from that time on she was a bride.'

Ovid's eerie description of the private rite of appeasing ancestral ghosts at the *Lemuria* in May is our only full account of this primeval superstition:[92]

'When now full midnight lends silence to sleep and the dogs and birds of every sort are hushed, the man, mindful of the old rite and fearing the gods, rises (no knot on his feet†) and makes a sign with fingers joined about his thumb,‡ lest in his silence an unsubstantial shade may meet him. After washing his hands clean in spring water he turns, and first takes black beans and throws them away with face averted, saying, 'Lo, these I cast; with these beans I redeem both me and mine'. This he says nine times without looking back; the ghost is believed to gather the beans, following unseen behind. Again he touches water and clashes Temesan bronze, and begs the ghost to depart from his house. When he has said nine times, 'Shades of my fathers, avaunt!' he looks back; for then he deems the rites duly performed.'

Other rites for the dead were performed at their tombs in February in the *Parentalia*:[93]

'The ghosts ask but little: they value devotion more than the richness of the offering: they are not greedy gods that haunt the

---

* In the men's baths. Only women of humbler rank did this.
† For knots as obstacles to magic see Frazer, *ad loc.*
‡ This is the only mention in ancient literature of a gesture against malignant influences still commonly used to avert the Evil Eye (Frazer, *ad loc.*).

Styx. A tile wreathed with votive garlands, a sprinkling of corn, a few grains of salt, bread soaked in wine and scattered violets— that is enough. Leave these on a potsherd in the middle of the road.'

There is something reminiscent of Jacob's sharpness in Numa's verbal wrestling with Jupiter, whom he has conjured down from the sky to his own terror. He has asked the god how to expiate thunderbolts and receives an oracular reply:[94]

> 'Caede caput' dixit: cui rex 'parebimus' inquit:
>   'caedenda est hortis eruta caepa meis.'
> addidit hic 'hominis': 'sumes' ait ille 'capillos'.
>   postulat hic animam. cui Numa 'piscis' ait.
> risit et 'his' inquit, 'facito mea tela procures,
>   o vir colloquio non abigende deum.'

> *'Cut off a head', said Jove. 'It shall be done',*
> *Said Numa, '—we will pluck an onion.'*
> *'A man's', said Jove. 'Yea, thou shalt have—his hair.'*
> *'A life I'll have.' 'A fish's life, I swear.'*
> *Jove laughed, 'Then those my bolts shall expiate,*
> *Man not to be repelled from gods' debate.'*

And whatever the true reason, the Romans did expiate a thunderbolt's fall with onions, hair and sprats.[95] We are here in the realms of magic rather than religion, as also in this scene from among the rites of the dead:[96]

' See, an aged hag seated among girls performs rites to Tacita, but herself is not taciturn. With three fingers she places three lumps of incense under the doorstep, where a little mouse has made its secret track. Then she binds enchanted threads together with dark lead and chews seven black beans; and sewing up and sealing with pitch a small fish's head, pierces it with a bronze needle and roasts it over a fire; wine too she pours on to it, and any there is left she or her companions drink (but she has most). "We have bound hostile tongues and enemy mouths", she says as she departs: then exit drunk.'

Such passages take us far from our world, but there are not a few in which we recognize customs that have counterparts or survivors in modern times. The votive tablets for services rendered and the candles dedicated by grateful women in the shrine of Diana are now offered in many places to another Virgin.[97] We have a passing reference to what would surely have been the climax of the poem if Ovid had completed it, the Saturnalian festivities of December 'welcome to mirthful spirits' (*acceptus geniis*, III, 58). The Purification of the Virgin at Candlemas (February 2) may be a relic of the purificatory rites (*februationes*) from which, as Ovid tells us, the month took its name.[98] The bonfires which peasants in east Europe light, or till recently lit, on St George's Day, and those which Italians lit two thousand years ago on the *Parilia* two days earlier, have probably a common Aryan ancestor.[99] And our pagan rites of May Day are akin to those of the *Floralia*.[100]

Again, how reminiscent of a Bank Holiday crowd on Hampstead Heath is Ovid's description of the carnival of Anna Perenna, which took place beside the Tiber on the Ides of March, a picture worthy of Frith, and incidentally a piquant background to the murder of Julius Caesar:[101]

'The populace arrives, and scattering in knots all over the grass drinks, with each boy lying beside his girl. Some rough it in the open air, a few pitch tents, some make themselves huts of leafy boughs. Others again put up canes for uprights and stretch their gowns over them. With sun and wine they warm up and pray for as many years as they can drain cups, drinking by numbers. There you will find a man who can drink himself as old as Nestor, a woman whose bumpers would make her as old as the Sibyl. There too they sing snatches picked up in the theatre, and keep time to their song with waving hands, and tread uncouth measures around the bowl, while sweethearts in their best dance with streaming hair. On the way home they reel and provide amusement for the crowd, and all who meet them bless them. I met such a procession lately and thought it would make a good story: there was a drunk old woman dragging a drunk old man.'

The *Fasti*, considering their length, have less humour than we should expect from Ovid: he has become, in the words of Peeters, 'une sorte de *vates*, inspiré, grave, et respectueux', somewhat to our regret. There is some rather boisterous fun over the bald and fat Silenus standing greedily on his ass to eat honey from a hollow elm and suddenly mobbed by a swarm of hornets (how Bacchus and the Satyrs laughed!); and the dénouement of the merry tale of Faunus, who attempted to assault Omphale and found she had changed clothes with her bedfellow Hercules, smacks strongly of the *Reve's Tale* in Chaucer.[102] More typically Ovidian is the scene where the babies born of the Rape of the Sabines are being used by their mothers as peacemakers between their parents' families:[103]

> Qui poterat clamabat avum tum denique visum:
> et qui vix poterat posse coactus erat.

> *Those who could speak 'Dear Grandfather!' did cry:*
> *Those who could hardly speak were made to try;*

or the account of the shopkeeper's visit to the spring of that notorious thief Mercury:[104]

> Est aqua Mercurii portae vicina Capenae;
> si iuvat expertis credere, numen inest.
> huc venit incinctus tunica mercator, et urna
> purus suffita, quam ferat, haurit aquam.
> uda fit hinc laurus, lauro sparguntur ab uda
> omnia quae dominos sunt habitura novos;
> spargit et ipse suos lauro rorante capillos
> et peragit solita fallere voce preces:
> 'ablue praeteriti periuria temporis', inquit,
> 'ablue praeteritae perfida verba die;
> sive ego te feci testem falsove citavi
> non audituri numina magna Iovis,
> sive deum prudens alium divamve fefelli,
> abstulerint celeres improba verba Noti,
> et pateant veniente die periuria nobis,
> nec curent superi si qua locutus ero.

da modo lucra mihi, da facto gaudia lucro,
  et fac ut emptori verba dedisse iuvet.'

There is a fountain near the Capene Gate,
Hallowed by Mercury, its clients state.
The loose-clad vendor comes and, duly pure,
Takes water thence in fumigated ewer.
Some bay leaves dipped in this will sprinkle dew
On wares he destines for an owner new;
He sprinkles too with dripping bay his hair
And utters in his trickster's voice a prayer:
'Absolve me from my lies in times gone by;
Absolve me from this day's duplicity;
Whether I called thyself to witness or
By Jove, too high to hear me, falsely swore,
Or against any god with knowledge sinned
Or goddess, may my words be as the wind;
And may the coming day bring scope for lies,
Nor any god regard my perjuries.
Give me but gain and joys that gain confers,
And make it pay to have tricked my customers.'

The graceful rococo charm of the *Metamorphoses* is seldom given play in the *Fasti*, but once or twice it appears when the poet is describing his fictitious relations with the various deities from whom he seeks information. The opening of Book IV on April, the month of Venus, gave an obvious chance, and Ovid handled it to perfection:

'Alma, fave' dixi 'geminorum mater Amorum!'
  ad vatem voltus rettulit illa suos:
'quid tibi' ait 'mecum? certe maiora canebas.
  num vetus in molli pectore vulnus habes?'
'scis, dea' respondi 'de vulnere'. risit, et aether
  protinus ex illa parte serenus erat.
'saucius an sanus numquid tua signa reliqui?
  tu mihi propositum, tu mihi semper opus.'

'Be gracious, Mother of twin Loves', I said.
The goddess to her poet turned her head:
'What would'st with me, pledged to a higher strain?
Doth that soft heart still feel some ancient pain?'
'Thou know'st about the pain', I answered: she
Laughed, and thereat half heaven of clouds was free.
'Wounded or whole, allegiance still I pay
To thee, my earliest theme, my theme for aye.'

Ovid pleads that more serious themes befit his present age, and Venus graciously gives him both absolution and inspiration.

The same quality appears in the exordium to Book VI. After a mock-serious claim that he is directly inspired, though some will say he is lying, he narrates how he was musing in a sequestered grove on the origin of the name of June when three goddesses appeared. The first was Juno, whom he represents not without burlesque as being sensitive as ever about her dignity and rehearsing her titles to pre-eminence; in an eloquent speech she claimed that the month was named after her, just as May was from *Maia*. Her daughter Hebe followed, modestly professing that she would not argue for this honour but only plead as wife of Hercules, Rome's benefactor. She is Youth, and June is derived from *iuvenes* as May was from *maiores*. There was danger of unnatural strife arising between mother and daughter when Concord came and healed it—by propounding a third solution: in June the Romans and Sabines were *iuncti*. Ovid tactfully declines to assume the role of Paris, gives no judgement and leaves it at that.[105]

Occasionally he shows how even the astronomical lore could be presented in a lively way. At VI, 785–90 the device he chose was happily appropriate, since the information conveyed is not quite accurate for June 25:

> Ecce suburbana rediens male sobrius aede
> ad stellas aliquis talia verba iacit:
> 'zona latet tua nunc, et cras fortasse latebit:
> dehinc erit, Orion, aspicienda mihi.'

at si non esset potus, dixisset eadem
    venturum tempus solstitiale die.

Lo, one returning tipsy from a shrine
Without the walls thus hails a starry sign:
'Your belt to-night, to-morrow too maybe,
Unseen, Orion, after that I'll see.'
He might have added, had his head been clear,
'On that same day the solstice will be here.'

On another occasion history is happily linked with astronomy.[106]
The calendar gave for April 6 the Battle of Thapsus, the setting of
Libra, and the expectation of rain: Ovid combines the three:

Tertia lux (memini) ludis erat, ac mihi quidam
    spectanti senior continuusque loco
'haec' ait 'illa dies, Libycis qua Caesar in oris
    perfida magnanimi contudit arma Iubae.
dux mihi Caesar erat, sub quo meruisse tribunus
    glorior: officio praefuit ille meo.
hanc ego militia sedem, tu pace parasti,
    inter bis quinos usus honore viros.'
plura locuturi subito seducimur imbre:
    pendula caelestes Libra movebat aquas.

'Twas on the games' third day: I well recall
My oldish neighbour at the festival,
Who said, 'This day it was, on Libya's coast,
That Caesar crushed proud Juba's treacherous host.
He was my captain, and it is my pride
As tribune to have served him at his side.
This seat of honour war on me confers,
But peace on you and all your Decemvirs.'
A sudden shower cut short this episode:
The Balance hung in heaven shed its load.

In spite of its middle-aged conventionality there are plenty of
traces of Ovidian freshness in the *Fasti*. There are phrases which

stick in the memory, whether for their charm (χάρις) of thought
—*aves, solacia ruris,* or of sound—*Chloris eram quae Flora vocor.* My
first encounter with Latin verse was when I opened a small blue
book of extracts for schoolboys and spelt out

> Puppibus egressus Latia stetit exul in herba;
> felix exilio cui locus ille fuit![107]

*Disembarking, the exile stood on Latin turf; happy the man
who had that place for his banishment!*

I had no idea that the poet was now himself an exile, the second
line a poignant cry of nostalgia. But there was something nimble
and bracing in the rhythm and sound, something fresh and compelling in the picture of this unknown hero disembarking on what
I imagined as our own 'Grassy Beach' by the Firth of Tay, so that
the couplet, which might seem like any other, has haunted me
ever since. There is also something essentially musical about a line
such as

> inter Hamadryadas iaculatricemque Dianam.[108]

It goes without saying that there are passages full of euphonious
names, especially Greek names, whose sound appealed to the ear,
and associations to the romanticism, of Roman listeners;

> Amphiareïades Naupactoö Acheloö[109]

sounds like a transliteration of some Hellenistic line;* Greek forms
enhance the melody of the couplet

> Dindymon et Cybelen et amoenam fontibus Iden
> semper et Iliacas Mater amavit opes,[110]

as of several longer passages.[111]

Nearly a third of the *Fasti* consists of narrative pieces of from
twenty to two hundred lines each. In content many of these
stories are only moderately entertaining for sophisticated readers,

---

* Cf. Virgil, *Ecl.* II, 24,
> Amphion Dircaeus in Actaeo Aracyntho.

being in any case familiar, and much depends on the telling. Heinze, in his classic work already cited, has examined minutely the difference between Ovid's elegiac and his epic narrative style, taking as his basis the story of Ceres and Proserpine, the longest elegiac narrative we possess, and its counterpart in the contemporary *Metamorphoses*,*¹¹² and proceeding with other stories that occur in both works. Briefly, his conclusions are that in the epic we find strong, active emotions with emphasis on τὸ δεινόν; in the elegiac more tender feelings, complaints and sympathy, with emphasis on τὸ ἐλεεινόν; in the epic the divine majesty of the gods is heightened, in the elegiac godhead is humanized; the epic observes rhapsodic objectivity, the elegiac is personal and contemporary in outlook.†¹¹³ I have already suggested that in the matter of divine personages this contrast has been pressed too far,‡ and the attempt to distinguish the scenery of the *Metamorphoses* as impressive (*feierlich*) from that of the *Fasti* as idyllic also seems unconvincing;§¹¹⁴ but in general it must be acknowledged that Heinze has drawn attention to a pervading distinction and analysed it with the thoroughness and perception one would expect of the author of *Vergils Epische Technik*. In explaining how the end-stopping of the contemporary elegiac couplet‖ hindered the building up of periods, he suggests that it was because the characteristics of elegiac narrative are such as he has diagnosed that Ovid did not feel this as an intolerable restraint.¹¹⁵ He might, perhaps, have gone further and said that to a large extent it was the nature of the metre itself which conditioned those characteristics. In particular, it is less easy to be majestic in so staccato

---

* Heinze (p. 1) thinks Ovid told this story twice precisely because it could be treated differently in the two styles, since the ostensible occasion in the former, the origin of ploughing, occupies only one couplet (559–60), and in the latter it is only the frame for some stories of transformation (Arethusa, etc.).

† Other traits of the *Fasti* include a playing-down of war (few battles described, warrior side of Romulus not stressed) and of the miraculous, sublime or heroic in general; similes are few, settings not elaborate.

‡ See pp. 196–9.

§ For 'idyllic' scenery in the *Metamorphoses* see pp. 180–4 above. ‖ See pp. 30–1.

a medium, whereas it is easier to be flippant. The freely flowing metre of the *Metamorphoses* allows the expression to adapt itself to the subject, whereas the fetters of the couplet allow the *Fasti* to succeed fully in one kind of narrative only, the swift and exciting. Here indeed it does excel, with its rapid fire of direct speech, commands, apostrophes, questions, interjections, parentheses, and short dialogue. One is reminded of those stories in Livy where, as the tension increases, he breaks into a panting movement of short sentences, often with use of the historic infinitive. No story was better suited to this style than that of Lucretia, which may serve as a specimen of Ovid's narrative power in elegiacs at its best.* It is too long to give in full, but I will summarize it and quote the most characteristic passages.

The last of the Tarquins is king, and the Romans are conducting a tedious siege against Ardea. While they are beguiling the time in talk, the king's son Sextus raises the question, 'Are we as dear to our wives as they to us?', and a lively contest of wife-praising ensues over the wine, till Collatinus, the husband of Lucretia, proposes a simple solution:

> Surgit cui dederat clarum Collatia nomen:
>   'non opus est verbis, credite rebus!' ait.
> 'nox superest: tollamur equis urbemque petamus!'
>   dicta placent, frenis impediuntur equi,
> pertulerant dominos. regalia protinus illi
>   tecta petunt: custos in fore nullus erat.
> ecce nurus regis fusis per colla coronis
>   inveniunt posito pervigilare mero.
> inde cito passu petitur Lucretia: nebat,
>   ante torum calathi lanaque mollis erat.
> lumen ad exiguum famulae data pensa trahebant,
>   inter quas tenui sic ait illa sono:
> 'mittenda est domino (nunc, nunc, properate, puellae)
>   quam primum nostra facta lacerna manu.

---

* II, 721–852. For a good analysis of this episode see A. G. Lee in *Greece and Rome*, 1953, pp. 107–18.

quid tamen auditis? nam plura audire potestis:
  quantum de bello dicitur esse super?
postmodo victa cades: melioribus, Ardea, restas,
  improba, quae nostros cogis abesse viros.
sint tantum reduces! sed enim temerarius ille
  est meus, et stricto qualibet ense ruit.
mens abit, et morior, quotiens pugnantis imago
  me subit, et gelidum pectora frigus habet.'
desinit in lacrimas intentaque fila remittit,
  in gremio vultum deposuitque suum.
hoc ipsum decuit: lacrimae decuere pudicae,
  et facies animo dignaque parque fuit.
'pone metum, veni!' coniunx ait. illa revixit
  deque viri collo dulce pependit onus.

Up rose Collatia's namesake and its pride:
'Why bandy words? Believe your eyes!' he cried;
'Night lingers yet: to horse, and let's to Rome.'
Agreed, they saddled horse and soon were home.
There first they sought the royal residence.
Without they found no guard in evidence;
Within the princely matrons met their sight,
Garlanded, wassailing the livelong night.
Thence to Lucretia straight. Behold, she span,
Baskets of wool in front of her divan.
Her maids around by frugal lamplight plied
Their stints allotted, while she softly cried:
'Come, hasten, girls: this cloak our hands have wrought
Must to your master presently be brought.
But what's the news? You can hear more than I.
How much more fighting do they prophesy?
Soon, Ardea, you to better men must bow:
Wretched, why keep them absent from us now?
Ah, safe return is all: for mine is rash
And, sword in hand, through thick and thin will dash.
I faint whene'er his image I behold
Fighting, and in my heart my blood runs cold.'

Tears drowned the rest; she dropped her stretchèd thread
Of yarn and on her bosom sank her head.
E'en this became her: tears lent virtue grace,
And worthy of her heart appeared her face.
'Fear not; I've come!' her husband cried. She flung
Her arms around his neck and cherished hung.

But Sextus meanwhile is fired with love for Lucretia, and not least by the challenge of her chastity:

> Verba placent et vox et quod corrumpere non est,
>   quoque minor spes est, hoc magis ille cupit.

The young men return to the camp before Ardea, but he cannot get her out of his mind: ever fresh and pleasing images of her keep recurring:

> Sic sedit, sic culta fuit, sic stamina nevit,
>   neglectae collo sic iacuere comae,
> hos habuit vultus, haec illi verba fuerunt,
>   hic color, haec facies, hic decor oris erat.

Love continues to surge in his heart like a wave in the sea raised by a wind which has now dropped, and he begins to plot the rape. He mounts, and rides at sunset into Collatia:

> Hostis ut hospes init penetralia Collatini:
>   comiter excipitur; sanguine iunctus erat.
> quantum animis erroris inest! parat inscia rerum
>   infelix epulas hostibus illa suis.
> functus erat dapibus: poscunt sua tempora somnum;
>   nox erat et tota lumina nulla domo;
> surgit et auratum vagina liberat ensem
>   et venit ad thalamos, nupta pudica, tuos.
> utque torum pressit, 'ferrum, Lucretia, mecum est.
>   natus' ait 'regis Tarquiniusque loquor!'
> illa nihil: neque enim vocem viresque loquendi
>   aut aliquid toto pectore mentis habet,

sed tremit, ut quondam stabulis deprensa relictis
  parva sub infesto cum iacet agna lupo.
quid faciat? pugnet? vincetur femina pugnans.
  clamet? at in dextra, qui vetet, ensis erat.
effugiat? positis urgentur pectora palmis,
  tunc primum externa pectora tacta manu.
instat amans hostis precibus pretioque minisque:
  nec prece, nec pretio nec movet ille minis.
'nil agis: eripiam' dixit 'per crimina vitam:
  falsus adulterii testis adulter ero:
interimam famulum, cum quo deprensa fereris.'
  succubuit famae victa puella metu.

As friend this foe to Collatinus' hall
Was welcomed: kinship made it natural.
Ah, human blindness! All unwitting she
Prepared a banquet for her enemy.
The feast was done, and sleep its hour claimed.
Night fell, and through the house no taper flamed.
He rose, and drew his gilded sword, and hied
Straight to the chamber of that innocent bride,
And kneeling on the bed, 'Lucretia', breathed,
''Tis I, Prince Tarquin, with my sword unsheathed!'
She nothing spake: she had no power to speak,
Nor any thought in all her heart to seek,
But trembled, as a lamb from sheepfold strayed,
Caught by a wolf, lies under him dismayed.
What could she do? Struggle? She could not win.
Cry out? His naked sword would intervene.
Escape? She felt his hands upon her breast,
Never before by hand unlawful pressed.
With prayers and bribes and threats he sought to assail:
No prayer or bribe or threat could aught avail.
'What use? I'll mingle death and calumny,
Rape, and accuse you of adultery;
A slave I'll kill, say you were caught in sin.'
Fear for her name prevailed, and she gave in.

Morning comes and she summons her father and husband from the camp. At first she cannot bear to tell them of her shame, but finally she forces herself. They forgive her, but she cannot forgive herself, and straightway stabs herself and dies. Brutus appears, and snatching the dagger from her body swears to avenge her. Her wound is shown to the people, and in fury they drive the Tarquins out of Rome.

This story was, of course, well known already: Livy had told it in his first book (57–9), and at times Ovid echoes his very words, as for instance, 'Tace, Lucretia', inquit, 'Sextus Tarquinius sum: ferrum in manu est'. But no prose could equal the swift economy of Ovid. How well he uses the figures of speech which were the rhetorician's stock-in-trade! In a scene so dramatic as this neither they nor even the occasional conceits seem forced. It is a masterpiece of writing, and no wonder the young Shakespeare was impressed.

CHAPTER IX

BANISHMENT: 'TRISTIA' I AND II

REPERTUS EGO

URSUIT of the story of the *Fasti* down to the abortive revision has led me to anticipate. Before coming to the crisis of Ovid's life I must pick up the thread where I left it at the end of Chapter I. By A.D. 8, when the *Metamorphoses* were virtually completed and the *Fasti* half completed, his brief marriage with his second wife had ended, whether through death or divorce, which was commoner at Rome than it is in Europe to-day and implied no stigma; and he had now been married for some time to a third, who proved as loyal to him, in success and in disaster, as he was devoted to her.[1] She had a daughter, who married P. Suillius Rufus.[2] He speaks also of his parents with warm affection, of whom his father had lately died a nonagenarian, followed by his mother.[3] His daughter, twice married already, has had a child by each husband.[4]

The nineteenth century, which to a large extent is still with us, dealt harshly with Ovid's character.* It recognized no love that was not romantic, and it made 'morality' mean chiefly conventional sexual standards. For both these reasons the *Ars Amatoria* ('*L'art d'aimer sans amour*', as Ripert calls it) was naturally condemned, not to mention the *Amores*. Again, it was for the most part an age of piety, in which pagans who treated their religion with reverence earned more marks than those who did not, especially when, as in the case of Virgil, there were signs of a groping after monotheism and of a sympathy with speculations about human survival of death. Finally, it was an age of patrio-

---

* Norden's estimate in his *Die römische Literatur* (5th edn. 1954) is as harsh as any. For a good and much more sympathetic account see T. F. Higham, *C.R.* 1934, pp. 105–16.

tism, and in Britain especially, of imperialism, so that enthusiasm for the beneficent power of Augustan Rome found a ready echo, and those who, like Ovid, were tardy in toeing the line did not obtain full credit. In fine, the Stoic type was at a premium, the Epicurean at a discount. For this kind of reader, Horace mended his ways in time, but Propertius' character was too deeply compromised for him to be appreciated as the exciting poet that he is, and Ovid was still more reprehensible.

Let us admit immediately that Ovid could not be called a man of principle. He had the rhetorician's facility for maintaining whatever suited the purpose in hand, and no doubt he was irresponsible about the possible social effects of his earlier works. His generation, unlike that of Virgil and Horace, which came through the horrors of the Civil War, had grown up under the Pax Augusta, so that he took it and the endeavour that had gone to its making for granted. He had not the passion of a Lucretius for truth, nor any mission to redeem his fellow-men or to wrestle with the problems of metaphysics. But there are many people who, having all those virtues and offending no conventional code, are nevertheless immoral in the true sense of the word and unpleasant into the bargain. Let us scrutinize our values before we condemn Ovid's character. His salient characteristic was *humanitas*, humane good feeling akin to that charity without which, we are assured, all other qualities are as nothing.*

Again, though we have no evidence that he was a systematic thinker, he had a respect for the intellect. We have seen evidence

---

* His own word for this was *candor* (*Tr.* II, 467; 565; III, 6, 7; IV, 4, 3–4; V, 3, 53). Cf. Horace's use of *candidi animi* for Virgil, Varius and Tucca, *Sat.* I, 5, 41. Fränkel is right in seeing something in common between Ovid's good nature and the ideals of Christian ethics; but there had no doubt been many equally humane pagans (Virgil was one and Horace another, not to mention Socrates), so that there is nothing unique about his position. It is a relief, after Victorian censoriousness, to turn back to Macaulay's summing up: 'He seems to have been a very good fellow; rather too fond of women; a flatterer and a coward; but kind and generous, and free from envy, though a man of letters sufficiently vain of his literary performances. The *Art of Love*, which ruined poor Ovid, is, in my opinion, decidedly his best work' (Trevelyan, *op. cit.* p. 726).

of this in his deliberately making the clever Ulysses triumph over the stolid Ajax.* He trusted in reason and spoke slightingly of augury† and of superstitions such as belief in spells and witchcraft,[5] which Propertius had treated with solemnity in some of his most imaginative passages. Lucretius himself would have approved of his outburst against the idea of ritual purification from murder:[6]

> A ! nimium faciles, qui tristia crimina caedis
> fluminea tolli posse putatis aqua !

> *Ah, men too lax, who think that the gloomy crime of murder*
> *can be washed away by river-water!*

He must also have lived a life of intense and incessant intellectual activity, always reading and composing, a bee, not a butterfly. The Italian attitude of *dolce far niente* was not for him—*mors nobis tempus habetur iners* ('the time for us to be idle is after death')—nor did he care for gaming or even for the all-night drinking parties of Roman society, being, as he reminds a friend from exile, almost an abstainer.[7]

As for beauty, we have had abundant evidence of his love of it as displayed in nature, especially where it is associated with peacefulness. In everything aesthetic he gives an impression of good taste. What he liked to see in women was *cultus*, which the French call *chic*, the opposite of *rusticitas*. This did not involve expensive adornment, as the vulgar imagined; the tasteful simplicity which made Horace's Pyrrha irresistible was his ideal: *munditiis capimur*. A touch of the hand can make or mar a coiffure; and what suits one woman may not suit another. As for men, they too should rely on *mundities*—neatness and cleanliness both of person and dress.[8] But what mattered most in both sexes was personality and character, the only sure basis of lasting affection. *Certus amor morum est;* and again, *ut ameris, amabilis esto.*[9]

---

* See pp. 234-5.

† *Augurium ratio est et coniectura futuri*, i.e. '*I* divine things by reason and calculation' (*Tr.* I, 9, 51).

'*Amabilis*': that was just the word used by Seneca to describe Ovid's own showing in the oratorical schools: *habebat ille comptum et decens et amabile ingenium* (his style was elegant, neat and attractive).[10] His good taste extended into the sphere of conduct. How heartily one assents to the eloquent passage in which he abjures lovers not to boast of their experiences, or still worse, their fictitious experiences![11] More than once he asserts his belief in the civilizing power of love.[12] Lovers are bound to each other, not by law, but by their love (as those should remember who defend Aeneas on the ground that he was not legally married to Dido):

> fungitur in vobis munere legis amor.[13]
>
> *in you love performs the office of law.*

Unlike Propertius and Tibullus, he thinks constantly of the woman's point of view. He bids a man be chivalrous in forgetting, and helping her to forget, any blemishes she may have, especially if she is past her prime, and insists that in the act of love the woman should have equal pleasure with the man.[14] Nor does he forget to put in a word for the lady's maid, so often ill-treated by her mistress in a fit of temper as she does her hair.[15] And in a striking passage he pleads that, if love must end, it should fade decently with mutual goodwill, not explode in a quarrel or law-suit and leave rancour behind:[16]

> Sed modo dilectam scelus est odisse puellam:
>   exitus ingeniis convenit iste feris.
> non curare sat est: odio qui finit amorem,
>   aut amat, aut aegre desinet esse miser.
> turpe vir et mulier, iuncti modo, protinus hostes;
>   non illas lites Appias ipsa probat.
> saepe reas faciunt, et amant: ubi nulla simultas
>   incidit, admonitu liber aberrat amor.
> forte aderam iuveni; dominam lectica tenebat;
>   horrebant saevis omnia verba minis.
> iamque vadaturus 'lectica prodeat!' inquit;
>   prodierat: visa coniuge mutus erat;

et manus et manibus duplices cecidere tabellae;
  venit in amplexus atque 'ita vincis !' ait.
tutius est aptumque magis discedere pace,
  nec petere a thalamis litigiosa fora.
munera quae dederas, habeat sine lite, iubeto:
  esse solent magno damna minora bono.

To hate a girl once loved's a rank offence,
An end more fit for beasts than men of sense.
Indifference is enough: who ends in hate
Loves still, or else will shed his misery late.
Woman and man, now one, then foes straightway!
'Shame on such strife!' would even the Appian say.*
The man who sues his girl may love her yet:
Where there's no grudge, love fades and both forget.
One for whom I was acting, while his wife
Stayed in her litter, seethed with threats of strife;
When his turn came to accuse her, 'Let her come
Forth!' he exclaimed: she came, and he was dumb;
Dropping his hands, dropping his tablets twin,
He took her in his arms and cried 'You win!'
Surer and seemlier 'tis to part in peace
Than sink from marriage-vows to court-decrees.
Unchallenged let her all your gifts retain:
A little loss is oft a greater gain.

So even the ostensibly cynical author of the *Amores, Ars* and *Remedia* sometimes betrays that he has really a heart; and when in the later poems he emerges in his own person, we find him a loved and loving husband and father. We are often warned, and as often forget, that Roman erotic poets did not expect their characters to be judged from their poetry.†

Ovid's third wife was possibly by birth, and certainly by personality, a woman of some consequence, who had early won

---

* Venus Appia, conceived as being accustomed to look down on the strife of the law-courts from her temple in the Forum Iulium.

† See S. G. Owen, edn. of *Tristia* II (1924), note on 353–4. Ovid says boldly that no scandal has ever attached to his name (*ibid.* 349–52).

the approval and friendship of Augustus' aunt, the younger Atia, and paid court apparently in person to the Empress Livia.[17] She was a member of the household of Paullus Fabius Maximus, in what capacity we cannot tell; she was at all events a beloved protégée of his wife, Marcia, the daughter of Atia.*[18] She had herself already a daughter by another husband when he married her, but was still young enough for him to think of her as 'iuvenis' at the time when he went into exile.[19] His letters from exile contain many expressions of his love for her, and tributes to her devotion, loyalty and competence as guardian of their property.[20]

Paullus Fabius was an influential noble, consul in 11 B.C. at the earliest age of eligibility. He provides an interesting link between Horace and Ovid. When Horace published the last book of his *Odes*, some time after 14 B.C., he placed first in it a wistful poem deprecating the renewal of Venus' assaults upon him now he is close on fifty. He bids her go revelling *in domum Paulli Maximi*, who is ripe for love: for he is noble and good-looking and an eloquent pleader for anxious prisoners at the bar, and a young man of a hundred talents; he will carry far and wide the standards of her warfare. When she did finally triumph in the young man's marriage, it was his contemporary Ovid, already approved by him as a poet and perhaps already married to a member of his *entourage*, who composed the wedding hymn.[21] Later Horace's phrase

et pro sollicitis non tacitus reis

was to wake a poignant echo, when the exile begged Paullus to plead with the Emperor for him,

Vox, precor, Augustas pro me tua molliat aures,
auxilio *trepidis* quae solet esse *reis*.[22]

May your voice, I pray, soften for me the imperial ears, your voice so often an aid to trembling prisoners.

* There is no ground for the often-repeated assertion that she was *related* to Fabius; she seems however to have had some connexion with Pompeius Macer, the companion of Ovid's youthful Grand Tour (*P.* II, 10, 10).

But Ovid's first allegiance was to the house of his patron
Messalla,* on whose death he composed, only a few months before
his banishment, the elegy to be recited in the Forum.²³ Though a
devoted adherent of Augustus, Messalla had resigned the new post
of Praefectus Urbis after a few days and devoted himself thence-
forward to the bar and the patronage of literature. His elder son,
Messallinus, inherited his rhetorical talent; but though a few years
younger than Ovid, he knew him only as one of his throng of
clients, and the exile, when he seeks his support, is embarrassed by
the recollection that he had not waited on him as often as he might
profitably have done.²⁴ But if Messallinus was to him remote 'as
a Caesar', it was far otherwise with his brother, Cotta Maximus,
who was some twenty years younger than the poet and was born
after he had joined Messalla's circle. He was a gentle soul (*mitis*),†
and a poet who could be addressed as 'iuvenis studiorum plene
meorum', whose generosity to poets was indeed proverbial to
Juvenal nearly a century later.²⁵ Ovid always addresses him with
deep gratitude and affection, as at *P.* ii, 3, 69–82:

> Movit amicitiae tum te constantia longae,
>   ante tuos ortus quae mihi coepta fuit,
> et quod eras aliis factus, mihi natus amicus,
>   quodque tibi in cunis oscula prima dedi.
> quod, cum vestra domus teneris mihi semper ab annis
>   culta sit, esse vetus me tibi cogit onus.
> me tuus ille pater, Latiae facundia linguae,
>   quae non inferior nobilitate fuit,
> primus ut auderem committere carmina famae
>   impulit; ingenii dux fuit ille mei.
> nec quo sit primum nobis a tempore cultus
>   contendo fratrem posse referre tuum.
> tu tamen ante omnes ita sum complexus, ut unus
>   quolibet in casu gratia nostra fores.

* S. G. Owen conveniently summarizes what is known of Ovid's patrons and
friends (*Tristia* I, pp. xxvii–xlix).

† *P.* iii, 2, 103 (cf. *Tr.* v, 9, 7, if he was the recipient); *P.* ii, 3, 29–40 (*mitius*,
l. 39). *P.* i, 2 is also addressed to Cotta Maximus and probably *Tr.* iv, 4.

Then were you moved by friendship's constancy,
Which even before your birth began for me,
Remembered you were born my friend, not made,
And how I kissed you in your cradle laid,
From youth devoted to your family—
So old was your responsibility.
Your noble father, Latin eloquence
Incarnate, owning like pre-eminence
In speech and birth, first bade me dare confide
My verse to fame: he was my genius' guide.
Your brother too will scarce remember now
The distant day when first I made my bow.
But you especially I did embrace:
Whate'er befell, you were my only grace.

He had other patrons in high places whom he was to remember in time of need, the wealthy Sextus Pompeius, consul in A.D. 14, last scion of the house of Pompey the Great, Graecinus,* *consul suffectus* in 16, and his brother Flaccus, consul in 17; but, apart from Cotta and Fabius, his closest friends were naturally men of similar social status to himself, of whom we know nothing from elsewhere, particularly Celsus, a member of Cotta's circle,† a certain Brutus, and one Atticus,‡ of whose companionship he gives a lively picture in recollection at *P.* II, 4, 9–20:

Seria multa mihi tecum conlata recordor,
    nec data iucundis tempora pauca iocis.
saepe citae longis visae sermonibus horae,
    saepe fuit brevior quam mea verba dies.
saepe tuas venit factum modo carmen ad aures
    et nova iudicio subdita Musa tuo est.
quod tu laudaras, populo placuisse putabam;
    hoc pretium curae dulce regentis erat.

---

* Perhaps the Graecinus addressed in *Am.* II, 10.
† *P.* I, 9. Celsus is probably the Albinovanus Celsus of Horace, *Ep.* I, 8, 1–2 and I, 3, 115, and father of Pedo.
‡ Perhaps the Atticus addressed in *Am.* I, 9.

utque meus lima rasus liber esset amici,
　　non semel admonitu facta litura tuo est.
nos fora viderunt pariter, nos porticus omnis,
　　nos via, nos iunctis curva theatra locis.

Much of our time in serious talk we spent,
Nor little, I recall, in merriment;
Often our converse made long hours fly;
Days were too short for my garrulity.
Often my latest song was read to you,
Your judgment sought upon some poem new;
What you had praised I deemed the world approved,
And this reward for guiding care you loved;
To make erasures your advice I took,
That a friend's file might polish up my book.
Together we appeared in squares and streets
And porticos and curving theatre's seats.

Of his less intimate friends, men like Gallio, Rufinus and Salanus, some were naturally fellow-poets. From Macer, the companion of his youthful Grand Tour and indeed some connexion of his own wife, he had somehow drifted apart;[26] but there remained Carus, Albinovanus Pedo, Cornelius Severus and Tuticanus. Roman poets were by no means always free from jealousy, but from the very first Ovid shows generous enthusiasm for his colleagues. As a young man he looked up to his elders as gods:

Temporis illius colui fovique poetas,
　　quotque aderant vates rebar adesse deos.

Propertius, Tibullus, Varro of Atax—he speaks appreciatively of all the other elegists of that generation, and particularly of the dead and disgraced Gallus, to whom he insists on giving the benefit of the doubt,

si falsum est temerati crimen amici,

if the charge of treachery to your friend is false,

refusing to be silenced by any *damnatio memoriae*.[27] From exile he asks the poets at home to drink his health, but only if he has deserved their favour by his kindness and done no harm to letters by any criticism, and if he has not fallen into the common fault of disparaging modern writers because of his reverence for the ancient.[28] Of these moderns he gives a complimentary, and no doubt over-indulgent, list in his last Pontic Epistle.* It would appear that there was a society (*sodalicium*) of poets, and it has been suggested that *Tristia* IV, 3 reflects an annual custom of meeting at the Liberalia under the patronage of Bacchus, long recognized as an inspirer of poetry.[29]

I have already indicated a certain analogy between the circle of Ovid and that of Oscar Wilde. The *Ars Amatoria* was not written in a vacuum; it was the reaction of a witty and high-spirited member of a sophisticated circle to a puritanical and sometimes hypocritical orthodoxy backed by power. Half the point would have been lost if there had been no respectable people to shock. But whereas Wilde was secure, so long as he did not break the law, because he risked only the disapproval of Society, Ovid lived under a velvet-gloved despot who had personally initiated a not very successful campaign against sexual irregularity.

It is scarcely surprising that there is no evidence of a personal relationship between Ovid and the Emperor—if there had been one, he could hardly have failed to mention it in his appeals from exile. His early attachment had been to Messalla, and in any case Maecenas, who might have won him betimes for Augustanism, as he won the equally unpromising Propertius, and introduced him to Court, had fallen from grace in 23 and died in 8 B.C. The advances tardily made by the poet in the *Metamorphoses* and *Fasti* could not efface the strong impression of indifference or even contempt which the work of his first forty-five years had created, even though he was now without doubt the most famous and talented poet in the Empire. In face of the eulogies in Virgil and

---

* Quintilian however says that he wrote a book of epigrams against bad poets of his day (VI, 3, 96).

Horace of the hardy old Sabine way of life he had scoffed in the *Medicamina Faciei* (11–12);

> Forsitan antiquae Tatio sub rege Sabinae
> maluerunt quam se rura paterna coli;

> *Old Sabine dames preferred at Tatius' date*
> *Their holdings, not themselves, to cultivate.*

For himself, he rejoices that he has been born into a latter age of sophistication:

> Prisca iuvent alios: ego me nunc denique natum
> gratulor: haec aetas moribus apta meis.[30]

> *Others may crave old times; thank God, I thrive*
> *In these: to-day 'tis bliss to be alive.*

One wonders how the Emperor liked to read in the *Ars Amatoria* that his famous mock naval battle had been a splendid occasion for picking up foreign girls, or that the porticos dedicated by his sister in memory of Marcellus and by himself in honour of his wife were among the gallant's best hunting-grounds.[31] Not that he would have minded about casual affairs with freedwomen; but despite the poet's repeated assurance that he was only concerned with this class,[32] the greater part of the poem could apply equally well to wives of citizens,[33] especially as the assumption is often made that the girl will have a *vir* who has first claim on her. Sometimes too Ovid seems to forget his disclaimers, as when he recommends the theatre as a place often fatal to *castus pudor*, refers to the intrigues he is facilitating as *crimen, culpa, peccare*, compares the married state adversely with free association, or assumes that even a bride can scarcely hope to enjoy her bridegroom for long without rivals, and that wives regularly deceive their husbands.[34]

He was aware that the *Ars Amatoria* had provoked criticism in some quarters, but feeling secure in his profession that he was dealing only with *libertinae* and in the applause of society, he castigated his critics with hybristic gusto in the *Remedia Amoris* (379–96):

> Blanda pharetratos Elegeia cantet Amores
> et levis arbitrio ludat amica suo.
> Callimachi numeris non est dicendus Achilles;
> Cydippe non est oris, Homere, tui.
> quis feret Andromaches peragentem Thaïda partes?
> peccat, in Andromache Thaïda quisquis agat.
> Thaïs in arte mea est; lascivia libera nostra est;
> nil mihi cum vitta: Thaïs in arte mea est.
> si mea materiae respondet Musa iocosae,
> vicimus, et falsi criminis acta rea est.
> rumpere, Livor edax: magnum iam nomen habemus;
> maius erit, tantum quo pede coepit eat.
> sed nimium properas: vivam modo, plura dolebis;
> et capiunt animi carmina multa mei.
> nam iuvat et studium famae mihi crevit honore;
> principio clivi noster anhelat equus.
> tantum se nobis elegi debere fatentur
> quantum Vergilio nobile debet epos.

> *Let charming Elegy sing quivered Loves*
> *And lightly wanton as the spirit moves;*
> *Achilles in Callimachēan verse,*
> *Cydippe in Homeric—which is worse?*
> *Who could endure the offence, if in a play*
> *Andromache should Thaïs' part portray?*
> *My theme is Thaïs: here free love's supreme:*
> *No fillets here, for Thaïs is my theme;**
> *If but my Muse this playful part sustain,*
> *I triumph, and my critics' charge is vain.*
> *Burst, Envy, burst: e'en now my name is great,*
> *Greater to be, so it maintain this rate.*

---

* The fillet was the badge of respectable women. Thaïs was the famous Athenian courtesan who went on Alexander's expedition to the East.

But stay! I hope to live to vex you more:
My mind has many another song in store.
For fame is sweet and honour spurs intent;
My panting steed has scarce begun the ascent.
Elegy owns a debt to me no less
Than epic doth to Virgil's self confess.

That was written about A.D. 2, when Ovid was at the height of his popularity,* and already Nemesis had her eye on Hybris. It was just about the time when the first book of the *Ars Amatoria* took Rome by storm that Augustus discovered that his daughter Julia was a notorious adulteress. It is hard to imagine a more devastating blow. He had made such a point of the sanctity of marriage, and himself sponsored the *Lex Iulia de adulteriis*.† And now his own daughter, the apple of his eye, had not only violated it, but done so in the most dignified of public places in Rome; and her paramours included Antonius Iullus, son of his old enemy Mark Antony and Fulvia, whom Octavia had induced him, with rare generosity, to bring up with the other children of the palace.‡ He relegated Julia to the Isle of Pandataria, and banished her known adulterers, except for Iullus, who was driven to suicide. When he imagined the mocking *Schadenfreude* of fashionable society, he could hardly help thinking of it as crystallized and perpetuated in the *Ars Amatoria*, now on everyone's lips.§ For the moment he took no action against Ovid, whereas he might have deprived him of his knighthood at the periodical review of the knights;[35] but for some years he brooded, and it is possible that the extravagant flatteries of the *Fasti* and *Metamorphoses* were motivated by palpable grounds for anxiety.

* One of the consuls of that year, P. Vinicius, is called by Seneca *summus amator Ovidii* (*Contr.* X, 4, 25). For Ovid's popularity as poet cf. *Tr.* II, 115–20; IV, 10, 121–8.

† For difficulties over his legislation on marriage see Propertius II, 7; Dio Cass. LIV, 16; Tacitus, *Ann.* III, 25.

‡ He is the addressee of Horace, *Odes* IV, 2.

§ Cestius said of Ovid, 'hoc saeculum amatoriis non artibus tantum sed sententiis implevit' (Seneca, *Contr.* III, 7).

A second blow fell in A.D. 8.* Augustus found that Julia's daughter, also called Julia, was in her turn committing adultery. Her paramour, Junius Silanus, went into voluntary exile on being declared no longer *persona grata*, and she herself was banished to the island of Trimerus off Apulia.†[36] But these penalties were light compared with the doom that fell upon Ovid at this time. For nearly two thousand years men have been speculating on the cause. No new evidence is likely to come to light, and the poet himself remains our sole authority, so all we can do is to steer clear of wild imaginings and support what seems the most plausible conjecture.

It is probable that, as Boissier thought, the *Ars Amatoria* was the true as well as the official cause. Fourteen times Ovid speaks of his poetry as being responsible for his downfall, on four occasions specifying the *Ars*.‡ Incensed at his continued failure to reform society, Augustus chose the most obvious representative ('*repertus ego*') of what he wished to crush, and made him a scapegoat in a most public and extreme way. The 'error' to which Ovid recurs even more often, and round which the curiosity of later ages has buzzed, was probably only the occasion. A long chain of circumstances had led to his being present and accidentally witnessing something culpable. His offence was shameful, but not heinous. He attributes it to *simplicitas*—naïveté,§ aggravated afterwards by what he has to call timidity (which may simply have been a decent

* For the chronology see Owen, *Tristia* II, pp. 9–10. We know that Ovid set out on his long journey in December (*Tr.* I, 11, 3) and he could not have got to Tomis till spring had begun. He indicates that in October of 14 A.D. he has already spent five winters 'in Scythia' (*P.* IV, 6, 5–6, 15–16). See further W. Kraus, 'Ovidius Naso', in R.-E., Col. 1918.

† It was called adultery, though she was actually a widow.

‡ Owen, *op. cit.* pp. 10–11. For a full discussion of Ovid's banishment see his Introduction, pp. 1–47.

§ He uses the obvious *exemplum* of punishment for an unintentional offence, Actaeon (*Tr.* II, 105):

inscius Actaeon vidit sine veste Dianam.

This led to the crowning absurdity, the theory that he was banished for accidentally seeing the Empress in her bath (Dryden, Pref. to Trans. of Ovid's Epistles (1680); Deville, *Essai sur l'exile d'Ovide*, 1859).

disinclination to tell tales). Yet although, if he could explain all, his guilt would be seen to have been trifling, for reasons he cannot explain he must forbear even long after to go into details. It was natural that the Emperor should resent his error, but he had meant no harm and broken no law.[37]

Since all must be obscure because Ovid intended it to remain so, let us not waste many words where too many have been wasted down the ages. There are only two theories that deserve mention, though each has variations. One is that the poet became involved in the dynastic tension between the Julians and the Claudians. The former were represented by Agrippa Postumus, son of Agrippa and the elder Julia, whose ill-temper, which disqualified him for succession, had been aggravated by indiscretion resulting in his banishment in A.D.7; the ageing Emperor is reputed to have continued to nurse an affection for him. The latter were represented by Tiberius, son of the Empress Livia, adopted in A.D. 4 by Augustus and made heir apparent. Ovid's offence might have been that he became involved with the cause of Agrippa, perhaps through Paullus Fabius Maximus, and so offended Livia.* But it is hard to imagine in that case how his offence could have been, as he so often asserts, to have *seen* something wrong. In any case he had long since withdrawn, almost ostentatiously, from public interests.

The second theory is that Ovid became undesignedly an accessory to Julia's adultery.† It has the advantage of establishing

---

* The arguments for this theory are set out, e.g., by Némethy, *Comm. exeg. ad Ovidii Tristia* (1913), pp. 133 ff.; cf. Ripert, *op. cit.* pp. 179 ff.; Owen, *op. cit.* pp. 26–31; Zimmermann, *Rh. Mus.*, 1932, pp. 263–74. There was a story that in A.D. 13 or 14 Augustus paid a secret visit to Agrippa Postumus, accompanied only by Fabius, and that Livia got to know of it through Fabius' wife, her friend Marcia, who was also the friend of Ovid's wife (Tacitus, *Ann.* I, 5; *Dio Cass.* LVI, 30; Pliny, *N.H.* VII, 150). Owen inclines to think that at all events the cause was political (p. 31). Charlesworth throws doubt on the story (*A.J.P.*, 1923, pp. 145 ff.).

† Of this Boissier is the best representative: *L'opposition sous les Césars²* (1885) pp. 140 ff. (His interpretation of *Tr.* IV, 10, 101, *comitumque nefas famulosque nocentes*, as indicating that Ovid's companions put the blame on him and his servants betrayed him, is probably a misapprehension: the words refer to their treatment of him *after* he was banished; see Owen, *op. cit.* p. 26.)

a connexion with the other charge, concerning the *Ars Amatoria*, and so accounting psychologically for the surprising savagery of the Emperor; for the poem had gone unpunished for some eight years, and it is clear that the other offence, however misconstrued, was not in itself sufficient to warrant so extreme a penalty, being one of complicity rather than action and not a legal crime. Ovid makes it clear that the *Gens Iulia* was involved: 'Such is your family feeling for all who bear the Julian name that you think yourself injured when any member of it is injured.'* Either of the theories would square with that; my own inclination is towards the second.

When the storm burst Ovid was on Elba, with Cotta Maximus. Rumours soon reached the Island, and he was questioned by his young friend and patron. In a touching passage written long afterwards from exile he recalls the scene to him:[38]

> Ultima me tecum vidit maestisque cadentes
>   excepit lacrimas Aethalis Ilva genis:
> cum tibi quaerenti num verus nuntius esset,
>   attulerat culpae quem mala fama meae,
> inter confessum dubie dubieque negantem
>   haerebam, pavidas dante timore notas,
> exemploque nivis, quam mollit aquaticus Auster,
>   gutta per attonitas ibat oborta genas.

> *Aethalian Elba last saw me with you,*
> *Whose soil my tears of misery did bedew.*
> *When you demanded whether the report*
> *Was true, that evil rumour of me brought,*
> *Half I denied yet half did I confess,*
> *And wavered, fear betraying my distress;*
> *And as when watery Auster melts the snow,*
> *Down my numb cheek a welling tear did flow.*

* *P.* II, 2, 21–2.

> Quaeque tua est pietas in totum nomen Iuli,
>   te laedi, cum quis laeditur inde, putas.

Cotta was angry at first, but Ovid claims to have heard that the anger turned to sympathy when he learnt the full story of his 'error'; he was one of the first to send him a letter of consolation and raise his hopes that Augustus might relent;[39] and he even (if, as seems probable, he is the addressee of *Tristia* IV, 5) undertook to finance him in the event of his property being confiscated (ll. 7–8).

There could be no question of a public hearing: one charge was too general and the other too embarrassing for such treatment. Ovid was summoned to appear before the Emperor who, after delivering a stern rebuke,* issued an edict that, being guilty of *maiestas*[40] (degradation of the national dignity or insult to the imperial family), he was to retire to Tomis. Technically his punishment was *relegatio*, not the severer *exilium* (*aquae et ignis interdictio*), though he sometimes loosely calls it exile;[41] he thus retained his property and civic rights, but in other respects the penalty was crushing. Tomis, in Moesia, was a bleak outpost on the Black Sea, at the site of the modern Constanza, insecurely held against the barbarians of the steppes. We may gather that he was given no opportunity of publicly stating his case,† and the result was unfortunate for him as for us, at least as regards the second charge, which he himself conceived to be the chief. Instead of getting it out of his system, he spent the rest of his life in chewing it over, unable to turn to fresh pabulum. The necessity of concealing the details of his 'error' drove him to the futile alleviation of dropping hint after hint.

His poems were removed from the public libraries,[42] and though no steps were taken against privately owned copies,‡ such censorship had been most unusual in Republican Rome.§ With regard to these he had a case that could be openly stated, but it was based on general principles and required time and leisure for its organiza-

---

* *Tristibus invectus verbis (ita principe dignum)*: P. II, 7, 56.[43]
† He was tried, if trial it was, by the Emperor *in camera*.[44]
‡ With the possible exception of the *Ars Amatoria*.[45]
§ *Res nova et inusitata, supplicium de studiis sumi*: Seneca, *Contr.* X, praef. 5, on T. Labienus, who died in 45 B.C., having his books burnt at the instigation of his enemies.

tion. It reached Rome towards the first summer of his exile as Book II of the *Tristia*, a single poem 578 lines long addressed to Augustus. Like Cicero's *Pro Milone*, it is a 'backstairs' speech for the defence, all the more elaborate and effective for being matured after the event.

Though written afterwards, perhaps on the voyage to Tomis, it bears on the time of the edict, when ideally it should have been delivered, so that we may properly anticipate and deal with it here. It is duly arranged according to the principles of the rhetorical Schools, with *exordium* to conciliate the court (1–26), *propositio* to explain what was to be attempted (27–8), and *tractatio* to develop the argument (29–578). The argument in turn is divided into *probatio* to prove that mercy would be appropriate (29–154), with its *epilogus* requesting a lighter penalty (155–206), and *refutatio* to refute the charge against the *Ars Amatoria* (207–572), with another brief *epilogus* (573–8).[46] The narration which usually followed the exordium is omitted; all the background was known to the judge, and much could not be revealed to the public.

The first part (1–210) is servile in tone. The poet reproaches himself with being, in Wilde's phrase, 'the spendthrift of my own genius', and his pleas are pathetic conceits: If I had not sinned, Caesar, what would you have had to pardon? My plight has given you an opportunity of showing mercy. If Jupiter hurled his bolt whenever men sinned, he would very soon be weaponless; as it is, he frightens the world with a warning thunder-clap and then clears the sky (31–6). Such clemency you have shown, even to those who have openly opposed you (37–52); whereas I have duly worshipped your divinity and praised you in my poems—not that anything could increase your glory, especially so humble a poet's verses, but after all, Jupiter too is glad of praise (53–76). Yet my world has collapsed around me; following your lead, as, of course, they should, men have come to hate me for my verse (77–88). My life has otherwise been blameless and even creditable; I might have lived down my early poems, if only I had not witnessed what I should not. That one day ruined my house, which had been honourable for generations and made more honourable by my world-wide fame (89–124). I was lucky indeed to be left alive and with my goods unconfiscated, not condemned by Senate or Grand Jury. My remorse itself is punishment enough, but your leniency gives me hope against hope (125–54). By the gods, by our father-land, by your family, so may victory ever be theirs, I beg for mercy—not yet for return, but for a place of exile less dangerous and desolate than Tomis (155–206).

This *probatio*, for all its eloquence, repels us by its abjectness, though it derives a certain interest from the incidental information it gives about the nature of the poet's previous life, his sentence and its cause. With the *refutatio* a remarkable change comes over the poem. We all know how hard it is, when we are indignant and wish to get a decision reversed, to imagine the reactions of the person to whom we are appealing and address him with tact and moderation that may have some chance of achieving the desired end, giving him an opportunity to save his face, refraining from putting him in the wrong or making him feel foolish. How irresistible is the temptation to let ourselves go, making the most of our case and scoring every conceivable point! To this temptation Ovid now yielded, vainly imagining that a seasoning of gross flattery would counteract the effect; and at this distance our anxiety at the harm he risks doing thereby to his own fortunes is overcome by our delight at seeing the old Ovid re-emerge from the wastes of the Dobruja to discomfort his not invulnerable oppressor. He may even have fondly believed at this time that his cause might be helped if he appealed over the Emperor's head to public opinion.

Leaving out most of the flattery, his gist is as follows. There are two offences, *carmen et error*. I must not reopen your wounds by dealing with the latter, but will defend myself against the charge of encouraging adultery by my *Ars Amatoria*. Even divine minds can sometimes be mistaken; they have so much else to think about, without reading what are only intended as *ioci*. If you had ever had time to do so, you would have found my *Ars* innocuous, if

frivolous. It counsels nothing illegal, being concerned only with
lawful affairs with courtesans, as I made clear in four lines of
Book I[47] (207–52).

Ovid now proceeds to answer criticisms severally:

'At matrona potest alienis artibus uti,
　　quoque trahat, quamvis non doceatur, habet.'
nil igitur matrona legat, quia carmine ab omni
　　ad delinquendum doctior esse potest.
quodcunque attigerit siqua est studiosa sinistri,
　　ad vitium mores instruet inde suos.
sumpserit Annales (nihil est hirsutius illis)
　　facta est unde parens Ilia nempe leget.
sumpserit 'Aeneadum genetrix' ubi prima, requiret
　　Aeneadum genetrix unde sit 'alma Venus'.

'But wives can emulate the not so pure
And learn, though not addressed, the art to allure.'
Then let a wife read nothing, for there is
No poem but can tutor her amiss:
Whate'er she touch, if she be bent on sin,
She'll find encouragement to vice therein:
Opening the Annals (what could be more stern?).
The cause of Ilia's motherhood she'll learn;
Beginning 'Mother of Aeneas' race',
She'll ask how Venus came to have that place. *

Nothing benefits that cannot also do harm. My poem can harm
no one, if it is read in the right frame of mind (253–76). But supposing it could: by the same token you must condemn all sorts of
innocent places used for assignations, and also temples, where one
is constantly reminded of the gods' adulteries. (Ovid does not

---

* The *Annals* of Ennius, a pattern of rugged ('hirsute') virtue, included the
seduction by Mars of Ilia, the mother of Romulus and Remus. The *De Rerum
Natura* of Lucretius begins,

　　　Aeneadum Genetrix, hominum divumque voluptas,
　　　Alma Venus...,

Aeneas being Venus' son by her liaison with Anchises.

check himself to consider whether the great restorer and builder of temples would mind the suggestion that they are open to such criticism, with Mars Ultor singled out as *tua munera*—even granted that it is intended as a *reductio ad absurdum*: Greek mythology had grown by a process of identification and interconnexion which made divine adulteries an inevitable and ubiquitous ingredient, and he takes full advantage of this):

Ut tamen hoc fatear, ludi quoque semina praebent
    nequitiae: tolli tota theatra iube.
peccandi causam multi quam saepe dederunt,
    Martia cum durum sternit harena solum!
tollatur Circus; non tuta licentia Circi est:
    hic sedet ignoto iuncta puella viro.
cum quaedam spatientur in hoc, ut amator eodem
    conveniat, quare porticus ulla patet?
quis locus est templis augustior? haec quoque vitet
    in culpam siqua est ingeniosa suam.
cum steterit Iovis aede, Iovis succurret in aede,
    quam multas matres fecerit ille deus.
proxima adoranti Iunonis templa subibit
    paelicibus multis hanc doluisse deam.
Pallade conspecta, natum de crimine virgo
    sustulerit quare, quaeret, Erichthonium.
venerit in magnum templum, tua munera, Martis,
    stat Venus Ultori iuncta, vir ante fores.

But grant it: are not our dramatic shows
Suggestive too? Then every theatre close.
Many must answer for liaisons planned
While gladiators battle on their sand.
The Circus is a snare—away with it!—
For there strange men beside a girl may sit.
Should colonnades be open, just the place
Where women keen to meet a lover pace?
Temples are holy ground, but let her fly
Even from these, who tends to lechery:

> *Standing in Jupiter's, she will recall*
> *The women Jupiter made mothers all;*
> *Near by in Juno's worshipping, reflect*
> *How Juno grieved her rivals to detect;*
> *At sight of virgin Pallas, ask why she*
> *Reared Erichthonius, child of infamy;* *
> *In Mars the Avenger's, your own gift, behold*
> *Venus with Mars, her husband in the cold.†*

And after all it is no crime, he continues, to read amorous verses; pure women may read of many things they must not do, just as severe matrons and Vestals often see prostitutes exposed naked, yet brothel-keepers are not prosecuted (277–312).

'But why is your book excessively wanton, and why does it encourage *anyone* to love?' I admit the criticism, but not the implication that I should rather have written epic or panegyric, for which I am unsuited. I should have feared to treat of your own deeds, in case I could not do them justice (313–42).‡ You think I instructed wives in adultery, but I never addressed them, and indeed I have no knowledge of the subject, having never been under suspicion of that crime. No one should judge my character or any poet's from what he writes; or are we to suppose Accius was grim, Terence convivial, poets of war warlike? (341–60.)

Ovid then embarks on a list of all the famous poets of love whose work has gone unpunished, a list which acquires a touch of irony

---

* I.e. why did Pallas rear Erichthonius if he was, as alleged, not her son, but sprung directly from Vulcan while she was struggling to protect her virginity against him?[48]

† Venus, as ancestress of the Julian house, had a place of honour by Mars in Augustus' new temple, while her husband Vulcan's statue apparently stood outside the door. Ovid mischievously adduces the notorious intrigue of Mars and Venus.

‡ This is simply a variation on what was by now the stock theme of *recusatio*, familiar from Propertius and even Horace:

> dum pudor
> imbellisque lyrae Musa potens vetat
> laudes egregii Caesaris et tuas
> culpa deterere ingeni.[49]

from its similarity to the eulogistic roll in *Amores* I, 15, and is, as usual with him, too long because he cannot resist bringing in everyone. Anacreon taught men to make love while deep in wine. What did Sappho teach her girls but to love? Callimachus often confessed to his amours, and Menander is full of love, yet he is given to boys and girls to read. The *Iliad* itself is simply a tale of adultery, first between Paris and Helen, then between Agamemnon and Briseïs. The *Odyssey* is a story of suitors attempting to seduce the wife of an absent husband. And who but Homer told of the adultery of Mars with Venus, of Odysseus with Calypso and Circe? Even the most serious genre, tragedy, is full of such affairs —Hippolytus, Canace, Hippodameia and others (to the tune of twenty-six lines)—while satyric drama is deliberately coarse, not to mention the Milesian Tales of Aristides and such like (361–420):

> Suntque ea doctorum monumentis mixta virorum
> muneribusque ducum publica facta patent.

> *These stand on the open shelves mingled with great works of literature, made available to the public by the generosity of our leading citizens.**

There have been many Roman writers equally wanton— Catullus, Calvus, Memmius, Ticidas, Cinna, Anser, Cornificius, Valerius Cato, the singers of Metella, Varro of Atax, Hortensius, Servius. Catullus' verse openly admitted his adultery; and, on the other hand, who could be such a warrant of immunity as the highly respected Hortensius or Servius? Sisenna had translated the lascivious tales of Aristides without penalty, and Gallus suffered, not for celebrating Lycoris, but for not holding his tongue when

---

* Asinius Pollio started the first public library at Rome in 39 B.C., and Augustus included a public library in the precincts of his shrine of Palatine Apollo; Ovid's bitterness at the removal of his books from them is natural, but his way of expressing it was hardly calculated to convert the Emperor. I think these are the *duces* Ovid is referring to, rather than the old generals who fought in Greece, such as Aemilius Paulus and Sulla, who cannot be said to have made public the libraries they brought back to Rome.

drunk. As for Tibullus, he devotes a great deal of attention to hoodwinking his mistress's husband, and Propertius is similar. (Ovid characteristically underlines his refusal to mention names of living poets—not that it would be beyond Augustus' wit to think of appropriate ones.) But all have been spared, both in life and libraries, save him alone (421–70).

He turns next to those who have written with impunity on games of hazard. It is true that technically these were forbidden, except at the Saturnalia or for old men, and Horace in one of his more censorious odes refers to *vetita legibus alea*;[50] but the law was already becoming a dead letter, as such laws are apt to do.[51] Why does Ovid make so much of it? Partly, it would seem, because he enjoyed the mental gymnastic of bringing the various games into verse, and, having incurred possible reproach by doing so in the *Ars Amatoria*[52] is glad to seize the opportunity of doing so again; but partly also, one may suspect, because Augustus was known to be so keen a player (471–92).*

Suppose he had written mimes, he continues. These are all about adultery, very indecent and very popular. Praetors pay high prices to put on 'tanta crimina', and not merely praetors (509–14):

> Inspice ludorum sumptus, Auguste, tuorum;
>   empta tibi magno talia multa leges.
> haec tu spectasti spectandaque saepe dedisti
>   (maiestas adeo comis ubique tua est),
> luminibusque tuis, totus quibus utitur orbis,
>   scaenica vidisti lentus adulteria.

> *Augustus, scan your sums on games defrayed:*
> *High prices for such shows you've often paid,*
> *Watched them in person and produced them free*
> *(So genial ever is your majesty),*
> *And with those eyes that all the world engage*
> *Smiled at adulteries upon the stage.*

---

* Suetonius, *Aug.* 71, based on letters of Augustus in the imperial files.

Indeed, Ovid's own poems have been performed as mimes, and sometimes before the Emperor. Even the fortunate, favoured Virgil in his youth wrote of Phyllis and Amaryllis, and the most popular part of the *Aeneid* is that in which (irreverent phrase!)

> contulit in Tyrios arma virumque toros,
> *Arms and the man were put to Dido's bed*

(though the characterization of that love as 'non legitimus' is rather disingenuous in this context). Why should he now be punished for juvenilia, especially as he has written major works since then which are full of tokens of his loyalty? Having attacked no one, he divines that no one at Rome is glad of his troubles and many are sorry (495–572).* In conclusion, he pleads that his penalty be mitigated so as to be commensurate with his offence.

This *refutatio* is rather patchy and cavalier as a defence, if the charge is taken seriously. To tell someone not to read a book is to ensure that she reads it, whoever it claims to be intended for, and there is little difference between the technique of *legitimus amor* and that of adultery. The fact that Penelope was a wedded wife did not prevent Ovid from citing her as an illustration in the *Ars*.[53] As for the contention that even the most solemn and approved works might suggest adultery, one cannot seriously maintain that the words *Aeneadum genetrix* with which Lucretius begins his *De Rerum Natura*, referring ultimately to Venus' legendary amour with Anchises, are in the same class as an incentive to, or sanction for, adultery as the *Ars Amatoria*. To the assertion that the latter has in fact corrupted certain matrons Ovid opposes a simple denial—*quicumque hoc concipit, errat.* Such accusations are seldom easy to substantiate, though they are familiar to us from the periodical strictures of magistrates on the cinema. It cannot be denied that books have on occasion led to deeds:

> Galeotto fu il libro e chi lo scrisse;

* This hint of the unpopularity of Augustus' action reverses what is said in the servile portion (ll. 77–88).

but how often, and in what circumstances, and with what kinds of character? Ovid has an answer to the last question at least:

> omnia perversas poterunt corrumpere mentes.

But though 'to the pure all things are pure' sounds a conclusive motto, it does not square entirely with human nature. On the other hand, though a colonnade may be a convenient place for an assignation, there are other places nearly as good, and to allow is not the same as to encourage. As for the argument about the suggestivity of temples due to the legends told of the gods, it is on a par with that about the opening of the *De Rerum Natura*.

When he proceeds to deal with the question why his Muse has *nimia lascivia* and why it encourages anyone at all to love (313 ff.), it may well be that he is introducing a charge never strictly made, in order to broaden the basis of his defence. He cannot deny it, but he can rope in everyone else as equally guilty or more so, and thus make it seem that he is being unfairly singled out. There was hardly a great man in recent Roman history to whom indecent verses were not ascribed,* let alone the famous Greek and Roman poets of the past. His excursus on Tibullus as an advocate of adultery is slightly disingenuous, since the word *coniunx* in his elegies need not mean a husband, *maritus* (457), but merely, as K. F. Smith says, 'the man who at the time happens to be furnishing the mistress of the elegiac lover with a house door';[54] and Ovid was surely aware of this. The games of hazard are a red herring. On the other hand, the final plea, that he is being punished for an offence committed too long ago, has force, to our way of thinking.

The whole rebuttal is more akin to satire in spirit than to anything else. The case against Ovid rested on degree; the *Ars Amatoria* was in a class by itself because of its exclusive and expressed intention, its scope and its shamelessness. His reply depends largely on mischievous and fantastic disregard of degree;

---

* The younger Pliny, in a similar context (*Ep*, v, 3, 2), gives a long list which includes Cicero, Pollio, Brutus, Messalla, Sulla, Scaevola, Servius Sulpicius, Varro, Julius Caesar and Augustus; cf. IV, 14, 4.

it is a riotous *reductio ad absurdum*, and what is meant to seem absurd is the attitude of the Emperor. It must have been all the more discomfiting because of the personal record of that upholder of the sanctity of the marriage tie, on which the poet could hardly touch. In his youth, having fallen in love with Livia, he had forced her devoted husband to surrender her, though she was pregnant; and later he had, for dynastic ends, made first Agrippa and then Tiberius divorce a wife to marry his daughter Julia. Suetonius says that even his friends excuse rather than deny his adulteries,[55] though we must be duly suspicious of the examples he quotes. Various writers mention him as author of indecent verses (Martial quotes an alleged specimen),[56] and indeed he would have been exceptional if, at least in his younger days, he had not followed this fashion.[57] Ovid may have gone further than others in the *Ars Amatoria*, but his surprise at the reaction is perfectly understandable. He was a real scapegoat, a vicarious expiator of the sins of others as well as a conspicuous warning. There may well be justice in Aurelius Victor's remark in this connexion, that Augustus was 'a most severe punisher of vice, in accordance with the way of men, which makes them be harsh in punishing those vices in which they themselves most freely indulge'.[58]

A time limit was set for Ovid's remaining in Italy, and he stayed till the last moment, paralysed into inaction while others bustled around him. Many supposed friends avoided contagion with him, but a few were notably loyal, and if he ever seriously thought of suicide, a friend talked him out of it.[59] Some of his slaves were to go with him (we hear nothing of their feelings about this, and should be surprised if we did). His wife begged and begged to accompany him, but it was essential that she should remain to keep the home together and work for his return.* The

---

* One is constantly reminded of the events and emotions of Cicero's exile: e.g. 'mulierem miserrimam, fidelissimam coniugem, me prosequi non sum passus, ut esset quae reliquias communis calamitatis, communes liberos tueretur' (*Ad Q.F.* I, 3, 3); and his charge to Terentia herself; 'si est spes nostri reditus, eam confirmes et rem adiuves' (*Ad Fam.* XIV, 4, 3).

famous poem[60] recalling his last night in Rome sounds as sincere as anything he wrote. It has hardly a trace of the old artificialities. Instead of the piled-up *exempla*, we have isolated and passing references to the desolation of the last night of Troy, limned for ever by Virgil in everyone's imagination, to the loyalty of Theseus, to Mettus, torn in two by horses; but that is all, in over a hundred lines. More significant, there is hardly a trace of straining after epigram or point—perhaps only in two couplets (61-2, 85-6)—for the points emphasized by verbal repetition in 63,

> uxor in aeternum vivo mihi viva negatur,

> *my wife, though alive, is denied for ever to me, though alive*

and 82,

> te sequar et coniunx exulis exul ero,

> *I will follow you and be the exiled wife of an exile*

are such as came naturally to anyone who spoke the Latin tongue. It is a sincere and vivid record of a poignant personal experience, a thing rare in ancient poetry, except on the subject of love or death, though Cicero's Letters offer us counterparts in prose. It is too long to quote in full, but a short selection may convey its quality (5-26):

> Iam prope lux aderat qua me discedere Caesar
> finibus extremae iusserat Ausoniae.
> nec spatium nec mens fuerat satis apta parandi:
> torpuerant longa pectora nostra mora.
> non mihi servorum, comites non cura legendi,
> non aptae profugo vestis opisve fuit.
> non aliter stupui quam qui Iovis ignibus ictus
> vivit et est vitae nescius ipse suae.
> ut tamen hanc animi nubem dolor ipse removit
> et tandem sensus convaluere mei,
> alloquor extremum maestos abiturus amicos
> qui modo de multis unus et alter erat.
> uxor amans flentem flens acrius ipsa tenebat,
> imbre per indignas usque cadente genas.

nata procul Libycis aberat diversa sub oris,
    nec poterat fati certior esse mei.
quocunque aspiceres, luctus gemitusque sonabant,
    formaque non taciti funeris intus erat.
femina virque meo, pueri quoque, funere maerent:
    inque domo lacrimas angulus omnis habet.
si licet exemplis in parvis grandibus uti,
    haec facies Troiae, cum caperetur, erat.

The day drew near when Caesar's firm decree
Compelled me leave the bounds of Italy.
Nor time nor spirit had I to prepare:
My mind was atrophied by long despair.
Of slaves, of company I took no heed,
Or clothes or comfort for an exile's need,
But stunned I was, like one by lightning hit
Who lives but yet is unaware of it.
When pain at length itself had cleared my brain
And all my senses were restored again,
I said my last farewells to one or two—
Of all those former friends alas how few!
My loving wife wept loud in our embrace,
Tears undeserved ran streaming down her face.
My daughter, somewhere far on Libya's shore,
Could not be told about my fate in store.
From every side laments and groans arose,
Filling the house as with funereal woes:
In every corner men and women all
And children wept at this my funeral.
If little things to great we may compare,
Troy's aspect on her fatal night was there.

Then follows one of those touches of vivid imagination that suddenly lift Ovid's verse on to an altogether higher plane (27–34):*

Iamque quiescebant voces hominumque canumque,
    Lunaque nocturnos alta regebat equos.

* Goethe, on his last night in Rome, paced the Colosseum in the moonlight declaiming this passage (*Italienische Reise* III, pp. 336–7, Sophien Ausgabe, Bd. 32).

hanc ego suspiciens et ad hanc Capitolia cernens,
    quae nostro frustra iuncta fuere Lari,
'numina vicinis habitantia sedibus', inquam,
    'iamque oculis numquam templa videnda meis,
dique relinquendi, quos urbs habet alta Quirini,
    este salutati tempus in omne mihi...'.

At last all noise of men and dogs was still.
The moon was driving high o'er heaven's hill.
I looked at her and, silhouetted plain,
The Capitol, our neighbour all in vain:
'Divinities whose fanes we dwell beside
And temples I shall never see', I cried,
'Gods of Quirinus' city reared of yore,
Hail and farewell for ever, ever more....'

It is true that the image serves a practical purpose, to enlist the all-seeing gods of the Capitol to intercede with the new god of the Palatine, who has been misled; but who can doubt, in this case at least, that the poet had really seen that vision of the Capitol with its temples outlined in the moonlight, towering above his home? The stars revolved, and night sped on relentlessly (47-8); did Ovid, like Marlowe's Faustus, recall with poignant irony on that last night the prayer in his youthful *aubade* of love—*lente currite, noctis equi?*[61] The whole house was in mourning, the symbolic fire before the Lares extinguished. He tried to tear himself away from so much that was dear to him—*domus et fidae dulcia membra domus*—and snatched at any pretext for delay. His wife was distracted, and when she pleaded once more to accompany him (84),

      accedam profugae sarcina parva rati,

      I will be but a small additional burden to the ship of exile,

we hear again, and perhaps are meant to hear, an ironic echo of Briseïs begging to be taken too if Achilles sails away from Troy:[62]

      non ego sum classi sarcina magna tuae.

His last thought is of her, how he saw her behaving then, and how he heard she had behaved after he left.

Ovid was forced to sail, probably from Brindisi, in November, at a time of year when sailing was by no means safe or comfortable. The events of the voyage are told in the First Book of the *Tristia*, which seems to have been sent to Rome soon after his arrival at Tomis.* He assures us in the Epilogue (xi) that he composed on shipboard, even in the midst of storms:

> Saepe maris pars intus erat; tamen ipse trementi
> carmina ducebam qualiacumque manu.[63]

> *Ship might be inundated, yet I would*
> *With trembling hand write verse as best I could.*

Granted that he may have made phrases in his head, and even jotted them down, in such conditions, we should take this claim with a drop of salt water. The poems are ingeniously constructed; they average 67 lines apiece; and ii, which is ostensibly written at the height of a storm, extends to 110. Here the threatening waves serve in fact not only to arouse pity for his state, but as a metaphor for it and a text for reflexions on it. Certainly these descriptions, even if inspired by emotion recollected in tranquillity, are none the less vivid for that. With a rare use of onomatopoeic spondees and repetition Ovid brings before our eyes the slow, huge, relentless alternation of billow and trough:

> Me miserum, quanti montes volvuntur aquarum !
> iam iam tacturos sidera summa putes:
> quantae diducto subsidunt aequore valles !
> iam iam tacturas Tartara nigra putes.[64]

Yet the reflexions are the *raison d'être* of the poem. He begins by begging the gods of the elements not to abet but to mitigate the wrath of the god who has punished him (1–12). The complaint that the wind and waves will not let his prayer be heard leads into

---

* For a most useful excursus on the voyage see Fränkel, *op. cit.* pp. 230–1.

a description of the storm designed to emphasize his sufferings, and pity is heightened by his thoughts of his wife, the half of his life, bitterly bewailing his banishment without realizing that he has any more trouble than that (13–44). The sky thunders, and increases his terror; it is not so much death he fears as the horror of drowning in that terrible sea (45–56). He then turns to thoughts of his deserts. If Caesar has spared his life, the gods of the elements should concur; he could himself have drowned him, had he wished (57–70). Yet if his life is spared now, what sort of a life remains for him? He contrasts the pleasure of his youthful voyage, to study at Athens and visit the cities of Asia, with the bleak prospect of Tomis, and does not know what to pray for (71–90). He resolves to submit, acknowledges his fault while protesting his innocence in intention, and outlines the plea he was later to develop as the *probatio* in *Tristia* II (91–106). Finally he sees, or thinks he sees, signs that the gods have heard and the storm is abating (107–10). With considerable finesse he has woven themes suggested by the storm into an appeal to Caesar.

No. IV describes more briefly a storm in the Ionian Sea which with pathetic irony drives the ship back into sight of Italy and threatens to cast the exile back on the forbidden shores of his native land. Once again, the appeal is to pity, the description only a means to it.

Nos. X and XI enable us to trace the wintry voyage. From Italy the ship crossed to Greece and went up the Gulf to Corinth, putting in at its western port of Lechaeum. Thence Ovid crossed the Isthmus to Cenchreae and embarked on another ship, which crossed the Aegean by the stepping-stones of the Cyclades, and so reached the Hellespont. From there it made a diversion to Samothrace, where he left it to pursue its voyage to the Black Sea without him.

θάλασσα κλύζει πάντα τἀνθρώπων κακά—

'the sea', says Euripides' Iphigeneia, 'washes away all the troubles of men.' Ovid seems to have become attached to this ship, with its guardian image of Pallas, the patroness of poets, and its sign of the painted helmet, and the valediction he wrote to it, suggested by Catullus' poem on his yacht, which had made the same voyage in a happier direction, is almost serene:[65]

Est mihi sitque, precor, flavae tutela Minervae,
 navis, et a picta casside nomen habet.
sive opus est velis, minimam bene currit ad auram,
 sive opus est remo, remige carpit iter.
nec comites volucri contenta est vincere cursu,
 occupat egressas quamlibet ante rates,
et pariter fluctus ferit atque silentia longe
 aequora, nec saevis victa madescit aquis.
illa, Corinthiacis primum mihi cognita Cenchreis,
 fida manet trepidae duxque comesque fugae,
perque tot eventus et iniquis concita ventis
 aequora Palladio numine tuta fuit.
nunc quoque tuta, precor, vasti secet ostia Ponti
 quasque petit, Getici litoris intret aquas.

A painted helmet gives my ship her name.
Pallas, her guardian, guard her still the same!
Sailing, she runs before the lightest breeze;
Driven with oars, she makes her way with ease;
And not content her comrades to outstrip,
She overtakes the long-departed ship.
Both waves and calm expanse of ocean well
She cleaves, and ships no water in a swell.
I met her first at Corinth's Cenchreae;
Guide and companion of my exile she
Through thick and thin, though windswept billows chafe,
Under Minerva's aegis has been safe.
Still safe may she the Black Sea gateway cleave,
And on the Getic coast her goal achieve.

The landsman had apparently, however, had enough of the sea. He preferred the short passage from Samothrace to the mainland

opposite and the land journey across Thrace.[66] He later recalled
with gratitude that the wealthy Sextus Pompeius had, to save his
purse, thoughtfully provided him with means of protection for
this journey through bandit-ridden territory.[67] It is possible that,
as Fränkel thinks, he re-embarked on the other side; the Epilogue
at least affects to be written in a storm, and there are indications
that it may be on the Black Sea.*

The rest of the book is composed of letters written to individuals
who are not, apart from his wife, named, because he was still
uncertain whether it would harm anyone to be connected with
him;† but it is intended for the ear of the general public, and of
Augustus in particular, and each poem, directly or obliquely,
enlists sympathy for the poet. Thus IX, congratulating a friend on
some advancement, is a warning of how those whom prosperity
attracts desert a man in adversity, and an appeal for continued
fidelity, which Caesar himself would surely approve on principle.
VIII is a denunciation of a faithless friend, which has one or two
fine lines, such as (15),

> illud amicitiae sanctum et venerabile nomen,

> *that sacred and reverend name of friendship,*

but consists mainly of worn and mechanical *loci*. VII is to his
publisher, who has told him that he wears his likeness, the head
crowned with the Bacchic ivy of poetic inspiration, engraved on
the stone of a ring. In thanking him Ovid commends to him a
still better image of himself—his poems, particularly the *Metamorphoses*, happily preserved from his own despairing rage, which
will keep his memory green at Rome. That was the most important
thing; at all costs he must not simply be forgotten. But he was

---

* 'Nunc quoque' (XI, 19) seems to distinguish the present voyage from that
across the Aegean; and the terms of v, 61-4, though not conclusive, suggest that
he arrived at Tomis by sea (see Fränkel, *op. cit.* p. 230).

† scis bene, cui dicam, positis pro nomine signis   (v, 7);
hoc tibi dissimula, senti tamen, optime, dici   (VII, 5).

Those who wish may speculate about the identity of the persons addressed.

also anxious for his readers to know that the work is unrevised. In the central position, *honoris causa*, is VI, to his wife, who alone can enlist friends to protect the family fortunes against the designs of the sinister 'nescioquis' of line 13, a letter full of trust and affection. Even this has one eye on the Palatine, for he suggests that her uncommon virtue comes from association with the Empress (25–8). V is to a friend who had given him the first word of kindness in his downfall, and so the will to go on living; the calamity has at least had this good result—without it he would never have known the extent of that loyalty (17–18). The second half of this poem (57–84) is an exhaustive comparison of his lot with that of Ulysses, showing how on every count he is worse off. This defeats its own end; we find ourselves congratulating him on each new point he wins in this odd contest of rivalry. But the opening lines (1–18) are a simple expression of gratitude and affection, flowing on freely over the bounds of the couplets and so doubly reminiscent of the sincerity of Catullus:

> O mihi post ullos nunquam memorande sodales,
>   et cui praecipue sors mea visa sua est,
> attonitum qui me, memini, carissime, primus
>   ausus es alloquio sustinuisse tuo,
> qui mihi consilium vivendi mite dedisti
>   cum foret in misero pectore mortis amor—
> scis bene, cui dicam, positis pro nomine signis,
>   officium nec te fallit, amice, tuum—
> haec mihi semper erunt imis infixa medullis,
>   perpetuusque animae debitor huius ero,
> spiritus et vacuas prius hic tenuandus in auras
>   ibit et in tepido deseret ossa rogo,
> quam subeant animo meritorum oblivia nostro,
>   et longa pietas excidat ista die.
> di tibi sint faciles, tibi di nullius egentem
>   fortunam praestant dissimilemque meae.
> si tamen haec navis vento ferretur amico,
>   ignoraretur forsitan ista fides.

Friend whom no friend for me will e'er dethrone,
Who most have felt my trouble as your own,
Dearest, who first dared speak and comfort me,
I well remember, in my agony,
And gently wooed me life again to try
When my poor spirit only yearned to die,
Unnamed, you know by tokens whom I so
Address, and what you did for me you know.
Deep in my heart I'll keep remembrance due,
And always I shall owe this life to you;
Yea, this my breath shall into air expire
Leaving my body on the smouldering pyre,
Ere time the memory of your kindness blot
And your devotion be at last forgot.
To you may kindly heaven such fortune send,
Unlike to mine, as needs no helping friend;
Yet if a favouring gale still wafted me,
Should I have ever known that loyalty?

'Where there is sorrow there is holy ground.' One is reminded of that man, who likewise had to be anonymous, mentioned in *De Profundis* (p. 18), who raised his hat to Wilde as he passed handcuffed down a crowded corridor after his condemnation: 'I do not know to the present moment whether he is aware that I was even conscious of his action. It is not a thing for which one can render formal thanks in formal words. I store it in the treasure-house of my heart. I keep it there as a secret debt that I am glad to think that I can never possibly repay.'

These five poems, v–ix, are a cross-section of the verse Ovid was to write henceforward. It is something that he could write at all, that his Muse was maimed rather than murdered, and he tells us of the wonder and relief he felt when he found that, even amid the surge of the sea and of his troubles, his *ingenium* was still alive.[68] His conclusion is charming:

Improba pugnat hiems indignaturque, quod ausim
scribere se rigidas incutiente minas.

vincat hiems hominem! sed eodem tempore, quaeso,
   ipse modum statuam carminis, illa sui.

The storm, indignant that I dare to write
For all its menaces, pursues the fight.
To storm I'll yield—on terms of armistice,
That this my song and it together cease.

So, with a touch of his old wit, he ended his Epilogue; and to
round off the book he added a very skilful Prologue, giving
instructions to the volume itself, which, albeit in the garb of
mourning, plain and unadorned, can at least enter the city. By
this engaging device he was able without offence to make an
oblique appeal to the Emperor (69–104). This carefully arranged
plea for pity he despatched, perhaps accompanied by Book II, as
soon as he arrived at Tomis.

CHAPTER X

'TRISTIA' III–V, 'IBIS', 'EPISTULAE EX PONTO'

AMONG THE GOTHS

THE eighty-four elegiac epistles which Ovid sent home from exile after *Tristia* II range from 22 to 166 lines in length, and fill seven books (i.e. rolls—*libelli*) averaging about 750 lines each. In the *Tristia*, apart from his wife, the girl Perilla, and members of the Imperial family, he does not name those he addresses for fear of doing them harm by advertising their association with him. Modern scholars have tried to identify them where there is any hint of a clue. It seems fairly sure, indeed, that IV, 4 and 5 are to Messallinus and Cotta respectively, and perhaps the association of the poet with Messalla's house was too well known to call for more than a perfunctory concealment. But it is significant, for instance, as Bakker points out,* that in seventeen cases where Lorentz ventured to supply a name Némethy either did not venture or supplied a different one, and in the only case where they did agree they seem to be wrong.

The *Letters from the Black Sea* (*Epistulae ex Ponto*) follow hard on the heels of the *Tristia*,† and differ from them, as the poet him-

---

* See his comparative table, *P. Ovidii Nasonis Tristium V* (1946), p. 2. The lines III, 5, 17–8,

> Sum quoque, care, tuis defensus viribus absens:—
> scis 'carum' veri nominis esse loco,

would be a dangerous joke, making nonsense of the concealment whose necessity Ovid elsewhere emphasizes with regret, if they were addressed (as these two scholars suppose, following Heinsius) to the friend named Carus who is the recipient of *P.* IV, 13.

† Thus *Tr.* V, 10, 1, written when Ovid has seen three winters at Tomis (i.e. in the winter of 11–12) cannot anticipate by much *P.* III, 3, 86, where he has not yet heard of the triumph of Tiberius on 16 Jan. 13 A.D.

self avows, only in that they no longer conceal the recipients' names.[1] To a friend who is represented as having demurred to this publicity he protests that he had himself offended previously in crediting the Emperor with so little humanity as to suppose that he would persecute those who comforted an exile.[2] (Perhaps he had received a hint.) There is a curious passage at *Tristia* IV, 5, 10–2, probably addressed to Cotta, in which Ovid exclaims: 'In my enthusiasm I almost let out your name! But in any case you will recognize yourself, and fired with desire for honour would fain cry openly, "I am that man".' This is obviously a conceit, but a strangely inappropriate one if we are to suppose that the poem was sent to the recipient personally. Yet it is natural to assume that each poem addressed to an individual would be so sent, not kept in cold storage till the poet had enough of them by him to fill a volume; and in the case of the *Pontic Epistles* he tells us that this was in fact so.*[3] But each was intended also for circulation, as the occasional intrusion of *vos* or *o lector* sufficiently testifies.[4] And finally, each was intended for the imperial eye. Even in an invective against a detractor Ovid contrives to glance at Augustus' clemency and his certainty of apotheosis,[5] and few of the poems have no reference to him.

About once a year between A.D. 8 and 13 he made up a *libellus* of these elegies.†[6] In the books of the *Tristia* he arranged them, not chronologically, as a modern poet might do, but on principles

---

* The poem on a triumph mentioned at *P.* II, 5, 27–34 as possibly already in Salanus' hands may be identical with that which stands first in the same book. *Tr.* III, 11 is odd: it is addressed to an enemy,

> si quis es, insultas qui casibus, improbe, nostris,

(cf. l. 56, *quisquis is es*; l. 63, *quicunque es*). Surely we have here simply a lay figure invented to enable the poet to write an elegy contrasting with the previous one, which is addressed in general to

> si quis adhuc istic meminit Nasonis adempti.

† The chronology of composition and publication is conveniently set out by A. L. Wheeler in the Introduction to his Loeb edition (1924), pp. xxxiii–xxxv. It is based on the work of Graeber and others.

of variety and symmetry such as we find operating in other ancient collections of poems.* The dates emerge as follows:

A.D. 8–9	Tristia I
9	II
9–10	III
10–11	IV
11–12	V

The decision to mention his friends by name so stimulated Ovid's Muse that by the end of 13 he had enough *Pontic Epistles* (30) to fill three rolls. These he caused to be published together (as Horace in 23 B.C. had published together the first three books of his *Odes*) arranging them in no special order and consigning them in a prologue and epilogue to his friend Brutus.†

The poems in Book IV that can be dated fall between 13 and 16. Since it contains some 200 lines more than the others and, unlike them, has no prologue, it is presumed that they were collected and published after the poet's death in 17–18.

If we may believe Ovid, he sometimes had fits of rage or despair in which he burnt what he had written, as he had done on the eve of his exile. But just as the *Metamorphoses* had survived that holocaust so, he claims, it is relics saved 'by chance or stealth' from the flames that are preserved in these *libelli*.[7] He may, of course, only be trying to shock his readers by the thought of such losses to Latin literature, as one more stimulus for his recall; but there is nothing surprising psychologically if what he says is true. At all events, the surviving poems average one for every month. For all his facility, he did not find writing easy. He had no books to nourish his Muse, no privacy, no one to consult when at a loss for a word or name of person or place, no friendly circle of poets to listen and criticize, no audience to spur him with applause:[8] 'to write a poem you may not read to anyone is like dancing in the dark.'[9] Nor had he now a succession of new experiences, such

---

* This was established by K. Herrmann in an unprinted Leipzig dissertation *De Ovidii Tristium Libris V* (1924); his schemes are set out by Martini, *op. cit.* p. 52.

† *P.* I, 1; III, 9, 53, *utcumque sine ordine iunxi.*

as had diversified the first book of the *Tristia*, and obsession with his wrong precluded his seeking any. As time went on he felt that his genius, living on capital, was drying up;[10] and even so fastidious an artist found eventually that he had no longer the zest to face the labour of amending faults in his verse which he clearly recognized. Why cast pearls before the Getae?[11]

Whatever gleams of reviving spirits flickered in Ovid as his voyage proceeded, they were rudely quenched by the realities that confronted him on his arrival at Tomis. The Emperor had doubtless chosen the place because it was as far as possible from Rome; but he could not have chosen better if his object was to break the spirit of one who had thrived on the comfort and the pleasures of a brilliant capital. Ovid's charity or discretion preferred to suppose that he simply did not realize what he was doing.[12] Here was no frontier-fort built and garrisoned by the Romans, but an old Milesian colony which had no doubt seen better days, existing because it was the only port on a desolate coast, and sustained partly by fisheries, partly perhaps by the passage of goods from ships that would have entered the Danube but for delta-silt. It had no mineral wealth, and the only product the poet could find worth sending to Rome as a present was a quiverful of arrows. Brackish lagoons afforded distasteful and unhealthy water, carried in jars on women's heads, to one who had been used to the clear hill-streams that flowed through aqueducts into the fountains of Rome. Nor were there vines to produce so much as a *vin ordinaire*; indeed, marauders allowed little cultivation at all around the town; there was a certain amount of grazing, though the women had not learnt how to work or dye the coarse wool; for the rest, wormwood scrub and an occasional barren tree were all the vegetation on the vast no-man's-land of steppes that, with the leaden sea, extended to the horizon on all sides.*[13]

* The coastal lagoons are formed by Danube silt moving southward. Before the Dobruja was taken over by the Rumanians in 1878 most of it was, as in

In lines familiar to schoolboys Ovid has depicted the scene:[14]

Nix iacet, et iactam ne sol pluviaeque resolvant,
   indurat Boreas perpetuamque facit.
ergo ubi delicuit nondum prior, altera venit,
   et solet in multis bima manere locis;
tantaque commoti vis est Aquilonis, ut altas
   aequet humo turres tectaque rapta ferat.
pellibus et sutis arcent mala frigora bracchis,
   oraque de toto corpore sola patent.
saepe sonant moti glacie pendente capilli
   et nitet inducto candida barba gelu;
nudaque consistunt, formam servantia testae,
   vina, nec hausta meri sed data frusta bibunt.
quid loquar, ut vincti concrescant frigore rivi
   deque lacu fragiles effodiantur aquae?
ipse, papyrifero qui non angustior amne
   miscetur vasto multa per ora freto,
caeruleos ventis latices durantibus, Hister
   congelat et tectis in mare serpit aquis;
quaque rates ierant, pedibus nunc itur, et undas
   frigore concretas ungula pulsat equi,
perque novos pontes, subter labentibus undis,
   ducunt Sarmatici barbara plaustra boves.

Snow lies, and ere it melt in sun or rain
Comes Boreas and hardens it again;
Ere one dissolves, another fall is here,
In many a place to lie from year to year;
And Aquilo such fury can display,
'Twill level towers and carry roofs away.
Breeches and furs keep out the cruel cold:
No feature but the face can one behold.

Ovid's day, uncultivated steppe covered with brushwood, with frequent marshes
that made it unhealthy (*Guide Bleu*, 1933, p. 6). For a vivid account of the desolation of this region under the Turks see Ripert, *op. cit.* pp. 195–6, based on C. Allard,
La Dobroutcha (Paris, 1859).

Icicles tinkle when men shake their hair,
And rough beards glister with the rime they wear.
Stark stands the wine, the wine-jar's shape preserved,
And from it chunks instead of draughts are served.
What of the rivers bound in icy bonds,
And brittle water quarried out of ponds?
Danube himself, who mingles with the sea
Wide as the Nile through many mouths as he,
Feels his blue waters by the wind congealed
And creeps to ocean with his flow concealed.
Men cross on foot where ferries lately plied,
And horse-hooves echo o'er the frozen tide,
While on new bridges o'er the flood's domains
Sarmatian oxen haul outlandish wains.

Even the Black Sea was liable to freeze near the coast, and everything from fish to ships became ice-bound.[15] (Provoked by rumours that his readers at Rome are sceptical about this, Ovid launches into a discourse on the reasons: the prevailing wind is north-east, with no relief from the mild south-west; the great rivers pour into the almost land-locked sea fresh water which, being lighter than salt water, rises to the surface.)[16] No wonder the poet's health suffered. During his first winter he fell ill, and there were no suitable quarters for him, no medical attention or proper diet, no pure water, no one to talk to.[17] Next winter he is ill again, and doubtful of recovery; a year later he is suffering from pains in the side (? pleurisy) which he attributes to the cold.[18] Later, fearing he may have caused undue alarm by his account of his health, he reassures his wife; he has become inured in body, though not in mind.[19] Indeed, he is aware that his illness is largely due to psychological causes. He has no taste for his food, even when he is not actually ill, and meal times bring him no pleasure; at night he suffers from feverish insomnia, and from sheer fretting he has become emaciated and prematurely old. His own wife would scarcely recognize him now.[20]

The freezing of the sea and of the Danube, thirty-five miles

west-north-west at its nearest point, brought fear to aggravate
the attendant cold. Dacian barbarians on horseback poured over
these normal defences of the Empire to plunder:[21]

> Sive igitur nimii Boreae vis saeva marinas,
> sive redundantes flumine cogit aquas,
> protinus aequato siccis Aquilonibus Histro
> invehitur celeri barbarus hostis equo;
> hostis equo pollens longeque volante sagitta
> vicinam late depopulatur humum.
> diffugiunt alii, nullisque tuentibus agros
> incustoditae diripiuntur opes,
> ruris opes parvae, pecus et stridentia plaustra,
> et quas divitias incola pauper habet.
> pars agitur vinctis post tergum capta lacertis,
> respiciens frustra rura Laremque suum;
> pars cadit hamatis misere confixa sagittis:
> nam volucri ferro tinctile virus inest.
> quae nequeunt secum ferre aut abducere, perdunt,
> et cremat insontes hostica flamma casas.

So whether Boreas with bitter blast
Has gripped the sea or bound the river fast,
When dry North Winds have smoothed the Danube's back
Swiftly the mounted savages attack.
With horse and long-range archery supplied
The foe lays waste the country far and wide.
Some flee and leave their fields an open prey;
Their undefended wealth is driven away,
Poor country wealth such as a peasant has,
A creaking waggon and an ox or ass.
Some, caught and led away with pinioned arms,
Vainly look backward to their homestead farms;
Some, pierced by barbèd shafts, fall cruelly dead,
For poison clings to every arrowhead.
What cannot be removed is wrecked entire,
And harmless cottages are set on fire.

And it was not only Dacians taking such intermittent opportunities who were to be feared. The surrounding country was only
half pacified. While Tomis and the other towns of Greek origin
were self-governing outposts, under Roman law and subject to
the distant jurisdiction of the Governor of the province of
Macedonia, the hinterland was an outlying part of the half-
controlled dominions of the Kingdom of Thrace, a satellite of the
Empire.* Ovid gives us a vivid picture of the constant state of
emergency:[22]

> Innumerae circa gentes fera bella minantur,
>   quae sibi non rapto vivere turpe putant.
> nil extra tutum est: tumulus defenditur ipse
>   moenibus exiguis ingenioque loci.
> cum minime credas, ut aves, densissimus hostis
>   advolat, et praedam vix bene visus agit.
> saepe intra muros clausis venientia portis
>   per medias legimus noxia tela vias.
> est igitur rarus, rus qui colere audeat, isque
>   hac arat infelix, hac tenet arma, manu.
> sub galea pastor iunctis pice cantat avenis,
>   proque lupo pavidae bella verentur oves.

> *Unnumbered tribes around hold us at bay,*
> *Who count it shameful not to live on prey.*
> *Naught's safe without; even the fortress-height*
> *Has puny walls to reinforce its site.*
> *When least you think, like birds, a flock of foes*
> *Swoops down and, scarcely sighted, robs and goes.*
> *Often within the bolted gates' retreat*
> *We pick up poisoned arrows in the street.*
> *Few, then, dare till the soil, and they must farm*
> *One hand on plough, the other on their arm;*
> *Helmeted pipes the shepherd, and instead*
> *Of wolves, his sheep marauding warriors dread.*

* For a good account of the situation see Fränkel *op. cit.* p. 124.

And again:[23]

> Aspera militiae iuvenis certamina fugi,
>   nec nisi lusura movimus arma manu;
> nunc senior gladioque latus scutoque sinistram,
>   canitiem galeae subicioque meam.
> nam dedit e specula custos ubi signa tumultus,
>   induimus trepida protinus arma manu.
> hostis, habens arcus imbutaque tela venenis,
>   saevus anhelanti moenia lustrat equo;
> utque rapax pecudem, quae se non texit ovili,
>   per sata, per silvas fertque trahitque lupus,
> sic, siquem nondum portarum saepe receptum
>   barbarus in campis repperit hostis, habet:
> aut sequitur captus coniectaque vincula collo
>   accipit, aut telo virus habente perit.

> *In youth I shunned all horrid martial fray,*
> *Nor ever handled arms except in play:*
> *Now, middle-aged, a shield and sword I bear,*
> *And press a helmet on my grizzled hair.*
> *For when the look-out raises the alarm,*
> *We haste at once our trembling hands to arm;*
> *Ere long on panting horse the savage foe*
> *Circles the walls with poisoned shaft and bow.*
> *And as a ravening wolf through wood, o'er wold,*
> *Bears, drags a sheep surprised without the fold,*
> *So any man caught ere he can regain*
> *The gates' defence is by the invader ta'en;*
> *Then either, neck in halter, as a prize*
> *Is led, or by a poisoned weapon dies.*

The savage horsemen battered at the gate, and their arrows stuck bristling in the thatched roofs of the houses inside.[24] No wonder Ovid dared not venture much without, though he would have liked to kill time by his old recreation of gardening.*[25]

---

* He enlarges on this theme in the spirit of Tibullus (51–60), not very realistically.

Even within the precarious fortifications he felt none too safe. The Tomitans were originally Milesian Greeks, but by now more than half the population consisted of Getic or Sarmatian barbarians. With rough voice, grim face, unkempt hair and beard they rode up and down the streets, long bow and quiver of poisoned arrows on their shoulder and dagger at their side. Their law was jungle law; often their disputes in the forum were settled with the sword. He hints vaguely at plots against his life.[26] Moreover, 'even if you are not afraid of them', says the delicate Roman, 'you may well loathe the sight of their chests covered with hides or long hair.' More savage than wolves, they were scarcely worthy of the name of men. Even those credited with Greek descent had adopted (sensibly enough, in view of the climate) the native trousers which looked so outlandish to the toga'd race. They used the local languages among themselves, or spoke Greek with a Getic accent, and for some time Ovid could only make himself understood by signs. He, the master of the noble Latin tongue (*ille ego Romanus vates*), was here a 'barbarian', a man who spoke a language unintelligible as *bar-bar*, which made the oafish inhabitants laugh. Indeed, whenever they laughed (one recognizes here the phobia common among the deaf), he imagined it was at him, perhaps even at his being an exile; and they in turn suspected his every gesture. Not a soul knew the commonest Latin words; he had to talk to himself for fear of forgetting how to speak his native tongue; perhaps even his poems—horrid thought, had it been sincere!— might contain barbarisms undetected by him.[27] At length he could hold out no longer; he was compelled to learn to speak Getic and Sarmatian.[28]

In a striking passage, where each pentameter contrasts with its hexameter, he sums up the burden of his fate:[29]

> Artibus ingenuis quaesita est gloria multis:
>   infelix perii dotibus ipse meis.
> vita prior vitio caret et sine labe peracta est:
>   auxilii misero nil tulit illa mihi.

culpa gravis precibus donatur saepe suorum:
  omnis pro nobis gratia muta fuit.
adiuvat in duris aliquos praesentia rebus:
  obruit hoc absens vasta procella caput.
quis non horruerit tacitam quoque Caesaris iram?
  addita sunt poenis aspera verba meis.
fit fuga temporibus levior: proiectus in aequor
  Arcturum subii Pleïadumque minas.
saepe solent hiemem placidam sentire carinae:
  non Ithacae puppi saevior unda fuit.
recta fides comitum poterat mala nostra levare:
  ditata est spoliis perfida turba meis.
mitius exilium faciunt loca: tristior ista
  terra sub ambobus non iacet ulla polis.
est aliquid patriis vicinum finibus esse:
  ultima me tellus, ultimus orbis habet.
praestat et exulibus pacem tua laurea, Caesar:
  Pontica finitimo terra sub hoste iacet.
tempus in agrorum cultu consumere dulce est:
  non patitur verti barbarus hostis humum.
temperie caeli corpusque animusque iuvatur:
  frigore perpetuo Sarmatis ora riget.
est in aqua dulci non invidiosa voluptas:
  aequoreo bibitur cum sale mixta palus.

Many win glory by the liberal arts:
I have been ruined by my very parts.
My former life from vice and blame was free:
What help has that been in my misery?
Grave crimes are often pardoned at the suit
Of friends: for me all influence was mute.
Through being present some abate the worst,
But I was absent when my tempest burst.
Fearful were Caesar's anger even pent:
His stern rebuke made worse my punishment.
Seasons can soften exile: I am cast
On northern shores the Bear and Pleiads blast.

332

Often in winter ships have sailing fine:
Ulysses' barque had calmer seas than mine.
Comfort could spring from comrades' loyalty:
My faithless gang grew rich by robbing me.
Congenial place can cheer an exile: is
There bleaker spot between the poles than this?
'Twere something to be near one's native sky:
In furthest land of utmost earth I lie.
E'en exiles gain from Caesar's laurels peace:
This Pontic land lies close to enemies.
In gardening sweet pastime may be found:
Here savage foes forbid us till the ground.
Body and soul thrive in a temperate clime:
This Getic shore is chilly all the time.
Fresh water is a harmless luxury,
But brackish, briny marsh-water drink we.

Since Ovid is practically our only source of information on Tomis, we must be cautious about taking him too literally. Though he claimed credence because he had no motive for lying,[30] his perpetual object was to awake pity for his plight. He was naturally exasperated when he sensed that people sitting comfortably at Rome presumed he was exaggerating for effect as usual, and he appealed for confirmation to any visitor from civilization.[31] Sometimes, indeed, we may suspect that he is simply making picturesque use of literary data for his ulterior purpose, as when he enhances the horrors of Tomis by accepting the derivation of its name from the Greek word for 'to hew', with reference to the grisly story of Medea's hewing her brother in pieces near the Danube mouth and scattering his limbs to delay her pursuing father.[32] The comparative proximity of the Tauric Chersonese (Crimea) enabled him to use the story of Euripides' *Iphigeneia in Tauris* both to suggest that he is in a region notorious for human sacrifice, and to connect the legend of the devoted friendship of Orestes and Pylades and their happy escape back to civilization with the bonds between himself and friends at Rome and his hopes of a similar return through their good offices. Once, so he says, when he was praising Cotta's loyalty to a barbarian audience, an aged Scythian broke in with 'We too, stranger, know the word "friendship"', and then, claiming to have been born near the Tauric temple of Artemis, recounted the same legend. Surely Ovid's contemporaries, like us, would suspect he invented this incident as an effective piece of scene-setting.[33]

Several times he speaks as though he were in the far north, 'near the Great Bear',[34] though in fact he was no nearer to it than Florence is; and his Italian friends might well be sceptical about the rigours of a place which they may have vaguely known to be in much the same latitude as themselves. But there is in fact no reason to doubt the faithfulness of the general impression he gives. From modern experience the winters of the Dobruja might well paralyse an Italian. Icy north-east winds sweep down from the Russian steppes on to the unsheltered plateau, and the Danube does in fact freeze, sometimes for two or three months on end. The *Guide Bleu* describes the climate as 'très continental, assez proche du climat russe'. The winter is long, and the temperature can fall to $-30°$ or even $-35°$.[35]

It is clear that Ovid kept up a continual prose correspondence with his friends at Rome, with Severus for instance.[36] But he would have to rely on chance carriers, and letters might be held up or go astray.[37] He reckoned it might take a full year for a letter to come and a reply to be composed and to reach Rome.[38] One friend tried, in vain, to cheer him up by telling him that poems of his were being performed as dances to crowded houses at Rome.[39] Cotta sends him some speeches he has delivered in the Forum, and he reads them over and over again.[40] But he remains avid of any rumour from the civilized world. When spring breaks up the ice he looks forward to the arrival of ships again. Though they are unlikely to be more than coasters, or from the Sea of Marmora at the farthest, he will run down to greet their crew in the hope of finding someone who speaks Greek, or still better Latin, and can tell him some news.[41] 'Oh for the wings of a dove!'

334

In a wistful and beautiful passage Ovid recalls those legendary figures who had made their escape by flying—Triptolemus who had come himself to the Scythian shores with his new gift of corn, Medea and Perseus and Daedalus who were exiles like himself:*[42]

> Nunc ego Triptolemi cuperem consistere curru,
>   misit in ignotum qui rude semen humum;
> nunc ego Medeae vellem frenare dracones,
>   quos habuit fugiens arce, Corinthe, tua;
> nunc ego iactandas optarem sumere pennas
>   sive tuas, Perseu, Daedale, sive tuas:
> ut tenera nostris cedente volatibus aura
>   aspicerem patriae dulce repente solum,
> desertaeque domus vultus memoresque sodales,
>   caraque praecipue coniugis ora meae.

> *Oh in his heavenly chariot to stand,*
> *Who first put seeds into the virgin land!*
> *To harness now Medea's dragon-car*
> *Whereon she sped from Corinth's walls afar!*
> *Oh to be borne on wings impetuous,*
> *Soaring like Perseus or like Daedalus!*
> *That wafted through the yielding air above*
> *I soon might see the country that I love,*
> *My long-lost home, true friends about the place,*
> *And chief of all, my wife's belovèd face.*

Meanwhile, for lack of anything else to do, cooped up as he was and without company or means of enjoyment, he continued to do what he had done for the past thirty to forty years—write elegiac verse. He sings as the shackled farm-slave, the heaving barge-puller or the galley-slave sings, to lighten his toil.[43] After all, even Phalaris could not prevent Perillus from groaning when he was in torment in the heated brazen bull.[44] He finds writing verse an anodyne, and it fills up leisure which would otherwise be

* For a sensitive appreciation of this poem see A. G. Lee in *Greece and Rome*, 1949, pp. 113–20.

intolerable.[45] Besides, when he wrote he felt he was in some sense present with the friend he was writing for. 'You are here though you do not know it, and though absent you are most constantly present; from the midst of the City I can summon you to the Getae: do likewise for me, and since your country is the happier, keep me always there in your remembering heart.'[46] We may well believe that he had all these subjective motives for writing; but he had objective aims as well.

In the first place he could not bear to think of being forgotten at Rome, of coming home, if ever he did, to find that his world had passed on. Here is one effect of his exile for which we should be grateful. It made him dwell in his poetry on himself, partly from motives of self-pity and self-justification, but partly also to keep himself alive in Roman minds and excite sympathy. So his later poems contain pieces of autobiography, such as his recollections of his youthful grand tour with Macer,[47] and his detailed *curriculum vitae* in *Tristia* IV, 10 already cited, which are exceptional in ancient poetry and have special interest for our age, hungry for *personalia*; and they may also have encouraged other poets, ancient and modern, to tell their readers about themselves.

But his overriding object was to move the powers at Rome, either by arousing their pity and ingratiating himself through flattery or by provoking a public outcry for his recall. For tactical reasons he only asks in the first place for transference to a safer and more civilized place of relegation, though return to Rome was avowedly his ultimate hope:

> Quod petimus, poena est: neque enim miser esse recuso,
> sed precor ut possim tutius esse miser.
>
> *What I seek is a punishment; for I do not balk at suffering, but only ask to be able to suffer in more safety.**

Nearly all the poems come back to this:

> scribere saepe aliud cupiens, delabor eodem.[48]

* *Tr.* v, 2, 77–8; cf. *Tr.* II, 575–8, both addressed to Augustus.

There is, indeed, something distasteful in his reply to a letter from Cotta breaking the news that their friend Celsus is dead; though genuinely moved, he is soon improving the occasion by recalling how Celsus had constantly assured him that Cotta, such is his loyalty, could be relied on to work for his recall; a dead man's wishes must be respected.[49] But a sufferer must be pardoned his *idée fixe*.

His flattery of Augustus and members of the Imperial family knows no bounds. They are of course deified, and he is careful to mention that he has a shrine dedicated to them in his house at Tomis, in which he offers daily incense and prayer.[50] Nothing could be more fulsome than his poem acknowledging a gift from Cotta of a silver *objet d'art* with likenesses of the Caesars on it.[51] We may admire the ingenuity of his ideas—for instance, his use of the oak leaves decreed by the Senate to hang on Augustus' door *ob cives servatos* as text for an appeal to save just one more citizen[52] —but we can hardly be surprised that it had no effect. Such adulation, largely derived from that of Eastern monarchs, had for some time attached itself to the person of the Emperor, who was identified in this with the state; as Ovid says,

> Res est publica Caesar,
> et de communi pars quoque nostra bono est.

> *Caesar belongs to all, and I, even I, have a share in the commonwealth.*[53]

His flatteries differ from those of previous Augustan poets only in assiduity. Thus his differentiation between the supreme deities of Caesar and Jupiter,

> quorum hic aspicitur, creditur ille deus,

> *of whom the one is seen, the other believed, to be a god,*

recalls Horace's

> caelo tonantem *credidimus* Iovem
> regnare: *praesens divus* habebitur
>   Augustus adiectis Britannis
>   imperio gravibusque Persis;[54]

and he has nothing more fancifully extravagant than Virgil's invocation to the new god Caesar in the exordium of the *Georgics*. This phenomenon is distasteful to the modern mind, and was indeed to some of the ancients even under the Empire. Tacitus, no friend of Tiberius, put into his mouth words which are as fresh air in a room stifling with incense: 'I solemnly assure you, senators, and I wish posterity to be aware, that I am a mortal man limited to human functions, and that it is enough for me if I hold the highest place.'[55] It is painful to see a dog fawning on a master who is cruel to it. Ovid's adulation of Augustus is particularly nauseating because it is heaped on his oppressor; but we should be chary of blaming him, unless we have been through a similar experience.

What gave him hope was the fact that Augustus had deliberately prescribed for him what was considered to be the less severe of the two Roman forms of banishment. By not depriving him of his property or citizen's rights he seemed to envisage the possibility of his ultimate return.[56] In the event this proved to be a cruel mitigation. Full exile instead of relegation would probably have involved not coming within a prescribed distance from Rome;* but how gladly Ovid would have sacrificed all to be able to live, even in poverty, in some place of his own choice ! Instead, Fortune cheated him at every turn. The disaster to Varus and his legions in Germany in 9 A.D. distracted the Emperor's attention for some time, besides making it unlikely that his mood would become more benign; then, when the situation had been restored and the Pannonian triumph of Tiberius, finally celebrated on October 23, A.D. 12,† had generated an atmosphere which seemed more propitious,[57] Ovid lost the most likely and influential of his advocates by the death of Paullus Fabius Maximus in the summer of 14. Even so, he had fancied that Augustus had begun to relent, when on August 19 of that year he too died.[58]

---

* Thus Cicero was exiled in 58 B.C. to beyond a radius of 500 miles from Rome.

† For the date, established by a new fragment of the Praenestine Fasti, see W. Kraus, 'P. Ovidius Naso' in *R.E.* col. 1918.

From Tiberius personally he seems to have hoped for little, though he appeals briefly to him once amid prayers to his imperial stepfather,[59] and indicates that he has composed an elegy on his triumph, though in no mood for such themes.[60] He also composed a poem, which has not survived, on the apotheosis of Augustus.[61] His main hopes, however, were transferred to Germanicus, the nephew and adopted son of the new emperor. He does not seem to have known the prince personally, for he relies on the inter-cession of friends such as Salanus,[62] his tutor in rhetoric, Carus, the tutor of his children,[63] or Suillius, his quaestor, who worshipped him.[64] But he knew his reputation as a humane and affable man who was interested in literature and himself something of a poet. Already during the lifetime of Augustus he had put at the head of the Second Book of *Pontic Epistles* a poem addressed to Germanicus, congratulating him on assuming the triumphal insignia for his exploits against the Dalmatians a few years before. He now promised him a gift whose worth he would appreciate, a name immortal in poetry,[65] and took up the abandoned *Fasti* again in the hope of completing them in his honour.*

We may now explore this extensive corpus of verse for what we can find to interest or move us. In the first place, nostalgia for the life he had left behind sometimes allowed Ovid to escape for a while in imagination, and once more to compose in a major key. His brief autobiography and his memories of happy days with Messalla and Cotta, or with Atticus, have already been cited.† On another occasion, overcoming any bitterness for supposed neglect, he recalls his youthful tour with Macer:[66]

Te duce magnificas Asiae perspeximus urbes;
    Trinacris est oculis te duce visa meis.
vidimus Aetnaea caelum splendescere flamma,
    subpositus monti quam vomit ore Gigans,

* See p. 253.   † Pp. 290–3.

Hennaeosque lacus et olentis stagna Palici,
    quaque suis Cyanen miscet Anapus aquis.
nec procul hinc nymphe, quae, dum fugit Elidis amnem,
    tecta sub aequorea nunc quoque currit aqua.
hic mihi labentis pars anni magna peracta est:
    eheu, quam dispar est locus ille Getis!
et quota pars haec sunt rerum, quas vidimus ambo
    te mihi iucundas efficiente vias!
seu rate caeruleas picta sulcavimus undas,
    esseda nos agili sive tulere rota,
saepe brevis nobis vicibus via visa loquendi
    pluraque, si numeres, verba fuere gradu;
saepe dies sermone minor fuit, inque loquendum
    tarda per aestivos defuit hora dies.
est aliquid casus pariter timuisse marinos,
    iunctaque ad aequoreos vota tulisse deos,
et modo res egisse simul, modo rursus ab illis,
    quorum non pudeat, posse referre iocos.

The splendid Asian cities at your side
I toured, and Sicily with you for guide;
With Etna's flames we saw the heavens glow,
Vomited by the giant pinned below;
Saw Enna's lake, Palicus' pool that stinks,
And where of Cyane Anapus drinks,
And her who, Elis' river-god to flee,
Ran 'neath the waves, and still runs under sea.
There did I spend most of a gliding year
(Alas, how different that land from here!).
The merest fraction, this, of all we viewed,
While you with gladness all my ways endued,
Whether we clove the deep with painted keel
Or bowled along on rattling carriage-wheel.
Often our road seemed shortened by our talk:
We had more words to say than steps to walk.
Days proved too short, and we'd be talking yet
After the lingering summer sun was set.

340

'Tis something to have shared in dread of seas
And joined in prayer to ocean deities,
Done things together and, when later met,
Laughed over them with nothing to regret.

When at last spring comes to Tomis (but there promises little more than the melting of snow and ice), he thinks of the violets coming out in Italy, and the boys and girls going off to the meadows to pick flowers, the birds singing, the swallow building, the corn peeping above ground, the vines and trees budding; and then of the life of the city, the holidays when the business of the Forum gives way to a succession of festivals, contests on horseback or with arms, games with ball or hoop, young men after exercise bathing in the Aqua Virgo, and the intense dramatic activity and rivalries of the three theatres.[67] If Cicero, sent to govern Cilicia for a year, yearned for the life of Rome— 'urbem, urbem, mi Rufe, cole et in ista luce vive; omnis peregrinatio...obscura et sordida eis quorum industria Roma potest illustris esse'[68] ('stick to the City, the City, Rufus, and live in its limelight; all time spent abroad is dim and sordid to those by whose efforts Rome can be glorious')—how much more would Ovid, banished indefinitely to Moesia ! When he is in the act of protesting to Severus, *à propos* the latest barbarian raid, that safety, not the pleasures of city life, is all he asks, honesty checks him in mid-couplet:

> Nec tu credideris urbanae commoda vitae
> quaerere Nasonem—quaerit et illa tamen;

And do not think that Naso is missing the amenities of city life—
yet he does miss them;

and once again he reviews in imagination the piazzas, temples, theatres and porticos, the Campus with its green turf and the gardens, lakes, canals and fountains all about. He thinks too of his own gardens outside the city, of the plants he was not too grand to water himself, and of the trees he planted there, whose fruit another will be picking. In such surroundings, comforted by the love of his wife and the companionship of his friends, he had planned to spend his declining years; and he envies Severus, who can pass freely from Rome to his Umbrian home, or drive along the Appian way to his place in the Alban Hills:[69]

> Nescioqua natale solum dulcedine cunctos
> ducit et immemores non sinit esse sui.[70]

All men are drawn somehow by the sweet attraction of their native soil, which will not let them forget.

There is something particularly touching in the obvious sincerity of the passages in which the professed cynic of the *Ars Amatoria* comes at last to express a deep and genuine love—for his wife. When he lies ill and sleepless, her face keeps recurring to his disordered mind:[71]

> Omnia cum subeant, vincis tamen omnia, coniunx,
> et plus in nostro pectore parte tenes.
> te loquor absentem, te vox mea nominat unam;
> nulla venit sine te nox mihi, nulla dies.
> quin etiam sic me dicunt aliena locutum
> ut foret amenti nomen in ore tuum.
> si iam deficiam, suppressaque lingua palato
> vix instillato restituenda mero,
> nuntiat huc aliquis dominam venisse, resurgam
> spesque tui nobis causa vigoris erit.

> *Memories throng, but you prevail o'er all:*
> *Half of my heart and more you hold in thrall.*
> *To you far off I speak, name you alone;*
> *No night, no day without you have I known.*
> *When my mind raved in feverish eclipse,*
> *They say your name was ever on my lips.*
> *If I should faint, and tongue to palate cleave*
> *Till drops of wine could scarce my drought relieve,*
> *Yet if one said, 'Your lady's come', I'd rise*
> *And hope of you my limbs would vitalize.*

On her birthday, and on no other day of the year, he puts on the white clothing of good omen, builds an altar of turf, burns incense and pours wine upon it; pathetically he fancies that the smoke is wafted towards Italy.[72] Time and again he likens her to Penelope, the faithful wife whom the wandering Odysseus preferred to an unageing goddess; she may indeed have aged when they next see each other, but he will kiss her whitened hair and embrace her wasted body with joy, as beyond all hope they talk face to face again.[73]

She had wanted to come with him, and perhaps if he had been formally exiled, with no interests or property left at Rome, she would have done so;* as it was, her presence there was imperative, and her courage and vigilance achieved the difficult task of keeping their home together.[74] There were moments when, after several years of fruitless waiting, he doubted of her energy in pressing, through the Empress, for his return; but even when he urges her uncle, one Rufus, to spur her on, it is not without warm praise for her, and when he does once reply somewhat petulantly to her question, or supposed question, 'What can I do?', we discover that he is ill at the time.[75] The cumulative impression is of a devoted husband sure that his love is returned. In a beautiful letter to her, in which once again emotion flows over the limitation of end-stopped couplets, he sets his own mind at rest:[76]

> Magna minorque ferae, quarum regis altera Graias
>   altera Sidonias, utraque sicca, rates,
> omnia cum summo positae videatis in axe,
>   et maris occiduas non subeatis aquas,
> aetheriamque suis cingens amplexibus arcem
>   vester ab intacta circulus exstet humo,
> aspicite illa, precor, quae non bene moenia quondam
>   dicitur Iliades transiluisse Remus,
> inque meam nitidos dominam convertite vultus,
>   sitque memor nostri necne, referte mihi.

---

* For wives following husbands into exile see Tacitus, *H.* I, 3.

ei mihi, cur timeam? quae sunt manifesta, requiro.
    cur iacet ambiguo spes mea mixta metu?
crede, quod est et vis, ac desine tuta vereri,
    deque fide certa sit tibi certa fides,
quodque polo fixae nequeunt tibi dicere flammae,
    non mentitura tu tibi voce refer,
esse tui memorem, de qua tibi maxima cura est,
    quodque potest, secum nomen habere tuum.
vultibus illa tuis tamquam praesentis inhaeret,
    teque remota procul, si modo vivit, amat.

O *Great and Lesser Bear that never dip,*
Guide to the Greek and to the Tyrian ship,
Since set in highest heaven you witness all
Nor e'er beneath the western ocean fall,
And, circling with embrace the sky's whole girth,
Your orbit never stoops to touch the earth,
Look on those walls, I pray, which overbold
Remus the son of Ilia leapt of old;
Then on my lady shine, and bring me word
If she remembers or forgets her lord.

Ah, why be anxious when the answer's clear?
Wherefore this wavering from hope to fear?
Believe the pleasing truth, nor doubt what's sure:
Have faith secure that her faith is secure.
Expect no answer from the stars on high,
But tell yourself in words that cannot lie:
Your chiefest care is mindful still the same,
And—this she can do—cherishes your name;
Pores on your features, absent though you are,
And, if she lives, still loves you from afar.

Thinking of her lying sleepless and miserable as himself, constantly reminded of him by his empty place in their bed, he is torn between wishing her happy for her sake and unhappy for his; but he knows in his heart that she cannot be happy.[77] It makes him wretched to think that she who used to be so proud of him, indulgently so, may now blush to be called an exile's wife—yet she need not, for he has done nothing of which she need be ashamed.[78]

The Perilla to whom the charming poem *Tristia* III, 7 is addressed, a girl whose promise as a poetess Ovid had fostered, is apparently not, as is still sometimes assumed, his own daughter; for then he would hardly have said

> *utque* pater natae duxque comesque fui.

> *and as a father to a daughter I was your leader and companion.*

But she may possibly be his step-daughter, for the words *non patrio more* in line 12 seem, from the explanation in the next couplet (*mores pudicos*), to glance at Ovid's erotic verse, and a stepfather could perhaps refer to himself by courtesy as 'pater'.* At all events, the supposition that she belonged to his own household, so that her connexion with him was patent, would account better than her youthful innocence for the fact that she is the only person apart from the imperial house whom he ventures to call by name (whether it be true name or sobriquet) in the *Tristia*:

> Vade salutatum, subito perarata, Perillam,
>   littera, sermonis fida ministra mei.
> aut illam invenies dulci cum matre sedentem,
>   aut inter libros Pieridasque suas.
> quicquid aget, cum te scierit venisse, relinquet,
>   nec mora, quid venias quidve, requiret, agam.
> vivere me dices, sed sic ut vivere nolim,
>   nec mala tam longa nostra levata mora;
> et tamen ad Musas, quamvis nocuere, reverti,
>   aptaque in alternos cogere verba pedes.
> 'tu quoque' dic 'studiis communibus ecquid inhaeres,
>   doctaque non patrio carmina more canis?

---

* See Wheeler, *A.J.P.* 1925, pp. 27–8. The evidence for identifying her with the step-daughter (after Constantius Fanensis, fifteenth century) is not so cogent as he suggests.

nam tibi cum fatis mores natura pudicos
  et raras dotes ingeniumque dedit.
hoc ego Pegasidas deduxi primus ad undas,
  ne male fecundae vena periret aquae;
primus id aspexi teneris in virginis annis,
  utque pater natae duxque comesque fui.
ergo si remanent ignes tibi pectoris idem,
  sola tuum vates Lesbia vincet opus.
sed vereor, ne te mea nunc fortuna retardet,
  postque meos casus sit tibi pectus iners.
dum licuit tua saepe mihi, tibi nostra legebam;
  saepe tui iudex, saepe magister eram;
aut ego praebebam factis modo versibus aures,
  aut, ubi cessares, causa ruboris eram.'

Go, greet Perilla, letter swiftly writ,
True messenger my converse to transmit.
You'll find her sitting with her mother sweet,
Or mid her books and at her Muse's feet;
Whate'er it be, she'll leave her work for you,
Straight asking why you come, and how I do.
Say that I live, though thus to live not lief,
For all this time has not allayed my grief;
Still seek the Muses, though they brought this curse,
Marshalling words in alternating verse.*
'And do you still our old pursuits maintain,
Compose and yet avoid your father's bane?
For nature did both purity of heart
And rarest gifts of wit to you impart.
'Twas I that led to the Pierian Spring
That fertile rill, to save its perishing,
Which in your tender years I first descried,
And like a father was your friend and guide.
If in your breast that fire burns the same,
Then none but Sappho shall outshine your fame.

* I.e. elegiac couplets.

Yet do I fear my fate has set you back,
My ruin caused your ardour to grow slack.
Before, we read our poems, I to you
And you to me, your critic, teacher too,
Who lent my ear to each new verse you framed,
Or, if you idled, made you blush ashamed.'

* * *

The bulk of the poems from exile is so abject that one finds
relief in the occasional outbursts of indignation, whether real or
feigned. In the first poem that Ovid wrote to his wife after
leaving Italy, *Tristia* I, 6, he praises her in the following terms
(5–17):

'You are the pillar that sustains my tottering house: if I can count
myself anything, I owe it all to you. It is your doing that I am
not a prey, that I am not stripped by those who have tried to
snatch timbers from my wreckage. And as a ravening wolf
goaded by hunger and thirsty for blood tries to catch the sheepfold unguarded, or as a greedy vulture peers about to spy unburied
carrion, so a mean creature (*nescioquis*), treacherous in my time of
bitterness, would have come into my property, if you allowed it.
But your courage, with the help of stout friends, repulsed him.'

(The word *nescioquis* implies that the would-be peculator was a
nobody, not that Ovid did not know who he was.*)

Tristia IV, 9, written a year or two later, is a less specific poem
in the same vein. It is a spirited denunciation of an enemy, whose
name and offences Ovid will at present forbear to reveal, with
an incidental reminder that the Emperor has left him all his legal

---

* 'If his wife was such a Mrs Nickleby that she omitted the enemy's name in
relating his actions, Ovid would have written to ask for it; he would not have
sat down in easily remediable ignorance to pen 600 lines of verse and discharge
them at the circle of the horizon' (Housman, reviewing Rostagni's *Ibis* in
C.R. 1921, p. 68).

rights. The connexion between this poem and 1, 6 is through that strange composition, the *Ibis*,* written, as the opening line testifies, after Ovid had attained the age of fifty, and before he heard of the death of Augustus, who is referred to as alive in line 27—hence some time in the early years of exile.

Invective had been a recognized form of literature in the ancient world ever since Archilochus had brandished his iambics. From the Hellenistic Age we have fragments of *Imprecations* ('Αραί)† by Euphorion, who appears to have had considerable influence on the modernist poets (νεώτεροι) of Catullus' time and on Gallus. But nearer to Ovid's hand lay a poem of Callimachus called *Ibis*, in which he had denounced an enemy under that pseudonym. (The ibis was an Egyptian bird of unpleasant habits.) Here was a form of literature canonized by the Master which Ovid had not yet essayed, though he had approached it in some of the *Heroides*.

About Callimachus' poem we know singularly little.[79] We do not know who the victim was, for the identification with Apollonius Rhodius by 'Suidas' may rest on no firmer basis than a grammarian's guess. We do not even know in what metre it was written, though we may gather from lines 45–6 of Ovid's poem that elegiacs are excluded.‡ Ovid tells us that it was wrapped up in obscure tales (*historiis caecis involuta*, l. 57) and full of riddles (*ambages*, l. 59) and that it was short (*exiguo libello*, l. 449). His own poem, in elegiacs and 644 lines long, contains little that need have come from that of Callimachus, and more than one thing

---

* *Ibis* 18,

> naufragii tabulas pugnat habere mei,

is almost identical with *Tr.* 1, 6, 8; and the situation is the same: 'he who should have extinguished the sudden flames is seeking plunder himself from the fire, and endeavouring to deprive the old age of an exile of sustenance' (*Ibis* 19–22). Again, the prologue to the *Ibis* (1–66) closely resembles *Tr.* IV, 9. Cf. Fränkel, *op. cit.* pp. 245–6.

† Cf. the *Dirae* of the *Appendix Vergiliana*. To some extent Ovid seems to have taken ideas also from the *defixiones*, curses written on tablets by the superstitious, many of which have survived.

‡ *Modo* (l. 56) means 'manner', not 'measure'.

that cannot have done so;* and, in fact, he invokes the curses of his predecessor as an *addition* to his own (449–50).

The first 66 lines state his purpose. Hitherto his writings have hurt no one but himself—a just claim and a rare one. However, he will not yet denounce the offender by name, adopting rather the riddling style of Callimachus' *Ibis*, which he has previously avoided. But if the man continues in his ways, the poet, who has only been sparring so far, will attack in earnest with Archilochian iambics, and draw blood.[80] The alleged offence which purports to be the occasion of the poem is dealt with in the following terms, strongly reminiscent of *Tristia* I, 6, and it will be seen that even such a poem as this contrives to make its oblique appeal to the Emperor (11–28):

> Ille relegatum gelidos Aquilonis ad ortus
>   non sinit exilio delituisse meo,
> vulneraque immitis requiem quaerentia vexat,
>   iactat et in toto nomina nostra foro,
> perpetuoque mihi sociatam foedere lecti
>   non patitur vivi funera flere viri;
> cumque ego quassa meae complectar membra carinae,
>   naufragii tabulas pugnat habere mei;
> et qui debuerat subitas exstinguere flammas,
>   hic praedam medio raptor ab igne petit.
> nititur ut profugae desint alimenta senectae:
>   heu! quanto est nostris dignior ille malis!
> di melius! quorum longe mihi maximus ille est
>   qui nostras inopes noluit esse vias;
> huic igitur meritas grates, ubicumque licebit,
>   pro tam mansueto pectore semper agam.
> audiat hoc Pontus; faciet quoque forsitan idem,
>   terra sit ut propior testificanda mihi.

---

* The publication in 1934 from new papyri of prose digests (διηγήσεις) of parts of Callimachus' work has confirmed what had previously been asserted—that some of the references in Ovid's *Ibis* were suggested by Callimachus' *Aetia*. See F. Lenz in Bursian's *Jahresbericht 264* (1939), pp. 139–43.

He will not let me hide an exile's head
To the North Wind's cold birthplace banishèd,
Vexes my wounds that only crave repose
And still my name about the Forum throws,
Nor leaves my ever-constant wedded wife
To mourn her wretched husband's death-in-life.
Shipwrecked, the remnants of my barque I clasp:
He tries to wrest the salvage from my grasp,
The man who should have quenched the sudden blaze
Himself to plunder from the fire essays.
Who strives to rob an exile of his store
For age, deserves that penalty far more.
The gods forbade, of whom I most revere
Him who willed not I should be needy here;
To him deservèd thanks, where'er I may,
For this his mercy I shall ever pay.
Pontus shall hear—nay, he may yet allow
A nearer land to witness what I vow.

The invective that occupies the rest of the poem, apart from a six-line epilogue, falls into two parts, 67–250 and 251–638, uneven in merit as they are in length. The poet is discovered standing before an altar and in priestly fashion preparing to utter his solemn commination (97–8):

> Peragam rata vota sacerdos:
> quisquis ades sacris, ore favete, meis.

> *as priest I will perform due vows: speak no unseasonable word,*
> *ye who are present at my rites.*

He adjures the bystanders to do everything of ill omen they can, and bids the shrinking victim don the sacrificial fillet and prepare his throat for the knife. The invocation rises, in lines 75–80, to a solemnity worthy of Propertius (67–86):

> Di maris et terrae, quique his meliora tenetis
> inter diversos cum Iove regna polos,

huc, precor, huc vestras omnes advertite mentes
    et sinite optatis pondus inesse meis;
ipsaque tu tellus, ipsum cum fluctibus aequor,
    ipse meas aether accipe summe preces;
sideraque et radiis circumdata solis imago,
    lunaque, quae numquam quo prius orbe micas,
noxque tenebrarum specie reverenda tuarum
    quaeque ratum triplici pollice netis opus,
quique per infernas horrendo murmure valles
    imperiuratae laberis amnis aquae,
quasque ferunt torto vittatis angue capillis
    carceris obscuras ante sedere fores;
vos quoque, plebs superum, Fauni Satyrique Laresque
    fluminaque et nymphae semideumque genus:
denique ab antiquo divi veteresque novique
    in nostrum cuncti tempus, adeste, Chao,
carmina dum capiti male fido dira canentur
    et peragent partes ira dolorque suas.
annuite optatis omnes ex ordine nostris,
    et sit pars voti nulla caduca mei.

Gods of the sea and land, and ye who share
With Jove the wide, superior realms of air,
Hither, I pray, and lend me all your mind,
That force to my petitions be assigned;
And thou thyself, O Earth, thyself, O Sea,
Thyself, O highest Heaven, give ear to me;
Ye Stars, and Sun's bright image crowned with rays,
And shining Moon with ever-changing phase,
Night, awful in thy shadows, and ye Three
That spin the appointed web of destiny,
River of waters unforsworn that flow
With fearful murmur through the vales below,
And ye with snake-entwinèd locks that sit
Before the portals of the gloomy pit;
Ye lowlier powers, each Satyr, Faun and Lar,
All rivers, nymphs and demigods that are,

> Come, all divinities that have held sway
> From ancient Chaos to this latter day,
> Be present while a treacherous man is cursed
> And grief and anger do to him their worst;
> Assent to my petitions one and all,
> Nor let one jot of them unheeded fall.

There is a touch of the old Ovid here in the phrase *plebs superum*, which takes us back to the Olympian Palatine at the beginning of the *Metamorphoses* (1, 173), and again in his expression of the characteristically Roman prayer that anything he may inadvertently omit may be deemed to be included under a comprehensive clause (91–2):

> Quasque ego transiero poenas, patiatur et illas:
> plenius ingenio sit miser ille meo.

> *and whatever penalties I shall have omitted, may he suffer them too: may his misery be more perfect than my powers of imagination.*

The curses then follow, line upon line, every rift loaded with venom. The poet is clearly interested in his own hyperbolic ingenuity, not in the efficacy of his curses or even in verisimilitude. It is clear enough from his other works that Ovid despised superstition; yet never had he written more compact lines than here. There are pointed antitheses, such as

> noxque die gravior sit tibi, nocte dies,   (116)

> *may night be more grievous to you than day, day than night*

> causaque non desit, desit tibi copia mortis.   (123)

> *may you lack not good cause but good chance to die.*

Familiar things are expressed with a neatness that makes them fresh:

> Poma pater Pelopis praesentia quaerit, et idem
> semper eget, liquidis semper abundat aquis.

> *Pelops' father grasps at the fruit before him, and ever lacks yet ever has abundance of water.*

352

Aeacus will be ingenious in thinking of torments for Ibis' shade, but not more ingenious than the poet (167–74):

> Ipsae te fugient, quae carpunt omnia, flammae;
>   respuet invisum iusta cadaver humus.
> unguibus et rostro crudus trahet ilia vultur,
>   et scindent avidi pectora cruda canes,
> deque tuo fiet—licet hac sis laude superbus—
>   insatiabilibus corpore rixa lupis.
> in loca ab Elysiis diversa fugabere campis,
>   quasque tenet sedes noxia turba, coles.

> *Thee even the all-devouring flames shall leave,*
> *The righteous earth thy loathèd corpse upheave,*
> *A lingering vulture rend thy guts apart,*
> *And hungry hounds worry thy treacherous heart;*
> *Thy body—so much glory I permit—*
> *Insatiable wolves shall fight for it;*
> *Then, banished furthest from Elysium,*
> *To dwell with damnèd spirits thou shalt come.*

No one who has appreciated the *Metamorphoses* should imagine that there is anything serious here; the *Ibis* has the qualities of the winning entry in a competition in invective set by a literary magazine. Housman characterizes it justly as follows:

'In the poems of his exile Ovid often laments the monotony of his theme. But in III, 11 and IV, 9 and V, 8 he hit on a new subject, remonstrance with a persecutor; and it proved no bad variation, for IV, 9 contains some of his best lines. A longer effort, treating of the same matter in another vein, was a promising enterprise; for the vein itself, though new to Ovid, was congenial to the Roman fibre, and Roman poets had excelled in it. The 91st poem of Catullus and the 5th and 17th epodes of Horace, however little accordant with modern fashions, are masterpieces without which no anthology of Latin poetry is complete or representative. And the first 250 lines of the Ibis are another masterpiece. Ovid has written no passage of equal length which has equal merit.'[81]

The affinity with the grotesque and ghoulish Horatian epodes about the witch Canidia and her accomplices is well brought out by the following passage (225–48):

Protinus Eumenides lavere palustribus undis
    qua cava de Stygiis fluxerat unda vadis,
pectoraque unxerunt Erebeae felle colubrae,
    terque cruentatas increpuere manus,
gutturaque imbuerunt infantia lacte canino:
    hic primus pueri venit in ora cibus:
perbibit inde suae rabiem nutricis alumnus,
    latrat et in toto verba canina foro.
membraque vinxerunt tinctis ferrugine pannis
    a male deserto quos rapuere rogo:
et ne non fultum nuda tellure iaceret,
    molle super silices imposuere caput.
iamque recessurae viridi de stipite factas
    admorunt oculis usque sub ora faces.
flebat, ut est infans fumis contactus amaris,
    de tribus est cum sic una locuta soror;
'tempus in immensum lacrimas tibi movimus istas,
    quae semper causa sufficiente cadent.'
dixerat, et Clotho iussit promissa valere,
    nevit et infesta stamina pulla manu;
et ne longa suo praesagia diceret ore,
    'fata canet vates quae tibi', dixit, 'erit'.
ille ego sum vates: ex me tua vulnera disces,
    dent modo di vires in mea verba suas.

Forthwith the Furies washed him in a tank
Filled from the Styx with marshy water dank,
Smeared on his breast venom from snakes of Hell,
Thrice clapping bloody hands to aid the spell,
And wet his throat with bitch's milk, the first
Of foods on which his infancy was nursed
(Whence, from his foster-dam a heritage,
He fills the Forum with his barking rage).

354

His limbs they swathed in rags begrimed with fire
Snatched from a cursèd and abandoned pyre,
And lest bare earth pillow his tender head,
Laid it upon a heap of flints instead;
Then kindled torches, as a last surprise,
Made of green twigs and held them to his eyes;
The infant wept to feel the acrid smoke,
Whereat one sister of the three out spoke:
'Long shall thy tears we thus have started flow,
Nor ever lack sufficient cause in woe.'
She ended. Clotho bade her promise stand,
Spinning a dark thread with malignant hand,
And, loth so long a presage to relate,
Added, 'A bard shall rise to chant thy fate.'
That bard am I: from me you'll learn your Hell,
If the gods grant me strength the tale to tell.

Who was Ibis? Was he more than a shadow? We have already allowed Corinna to be a fiction, despite the traits that seem too realistic to be feigned—wool drawn over our eyes by the poet.* We have suspected the same of the enemy attacked in *Tristia* III, 11, whose offence is traducing Ovid in the Forum.† Invective would be a relief from incessant lamentation, and it was popular with Roman readers. Shall we not then assume with Housman (who had edited the text for Postgate's *Corpus* in 1894)‡ that here too the subject is a fiction, that he is a conflation of the peculator of *Tristia* I, 6 and IV, 9 and the malignant orator of III, 11? To do so disposes of the awkward question, 'Why does Ovid decline to specify the name and offence of his victim?'

Let us have Housman's own words:[82]

'Who was Ibis? Nobody. He is much too good to be true. If one's enemies are of flesh and blood, they do not carry complaisance so far as to choose the *dies Alliensis*§ for their birthday

---

* P. 52.   † P. 323 n.   ‡ The text used in this chapter.
§ July 18, the date of the defeat of the Romans by the Gauls at the Allia in 390 B.C., observed as a perpetual day of mourning and ill-omen: see l. 219.

and the most ineligible spot in Africa* for their birthplace. Such order and harmony exist only in worlds of our own creation, not in the jerry-built edifice of the demiurge. Nor does a man assail a real enemy, the object of his sincere and lively hatred, with an interminable and inconsistent series of execrations which can neither be read nor written seriously. To be starved to death and killed by lightning, to be brazed in a mortar as you plunge into a gulf on horseback, to be devoured by dogs, serpents, a lioness, and your own father in the brazen bull of Phalaris, are calamities too awful to be probable and too improbable to be awful. And when I say that Ibis was nobody, I am repeating Ovid's own words. In the last book that he wrote, several years after the *Ibis*, he said (*P.* IV, 14, 44),

> extat adhuc nemo saucius ore meo.

> *there is no man living that my tongue has so far wounded.*'

We may grant the brilliance of the writing, but readers who are repelled by the Ibis because its subject-matter is 'little accordant with modern fashions' (i.e. those of 1920) may feel that Housman has overpraised it because it was accordant with his own highly personal taste for invective. All will agree with him, however, in considering the second part of the poem (251–644) to be merely a display of erudition. If it were not that Ovid had told us that Callimachus' *Ibis* was obscure and riddling, we might be tempted to think that he had deserted his master to follow after Euphorion. Once again, I cannot do better than quote Housman's words:[83]

'Ovid, at the date of his exile, was bursting with information rather recently acquired. In his young days he had been by no means a learned poet; and Propertius, in the days of their sodality, must often have exhorted him to lay in a larger stock of those examples from mythology with which his own elegies are so much embellished or encumbered. But by the time he was fifty he had at his disposal more examples from mythology than he knew what to do with. His studies for the *Metamorphoses* and

---

* The African river Cinyps (22, 2), perhaps notorious for snakes; cf. *M.*VII, 272.

some of his studies for the *Fasti* (notably in the *Aetia* of Calli-machus) had furnished him with a far greater number of stories and histories than could be crowded into those two poems; and he felt the craving of the ὀψιμαθής to let everyone know how learned he had become. Here was his chance: history and mythology alike are largely composed of misfortunes as bad as one could wish for one's worst enemy; and he could discharge a great part of his load of knowledge through the channel of imprecation.'

At the close of his poem to Perilla (*Tr.* III, 7) Ovid exhorts her, not without a warning against love as a subject, to gather rosebuds while she may—from the garden of the Muses; they alone do not wither. As he writes, his old enthusiasm for poetry, which had inspired the envoy to his first book, *Amores* I, comes over him again, and for a moment, his heart getting the better of his head, he gives us a glimpse of his real feeling about the oppressor of his genius,*

> Caesar in hoc potuit iuris habere nihil,
>
> *Caesar could have no jurisdiction over this,*

and our sympathy for him, dulled by his flatteries, revives. Gone is the mood of III, 4,

> vive tibi, quantumque potes praelustria vita
>
> *live your own life, and as far as you can avoid the limelight:*

> Singula ne referam, nil non mortale tenemus
>   pectoris exceptis ingeniique bonis.
> en ego, cum caream patria vobisque domoque,
>   raptaque sint, adimi quae potuere mihi,

* One is reminded of Propertius' outburst against Augustus' attempts to impose conditions on relations between men and women nearly forty years before:

> 'At magnus Caesar'. Sed magnus Caesar in armis:
>   devictae gentes nil in amore valent.

('But Caesar is powerful', you say. Yes, but it is in arms that Caesar is powerful: to have conquered nations gives no power in matters of love'): II, 7, 5–6.

ingenio tamen ipse meo comitorque fruorque:
    Caesar in hoc potuit iuris habere nihil.
quilibet hanc saevo vitam mihi finiat ense,
    me tamen extincto fama superstes erit,
dumque suis victrix omnem de montibus orbem
    prospiciet domitum Martia Roma, legar.
tu quoque, quam studii maneat felicior usus,
    effuge venturos, qua potes, usque rogos![84]

In sum, no human blessing will abide
Save those that mind and spirit do provide.
Lo I, of country, home and you bereft,
With nought that could be taken from me left,
Have still my mind's own company to enjoy:
No Caesar's interdict could that destroy.
Aye, and though sword should take away my breath,
Yet shall my fame outlive my body's death:
While Rome shall from her hills survey outspread
The conquered world, so long shall I be read.
You too may happier themes than mine inspire
To shun, for so you can, the approaching pyre.

In splendid lines at the close of his autobiographical poem he gives
thanks to the Muse who can transport him from the Danube to
Helicon:[85]

Tu mihi, quod rarum est, vivo sublime dedisti
    nomen, ab exequiis quod dare fama solet.
nec, qui detractat praesentia, Livor iniquo
    ullum de nostris dente momordit opus.
nam tulerint magnos cum saecula nostra poetas,
    non fuit ingenio fama maligna meo,
cumque ego praeponam multos mihi, non minor illis
    dicor et in toto plurimus orbe legor.
si quid habent igitur vatum praesagia veri,
    protinus ut moriar non ego, terra, tuus.
sive favore tuli, sive hanc ego carmine famam,
    iure tibi grates, candide lector, ago.

Thou, Muse, hast given me in life what Fame
Gives rarely this side death—a glorious name.
Envy, that crabs the living, yet hath bit
With spiteful tooth no work that I have writ;
Nor, though our age has mighty poets seen,
Has Fame malignant to my genius been:
While many I count greater, I am said
To be as great, throughout the world am read.
Therefore, if bards can truly prophesy,
Earth, I shall not be thine, whene'er I die.
But be this fame to worth or favour due,
I owe, my gentle reader, thanks to you.

Passports to immortality these epistles from exile have indeed turned out to be. It was a consolation to Ovid that there was at least this one thing he could do for his wife. Paradoxically, many would envy her despite her husband's calamity, but for which indeed it would probably never have occurred to him that she deserved to be so honoured.[86] And when at last it proved to be safe to reward his faithful friends also in this way, he was anxious that not one of them should be left out.[87]

How do the poems from exile strike the modern reader? In giving our judgement we must be careful to make some distinctions. The first two books of the *Tristia* (as well as the *Ibis*) should be considered apart; for the changing scenes of the voyage give variety to the first book, and the second is a full-scale apologia. The remaining seven books of epistles may be treated as an entity, for they are all too homogeneous. The indulgence for which Ovid pleads is readily granted to him as a person by sympathetic critics; but too often, I feel, it has betrayed them into suggesting that these books as a whole are better reading than they are. '...much in them is superfluous: much however we could not afford to lose', says Wight Duff;[88] '...they contain much that is admirable', says Wheeler;[89] 'There is a great deal of excellent poetry in Ovid's elegies from exile', says Fränkel.[90] This praise is in each case attached to grave criticisms, but might it not mislead the prospective reader? 'Much' and 'a great deal' are relative terms. These books contain 5412 lines: a generous selection based on interest and literary merit would barely include a third of that total.

The chief trouble is that, although each poem is generally well constructed, ingenious and polished, they suffer as a collection, just as the *Heroides* do, from monotony of subject. It is generous but idle to deny this:* Ovid recognized it himself, in his epilogue to *Ex Ponto* I–III: 'Though the words are always the same, I have not written to the same persons: in one voice I seek help through a number of people. Should I, lest the reader twice find the same matter, petition you alone, Brutus, of all my friends? That would not be worth the sacrifice—pardon the confession, men of letters: my salvation means more to me than the reputation of my work. In sum, when a poet thinks of his subject-matter for himself, he can introduce as much variety as he fancies; but my Muse is all too true an index of my troubles, and has all the weight of an incorruptible witness. My purpose and care was that each friend should receive his letter, not that a book should result. Do not imagine this work is a selection: I simply collected the letters afterwards and put them together unarranged. So be indulgent to my writings; for their object has been to secure, not personal glory, but advantage for myself and for others their due.'[91]

Nor is it only the subject, but the treatment also, that is monotonous. The old formulae and stock-in-trade of elegy, the hard-worked figures of thought and figures of speech, recur again and again. Must we wade through eight couplets full of examples of the healing power of time before being told that Ovid's pain is not healed by it, or eight couplets of examples of legendary heroes more fortunate in that their place of exile was somewhere intrinsically desirable?[92] The wit that seasoned with its salt the poems of his happier days is still there, but it has lost its savour. When he remarks that Leander, had he lived among the Getae, could have walked over ice instead of swimming to his love, or that Acontius would have found there no apple to inscribe as a

---

* As, for instance, F. Plessis does (*La poésie Latine* (1909), p. 455).

trap for Cydippe,[93] we may admire his effort to smile even so wryly, but the pathos of his situation somehow precludes enjoyment; the contrast is too poignant. True there is some compensation in a new sincerity, especially in the earlier poems where the pain is fresh, but it is hard to agree that 'les élégies de l'exil restent toutefois les plus intéressantes que le poète ait écrites, parce qu'elles sont les plus sincères'.[94] Let anyone compare the picture he conjures up of the scenes at Tiberius' triumph and its counterpart in the *Ars Amatoria* and he will see the difference.[95] Ovid's genius was for composition in the major keys; forced by circumstances into the minor, he has a lowering effect after a time.

Gibbon observed that these poems have 'besides the merit of elegance, a double value. They exhibit a picture of the human mind under very singular circumstances; and they contain many curious observations, which no Roman, except Ovid, could have the opportunity of making.'[96] That is true, but the picture is exhibited far too often, while the observations are tantalizingly few. Some Romans, such as the Elder Pliny, enjoyed information about strange people and lands and customs for its own sake; Ovid in the first years of his exile only mentioned them in so far as they could be pressed into the service of his pleas for transfer or recall. It is natural that we, whose appetite for knowledge of all kinds has steadily increased since the Renaissance, should regret this. What light an educated observer could have thrown on an obscure corner of history if he had had the zeal and patience of an ethnologist! But at first Ovid would not reconcile himself to thinking of his quarters at Tomis as home; they were only *hospitium*, not *penetrale domusque*.[97] Had he not still a home in the Capital?

At last, however, after four or five years, there begin to be signs of resignation to his lot. In a notable poem (*P*. III, 7) he apologizes to his friends for having so long pestered them with letters whose contents, now known almost by heart, they must divine even before breaking the seal. He resolves to face the facts (21–4):

> Spem iuvat amplecti quae non venit irrita semper,
> ut, fieri cupias siqua, futura putes;

proximus huic gradus est bene desperare salutem
seque semel vera scire perisse fide.*

We hug our hopes when all are not deceived,
While we can fancy every wish achieved;
Next after this comes resolute despair
That faces ruin once for all aware.

Not that he ceased to beg for the intercession of his friends—as
he confesses, *res immoderata cupido est*;[98] but he began at last to show
signs of interest in what went on around him. He tells of the
surprise of Aegisos, an old walled city of the Odrysians high on
a hill near the Danube, by the Getae, who were in rebellion against
the King of Thrace;[99] and though his motive is still primarily to
give his friend Severus an illustration of the constant dangers of
Tomis, he adds a little picturesque detail and expresses his gratitude
and admiration to the King for restoring the situation. Apparently
he did not restore it without Roman help; for the interesting poem
IV, 7 seems to recall the same occasion. There we are told that
Vitellius brought troops down the Danube by boat to relieve the
town. This elegy is quite exceptional in Ovid's work. It is
addressed to Vestalis, a centurion sprung from Alpine chiefs who
had risen 'from the ranks', and is a citation of his act of gallantry
in leading the assault on the apparently impregnable site, regardless of the steepness and the hail of stones and poisoned arrows.
Though wounded, he led his men to close quarters and did
prodigies of valour in hand-to-hand fighting until the place was
recaptured. It would appear from lines 1–2 that he had sub-
sequently been given an administrative post in the area, which
would account for Ovid's coming to know him personally.

P. II, 9 is also addressed to a local character, Cotys, King of
Thrace, who claimed descent from Eumolpus, the legendary
founder of the Eleusinian Mysteries. Ovid credits this client-king
of the Empire with humane studies, and salutes him as a
fellow-poet.

* *venit...ut*, Camps.

If the fragment of 134 hexameters about sea-fish which is preserved as Ovid's by a ninth-century Viennese manuscript were
really by him, as some believe, it would provide further evidence
that he turned in his last years to local interests. Pliny indeed cites
this work more than once in Book XXXII of his *Natural History*,
ascribing it to Ovid's last years and supplying the name *Halieutica*.[100]
But despite picturesque surmises about his conversations with
Tomitan fishermen, the fact remains that the work seems to be
founded on a Greek treatise, and that some of the species mentioned
do not occur, nowadays at least, in the Black Sea. That Pliny
thought Ovid wrote it signifies little: Lucan, Statius and Martial
thought Virgil wrote the extant *Culex*, which is almost certainly
a forgery.[101] And even if Ovid's own words are adduced to show
that he eventually became less fastidious as an artist, the un-
Ovidian traits in the metre are too many; it is hard to believe that
such a practised metrist wrote, even in a rough copy, such a line
as (11)

> decidit adsumptamque dolo tandem pavet escam.

It is not impossible that the author of the *Medicamina Faciei* whiled
away his tedious hours by composing a didactic poem on this
subject; but if he did, it is unlikely to have been the one we have.[102]

More authentic as well as more interesting is the change that
occurred in Ovid's attitude to the Tomitans themselves. In the
earlier years of exile, when he had mentioned that he was learning
to speak Getic and Sarmatian, it was only to shock his readers.[103]
And he had remarked sardonically that he believed he could even
write a poem in Getic.[104] But at length, by his own account, he
not only learnt the language but actually wrote such a poem, on
the apotheosis of Augustus.[105] One may well wonder how he
reduced the barbarian language to the kind of prosody with which
he was familiar. He could of course have imitated, not the quantitative metre of the Greeks and Romans, but one of the accentual
metres native to Italy. But his synopsis of the subject-matter, so
laudatory of the imperial house, and his account of the reaction of

the approving circle of *inhumani Getae*, 'Since you write thus
about Caesar, you ought to be restored by Caesar's command',
are such as to arouse in those who know their Ovid enough
suspicion to console philologists for the absence from his literary
remains of any trace of so tantalizing a document.* At all events,
after some five years among the Tomitans he either became aware
of them as human beings or decided that there was no longer any
profit in proclaiming their savagery. They were not unnaturally
offended when they got wind of what he had told the world about
them in his poems; and his defence, that he had been misinter-
preted to them, that he had criticized the place, not the people,
will hardly bear scrutiny: 'let anyone', he protests, 'examine the
record of my work: my letters have made no complaint about
you.'[106] (One wonders how he would have explained away
Tristia v, 7 and 10.†) Yet they do not hate him; and, indeed, his
conduct has deserved no hatred, for he has retained his old
sobriety (*quies animi*) and modesty (*pudor*), and even in this lawless
country no man, woman or child has had cause to complain of
him. And he in turn now refers to them as loyal folk whom he
loves; their sympathy with him has shown that Greek blood still
flows in their veins. For his sake they wish he may leave them,
but for their own are eager he should stay. They have even
recently, despite his disclaimers, crowned him publicly with a

---

* Other works attributed to Ovid by himself or others which have not come
down to us are the following: the tragedy *Medea*; a book of epigrams, or perhaps
nugae like Catullus' and the Virgilian *Catalepton* (Priscian, *G.L.* II, 149, 13 App.;
Quintilian VI, 3, 96; IX, 3, 70); the epithalamium for Paullus Fabius Maximus
(*P.* I, 2, 131–2); the elegy on Messalla (*P.* I, 7, 30); the encomium on Tiberius'
triumph (*P.* II, 5, 27; III, 4, 3) unless this was identical with *Tr.* IV, 2 or *P.* II, 1;
and the Latin poem on the apotheosis of Augustus (*P.* IV, 6, 17–8; 9, 131–2).
Also the *Phaenomena* (Probus on Virgil, *G.* I, 138; Lactantius 2, 5, 24). The extant
Consolatio ad Liviam is agreed to be spurious. The *Nux*, in which a nut-tree makes
a formal complaint of being stoned by passers-by for its fruit, has been considered
spurious by many scholars from Aldus Manutius onwards. Its ascription to Ovid
is defended by Ganzenmüller, *Die Elegie Nux und ihr Verfasser* (1910), and other
more recent scholars, who take it as allegorical of the poet's fate. Its 182 lines
provide little internal evidence either way.

† See p. 331.

wreath; and not only they, but other neighbouring towns, have voted him the privilege, granted to no one else in that region *honoris causa*, of being exempt from taxation. Tomis is now as dear to him as Delos was to Latona, and he no longer refuses to call his house there 'domus', home.[107] He can even realize that a barbarian might wish to escape from Rome to Moesia.[108] We have no reason to doubt the truth of the information given here, for it is too specific to be false, nor the sincerity of the sentiments, for they are not such as would assist his pleas for recall. It looks as though the public honour accorded him by these simple people had surprised, touched, and perhaps shamed him.

When he first came to Tomis Ovid had dreaded the thought of dying far from home, where his wife could not comfort his final moments and perform the last rites for him:[109]

> indeploratum barbara terra teget.

> *a barbarian earth shall cover me unmourned.*

But at length he resigned himself bitterly to the idea:

> venimus in Geticos fines: moriamur in illis.[110]

> *we have come to the Getic land: let us die in it.*

The end came not long after that, late in 17 or early in 18.* We know nothing of the circumstances, but they must have been sadly different from those he had wickedly prayed for in the bravado of the *Amores*.[111] He had lived for fifty-nine years, eight of them in exile. We may be sure that the Tomitans gave honourable burial to one who had nevertheless affected to fear that, if there were any after-life, his shade would flit in terror amid wild Getic and Sarmatian shades.[112] He had confessed in the end that even his own Pelignian people could not have treated him more kindly;[113] and today his statue stands in Constanza, as it does in Sulmona.

---

* Jerome gives 17. For the evidence, such as it is, see Fränkel, *op. cit.* pp. 253–5.

CHAPTER XI

THE MIDDLE AGES

VENUS' CLERK OVYDE

WHEN Ovid claims in his autobiographical poem that, as he made a cult of the elder poets, so the younger made a cult of him,

utque ego maiores sic me coluere minores,

he is probably speaking no more than the truth. And neither his exile nor the banishment of his books from public libraries seems to have affected his popularity. Indeed, his vogue extended beyond the reading public. A friend wrote to tell him that he was having a success at Rome of a kind which he wearily disclaims having sought—passages of his works were being performed in the theatre to the applause of crowded houses,[1] as had sometimes happened before the eyes of the Emperor in happier days.[2] (These performances of literary selections by pantomimic dancers were a strange feature of popular variety shows at Rome; a chorus recited the words in unison with musical accompaniment, while the dancer interpreted them with elaborate gesture.*) Further evidence of his popularity is provided by quotations and echoes of his poems in inscriptions at Pompeii and elsewhere. Sometimes in these a line of Ovid is wedded to one from a different part of his works or from a different author, which suggests that the composer, or scribbler as we should in some cases call him, had them by heart and at his beck and call.[3] Ovid comes second only to Virgil in the frequency with which he is echoed in these scraps of verse from all over the Empire.†[4]

---

* See Owen's note on *Tr.* II, 519. Ovid alludes to them himself at *F.* III, 535–8.

† In metrical epitaphs of the Empire Ovid is echoed 125 times to Propertius 20 and Tibullus 12 (K. F. Smith, *Tibullus*, p. 60).

Whether artists who depict stories which he treated actually had him in mind we cannot tell. The painters of Pompeii were presumably Greeks, and it may be negatively significant that, whereas Greek legends of the *Heroides* and *Metamorphoses* have counterparts there, none of the Roman stories of the *Fasti* is featured.* A coin of Antoninus Pius shows the Vestal Claudia with the ship, as described in the *Fasti* (IV, 305–28), but we cannot be sure that the designer had Ovid in mind, though it is likely enough.[5] On the other hand, there is no doubt about the poets. Traces of his wording have been found in many of them throughout the early Empire.[6] He emerges as, after Catullus, the favourite poet of Martial, who also couples him in a line with Virgil *honoris causa*.[7] In the post-Augustan age poets did not innovate in metre: they chose a model, and Ovid was the favourite; he exercised an influence even greater than Virgil's as regards hexameter usage, while in the licence of polysyllabic pentameter endings few went much further than he had gone in his later works.[8] He was also early paid the pathetic compliment of the self-effacing forger, who forfeits his own chance of an immortal name in the hope of endowing his child with one. We have seen that the extant *Halieutica* is probably spurious, though already circulating as Ovid's by the time of the elder Pliny; one certain forgery, the *Consolatio ad Liviam*, seems to have been composed about a century after Ovid's death.[9] But the spate of forgeries did not begin until the Middle Ages. As for prose writers, it was natural that the younger Seneca, whose plays show his influence clearly enough, should have dwelt in his days of exile on the memory of the poet of Tomis.† Ovid's vogue in the rhetorical schools is amply testified by the elder Seneca.[10] There is no evidence however of his early use in secondary education, which is surprising, for while one can understand that the erotic poems might seem unsuitable,

* Peeters, *op. cit.* p. 89. But Schefold points out that the lyric (and amatory elegiac) poetry of the time, as well as the painting, confines its *exempla* almost entirely to the Greek world, which was idealized (*op. cit.* p. 24).

† A. Siegmund collects reminiscences, *Wien. Stud.*, 1900, pp. 156 ff.

one would expect the *Fasti* at least, if not also the *Metamorphoses*, to be seized on by schoolmasters. Among casual critics the historian Velleius spoke justly of Tibullus and Ovid as *perfectissimi in forma operis sui.*[11] Quintilian, however, was rather stuffy: while allowing that the *Metamorphoses* were 'to be praised in parts', he took the poet to task for being frivolous (*lascivus*) even in what purported to be epic.[12] But in any case he was writing a treatise on rhetorical education, not a work of literary criticism for adults.

The second century was an age of practical organization rather than literary activity; and in the third, following the death of Septimius Severus, there were constant civil wars and barbarian incursions, a foreshadowing of the Dark Ages. When, thanks to the reconstructive efforts of Diocletian and Constantine, learning and letters were able to revive in the fourth century and its successor, we find Ovid freely cited in the text-books of the grammarians who were characteristic of the age.* The literary criticism of these men is best represented by Servius' massive commentary on Virgil, which is two-thirds linguistic and for the rest consists mainly of detailed explanation of historical or mythological references.[13] Some of the information in the extant scholia on the *Ibis* may go back to this age, if not further,[14] and there are traces of an ancient commentary on the *Metamorphoses.*[15] Macrobius' *Saturnalia* (*c.* 400), valuable though it is, is related to this narrow tradition; but his commentary on the *Somnium Scipionis* of Cicero, with its exposition of neo-Platonism, stands out as the solitary representative until the Renaissance of literary criticism with a more philosophic outlook, dealing with the spirit of the work and with literary experience, in the rare tradition of Aristotle's *Poetics*, Cicero's later works, and the treatise *On the Sublime.*†[16]

Meanwhile, however, the basis of education, which the Flavian

---

* Index of citations in Keil, *Grammatici Latini*, vol. VII, pp. 609–10. For the grammarians of this age in general see M. L. W. Laistner, *Thought and Letters in Western Europe from A.D. 500 to 900* (1931), pp. 20–2.

† For brief accounts of the literary figures of the fourth and fifth centuries see Sir J. E. Sandys, *History of Classical Scholarship*, 3rd edn. 1920, Ch. XIII.

Emperors had first made a matter of state interest,[17] was broadening. A scale of pay for schoolmasters in an edict by Diocletian of A.D. 301 shows the rhetor as still indeed the best paid; but he is now nearly approached by the 'grammarian' and the geometrician, whereas two centuries before geometry had been very much a 'subsidiary' subject.[18] Provincial officials had to be taught correct (i.e. Golden Age) Latin, and this set a premium on grammarians. Quintilian in the first century had put forward his ambitious scheme for reforming education within its existing rhetorical framework; but it was not until the fifth century that the framework itself was challenged. Then three works appeared advocating, what there had never been before, a definite curriculum, to be based on 'The Seven Liberal Arts'. * The ancestor of this system was Cicero's contemporary Varro in his *Disciplinae*; but whereas Varro had merely organized knowledge, these writers were advocating educational action.

The first of them was Augustine. He has left us a list of the subjects he intended to treat,[19] but he died in 430 with the work unfinished, and only half of what he did accomplish has survived. The second, roughly contemporary, was Martianus Capella, whose fanciful *De Nuptiis Mercurii et Philologiae* contains an account of the branches of study which were to be the basis of later education. The third was Cassiodorus, whose encyclopaedic *Institutiones* was written more than a century later (II, pref. 5). Such evidence as there is suggests that all three were independent theorists, destined to influence the future rather than the entrenched system of the present. They were setting the pattern for the Middle Ages.[20]

Augustine and Cassiodorus are particularly significant as representatives of the new force that was shaping the future, Christianity. What was the attitude of such men to a writer like Ovid? St Paul on occasion had quoted pagan scripture to his purpose—

---

* In Augustine these were Grammar, Logic, Rhetoric, Music, Geometry, Arithmetic and Philosophy. Capella and Cassiodorus replaced Philosophy by Astronomy.

'Evil communications corrupt good manners' (Menander), 'For we also are His offspring' (Aratus); but among early Christians, from Tertullian onwards, there were extremists who condemned pagan literature outright. Yet even Arnobius, who attacked it bitterly in the time of Diocletian's persecution (*c.* 305), was a stickler for correct style who also appears to have known even so subversive a writer as Lucretius well enough to quote him by heart; and he had among his pupils Lactantius, 'the Christian Cicero', who, incidentally, often quotes from Ovid's *Metamorphoses* and *Fasti*.[21]

The Middle Ages took their cue in this matter from three outstanding men of differing gifts and temperaments, so that there was some latitude within the bounds of orthodoxy. Jerome, Augustine and Gregory the Great were all saints, and therefore safe as authorities. Jerome was a pupil of Donatus, the grammarian and commentator. The story of his Vision of Judgement, in which he was accused of being 'non Christianus sed Ciceronianus', did not fail to impress posterity. But he was an incurable lover of style in literature, who countenanced the reading even of the comic poets and satirists, and the scholarship which gave Christianity the Vulgate was clearly justified in the eyes of the Christian world. Those in later ages who were drawn to the study of literature could take refuge in the shadow of that great monument.*[22]

'To the inattentive all things are pure', as Bolgar remarks. But no one was ever less inattentive than Augustine of Hippo. He perceived exactly what in ancient literature was incompatible with Christianity and what was not; by judicious selection, harmless compendia of knowledge could be compiled, on the principle of 'spoiling the Egyptians'. However, it proved not always possible in practice to extricate the harmless from its context, and

* St Jerome was the counterpart in the west of the Christian humanists of the Eastern Empire in the tradition of Clement of Alexandria, St Basil of Caesarea and his own mentor at Constantinople, St Gregory Nazianzen, who treated the classics as a propaedeutic to the Scriptures.

the names and prestige of pagan writers were inevitably kept alive. Since Augustine did not live to supply such a compendium, the bizarre work of Martianus Capella remained the nearest approach to what he advocated until, more than a century later (*c.* 550), Cassiodorus produced for the instruction of his monks in the heel of Italy his *Institutiones*, the second part of which is an account of the seven liberal arts. This was to prove one of the great textbooks of the Middle Ages, though as such it was surpassed by the encyclopaedia of ancient learning which Isidore of Seville compiled in the early years of the next century.

The third authority, Gregory the Great, lived in the latter part of the sixth century. By then the situation had changed. A Christian literature had grown up with reputable poets in Prudentius, Paulinus and Sidonius; and authors no longer laboured to write Golden Latin simply in order to qualify for a place in the temple of the old classics. The Egyptians had been spoiled enough. Gregory took no pains to avoid barbarisms, considering it 'utterly unworthy to keep the language of the Divine Oracles in subjection to the rules of Donatus'. We find him writing to rebuke the Bishop of Vienne (it was in Gaul that enthusiasm for the Latin Classics survived longest) for using pagan authors in the education of schoolboys. This does not mean that he would have disapproved of the classics as a source of information such as filled the encyclopaedia of his friend Leander's brother, Isidore; but he is to be counted among their enemies, and was destined to play this role in many legends which circulated in the Middle Ages. In general, it may be said that, while the Eastern Church remained fairly tolerant of the Greek classics, the Western was, with certain exceptions, hostile to the Roman.[23] The average layman, however, would probably have been loth to exterminate paganism, if he realized that the cost might be the undermining of the Roman civilization he knew.

Throughout these two centuries Ovid continued to be cited by grammarians and to influence poets, not only pagans such as Claudian (*c.* 400),[24] the last important classic, but also Christians like Claudian's contemporary Prudentius.[25] But he could no longer compete with Virgil, amid whose praises in the seven books of Macrobius' *Saturnalia* he is not even mentioned. It is hardly surprising that he should fade out in a society becoming rapidly, and indeed forcibly, Christianized. Here, however, we should not forget the possibilities inherent in a feature of the period which presaged medievalism, the revival of the Stoic fashion of allegorizing myth and legend. Its absurdities pullulate in the commentaries; and the Christian writer Fulgentius, about the end of the fifth century, uses not only Virgil, but among other sources the *Fasti* and *Metamorphoses*, as a basis for his allegories in the *Mythologiae*.

The fifth century saw the final break-up of the Western Empire. Many provinces had already been invaded by barbarians, and now Rome itself was sacked by Alaric the Goth and Genseric the Vandal. Cassiodorus himself was in his earlier years a minister of the Ostrogoths, who put to death his less compliant contemporary Boethius, and brutal Lombards ruled much of the Italy in which St Gregory was Pope.

Two centuries of night separate Gregory and Charlemagne. In so far as literature flickered anywhere, it was in the remote islands of Britain to which the former had sent the second St Augustine.* The Latinate monks spreading from Canterbury met counterparts who emanated from the older Irish tradition through Columban's Iona, and were put on their mettle by the contact. And, indeed, in all the old provinces of the Empire Latin had to be kept alive by the Church among the barbarous-tongued provincials, otherwise the liturgy could not have been understood nor the Bible read, to say nothing of the study of theology.† But no amount of knowledge of Latin so acquired could have availed to preserve the classics had not Benedictine monks, under the impulse given by Cassiodorus, occupied their long leisure in transcribing manuscripts.

---

* In 668 a scholar, Theodore of Tarsus, became Archbishop of Canterbury; he and his colleague Hadrian were described by Bede as 'deeply learned in sacred and profane letters alike' (*Hist. Eccl.* IV, 2). Aldhelm was a pupil of Hadrian.

† For such learners Bede, Boniface and Taturine compiled simplified grammars.[26]

It was rarely Ovid's works, however, that were transcribed, no doubt through disapproval of the erotic poems.* Few early manuscripts of them have survived—for some of the poems none from earlier than the eleventh century; nor do their titles occur often in the library catalogues of the eighth to tenth centuries. Citations in this period are also very few;†[27] at the end of the seventh century Aldhelm of Malmesbury, Bishop of Sherborne, wrote a treatise on metre, but though he frequently gives examples from Virgil, for instance, he never refers to the great master of elegiacs.‡ Nor is Ovid mentioned, though Virgil, Lucan and Statius are, in the poem in which Alcuin gives an account of the Library of the School of York, where Latin verse composition formed part of the curriculum.[28]

The ecclesiastical schools begun in the seventh century were much improved in the eighth. In 789 the Aachen Capitulary advocated the establishment of schools by cathedrals as well as monasteries. Instead of busy bishops' giving what time they could to teaching, professional schoolmasters were introduced with regular curricula. Charles Martel and his Frankish successors saw the possibility of using these schools as a training-ground for administrators, and it was primarily with a view to turning out 'a supply of fit persons to serve God in Church and State' that Charlemagne reorganized the famous school which moved about with his court. In this school by far the greatest influence was exercised by Alcuin, summoned from England in 782 to be master. He was the most learned man of his time, and during his eight years of office he began the work of spreading the educational

---

* Nevertheless an Oxford MS contains, besides three other works, *Ars Amatoria I*. It once belonged to St Dunstan, who, before he became one of the strictest of disciplinarians, had been in love with a lady at the Court. He has drawn a portrait of himself on the opening page.[29]

† In Manitius' *Handschriften antiker Autoren in mittelalterlichen Bibliothekskatalogen* (1935) the comparative figures for references in ninth-century library catalogues emerge as: Virgil 27, Horace and Juvenal 4, Ovid and Persius 3, Terence 1; and in the tenth century he occurs only in the lists of Bobbio and St Gall.

‡ Nor, for that matter, to Horace or Statius.[30]

pattern of York all over Europe. No one did more to ensure the survival of learning by encouraging the transcription of books and educating people to read them.[31]

But the textbooks which Alcuin composed were for beginners; for mature students the Bible and other Christian writings were to be the main fare.[32] Cognizant though he was himself of pagan literature, he should not be thought of as a Humanist before his time, nor is it likely that he was the moving spirit in the revival of secular poetry in that remarkable circle of friends, which, as a by-product of its serious activities, staged a brief rehearsal of the Renaissance. In the Court School, where the pupils were the king and his sons and daughters, Alcuin taught all the arts with one exception: 'grammar' was, for some time at least, in the hands of the elderly Peter of Pisa.[33] This man, brought back from the Lombard kingdom as part of the booty of Charlemagne's wars, came from the one part of the Western Empire where Latin was the vernacular and there were men who had some hereditary knowledge of the classics. The members of Charlemagne's circle adopted biblical or classical nicknames; the king was 'David' or 'Solomon', Alcuin was 'Flaccus', though he had possibly never read Horace's *Odes*, while Angilbert, though he had certainly never read the *Iliad*, was 'Homer'. Einhard, who wrote the king's biography on Suetonian lines, was 'Bezaleel', Theodulf the Spaniard 'Pindar', and Modoin 'Naso'.

These writers did anticipate the Renaissance Humanists in that their poems tended to be personal and epistolary, not variations on school themes (and here Alcuin is as human as the rest). The poets who influenced them most were Virgil, Ovid and the Christian Fortunatus. The best of them, Theodulf, read his 'Naso loquax', wrote mainly in Ovidian elegiacs and often echoed Ovidian phrasing; and he has left a charming picture of the life of the court at Aachen in his poem *Ad Carolum Regem*, written about 796.[34] The civilized intercourse of these high ecclesiastics and their beloved patron, revealed to us against a background of centuries of violence, was surely influenced by the *anima cortese* of Virgil, the *candor* of Ovid, the *urbanitas* and *humanitas* of Horace. To what extent they knew the works of these ancients entire it is hard to determine; the apparent range of their reading may reflect some use of the anthologies (*florilegia*) which were already circulating and were naturally popular in those ages when books were scarce.* And it is noteworthy that the learned biographer of Charlemagne, Einhard, never quotes Ovid; nor is he mentioned by Servatus Lupus, a great borrower and lender of classical manuscripts.†

In any case, this brief springtime was nipped in the bud by Charlemagne's death in 814. Alcuin had long been gone, and others too. The new Emperor, Louis the Pious, had not the personality to keep a literary circle together; and indeed Theodulf was soon, on some suspicion of disloyalty, committed to prison, where he composed some verses which were to bring him more fame with posterity than all his secular poetry, the Palm Sunday hymn 'All glory, laud and honour'.‡ The poets of the ninth century, though still taking Virgil, Ovid and Fortunatus for their models,§ were barely as good as their predecessors. What did survive of Charlemagne's achievement was the network of monastic schools and the increased copying of manuscripts; and these were sufficient to preserve through the turmoil of the next century the possibility of another flowering.[35]

The barbaric invasions of Norsemen and Hungarians in the tenth century plunged the Carolingian empire into chaos again, but by the end of it the former at least had been assimilated, the Islamic danger had receded, and learning had somehow survived. Though the new reform of Cluny was suspicious of the classics, the great Benedictine monasteries of St Gall, near Constance, and Monte Cassino were at their most active, copying classical as well as Christian manuscripts, practising Latin verse composition, and studying Virgil and Ovid carefully along with the Christian poets.[36]

---

* They probably knew the fifth century 'African Anthology'.[37]
† According to Manitius and A. Kleinclausz, *Eginhard* (1941).
‡ *Gloria, laus et honor tibi sit, rex Christe redemptor.*
§ Ermoldus Nigellus imitated the *Tristia*.

In Italy teachers and pupils felt themselves to be the heirs of the great classics, as in Peter of Pisa's day; but it was chiefly in the cathedral schools of France that the humanistic spirit was kept alive, to reassert itself at the end of the century, with the gradual improvement of economic and social conditions, under the influence of such dynamic figures as Gerbert of Rheims and Fulbert of Chartres.[38] But Ovid is never mentioned by Gerbert, who quotes freely from classical authors; he was as yet a formal model for composers rather than a spiritual influence.

It is only with the late eleventh- and early twelfth-century renaissance that he comes into his own. The Carolingian age had been, in Traube's phrase, *aetas Vergiliana*; now begins the *aetas Ovidiana*.[39] Economic improvement has encouraged the lust of the eye and the pride of life, and turned men's thoughts to the varied interests of this world. The wit and point of satire and rhetoric, appreciated in the new courts, have become fashionable, and Martial, Persius and Juvenal also come to the fore.* Whether in their courtly poems in praise of beautiful ladies, or in their poetic epistles to friends, or in their versified tales from the Bible, the young poets of the cathedral schools made Ovid their master Here are some lines of complaint *De perfida amica*:

> Conquerar an sileam? monstrabo crimen amicae
>   an, quasi iam sanus, vulnera nostra tegam?
> non queror aut molles oculos aut aspera crura;
>   non vitio quovis exteriora premo.
> quod queror est animi; laudaret cetera livor:
>   verba fide, vitiis lubrica forma caret.

And here are some on a girl (is it Arethusa again?) entering the water to bathe:

> Tentat aquam; laudat tentatam; nuda subintrat
>   laudatam; nudam vidit uterque senum,
> vidit et incaluit.

---

* This movement is reflected in the library-catalogues (Manitius, *Handschriften*).

The former quotation is from a poem which has a moral ending attributed to Hildebert of Lavardin, friend of Henry I and chief poet of the age, who lived to be Archbishop of Tours, the latter is from a poem on St Susanna attributed to Petrus de Riga. Yet how Ovidian they are in technique!*[40]

Baudry (1046–1130) is a typical poet of the earlier part of this period. Though Abbot of Bourgeuil and later Bishop of Dol, he was primarily a humanistic man of letters. A Vatican manuscript contains 255 poems from his hand. Ovid was his favourite poet, and he composed exchanges of letters between him and Florus based on the *Tristia*, and between Paris and Helen based on the *Heroides*. He also composed elegiac epistles to a girl in a convent expressing Platonic love, whose piquancy was in the paradox of Christian chastity venturing in Ovidian garb. In an epitaph written in 1095 he described Godfrey of Rheims as 'second only to Ovid'.[41] Baudry was not a great poet, but he was a classicistic versifier of talent.

The elegiac and hexameter metres were used for all sorts of themes—philosophic, satirical, courtly, epic, historical, personal— by poets free to study the classical authors who were now becoming increasingly available. France and England, then one kingdom, were the chief sources of poetry in the twelfth century. Especially popular in England were the so-called 'comedies', tales with a happy end dealing mainly with amorous intrigue and cuckolded husbands, not without satire at the expense of women. The content might derive at first from ancient comedy, but as time went on matter as well as treatment owed more and more to the poet whose name appears in the title of two of the most erotic— *Ovidius Puellarum* and *Ovidius Trium Puellarum*. An anonymous versifier told the incestuous story of Tamar and Ammon in the guise of the *Metamorphoses*;[42] and some of Ovid's stories, Myrrha

---

* Some of Hildebert's poems have in fact from time to time been mistaken for work of the classical period. He had a genuine feeling for the past, rare in that age, which comes out in his elegy evoked by a visit to pillaged Rome:

Par tibi, Roma, nihil, cum sis prope tota ruina....

and Leucothoë for instance, reappear in the *De Nugis Curialium*, a medley composed by Walter Map at the court of Henry II.[43]

But side by side with this verse in the old quantitative metres had sprung up verse-forms based on equality of syllables, division into stanzas, rhyme and the rhythm created by speech-accent.[*] The first two features made them especially suitable for hymns,[†] such as Hildebert's

> Me receptet Sion illa,
> Sion David urbs tranquilla,

the second two released a fresh lyric poetry, for the rhyme made the verse sing, and the speech-rhythm encouraged natural, un-rhetorical expression of feeling. This Latin lyric was obviously so much nearer to the ephemeral popular poetry of the period, that it could share its music and be quickened by its lyrical impulse; at the same time it inherited the mythology and the ideas of classical poetry, and occasionally indeed its wording, as when the first line of the *Metamorphoses* is deftly adapted[‡] as

> In nova fert animus
> Dicere mutata
> Vetera, sed potius
> Sunt inveterata.

The twelfth century was the age of the *Clerici Vagantes*, the Wandering Scholars, begging their bread and wine from monastery to monastery and court to court, largely independent of Church discipline and often critical of Church ways. Many of them were minstrels with a repertoire of sacred and profane verse.

---

[*] For a concise analysis of this development see Wright and Sinclair, *op. cit.* pp. 273–81. Gottschalk (805–69) had rhyme both in lyrics and between the two halves of hexameters ('Leonines'). Speech-accent with rhyme appears in the anonymous ninth-century poem of a Veronese clerk to his favourite boy, in the *Cambridge Song-book*:

> O admirabile Veneris idolum,
> Cuius materiae nihil est frivolum...

[†] By the tenth century religious poetry had abandoned the ancient metres.[44]

[‡] Possibly by the leading Goliard Hugo 'Primas' of Orleans.[45]

Somehow or other, perhaps first in England, there developed among them, wholly unorganized though they were, the fantastic medieval conception of 'Golias'. Goliath of Gath was the antithesis of the holy singer David; and the medieval Golias was a sort of Bishop of Misrule (Master of a mythical *Ordo Vagorum*, a travesty of the monastic orders), on whom the Goliards fathered the products of their own gay, youthful impulse to *nequitia*.[46] Wine, women and song were their themes,* and nothing was sacred to them. They were condemned by a Council of 1227 for singing parodies of the Holy Office. They would begin a begging poem with '*Ecce homo* sine domo', and change the Hymn to the Virgin from '*Verbum*' to '*Vinum* bonum et suäve', or the Hymn for Prime to

> Iam lucis orto sidere
> Statim oportet bibere.†[47]

Prominent among them was the 'Archpoet' of Cologne, who wrote, in their characteristic metre, the famous burlesque confession beginning,

> Aestuans intrinsecus ira vehementi.

Their favourite poet was Ovid, and we can recognize the *bravura* of his

> At mihi contingat Veneris languescere motu,
> cum moriar, medio solvar et inter opus

in the Archpoet's

> Meum est propositum in taberna mori,
> ubi vina proxima morientis ori.‡

A few odd facts may serve to illustrate the vogue of Ovid at this period. There was a curious verse form styled *cum auctoritate*

---

* The title of a selection from their verse in translation by John Addington Symonds.

† An edict of the Provincial Council at Trèves in 1227 forbade such frivolities.[48]

‡ *Am.* II, 10, 35–6: 'But may it be my lot to die languishing in Venus' throes, and to be dissolved in the middle of the act'; *Confession*, 41–2: 'It is my intention to die in a tavern, where the wine will be nearest to my mouth as I die.'

wherein each Goliardic stanza ended with a classical quotation. In a twenty-stanza poem by Walter de Châtillon seven of the tags are from various works of Ovid; and in an *amorosa visione* Cupid appears in a vision by night and laments that the high standard set by Ovid's precepts is no more maintained, each stanza ending with a line from the *Ars* or *Remedia*.[49] In the famous poem depicting a (doubtless apocryphal) Council held at the convent of Remiremont, in which young nuns debate whether knights or clerks are the more adept in the art of love, a *quasi evangelium* is read from the works of that *doctor egregius*, Ovid.[50] Once he is even called 'the Pope' of love, whose decrees have authority.[51] But the chief evidence comes from the library catalogues, the numerous *Florilegia*, and the ubiquitous reminiscences in secular poems of all kinds, metrical and rhythmic, Latin and vernacular.[52] Ovid is also cited more frequently than any other poet by Vincent of Beauvais (d. 1264) in his encyclopaedic *Speculum Mundi*; and he provided a store of stock quotations for the monks of Canterbury.[53] Many spurious works, classical and contemporary, were fathered on him.[54]

An early example of a Wandering Scholar's collection is the *Carmina Cantabrigiensia*, a German's book copied at Canterbury in the eleventh century and now in the University Library at Cambridge.[55] It contained some fifty pieces ranging from excerpts of Virgil and religious 'sequences' to comic tales and songs of love and spring. The hand of a monkish censor has been at work, tearing out a whole page, and making erasures with a tincture of galls in several poems, including the famous tenth-century lyric

> Iam, dulcis amica, venito
> quam sicut cor meum diligo....

But no censor has mutilated the *Carmina Burana* in the famous Munich manuscript from the monastery of Benediktbeuern in Upper Bavaria. In this huge medley the dominant theme is love and spring, and Raby has characterized some of the rhythmical pieces as 'of unmatched obscenity', surmising that the collector may have been a prelate or abbot of high birth.*

Here is the medieval paradox for us with our puritan tradition, that neither profanity nor obscenity was felt to be so inconsistent with religion as it generally is today. The noblest cathedrals of the period are liable to flaunt grotesque and even obscene carvings. Compared with many Goliardic poems by ecclesiastics Ovid was demure, and we need not be surprised that he maintained his place in the forefront of recommended school-books, from the eleventh-century *Ars Lectoria* of Aimeric to the thirteenth-century schedule in the Library of Caius College, Cambridge, attributed to Neckham, Abbot of Cirencester.[56] There are twelfth-century introductions to, and glosses on, Ovid's works, not excluding the *Ars Amatoria*, which were intended for schools.[57] The cathedral schools were becoming more and more secular, the 'minor orders' of the inmates merely disguising this fact, and indeed the prestige of the classics they taught depended partly on their utility for such lay careers as law and medicine.[58] Even the 'comedies', for all their bawdiness, were studied in school; and in his *Registrum multorum auctorum* (1280) Hugo of Trimberg includes a notoriously lascivious work with a light-hearted comment:

> Sequitur Ovidius dictus puellarum,
> quem in scholis omnibus non credo fore rarum.

Next comes The Girls' Ovid, *which I do not think will be a rarity in any school.*[59]

But we must not press this point too far. There are instances enough of prelates who repented of their youthful tastes and indiscretions. Marbod, a famous poet and head of the classical school of Angers, apologized for his early love poems, and in old age published what amounts to a denunciation of Ovid and all his corrupting works that are beaten into schoolboys.[60] Peter of Blois

---

* Ed. Hilka and Schumann (1930). Guibert of Nogent, as a young monk, wrote verses of calculated obscenity.[61]

deprecated the 'lasciviores cantilenae' of his youth.[62] Herbert de Losinga, the first Bishop or Norwich, had a dream that compelled him to renounce the reading and imitation of Virgil and Ovid; and the dramatic conversion of the frivolous humanist and poet Serlo of Wilton by an apparition from Purgatory provided a parable for many a sermon.[63] Even Abélard, whose love-songs for Héloïse had been sung in every street of Paris, came eventually to ask, 'Why do the bishops and doctors of the Christian religion not expel from the City of God those poets whom Plato forbade to enter into his city of the world?'[64] Nor should we, through concentrating for our present purpose on poetry and pursuits which hark back to Ovid, forget that this was the great age of hymn-writing and cathedral-building, of Christian chivalry and the Crusades. Whatever the corruption of the Papacy, it was in general a theocratic age of faith and piety. Frequent Councils, especially in the thirteenth century, denounced loose clerics, *vagi* and Goliards.* The old suspicion of pagan literature as a whole, and immoral literature in particular, was easily awakened in many a Christian breast.[65] One of the chief differences which Gratian sought to reconcile in his *Concord of Discordant Canons* (*c.* 1140) was on the question whether priests should be acquainted with pagan literature or not, and after reviewing the authorities he concludes that they should not be.[66] In the same century we have protests from such men as Peter Damian, Conrad of Hirschau, Honorius of Autun, Manegold of Lautenbach and the famous Bernard of Clairvaux.

Naturally those who loved literature were at pains to defend it by every shift. The beginning of the *Metamorphoses* offered a cosmogony and cosmology that could be commended to Platonized Christians of the twelfth century. Poems of the period that purport to describe erotic experience may in many cases have been merely the product of school convention and a cleric's

---

* Texts in H. Waddell, *The Wandering Scholars*, Appendix E. An edict of the Council of Rouen in 1231 actually deprived them of their clerical status, a severe blow.

wishful dreaming,[67] and Baudry, like Catullus and Ovid before him, warns his reader against deducing his morals from his verse:

> Sed quicquid dicam, teneant mea facta pudorem,
> cor mundum vigeat mensque pudica mihi.

> *But whatever I may say, may my deeds be ever pure, and my heart flourish in cleanliness, my mind in purity.*[68]

Again, it was easy to pick out from Ovid's voluminous works many lines that were edifying, partly because he was in many ways a man of sound morality, and partly because he knew what morality was and could put appropriate sentiments, for instance, into the mouth of Helen rejecting the advances of Paris. The *Florilegia* used in schools were full of unexceptionable lines culled from him, often pure statements of observation, such as the ever-recurring

> nitimur in vetitum semper cupimusque negata,

which a chastened Abélard wistfully quoted to Héloïse, and Luther inscribed in a copy of St Anselm.* King James I of Aragon, at an assembly of barons and bishops, led off with a quotation from the *Ars Amatoria* (II, 13) under the impression that it was from the Bible.[69]

More strange is the attribution of moral purpose to Ovid himself. Of the *Heroides* we hear that 'the author's intention is to condemn illicit loves, to brand the frivolous and commend those whose passions are of the right kind'.† The *Remedia Amoris* was taken seriously as an aid to chastity; it is pleasant to think of Brother Bertrand Ginesse settling down to transcribe it at 5.0 a.m. on the Vigil of the Conception and finishing his task at eleven o'clock that night 'to the praise and glory of the Virgin Mary'.[70] It was

---

* 'We strive ever for the forbidden, and desire what is denied to us.'[71]

† Poem in a thirteenth-century Berne MS quoted by Raby, *op. cit.* II, p. 214. Cf. E. H. Alton on the *Accessus* in the *Versus Bursarii Ovidii*, where the poet is credited with the highest moral intentions, even in the *Ars*—'Ethicae supponitur'. ('Ovid in the Medieval Schoolroom', *Proc. Class. Ass.* 1937, p. 33.)

also taken seriously by medical writers, and cited for cures for 'the loveres maladye of *hereos*' or *heroys*, defined as 'an alienation of the mind accompanied by immense and unreasoning concupiscence'.* If the moral was not obvious, recourse was had to allegorization, following the example of Fulgentius and the suggestion of Theodulf.[72] There were many such expositions of the *Metamorphoses* in the twelfth century, the most famous being the *Integumenta* of John of Garland; even the love-stories of the gods and goddesses were allegorized for the use of nuns, who were thus free to read the text of Ovid without necessarily accepting the interpretations offered.[73] One can see how the account of the Creation, Fall and Flood and the story of Philemon and Baucis 'entertaining angels unawares' would impress uncritical readers of the *Metamorphoses* nurtured on the Bible. They assumed that the author had had access to the material of the Old Testament. Early in the fourteenth century an anonymous author produced the *Ovide Moralisé*, in which a French translation of the *Metamorphoses* was encumbered with intellectual and moralizing commentary to the extent of 70,000 octosyllabic lines. This monstrous work was destined to have a great influence. A simpler, fundamentalist approach had relieved the conscience of Amarcius, a German poet of the eleventh century: unlawful loves had given ancient poets material for their songs, but though it was on the Muses that they called, it was God who had inspired them, for us to profit thereby.[74] This could, however, be a dangerous expedient, for in the same century one Vilgardus of Ravenna went to the stake for holding that certain ancient poets were to be believed throughout, and among doctors of Paris burnt in the next century for heresy were some who held that 'God hath spoken in Ovid, even as in Augustine'.[75]

As the thirteenth century proceeded the classics continued to be

* The word is derived from ἔρως. Chaucer, *Knight's Tale* (A), 1373–4. Definition in Arnaldus de Villanova (1240–1311), *Liber de Parte Operativa. R.A.* cited by Bernardus Gordonius (1295) (J. L. Lowes, *Modern Philology*, 1913–14, pp. 491–546).

copied, read and quoted. In the *Biblionomia* of Richard de Fournival,[76] a probably idealized library catalogue (*c.* 1250), all Ovid's genuine works are given a place, even the rarely mentioned *Medicamina Faciei*. The *Metamorphoses* ('Ovidius maior') remained the indispensable source of mythology, and it is as such that it played an important part in the composition of the *Divine Comedy*.* No poet, save Virgil, is so often echoed by Dante as Ovid. He is one of the *quattro grand'ombre*, with Homer, Horace and Lucan, encountered by the poets in Limbo.†[77] It was he who gave Dante Ulysses' noble line

> Considerate la vostra semenza,

with his

> este, precor, memores qua sitis stirpe creati.[78]

And yet Dante's whole approach to the classics is medieval rather than humanistic. He allegorizes, using Ovid's Orpheus as a typical example.[79] And though he shows in the *Vita Nuova* a knowledge of the poet of love, his peculiar conception of love has come to him refined through the Troubadours and the singers of the *dolce stil nuovo*, to be sublimated by his own religious vision.

In fact, during the thirteenth century there has been a shift of emphasis. The great humanistic schools of the previous century had been Chartres, home of philosophy as well as literature, where John of Salisbury from the flourishing English school of Canterbury had ripened into the outstanding Christian humanist of the age,‡ and Orleans, the more worldly society which had formerly numbered the Goliardic Hugo Primas among its canons, and which now heard Arnulfus Rufus lecturing on the *Fasti* with a wealth of antiquarian detail. By the middle of the century Orleans was the chief champion of the humanities, represented in Henri

---

* Dante recommends it as a model for style in the *De Vulgari Eloquentia* II, 6. For instances of Dante's borrowings see the index in A. Renaudet's *Dante, Humaniste* (1952).

† In describing a metamorphosis Dante boasts of outdoing Ovid.[80]

‡ Influenced by successors of Bernard, of whose teaching methods he has left an interesting account.[81]

d'Andeli's *Battle of the Seven Arts* as arraying the poets (Ovid and Hugo commanding the rearguard) in hopeless battle against the forces of Paris, Abélard's city, the stronghold of dialectic and law.[82] It was Aristotle who was driving the humanities out of Paris; there was now no time left for the *auctores*, when the *artes* had become so exacting, and by 1215 they had disappeared from the arts course there.[83] Next civil law, driven by papal decree in 1219 from Paris because it was strangling theology, was admitted by papal decree in 1235 to Orleans, where it proceeded to strangle literature.[84] The significant figure of the thirteenth century is not some humanist such as John of Salisbury had been, but St Thomas Aquinas.

Another setback to the classics was the appearance in 1199 of a popular Latin grammar, the *Doctrinale* of Alexander of Ville Dieu,* which supplanted Priscian. Alexander's work, instead of building up grammar by citing instances from classical works, tried to deduce it from logical principles. The examples he gave were largely made up by himself, so a fertile source of classical quotations hitherto common coin among educated people dried up. He also assumed that it was contemporary, not ancient, Latin that was to be learnt, a sign that one of the original excuses for Christians' reading classical authors at all, which was to train them to read the Vulgate and the Fathers, could no longer go unchallenged.[85] Fewer people than ever may thus have known Ovid at first hand just at a time when his *name* was becoming known far more widely; and inevitably he underwent the medieval metamorphosis of ancient worthies.† It was not merely among the peasants of his own Sulmo (for whom Ovidius survived as 'Uiddie', son of their eponymous founder Solymus the Trojan) that he was magician, necromancer, merchant, philosopher, paladin, prophet or saint.[86] He had studied with Cicero and travelled extensively with him, always coming out superior in

---

* He had a forerunner in Peter Helias (*fl.* 1140–50).

† Fancy played round him the more freely in that no ancient biography of him had survived.

their adventures.[87] But the Empress fell in love with him, and when he rejected her, played Potiphar's wife. The Emperor thereupon set him adrift in a ship, but granted his request for pen and paper which enabled him to write a *Tale of Troy* on board. On landing he sent back this more acceptable peace-offering than *Tristia* II, and was duly pardoned.[88] A famous poetic romance of the thirteenth century, the *De Vetula* ('The Hag'), which purported (not perhaps very seriously) to have been found in the tomb of Ovid at Colchis, was almost certainly written by Richard de Fournival, who must have known the real Ovid quite well. The poet himself is the hero; the hag is the nurse of the girl he loves; she deceives him by a stratagem borrowed from the *Fasti*[89] and he loses the girl. But twenty years later the girl is herself now a hag, and Ovid realizes that Learning is the only reliable love. This enables the book to close in medieval fashion with meditations on philosophy, astrology and religion.[90] In another legend popular with preachers, having been banished to the island of Tomos, providentially situated near Patmos, he is converted by St John and ordained bishop of the Tomitan land, which he evangelizes.[91]

Meanwhile local Latin dialects were developing at different paces into the vernacular languages, which triumphed in the thirteenth century. Latin might still be spoken at school, but it was ceasing to be spoken at home. About 1160 Chrétien de Troyes translated the *Ars Amatoria*. His version is now lost, but he had a host of successors among the poets of chivalry. The earliest extant version, by Maître Élie, expands the original here, abbreviates it there, and modernizes as well, Church taking the place of the theatre, and clerical mystery plays that of the racecourse, as suitable milieus for finding a mistress.*[92] The earliest vernacular version of the *Metamorphoses* was a free paraphrase in a little-known dialect of German produced in 1210 by Albrecht von Halberstadt. Translations might be prejudicial to classical studies, but they were influential in familiarizing a much wider public with classical stories and ideas. In *Flamenca*, a Provençal poem of 1234, there is

* The tourney was also recommended as an amorous hunting-ground.

a list of stories a minstrel would be expected to have in his repertoire. Most are classical myths, and of these the majority come from Ovid's *Heroides* or *Metamorphoses*.[93]

From the old popular poetry combined with the Latin heritage had emerged the songs of the Provençal Troubadours and the German Minnesingers. From Ovid, often no doubt by way of Latinate intermediaries, the Troubadours derived the conceptions of love as a sickness, as a form of warfare, and as a science that can be taught, besides various more particular motives.[94] But their knowledge of him was superficial, consisting of stories from the *Metamorphoses* and sentiments from the amatory works; and they differed from him in that they sang in *praise* of women, generally of higher birth, and that their love was a Christianized love involving service and sacrifice.[95] One type of song was the *alba* (*aube*) or *Tageliet*, which apparently arose from the medieval watchman's song of greeting to the dawn. It is not until the end of the eleventh century that the theme appears in it of lovers parted by the dawn and chiding

> Busie old foole, unruly Sunne.

Quite possibly this was introduced by some clerk who had read his Ovid.* In any case it may be refreshing to pause here for a moment and go back to the fountainhead (*Amores* I, 13):

> Iam super oceanum venit a seniore marito
>   flava pruinoso quae vehit axe diem.
> 'quo properas, Aurora? mane!—sic Memnonis umbris
>   annua sollemni caede parentet avis!
> nunc iuvat in teneris dominae iacuisse lacertis;
>   si quando, lateri nunc bene iuncta meo est.
> nunc etiam somni pingues et frigidus aer,
>   et liquidum tenui gutture cantat avis.

---

* Rand, *op. cit.* p. 121, says that it 'comes, it would seem, direct from Ovid'; but he gives no evidence or authority, and caution seems advisable. Cf. R. Schevill, *Ovid and the Renascence in Spain* (1913), pp. 24–5; Fränkel, *op. cit.* pp. 11–12. Ovid could have got his idea from Meleager, *A.P.* v, 171 and 172 St.

quo properas, ingrata viris, ingrata puellis?
   roscida purpurea supprime lora manu!
ante tuos ortus melius sua sidera servat
   navita nec media nescius errat aqua;
te surgit quamvis lassus veniente viator,
   et miles saevas aptat ad arma manus.
prima bidente vides oneratos arva colentes;
   prima vocas tardos sub iuga panda boves.
tu pueros somno fraudas tradisque magistris,
   ut subeant tenerae verbera saeva manus;
atque eadem sponsum multos ante atria mittis,
   unius ut verbi grandia damna ferant.
nec tu consulto, nec tu iucunda diserto;
   cogitur ad lites surgere uterque novas.
tu, cum feminei possint cessare lacerti,
   lanificam revocas ad sua pensa manum.
omnia perpeterer—sed surgere mane puellas,
   quis, nisi cui non est ulla puella, ferat?
optavi quotiens, ne nox tibi cedere vellet,
   ne fugerent vultus sidera mota tuos!
optavi quotiens, aut ventus frangeret axem,
   aut caderet spissa nube retentus equus!
invida, quo properas? quod erat tibi filius ater,
   materni fuerat pectoris ille color.
Tithono vellem de te narrare liceret;
   femina non caelo turpior ulla foret.
illum dum refugis, longo quia grandior aevo,
   surgis ad invisas a sene mane rotas.
at si, quem mavis, Cephalum conplexa teneres,
   clamares: "lente currite, noctis equi!"
cur ego plectar amans, si vir tibi marcet ab annis?
   num me nupsisti conciliante seni?
adspice, quot somnos iuveni donarit amato
   Luna, neque illius forma secunda tuae.
ipse deum genitor, ne te tam saepe videret,
   commisit noctes in sua vota duas.'

iurgia finieram, scires audisse: rubebat—
nec tamen adsueto tardius orta dies!

Lo, from her ancient spouse she comes away
Whose rimy car o'er Ocean brings the day.
'Stay, Dawn!—why hasten?—so may Memnon's shade
With yearly due of slaughtered birds be paid.*
Now most within my lady's arms to bide
I love, now most to feel her at my side;
Now also sleep is downy, air is cool,
And birds' clear-fluting throats with song are full.
Why hasten, both to men and maids a bane?
Check with thy rosy hand that dewy rein.
Before thy rising sailors better may
Their stars observe nor in mid-ocean stray;
Thy coming wakes the weariest traveller, and
Puts weapons in the soldier's hardened hand;
Thou first the mattock-laden peasant seest,
And summon'st to its yoke the tardy beast;
Thou sendest boys to school but half-awake,
On tender hands the cruel lash to take,
And halest many a sponsor into court
Where one small word huge forfeit may extort.
Thee every sort of lawyer vilifies,
For each to tackle some new case must rise,
And women's arms that might awhile have rest
Back to their stint of wool thou summonest.
All else I'd bear: but who that's not forlorn
Of love could bear that maids should rise at morn?
How oft I've prayed Night should not yield thee place,
Nor stars in rout scatter before thy face;
How oft I've prayed the wind should break thy wheel,
Or cloud-drifts cause thy stumbling steed to reel.

---

* Memnon, king of Ethiopia and hence black, was son of Aurora and Tithonus.
When Achilles killed him at Troy, his ashes became birds which yearly returned
to Troy on the anniversary of his funeral, and fought to the death over his grave,
on which they fell as offerings (see M. XIII, 600–22).

Jealous, why hasten? Sure, thy Memnon swart
Was proof of blackness in his mother's heart.
Would that Tithonus might tell tales of thee!*
No woman's fame in heaven would fouler be.
'Tis to escape thy all o'er-aged mate
Thou mount'st betimes the chariot he doth hate;
But if thy Cephalus thou didst embrace,
Then would'st thou cry, "Night's horses, check your pace".
Why should I suffer for thy spouse's age?
Did I, forsooth, your misalliance stage?
See now, what hours of sleep doth Moon allow
Her youth adored,† though not less fair than thou!
And Jove the Father, fain to see thee less,
Made two nights one to prosper his success.'‡
So did I chide, and you could swear she heard:
She blushed—but daybreak was no whit deferred.

The thirteenth century saw the appearance of a great poem in the French language—the *Roman de la Rose*. The Rose, guarded in a tower, is the girl whom the lover must pluck—and does, after more than 20,000 lines. The first 4266 lines were written by Guillaume de Lorris about 1225–30. 'Courtly' or chivalrous love was different from classical, involving courteous and submissive deference to the weak and the idealization of virgin purity. Yet Guillaume, a young and idealistic dreamer (the quest is presented as a dream), heralds his poem as one 'où l'art d'amors est toute enclose', and draws much on Ovid. In 1270 it was taken up by Jean de Meun and completed in a total of 22,700 (octosyllabic) lines. Jean was a scholar, philosopher, wit and satirist, and it is not surprising that he used Ovid still more; for his part of the poem is a vast intellectual treatise on subjects more or less connected with

---

* Aurora had prayed Jupiter that her husband Tithonus should be immortal, but forgot to ask that he should also be ageless. Cephalus was one of her many other loves.

† Endymion, the beautiful sleeper of the Latmian cave.

‡ In his affair with Alcmena.

the quest, and he puts, for instance, much advice from the *Ars* into the mouth of an old woman. In all, Ovid contributed about 2000 lines to the poem, which had a resounding success.[96]

The true spirit of Ovid, and much of his mythological subject-matter, lived on in the vernacular, helped by translations, to reach England late through Chaucer and Gower. Chaucer, captured by the French in 1359 when less than twenty years old, chivalrously treated and then ransomed, began his literary career by translating the *Roman de la Rose*. In an age when publication still consisted, as in Ovid's day, in recitation or multiplication of manuscripts or both, there was no idea of copyright.[97] Chaucer never thinks to mention Boccaccio, from whom he derived so much; but from across the Channel he was saluted with honour by Deschamps as 'Grand Translateur'. However, either a romantic and venial snobbery or reverence for the 'authoritee' of 'olde bokes' made an exception of the classics; and so it happens that he refers more often to Ovid by name, and to his works, than to any other author.* In *The Hous of Fame* (1486–9) he gave him a statue with Virgil, Lucan and Claudian:

> And next him on a piler was
> Of coper, Venus clerk, Ovyde,
> That hath y-sowen wonder wyde
> The grete god of loves name.

In the same poem (712) he refers to his 'owne book', the copy of the *Metamorphoses* he possessed in an age when private libraries were small, and which he had had within reach at his bedside that night when he sought to beguile his sleeplessness by reading the tale of Ceÿx and Alcyone.[98] 'Ovydes Art' was one of the books owned by the fifth husband of the Wife of Bath.[99] Chaucer's literal renderings, some involving variant readings, are proof enough that, however much of his classical lore he may have

---

* W. W. Skeat on *The Hous of Fame*, l. 1487; E. Shannon, *Chaucer and the Roman Poets* (1929), p. 318. In the latter book 315 pages deal with Chaucer's borrowings from Ovid and Virgil (mostly Ovid), while 54 suffice for all other classical writers together.

taken at second-hand from French and Italian poets, he did use Latin texts.[100] But equally his translation of Boethius shows that he was by no means an impeccable Latinist.[101] In his earlier period he shows knowledge of Ovid's *Metamorphoses*, *Heroides* and *Fasti*, and of the *Aeneid*, Statius' *Thebaid*, and Cicero's *Somnium Scipionis* in Macrobius' commentary. But his reading seems to have been the skimming of a poet, not the study of a scholar, and he naturally had no true perspective of the classical world such as Shakespeare shows in his plays based on North's Plutarch. He can be defended (if defence be needed) against the accusation of mistaking 'Metamorphoseos' and 'Corinne' as *authors* of the works that concern them, but Lollius, his alleged ancient authority for the Tale of Troy, must be not only a fiction, but a fiction born of a blunder, whether his own or someone else's;*[102] and he is capable of rendering *pernicibus alis* as 'partriches wings'.[103] On the other hand, he seems, like Ovid, to have had a remarkable memory for what he read, for it is most unlikely that he composed at a table covered with the various books which he uses on occasion within a few lines; and, as with Ovid, his very slips are an indication that he is relying on memory.[104]

The more obvious cases of his borrowings from Ovid of ideas, descriptions or stories have often been catalogued.[105] The Man of Law in the *Canterbury Tales* (47 ff.) maintains that Chaucer has told more tales even than Ovid, and then gives a list which reveals with charming irony that Ovid was in fact his chief source for them. There is still room for some debate as to how much came at second-hand, but no one can deny that the mature Chaucer relied mainly on the Latin originals.[106] Like Ovid himself, he did not hesitate to select, alter, conflate, elaborate and invent. In *The Hous of Fame* the walls of the temple of Venus are painted with scenes from the *Aeneid*, which are briefly enumerated. But when we

---

* Shannon, *op. cit.* pp. 307-12, defends the form *Metamorphoseos* as title of the book, and, pp. 17-28, 'Corinne' as a current title for the *Amores*. But why does Chaucer speak as though the former were a person, and why does he say he will follow Corinne and then not follow the *Amores*?

come to Aeneas' desertion of Dido, we are launched into a full-scale disquisition on the betrayal of a pathetic heroine in which the 'traitor' himself is hardly heard, while the plight of his victim is emphasized (239–432). 'The Epistle of Ovyde' has drowned the voice of 'Virgile in Eneidos'; and eight other of the *Heroides* are incidentally adduced as *exempla*.*

The unfinished *Hous of Fame* is a transitional poem. *The Book of the Duchesse* (1369–70) had been in the French medieval tradition, and the story of Ceÿx and Alcyone from the *Metamorphoses* plays only a casual part in it. But in 1372 and again in 1378 Chaucer had visited the Italy of Petrarch and Boccaccio; and *The Hous of Fame*, though still in the old tradition, teems with Renaissance ferment and undigested classical lore. It was followed by a masterpiece, *Troilus and Criseyde*, full, as a love story was sure to be, of reminiscences of Ovid. Though based on Boccaccio's *Il Filostrato*, it breaks free through the entirely new characterization of Troilus, Pandarus and Criseyde, which in turn necessitated the invention of new episodes. It is clear that the *Heroides* had already stimulated Chaucer's interest in feminine psychology, and the yielding of Criseyde, more subtle and lifelike than any treatment in medieval poetry of such a theme, was undoubtedly influenced by the yielding of Helen to Paris in Epistle XVII.[107]

Troilus seems to have shocked conventional society, or at least the feminine half of it, for it represents a challenge to the whole conception of courtly love. *The Legend of Good Women* (1386), his commissioned palinode, consists largely of stories from the *Heroides* or elsewhere in Ovid which deal with the constancy of 'Cupid's Saints', including Lucretia and the ever-popular Pyramus and Thisbe. How closely he sometimes followed his original may be seen from a specimen based on a passage already quoted (p. 102), about Ariadne:[108]

> Right in the dawening awaketh she,
> And gropeth in the bedde, and fond right noght.

* The influence of the *Heroides* is already traceable in Chaucer's *Anelinda and Arcite*.[109]

'Allas!' quod she, 'the ever I was wroght!
I am betrayèd!' and her heer to-rente,
And to the stronde bar-fot faste she wente,
And cryèd, 'Theseus! myn herte swete!
Wher be ye, that I may nat with yow mete,
And mighte thus with bestes been y-slain?'
The holwe rockes answerde her again;
No man she saw, and yet shinèd the mone,
And hye upon a rocke she wente sone,
And saw his barge sailing in the see.
Cold wex her herte, and right thus seide she.
'Meker than ye fynde I the bestes wilde!'
Hadde he nat sinne, that her thus begylde?
She cryed, 'O turne again, for routhe and sinne!
Thy barge hath nat al his meiny inne!'

This is his last work to show much Ovidian inspiration, for although the *Knight's Tale*, adapted from Boccaccio, has a number of details traceable to the *Metamorphoses*, the liberating influence of the renaissance spirit, itself fostered by study of the classics, had already broadened his horizon and encouraged him to stand on his own feet. The lively episode of Deïphobus' dinner-party and the thunderstorm in *Troilus*, his own invention, presages the *Canterbury Tales*.

The Legend of Good Women is significant in another way for our subject: in it the Heroic Couplet, destined to be inseparable from our idea of Ovidian elegiacs, makes its first appearance in English literature. But as yet it is curiously un-Ovidian, when we consider that the *Heroides* were being closely studied for their subject-matter; it is *enjambé*, and devoid in general of balance, antithesis, parallelism and the rhetorical figures of speech. There are of course instances in Chaucer, such as the couplet quoted by Dryden:

> Winsinge she was, as is a joly colt,
> Long as a mast, and upright as a bolt;[110]

but they amount to little in the great bulk of his work in this metre.

Fortune was kinder to Chaucer than to Ovid. When he offended the court on the subject of love he was not banished, but simply received an injunction from King Richard's queen to make amends by praising the faithful women of legend; and instead of writing an apologia, he contented himself with a certain irony in his rather bored presentation of these 'Good Women' (among whom he included Cleopatra and Medea!):*

> She fledde her-self into a litel cave,
> And with her went this Eneas al-so;
> I noot, with him if ther wente any mo;
> The authour maketh of hit no mencioun.[III]

Again, his reversal of prosperity when his patron John of Gaunt went abroad in 1384 was comparatively mild; without quenching his spirit it gave him leisure, and the result was that he produced *Canterbury Tales* rather than *Tristia*.

It was Dryden who first drew attention to a similarity between these two:

'Both of them were well-bred, well-natured, amorous and libertine, at least in their writings, it may be also in their lives.... Both writ with wonderful facility and clearness; neither were great inventors; for Ovid only copied the Grecian fables, and most of Chaucer's stories were taken from his Italian contemporaries, or their predecessors....Both of them understood the manners; under which name I comprehend the passions, and, in a larger sense, the descriptions of persons, and their very habits.'[112]

He was conscious, in his age, of defending a paradox when he went on to say that 'the figures of Chaucer are much more lively, and set in a better light', and for preferring Chaucer's thought, as distinct from his words, and deploring Ovid's 'boyisms' of untimely wit. But while we may now readily agree with him, we should not forget that in those touches which give life to a

---

* *Incipit legenda Cleopatrie Martyris*, says the rubric in three MSS. For the ironies of the *Legend* see Coghill, *op. cit.* pp. 86–105.

description Ovid surpassed his known predecessors as Chaucer surpasses him. In several respects we may extend the comparison between the two. The kaleidoscopic variety of mood which we noted as characteristic of the *Metamorphoses* is to be found in the (alternative) Prologues to *The Legend of Good Women*, and the Ovidian sense of fun and mischief in that work as a whole (and in both poets these traits have too often gone unrecognized).[113] Both are sophisticated men given to an ironical affectation of naïveté. The element of burlesque so common in Ovid appears in Chaucer's own Canterbury Tale of *Sir Thopas*, while the ribaldry of Faunus' discomfiture in the *Fasti* (II, 303–56) bursts out in the kindred dénouement of the Reve's Tale and in those other *fabliaux*, the Miller's and the Cook's Tale. Both also discovered in mid-career that their *métier* was story-telling; and both were intensely interested in psychology, especially that of women.

I doubt whether we should attribute those similarities to direct influence of Ovid on Chaucer so much as to innate sympathy of temperament (Chaucer shows other marked affinities to Horace, with whose works he was not familiar).[114] Nor should we stress them without also stressing the differences. Chaucer deliberately avoids the divine machinery and miraculous happenings that he found in his originals, thereby making his characters more serious and responsible human beings. Thus his practice of omitting metamorphosis begins in his earliest work; it would have marred his tale of Ceÿx and Alcyone in *The Book of the Duchesse* because that is introduced as a prototype of the conjugal love of John of Gaunt and his first duchess Blanche, who had died in 1368 at the age of twenty-nine. Chaucer has better taste than Ovid, and far more concern for morality. The high seriousness which prompted him to translate Boethius is evident in Troilus' musings on predestination, in the Dantesque close of that poem, and in the Prioress', Second Nun's, and other Canterbury Tales. He has a sincere, if fitful, strain of religion.

The classical world he sees largely through medieval spectacles.[115] His Dido and Procne go on pilgrimages; his Janus resembles a contemporary yeoman, his Aeneas a contemporary knight. And yet he is a bridge to the Renaissance. His Troy may be largely medieval, but significantly he added touches of true classical colour not found in *Il Filostrato*, so as to maintain the playful fiction that he is following an ancient authority.[116] This is a first step towards getting the classical world into perspective. On the other hand, he actually relies less in his later work on classical authorities, for the renaissance spirit opened his eyes to the world around him, awakening him from medieval dreams of allegorical gardens to the observation of contemporary life and character, and into his Troy bursts the Shakespearian figure of Pandarus, forerunner of such realistic creations as the Wife of Bath.

CHAPTER XII

THE RENAISSANCE

SWEET WITTY SOUL

THE phenomena we think of as being respectively medieval and renaissance spring from deep in the human heart, and co-exist perpetually in the same century, the same country, even the same individual; we can only say that in most centuries, countries and individuals the one or the other spirit is dominant. Thus in the twelfth century Palermo had a luxurious court bent on pleasure, such as we associate with the sixteenth. In the humanistic Florence of the Medici Savonarola struck a discordant note: 'You will say, "yet the Ovid of the *Metamorphoses* is good". I answer you, "Ovid the story-teller, Ovid the madman!";'[1] and in the France of Louis XIV the austere Fénelon stood out against the prevailing Ovidian craze.[2] In the sixteenth century alchemists were yet busy with the *Metamorphoses*;[3] while far into the seventeenth and even beyond, we come across such typically medieval titles as *Les Fastes de l'Église, L'Arte d'Amar Dio, De Arte Amandi S. Mariam.*[4]

Petrarch (1304–74) and Boccaccio (1313–75) are the significant figures of what may nevertheless be called the transitional period, each retaining a fair admixture of the medieval with what we recognize as forward-looking. Petrarch was steeped in Ovid. He took many of his mythological ideas from the *Metamorphoses*, the story of Daphne haunting him particularly because of the association of *laurus* with Laura. But most of his borrowings in his early, amatory period were from the erotic poems. His *Trionfo d'Amore*, for instance, was suggested by *Amores* I, 2, 19 ff. Later he became more critical of 'lascivissimus poetarum Naso', denouncing the

Ars Amatoria roundly.* Yet although he now cited him less frequently than Virgil, or even Horace, his echoes of Ovid betray the extent of his familiarity.[5] Boccaccio in his youth was much more pagan. Steeped likewise in Ovid, he drew upon him freely in the early part of *Fiammetta*, where Venus is persuading the heroine to yield; nor can we dissociate the spirit of the author of the *Decamerone* from that of the author of the *Amores*. But in 1361 he was reconciled to Christianity, and turned his back on such frivolities.[6]

For a hundred years after the death of these two no considerable poet appeared in Italy, nor for that matter in France, apart from Villon. But this was the springtime of Italian painting, and we may pause here to consider the role of Ovid in the visual arts. Even in the Middle Ages there were artists familiar with his stories. Pyramus and Thisbe were carved, about 1200, among the figures on the cathedral of Basel,[7] and on the Royal and West Portals of the cathedral of Chartres, built in the episcopate of the widely read John of Salisbury, appear incidents from the *Metamorphoses* involving centaurs.[8] The great textbook for artists of the High Middle Ages was the *Liber Ymaginum Deorum* of one 'Albricus', whom there is a fair case for identifying with the Englishman Alexander Neckham already mentioned (d. 1217).† Descended indirectly from this essentially medieval, moralizing work is the *De Deorum Imaginibus Libellus*, confusingly bound up with its predecessor in the Vatican manuscript, and also there attributed to 'Albricus'. The unknown author, about 1400, abstracted the descriptions of the gods from the Latin *Metamorphosis Ovidiana moraliter explanata* composed about 1340 by Petrarch's future friend Bersuire, and in a purely secular and

* 'Ille mihi magni vir ingenii videtur, sed lascivi et lubrici et prorsus mulierosi animi fuisse, quem conventus feminei delectarent usque adeo ut in illis felicitatis suae apicem summamque reponeret. Itaque amatoriam artem scribens, insanum opus et meritam, nisi fallor, exilii sui causam,' etc.[9]

† P. 381. The work has other titles—*Mythographus Tertius, Poetarius, Scintillarium Poetarum*.

iconographic spirit prescribed how each should be depicted.* His great handbook soon received the attention it invited from illustrators (the Vatican copy has pen sketches from about 1420), played no small part in enabling the pagan gods to regain their sovereignty in art, and fixed their attitudes authoritatively for the artists of the Renaissance. Once established, an iconographic type was seldom varied. The first illustrated edition of Ovid's *Metamorphoses* was produced at Bruges in 1484 by the city's pioneer in printing, Colard Mansion, with a French text based on Bersuire. The illustrations were medieval in spirit, with costumes belonging to the period and district. This was followed in 1497 by another, with Italian translation, published at Venice by Zoane Rosso, one of the finest of all Renaissance books, which was to exercise great influence on Italian artists for half a century, particularly on Giorgione and Mantegna.[10] Many others appeared; indeed, no ancient author so often received this tribute.

It was the same with the large-scale arts. There were numerous tapestry workshops operating in the north from the mid-fifteenth to mid-sixteenth centuries, at Arras, for instance, as the name reminds us. The subject and spirit of their work were suddenly transformed by a wave of influence from Ferrara that swept through Brussels over the Low Countries and France. From being medieval they became mythological, the whole inspiration coming from Ovid's *Metamorphoses*.[11]

Meanwhile in 1445 Filarete, carving the bronze doors of St Peter's, introduced sixteen stories from Ovid among those of the Christian tradition. The bridal chests of the period were mostly decorated, Vasari tells us, with scenes from Ovid and other poets or tales from Greek and Roman history.[12] Painters in general began to turn their attention to secular subjects, among which the stories of pagan mythology were especially popular. It may be no coincidence that this fashion became widespread in the years immediately following the publication of the first printed

---

* For a clear exposition of this once tangled matter see J. Seznec, *La Survivance des Dieux Antiques* (1940), pp. 147-56.

Ovid in 1471. Early in the sixteenth century it reached a climax at Rome in Peruzzi's *Villa Farnesina*, where Raphael painted his *Galatea* and Sebastiano del Piombo decorated the lunettes with scenes from the *Metamorphoses*. The passion for mythology affected all the great masters of the High Renaissance, especially those of Venice, among whom Titian stands out as an admirer of Ovid and an inheritor of his spirit.* The French kings in the middle of the century commissioned Rosso and Primaticcio to decorate the Palace of Fontainebleau with Ovidian pictures. Bernini's famous statue of Apollo and Daphne, and Rubens with his great series from the *Metamorphoses*, commissioned by Philip IV of Spain,† carry us on into the next century, when the passion gradually spent itself. From the lusty exuberance of Rubens' treatment we pass to the nostalgic, detached calm of Poussin and Claude.

In the arts it is especially difficult to determine in any particular case whether Ovid or any other writer is the direct source, for the myths became widely familiar through the handbooks. But we may justifiably assume considerable direct influence, and here and there we chance upon a significant clue. In some cases, of course, there is documentary evidence; in others an odd detail may be unmistakably derived. I can only give a few instances I have come across. In Raffaello Borghini's well-known dialogue *Il Riposo* (1584) one of the characters takes Titian to task for not following Ovid faithfully in representing Adonis seeking to elude the embrace of Venus.[13] Again, Piero di Cosimo, about 1498, painted a Bacchanalian scene in which Satyrs and others are making a noise to collect bees. Would anyone have thought of connecting Satyrs

---

* A. Lombard, *Un Mythe dans la Poésie et dans l'Art* (Europa) (1946), p. 36; Salomon Reinach, *La Mythologie Figurée et l'Histoire Profane dans la Peinture Italienne de la Renaissance* (1915), p. 73. This last work is an interim gleaning from catalogues of titles of such pictures painted before 1580. Sir Robert Witt added a supplement in 1919.

† For the Torre de la Parada, 1636-8. Most of the 112 subjects were from the *Metamorphoses*; the sketches were made by Rubens, but he himself painted only some of the large works, leaving the rest to collaborators. This is the most grandiose artistic enterprise of all those based on Ovid (L. de Puyvelde, *The Sketches of Rubens*, 1947, pp. 41-3).

with this process who had not been reading *Fasti* III, 735–62?* In the seventeenth century two great technical works, one Dutch and one German, containing all that an artist should know, both conclude with a complete prose translation of the *Metamorphoses*.[14]

Let us now return to literature. It was in Italy that bourgeois life had most chance to develop, and her cities had a tradition of culture more favourable to the revival of the classics than that of the courts of chivalry. In 1444 Aeneas Silvius Piccolomini, the future Pope Pius II, produced a Latin romance much influenced by Ovid, the *Historia de duobus amantibus*.[15] This was translated into Italian some years later, and took its place with Boccaccio's *Fiammetta* in popular esteem. But it was the invention of printing that did most to spread classical influence in general. The *editio princeps* of Ovid appeared at Bologna in 1471, followed in the same year by an edition published at Rome, and in 1478 by a prose *Heroides* in Florentine dialect published at Naples. The earliest annotated edition of the *Metamorphoses*, by Raphael Regius, was published at Venice in 1492, and immediately became a standard work.

Boccaccio, with his *Ameto* (c. 1341) had reintroduced ancient pastoral poetry into European literature. His rustic hero comes upon some nymphs and hears them tell of their loves. Everything is on a sensual plane until the sudden revelation that this is all an allegory of sacred love.[16] It is easy to see how a purely secular romantic literature could develop from such beginnings and a good example is the *Arcadia* of Sannazaro, which was circulating in manuscript by 1481 and had enormous influence.†[17] Sixteenth-century Italy developed a flourishing literature of this kind with major poets in Ariosto, Boiardo and Tasso. Pastoral and mythological elements were blended, and many versions were made of tales from the *Metamorphoses*, while the *Amores* and *Heroides* contributed erotic colour. Douglas Bush has characterized the

---

* The 'Sebright Panels'.[18]

† Sannazaro was one of the chief among many neo-Latin poets of the period.

mythological poems thus: 'In their pictorial richness, artificial rhetoric, erotic themes and general slightness of content, they were typical young man's poetry, beautiful words about beautiful things, things and bodies which can be seen and touched.'[19]

In France meanwhile Ovid became a favourite of the Pléiade, with Joachim du Bellay aspiring to the title of 'l'Ovide français' and drawing on the *Tristia* for his *Regrets*.[20] Ronsard, the greatest of the group, was much influenced by the Roman elegists, admiring Ovid most of the three, and taking from him hints for his love poems to Cassandra Salviati; but he owed still more to the *Metamorphoses*, especially in his *Odes*.[21] In the first half of the sixteenth century boys in Paris schools read Ovid in the eighth class, and in 1551 we find the *Tristia* and *Ex Ponto* prescribed for the seventh class in Jesuit colleges. St Ignatius himself was interested in the production of expurgated classics for schools.[22]

Spain had already felt the Ovidian influence in the Middle Ages, more from the erotic poems at first than from the *Metamorphoses*. A notable example is the *Pamphilus de Amore*, a Latin novel in dramatic form based on the *Ars Amatoria* and attributed to the poet himself. Another work of the late Middle Ages, the highly humanistic *Libro de Buen Amor* of Juan Ruiz (*c.* 1330), notoriously owes much to him, as well as the lyric *Cancioneros* of the fifteenth century.[23] The stock comic figure of the Bawd, derived from *Amores* I, 8, became through Ruiz a popular feature of Spanish poetry, notably in the famous dramatic dialogue *Celestina* of F. de Rojas (1499).[24] Piccolomini's romance was translated into Spanish in 1496, and had great influence in Spain;[25] and numerous stories of the sixteenth century drew upon Ovid himself, though the aristocratic, chivalrous tradition at first remained dominant, and the Inquisition forbade the translation of the *Amores* and *Ars Amatoria*.[26]

There are many other great European writers of the Renaissance who have been found to show Ovidian influence to a notable degree, such as Cervantes, Lope de Vega, Calderón and Camoëns. Montaigne, brought up by his father to speak Latin before French, first discovered the joy of reading when he came across the *Metamorphoses* at the age of seven or eight, though other writers were to please him more when he came to maturity.* But with the French I will deal later. Apart from them, Ovid's last and most distinguished devotee on the Continent was Goethe, who echoes him often in his *Roman Elegies* and whose journals constantly record that he has been rereading the *Metamorphoses*. In the vision of life at the end of *Faust* appear Philemon and Baucis.

An interesting side-line of the Ovidian tradition was operatic libretti. The first experiment in opera, made at Florence in 1594, was a dramatization by Ottavio Rinuccini of the story of Apollo and Daphne, with music by Peri and Caccini. *Daphne* was followed in 1600 by *Eurydice*. The novelty was that these works consisted of 'a magic circle of unbroken musical sound from the beginning of the story to its end'.[27] Monteverdi, Gluck and others later exploited the same inexhaustible source of plots.

Yet while few would deny the pervasive influence of Ovid in the Renaissance, it is often difficult in literature to determine whether it is direct, though less so than in the visual arts because of the clues provided by verbal echoes. Boccaccio's *De Genealogia Deorum*, the great link between medieval and renaissance mythology, for which he used and collated ancient sources, was followed by many another handbook.† A late instance of this dilemma is provided by Keats; we know that he was indebted to Sandys' translation, with allegorical verses and commentary, of the *Metamorphoses* (1632), but we also know that he pored over Lemprière's *Classical Dictionary*.[28]

In each country the Renaissance achieved for a time a harmony between Christianity and paganism, but this depended on a certain naïveté, and could not maintain itself for long against sapping of various kinds. The allegorical interpretation of the classics, or at

---

* *Essays*, I, 25. The following count has been made of his quotations: Lucretius 149, Horace 148, Virgil 116, Ovid 72 (P. Villey, *Les sources et l'évolution des essais de Montaigne*, 1908, vol. I, under the respective names).

† Seznec, *op. cit.* pp. 246–7. He gives a list. Boccaccio also produced a *De claris mulieribus* and a *De viris illustribus*.

least its feasibility, was accepted with varying degrees of sincerity. At least a perfunctory claim to be edifying was advisable until quite late in the period.* But those who had religion most at heart, from Luther to the compilers of the Index of Trent, denounced even the well-meaning *Ovide moralisé*. Meanwhile the rationalistic spirit began to see through the allegorical fog, Rabelais deriding in the prologue to *Gargantua* the obscurantist interpreter of Homer and Ovid. It was a small step from this to travesty of mythology itself, which became fashionable in the seventeenth century following the publication in 1644 of Scarron's *Tryphon*, with such works as Richer's *Ovide bouffon* and d'Assoucy's *Ovide en belle humeur*.[29] Finally, the authority of the classics in general was weakened by the spirit that led to the famous quarrel of the Ancients and Moderns in the France of Louis XIV.[30]

But to explore the fortunes of Ovid in renaissance Europe as a whole would be the work of more than a lifetime. In a book intended primarily for English readers I may be pardoned if I limit myself henceforward to some aspects of his influence on English literature and to his reputation in England, especially since, apart from the geniuses of Shakespeare and Milton, the insular development roughly paralleled the continental, with a certain time-lag.

After Chaucer and Gower, whose *Confessio Amantis* is full of stories borrowed from Ovid,[31] there followed a medieval twilight of a century and a half, during which, although some knowledge of Ovid was part of the school and university curriculum,[32] the classical stories were known mainly through medieval redactions, or through paraphrases of these by Lydgate and Caxton. In 1480 Caxton made an English prose version of the *Metamorphoses* from the French, which, however, was probably never printed.†

---

* Similarly we find Cervantes asserting that his *novelas* have a lesson, but adding that his object is that his readers should entertain themselves, though without prejudice to body or soul.[33]

† Only Books x–xv survive, in a MS in the Pepysian Library at Magdalene College, Cambridge (reprinted in 1924 by S. Gaselee and H. B. F. Brett-Smith). Gaselee (p. xxii) doubts whether it did reach the press, since no reference to it

We may make a fresh start with the establishment of a national system of education in the sixteenth century. In 1512 Colet founded St Paul's School (statutes 1518), which was destined to serve as a model for many, with a curriculum based on the *De Ratione Studii* of his friend Erasmus. Of the six Latin authors prescribed for reading in selection Ovid was not one; but Erasmus had elsewhere recommended the *Heroides* as an aid in the exercise of letter-writing (it was being so used at Eton about 1528), and Ovid in general as chief master for the final exercise of rhetoric; and soon, in Wolsey's instructions for Ipswich School (1529), the *Metamorphoses* and *Fasti* were added to the schedule.[34] Even Sir Thomas Elyot, in his programme for the education of a Utopian prince entitled *The Governour* (1531), grudgingly admitted these two works, if suitably moralized, though, like Ascham, he would have preferred to elevate Horace to the position next after Virgil; and the future Edward VI may have read the *Heroides* with an Italian translation opposite. Sturm (1538) thought that only the *Fasti* required class work, the *Metamorphoses* being easy enough to be read at home.[35] The *Tristia* makes its first appearance at Bury St Edmunds School in 1550; it soon became a staple, and Eton boys in 1560 were reading it along with the rules of versification (the study of Ovid was often deferred until this form of exercise began).[36] In 1530 we find Winchester boys learning twelve lines of the *Metamorphoses* by heart every week.[37] Beginners might meet Ovid first in some anthology such as Mirandula's *Flores Poetarum*, which Brinsley recommended; in higher forms the *Metamorphoses* were read in every school, with *Fasti*, *Heroides* or *Tristia* added according to taste.[*38]

Such was the grammar-school grounding in Ovid that we may expect an Elizabethan poet to have had. To many his characters and stories would also be familiar from pageants, often a curious

occurs anywhere in Tudor literature. The French original seems to have been identical with that used by Caxton's old collaborator Colard Mansion (see p. 401).

* Wynkyn de Worde, in 1513, published *The flores of Ovide de arte amandi with theyre englysshe afore them*, but this was presumably not intended as a school book.

mixture of pagan with Christian elements, and from tapestries, though pictures were still rare in England.[39] His immense vogue in the poetry of the age begins with the anonymous publication, in 1560, of a fairly close translation in seven-line stanzas of his story of Narcissus (some 200 lines of narrative being supplemented, in the manner of the day, by some 900 lines of moral).[40] In 1565–7 appeared Golding's complete translation of the *Metamorphoses* into fourteeners, and also Turberville's *Heroycall Epistles*, followed in 1569 by Underdowne's *Ibis* and in 1572 by Churchyard's *Tristia*.*

From now onwards his influence is paramount throughout the Elizabethan Age.† We may consider it under three headings, Literary Form and Subject-matter, Spirit and Treatment, and Technique. Discussions of influence usually concentrate on borrowings, perhaps because these are the most tangible and demonstrable form of evidence; but spirit is surely more important and interesting, in spite of the danger of subjectivity.

Of literary forms little need here be said. Spenser's *Shephearde's Calendar* (1579), though the idea of its division into monthly books may have come from the *Fasti*, is pastoral poetry owing little or nothing to Ovid. More to the purpose is Michael Drayton's most popular work, *England's Heroical Epistles* (1597). Instinctively the poets who imitated the *Heroides* turned for inspiration to the double letters, with their live situations and contest of wits. Beginning with the Fair Rosamond and Henry II, Drayton matched couples from history almost down to living memory. Still more important was the vogue of retelling Ovidian stories, spinning them out with rhetoric and Italianate embroidery.‡

* Marlowe's *Amores* was not published until 1597, under the title *Elegies*. Thomas Heywood translated the *Remedia* and *Ars*. Browne translated the *Remedia* in 1599. The *Fasti* had to wait for John Gower's version of 1640.

† At Elizabethan dinners select transformations from Ovid's *Metamorphoses* were exhibited in confectionery.[41]

‡ Among the most popular were Pyramus and Thisbe, Cephalus and Procris, Narcissus and Echo, Apollo and Daphne, and Philomela.

From 1560 to 1575 this was commonly done in ballad form, but later we have poems in stanzas or couplets which are akin to the Greco-Roman epyllia, of which, as we have seen, the *Metamorphoses* may be considered to be a congeries.

The finest example of these last was actually based on a Greek epyllion of the fourth or fifth century A.D., Musaeus' *Hero and Leander*, well known and of great prestige because the author was naïvely identified with Orpheus' legendary pupil of that name. Marlowe's poem in couplets, of which he only completed two books, was entered in 1593. He blended the unadorned story of Musaeus* with Ovidian elements taken either from the Hero-Leander letters in the *Heroides* or from elsewhere.[42] Thus the temple of Venus, on which Musaeus spent one epithet, provides the occasion for a brilliant description imitated from Ovid's palace of the Sun and web of Arachne:[43]

> So fair a church as this had Venus none.
> The walls were of discoloured jasper stone,
> Wherein was Proteus carvèd, and o'erhead
> A lively vine of green sea-agate spread,
> Where by one hand light-headed Bacchus hung
> And with the other wine from grapes out-wrung.
> Of crystal shining fair the pavement was;
> The town of Sestos called it Venus' glass.
> There might you see the gods in various shapes
> Committing heady riots, incests, rapes:
> For know that underneath this radiant floor
> Was Danaë's statue in a brazen tower,
> Jove slyly stealing from his sister's bed
> To dally with Idalian Ganymed,
> And for his love, Europa, bellowing loud,
> And tumbling with the Rainbow in a cloud;
> Blood-quaffing Mars heaving the iron net,
> Which limping Vulcan and his Cyclops set;

---

* Probably using a Greek text with Latin version.

Love kindling fire to burn such towers as Troy;
Silvanus weeping for the lovely boy
That now is turned into a Cypress tree,
Under whose shade the Wood-gods love to be.[44]

By 1590 most poets were borrowing freely from Ovid, whether directly or indirectly. The greatest of them, Spenser, took allegorical and other descriptions from him;* but he owed more perhaps to Virgil in *The Faerie Queene* (Books I–III, 1590). Marlowe's *Hero and Leander* was followed immediately by Shakespeare's *Venus and Adonis* (1593) and *The Rape of Lucrece* (1594). The former is based on the story in *Metamorphoses* X, with the description of the boar from VIII and the reluctance of Adonis imported perhaps from that of Narcissus (III) or Hermaphroditus (IV), though the debt to Ovid in detail is not great;† the latter follows Livy I, but borrows also from the story in *Fasti* II (see pp. 280–4). In 1595 the craze for Ovid was at its height, stories being especially popular in which the female, for a change, pursued the male, as in *Venus and Adonis*.‡

And so we come to Shakespeare's plays. It has been estimated that he echoes Ovid in these four times as often as Virgil. He draws on every book of the *Metamorphoses*, and there is scarcely a play which shows no trace of its influence, which is found particularly in the lighter scenes.[45] At first he used mythology like any other renaissance poet as a new and delightful toy; later a hint of burlesque and mockery creeps in, and still later, a sense

---

* Thus an Ovidian forest becomes the Wood of Error (*M.* x, 86 ff.; *Faerie Queene* I, i, 7–9). In *Muiopotmos* he blends two passages about Europa, *M.* VI, 103 ff. and II, 873 ff. We have already visited the Cave of Sleep (p. 185). The description of Chaos in the Garden of Adonis (*F. Q.* III, vi) is based on *M.* xv, 252 ff. The seduction by Paridell of Hellenore (*F.Q.* III, ix–x) is partly based on the Paris-Helen letters in the *Heroides*, hence the names.[46]

† The reluctance of Adonis appears also in *The Passionate Pilgrim* VI, and in *The Taming of the Shrew*, Induction, ii, 51–5, where in both cases he is again assimilated to Hermaphroditus, and Venus to Salmacis.

‡ E.g. Heywood's *Oenone*, Drayton's *Endymion and Phoebe*, Edwards' *Narcissus* and *Cephalus and Procris*. See Hallett Smith, *Elizabethan Poetry* (1952), pp. 92–3.

of deeper significance in it.[47] Let us marshal a few well-known instances in such a way as to display his attitude.*

At *Much Ado About Nothing* II, i, 99 occurs the following exchange:

Don Pedro. My visor is Philemon's roof; within the house is
Jove.
Hero. Why, then, your visor should be thatched.
Don Pedro. Speak low, if you speak love.

No one can doubt the source of that: the cottage of Philemon and Baucis in Ovid was *stipulis et canna tecta palustri.*† Yes, but Golding had used the same word in his translation,

The roofe thereof was *thatchèd* all with straw and fennish reede;

and what is more, in a scene written in prose, these lines break into Golding's metre. Did Shakespeare then read Ovid in the original at all?

Quotations in Latin are rare in the plays. Nevertheless, it is made clear in T. H. Baldwin's masterly survey of this much-discussed topic that he did use the original *Metamorphoses* habitually along with Golding;‡[48] and further that, although there is no direct evidence that he had or completed a grammar school education, his 'small Latine and lesse Greek' amounts to just so much as could be gleaned from the grammar-school curriculum of the Elizabethan

---

* Highet, *op. cit.*, has an excellent chapter (XI) on Shakespeare's Classics. The classical references in the plays are conveniently listed with comment, play by play, in J. A. K. Thomson, *Shakespeare and the Classics* (1952), pp. 47–224. Unfortunately this book lacks an index of proper names.

† *M.* VIII, 630. At *As You Like It* III, iii, 10, Jaques reacts to Touchstone's reference to 'honest Ovid among the Goths' with an aside: 'O knowledge ill-inhabited, *worse than Jove in a thatched house*'.

‡ Even the cautious Thomson allows this (*op. cit.* p. 154). Thus Holofernes' 'Cerberus, that three-headed canis' (*L.L.L.* v, ii, 593) is from Ovid's 'tria colla canis' (*M.* x, 65–6), not from Golding. *The Rape of Lucrece* uses both Livy and the *Fasti*, though neither is known to have been available in English in 1594 (Thomson, *op. cit.* pp. 43–4). Baldwin and Thomson owe much to R. K. Root's work mentioned above. See further P. Simpson, *Studies in Elizabethan Drama* (1955), pp. 24–40.

Age, which included the regular learning of passages by heart.* This opens up some interesting speculations. Suppose he began his classical reading, as so many did, with Mirandula's *Flores Poetarum*. The first excerpt he would come upon was from *Amores* I, 15, and it ended precisely with the couplet he prefixed to his *Venus and Adonis*:

> Vilia miretur vulgus: mihi flavus Apollo
> pocula Castalia plena ministret aqua.

He would come across the name Titania, which Golding does not use,† and also Autolycus, *furtum ingeniosus ad omne* ('adept at all kinds of thieving').[49] Again, the heading of two excerpts from Ovid in the *Flores* reads 'Lachrymas puellarum arma esse'— 'Women's weapons, waterdrops' (*Lear*, II, iv, 280).[50] If he reached the highest forms, he would probably learn rhetoric from the standard Tudor textbook, Erasmus' *Copia* in Veltkirchius' annotated edition of 1536. 'Copy' of *words* was the faculty of varying the same *sententia*—one thinks of Ovid's Ulysses:

> ille referre aliter saepe solebat idem;—

it depended, of course, on richness of vocabulary, in which of all poets Shakespeare stands supreme. 'Copy' of *things* was nurtured on the topics of dialectic. Erasmus' supreme example of an author who was copious, even to excess, was Ovid,[51] and it is perhaps significant that Veltkirchius selects as an example Hecuba in *Metamorphoses* XIII, 483–575; for she is mentioned more than once in the plays as she appears there, though 'the mobled queen' of the Player Scene in *Hamlet* derives ultimately from Virgil.‡

---

* A lesson from Lily's Latin Grammar is burlesqued in *The Merry Wives of Windsor*, IV, I.

† It can refer to any daughter or grand-daughter of a Titan, as Pyrrha (*M.* I, 395), Diana (*M.* III, 173), Latona (*M.* VI, 346), Circe (*M.* XIV, 382, 438).[52]

‡ *Cymbeline* IV, ii, 313 ('All curses madded Hecuba gave the Greeks, And mine to boot, be darted on thee!'); *Titus Andronicus* I, i, 136; IV, i, 20 ('And I have read that Hecuba of Troy Ran mad for sorrow'). A copy of the *Metamorphoses* is a stage-property in *Titus* (IV, i, 42).[53]

On the other hand, critics from Richard Farmer in 1767 onwards have pointed out apparent echoes of Golding's translation:

> Gallop apace, you fiery-footed steeds,
> Towards Phoebus' lodging; such a waggoner
> As Phaëthon would whip you to the west,
> And bring in cloudy night immediately.[54]

'Waggoner' is Golding's word for *auriga* though coincidence cannot be ruled out here.

> In such a night
> Medea gathered the enchanted herbs
> That did renew old Aeson.[55]

'Enchanted herbs' is Golding's phrase for *cantatas herbas*, though again it might be a coincidence. There are more certain echoes in *Venus and Adonis* and elsewhere, as we shall see. The use of a translation was no evidence of incompetence in Latin (Elizabethan schoolmasters had no prejudice against them, either for the boys or themselves); but if Marlowe at Cambridge could make the mistakes he did in rendering the *Amores*, we must not imagine that Shakespeare would read Latin with ease. However, he probably used Golding partly to cull *words* and the phrases or ideas that the words even of a mediocre writer can generate in the mind of a fertile poet. Like Chaucer, in fact, he skimmed.

The *Metamorphoses* was not the only work of Ovid that Shakespeare knew.* It has been suggested that he wrote of Cleopatra and Antony with Dido and Aeneas in mind,† particularly in the scene (I, iii) where he leaves her for Rome, alleging, like Aeneas, that 'the gods best know'. It was apparently Ovid's Dido rather than Virgil's, for Cleopatra uses words adapted from *Heroides* VII, 139,

> sed iubet ire deus: vellem vetuisset adire,
>
> *but a god bids you go: would he had forbidden you to come,*

---

* We have seen already from *Lucrece* that he knew the *Fasti*.

† Antony himself, before his suicide, shows himself conscious of the parallel:
> Dido and her Aeneas shall want troops,
> And all the haunt be ours.[56]

in taunting him with subservience to Fulvia:

> What says the married woman? You may go?
> Would she had never given you leave to come;

and like Ovid's Dido she hints that she is pregnant.[57]

We must not imagine Shakespeare, any more than Chaucer, as borrowing allusions from source-books open before him. Sometimes his very slips of memory indicate the contrary:

> In such a night
> Stood Dido with a willow in her hand
> Upon the wild sea banks and waft her love
> To come again to Carthage.[58]

When was this? Never, so far as we know. It seems to be a transferred recollection of Ariadne in the *Heroides*:

> Candidaque imposui longae velamina virgae
> scilicet oblitos admonitura mei.[59]

And I fixed a white veil to a long branch, to signal to those who had, it seemed, forgotten me.

Sometimes he might make a careful preliminary study of some source, such as a Life in North's Plutarch, but the casual allusions, accurate or inaccurate, probably leapt up at the touch of association from a deep, retentive memory.

So much for gleanings of subject-matter: but what of the absorption of spirit? For thirty years after the Ovidian revival of 1560 the medieval attitude predominated. Imaginative literature could only be justified by allegorical and moralistic interpretation. The hounds that rent Actaeon were his own passions; Narcissus was a parable of the fate of vanity. Golding prefixed a warning jingle to his translation:

> With skill, heed and judgement this book must be read,
> For else to the reader it stands in small stead,

and in a dedicatory Epistle and a Preface he proceeds to expound the inner meaning of the *Metamorphoses*. And the tradition died hard, for 'the greatest repository of allegorised myth in English was the commentary which Sandys added to the 1632 edition of his translation of the *Metamorphoses*', and despite the rationalistic criticisms of Hobbes and others there were some even in the eighteenth century who still paid at least lip-service to that form of interpretation, including Pope in the Preface to his *Iliad*.[60]

Spenser's tapestry is so vast that whole tracts are apt to be taken in without reference to their context. Thus in *The Faerie Queene* III, xi, we are conducted with Britomart along a 'goodly arras of great majesty', displayed through sixteen stanzas, in which are depicted the victories of Cupid, many of them over fellow-gods, as known from the *Metamorphoses* or works derived from it. We begin with Jove himself and his seduction in ram's form of Helle and in bull's form of Europa, and then proceed in stanzas of radiant beauty:

> Soon after that, into a golden shower
>   Himself he changed, fair Danaë to view,
> And through the roof of her strong brazen tower
>   Did rain into her lap an honey dew;
>   The whiles her foolish guard, that little knew
> Of such deceit, kept the iron door fast barred,
>   And watched that none should enter nor issue.
> Vain was the watch, and bootless all the ward
> Whenas the god to golden hue himself transferred.
>
> Then was he turned into a snowy swan,
>   To win fair Leda to his lovely trade.
> O wondrous skill and sweet wit of the man
>   That her in daffodillies sleeping made
>   From scorching heat her dainty limbs to shade!
> Whiles the proud bird, ruffling his feathers wide
>   And brushing his fair breast, did her invade,
> She slept: yet twixt her eyelids closely spied
> How towards her he rushed, and smilèd at his pride.

These last two lines, with their sly humour, might have come from Ovid's *Amores*, and the whole description is far from censorious. It is only later that we are reminded that this is the castle of the 'vile enchanter' Busirane, and that the worship paid to Cupid's golden statue by its inmates is 'foul idolatry'.

A still more surprising manifestation (though Boccaccio's *Ameto* might prepare us) is Chapman's curious poem, published in 1595, called *Ovid's Banquet of Sence*. Ovid is in love with Julia, the Emperor's daughter (Corinna to him). He hides in a garden, sees her bathing, and has the opportunity of gratifying in turn the five senses of hearing, smelling, seeing, tasting and—but he is interrupted before he can proceed to feeling. And to what is all this leading up? To the neo-Platonic conclusion, as opposed to the Stoic, that it is through the exercise of the senses that man must initiate his soul if he is to become capable of aspiring to the higher love and the vision of divine beauty!

There is no reason to suppose that these poets were hypocrites, however conscious they may have been that pagans could not be allowed to show their true faces in a Christian world. Nor should we impute cynicism to virtuous men such as Spenser who, steeped in Italian literature, lavished their gifts on sensuous and appetizing descriptions of what they were proposing to condemn: if their subconscious ran away with them, they were only, like Milton, 'of the Devil's party unawares'. Nevertheless, it is easy to see how descriptions of the sort they sometimes inserted would come to be relished without their context in a thoroughly pagan spirit, especially now that the pastoral tradition had become merged with the mythological. Thomas Lodge, in 1598, was the first to come out into the open with an epyllion pretending to no hidden meaning. His *Scillaes Metamorphosis* is a longish poem in sixain stanzas, with luscious anatomical and other descriptions in the Italianate manner. It is based on Ovid's tale of Scylla and Glaucus, though the scene is quaintly set on the banks of the Isis.[61] Itself a poem of little merit, it heralds four years in advance the lovely *Hero and Leander* of Marlowe.

It was not so long since Marlowe had been closely rendering the *Amores*, and indeed two dozen apparent reminiscences of that work have been detected in this poem. But more important is the spirit of the Ovidian erotic poems in general, which he has infused into the simple narrative of Musaeus. No sooner has Hero seen Leander kneeling in the temple

> (who ever loved that loved not at first sight?)

than she reacts like a sophisticated Corinna with a pert aside:

> Were I the saint he worships, I would hear him.

After he had declaimed at length against virginity in general, and hers in particular,

> Thereat she smiled, and did deny him so,
> As put thereby, yet might he hope for mo.

Her whole frame of mind recalls that of the already slipping Helen of *Heroides* XVII:

> These arguments he used, and many more,
> Wherewith she yielded, that was won before.
> Hero's looks yielded, but her words made war;
> Women are won when they begin to jar.
> Thus having swallowed Cupid's golden hook,
> The more she strived, the deeper was she strook;
> Yet evilly feigning anger strove she still,
> And would be thought to grant against her will.
> So having paused a while, at last she said:
> 'Who taught thee rhetoric to deceive a maid?
> Aye me, such words as these I should abhor,
> And yet I like them for the orator.'

Repelling his embraces, she volunteers the information where she lives, blushes to have let slip unawares a 'come thither', then later lingers on the way home, and even drops her fan, in case he may not succeed in following her. In Book II Leander, who knew

enough about 'Venus' sweet rites' in Book 1, is suddenly discovered to be an ignoramus in love (like the shepherd-boy Daphnis
in Longus' Greek romance), who

> Long dallying with Hero, nothing saw
> That might delight him more, yet he suspected
> Some amorous rites or other were neglected.*

The sole reason for this seems to be that it enabled the tantalizing
climax to be still further delayed, though in all conscience Hero
did her part in this:

> Treason was in her thought,
> And cunningly to yield herself she sought.
> Seeming not won, yet won she was at length,
> In such wars women use but half their strength.

And so at last to the point where Hero, like Corinna in *Amores* I, 5,
was 'all naked to his sight displayed'. And there Marlowe, for
whatever reason, broke off, leaving it to Chapman to add four
other books. He had written a poem of voluptuous beauty whose
whole intention was erotic as anything in Ovid.

Venus and Adonis, which appeared in the same year, is less
Ovidian, though still based on Ovid; it signally lacks his chief
characteristics as a story-teller, swiftness and simplicity; instead it
is spun out with conceit upon conceit, and the sugar that threatened
to cloy in Marlowe's poem has become saccharine.

> 'Thrice fairer than myself', thus she began,
> 'The field's chief flower, sweet above compare,
> Stain to all nymphs, more lovely than a man,
> More white and red than doves and roses are....'

So it goes on, redeemed however by Shakespeare's ear for word-
music and by occasional homely glimpses of the Warwickshire
countryside which are admittedly out of keeping. For the greater
part of the poem Adonis is simply a hearty, unfeeling boy with

---

* How like the end of some stanza in Byron's *Don Juan*!

no thought but for hunting with his friends. When he finally does, after 780 lines, give a reason, sympathetic at least and even touching, for his reluctance,

> Lest the deceiving harmony should run
> Into the quiet closure of my breast,
> And then my little heart were quite undone
> In his bedchamber to be barred of rest,

and distinguishes between lust and love,

> I hate not love, but your device in love,
> That lends embracements unto every stranger,

it comes too late, and by now seems out of character; it cannot deepen the significance of the poem, which appeals only to the senses. Such poetry is not at all like Ovid's, being rather a salient example of what Italianate renaissance poets made of him, and of what the emancipated late-Elizabethan public was ready to enjoy —phrase-making and rhetoric and conceits.

The Rape of Lucrece, which followed in 1594, dealt more seriously with chastity, a virtue which the condition of the reigning sovereign and the third book of *The Faerie Queene* may well have rendered topical at this period.* For its time it is archaic—indeed, it harks back to Chaucer. It is thirteen times as long as the episode in Ovid, being still more rhetorical, though less sensuous, than *Venus and Adonis*. Those who condemn Ovid as rhetorical might well read this poem before turning to him again.

Francis Meres, writing in 1598, made a well-known remark which no doubt represents the feeling of that decade: 'as the soul of Euphorbus was thought to live in Pythagoras, so the sweet witty soul of Ovid lives in mellifluous and honey-tongued Shakespeare; witness his *Venus and Adonis*, his *Lucrece*, his sugared sonnets among his private friends.'[62] We may feel rather that it is not so much in these poems as in certain of the plays that the true spirit of Ovid lives on, notably in *A Midsummer Night's Dream* and

---

* It was also glorified in Drayton's *Matilda* (1594).[63]

The Tempest, for both of which there is concrete evidence to support the impression.

The *Dream* is based on North's translation of Plutarch's Life of Theseus; but Professor Baldwin, discussing the phrase 'triple Hecate' in Puck's song at the end, has expressed his conviction that before Shakespeare wrote the play he had read Ovid's story of Jason and Medea in the *Metamorphoses* with some care, using along with Golding's translation an edition containing the notes of Regius.[64] And, indeed, it is natural that he should have turned to Ovid for ideas, since the scene is set in that prehistoric Greek world which was the background for so much of his masterpiece. Theseus is called a Duke, perhaps in reminiscence of Golding's phrase at *Metamorphoses* VIII, 405 (though Chaucer had called him so). In the hunting scene (IV, i) the hounds, as described by him, recall Actaeon's in Golding's version of *Metamorphoses* III, 206–25. Hippolyta has previously remarked,

> I was with Hercules and Cadmus once
> When in a wood of Crete they bay'd the boar
> With hounds of Sparta.

Why Cadmus, not at all a well-known hero? Because he was the grandfather of Actaeon, and the first 136 lines of this same third book are about him. But why Crete, with which he had no special connexion? Partly perhaps because of the provenance of Actaeon's hounds—

> This latter was a hounde of Crete, the other was of Spart—

and again

> The shaggy Rugge with other twain had had a syre of Crete
> And dam of Sparta;

but perhaps also from the chance association of the two names in the opening lines of the same book:

> The God now having layde aside his borrowed shape of Bull
> Had in his likenesse shewde himself, and with his pretty trull

Tane landing in the Ile of *Crete*. When in that while her Sire
Not knowing where shee was become, sent after to enquire
Hir brother *Cadmus*.

Here then is another longish passage in the *Metamorphoses* that
Shakespeare had been reading. And the whole performance of
Pyramus and Thisbe in the last act follows *Metamorphoses* IV, 45–166
closely, while the list of 'Sports' supplied to Theseus in the same
act[65] may equally have been suggested by various passages in
Ovid.

So much for the activities of the mortals. But what of the
uncanny agencies that play tricks on them? Here we can put our
finger on nothing tangible that is Ovidian save for the name
Titania; and yet the whole atmosphere is extraordinarily reminiscent of the *Metamorphoses*—the magic and the freedom, the
Puckish element, the blend of charm and moral irresponsibility,
the sense that nothing that happens is really serious because it is
all a dream, the interplay of pathos and humour, cruelty and love,
the natural and the supernatural, the grotesque and the beautiful,
Bottom with his Midas-ears fondled by the demi-goddess Titania.

It is just such a shifting world of fantasy and magic in *The
Tempest* that reminds one again of the *Metamorphoses*—the
mercurial spirit of Ariel changing from one shape to another, the
beauty of the island, the boisterous humour of Stephano and
Trinculo, the conjuring up of Iris, Ceres, Juno and the nymphs,
the grotesque Caliban and the innocent love of Ferdinand and
Miranda. This fairyland at least can produce evidence of direct
descent; for it was recognized long ago by Farmer that Prospero's
incantation is prompted by Medea's in Golding's Ovid:[66]

> Ye elves of hills, brooks, standing lakes and groves;
> And ye that on the sands with printless foot
> Do chase the ebbing Neptune and do fly him
> When he comes back; you demi-puppets, that
> By moonshine do the green sour ringlets make
> Whereof the ewe not bites; and you, whose pastime

Is to make midnight mushrooms; that rejoice
To hear the solemn curfew; by whose aid—
Weak masters though ye be—I have bedimmed
The noontide sun, called forth the mutinous winds,
And 'twixt the green sea and the azured vault
Set roaring war: to the dread-rattling thunder
Have I given fire, and rifted Jove's stout oak
With his own bolt; the strong-based promontory
Have I made shake; and by the spurs plucked up
The pine and cedar; graves at my command
Have waked their sleepers, oped, and let them forth
By my so potent art...

And now Golding's translation of Ovid:

Ye Ayres and Windes; ye Elves of Hills, of Brookes, of Woods
    alone,
Of standing Lakes, and of the Night, approche ye everychone.
Through help of whom (the crooked bankes much wondring at
    the thing)
I have compellèd streames to run cleane backward to their spring.
By charmes I make the calme Seas rough, and make ye rough
    Sees plaine
And cover all the Skie with Cloudes, and chase them thence
    againe.
By charms I rayse and lay the windes, and burst the Vipers jaw,
And from the bowels of the Earth both stones and trees do
    drawe.
Whole Woods and Forestes I remove: I make the Mountains
    shake,
And even the Earth itselfe to grone and fearfully to quake.
I call up dead men from their graves; and thee, O Lightsome
    Moone
I darken oft, though beaten brasse abate thy perill soone.
Our Sorcerie dimmes the Morning faire, and darkes ye Sun at
    Noone.

Clearly Shakespeare had Golding in mind, but it can be shown that he derived even more from the original.*[67]

All the Elizabethan poets borrowed from Ovid, but it was Shakespeare who knew best how to value him. In *Love's Labour's Lost* Holofernes comments severely on Berowne's verses:

'Here are only numbers ratified; but, for the elegancy, facility, and golden cadence of poesy, caret. Ovidius Naso was the man: and why, indeed, Naso, but for the smelling out of odoriferous flowers of fancy, the jerks of invention? Imitari is nothing: so doth the hound his master, the ape his keeper, the tired horse his rider....I will prove these verses to be very unlearned, neither savouring of poetry, wit, nor invention.'

He is judging according to the principles of Quintilian, who was studied in the higher forms of the grammar schools. He may be a burlesque character, but the qualities he ascribed by implication to Ovid, 'elegancy, facility and golden cadence', are so aptly chosen that we may assume that he speaks here for Shakespeare. As Professor Baldwin says:

'Shakspere agreed also with Quintilian that while the fundamental things in a writer are not mechanically imitable, yet an admired writer should be so mastered as to absorb his inimitable spirit. It was in this fashion that Shakspere had mastered Ovid, whom Quintilian would never have advised (Virgil was his favourite). But Holofernes—and Shakspere—thought that Ovid excelled in poetic invention and the other inimitable virtues'.[68]

In the sphere of technique we may trace the influence of Ovid on the development of the heroic couplet. We have already noted (p. 395) the general absence in Chaucer's myriad couplets of

---

* Some of the ingredients in the witches' cauldron in *Macbeth* come from Medea's recipe (*Macb.* IV, i, 4 ff., *M.* VII, 262 ff.), and Hecate there is Ovidian. Prospero's other famous speech (IV, i, 148–58),

'These our actors,
As I foretold you, were all spirits...'

also derives ultimately from Ovid, through Palingenius.[69]

closure, balance, antithesis, parallelism and rhetorical figures of speech, which are the distinguishing marks of the couplets of Ovid, as of Pope. In Tudor times it was the fashion to write Latin poems in various metres, but especially elegiacs; and from this developed the practice of imitating the Latin forms in English poems. From the period 1557–90, in forty-seven such poems, it has been observed that, whereas hexameters are hardly ever imitated by *rhymed* verse, elegiacs nearly always are.* During that period, moreover, the couplets that show signs of the features mentioned above tend to be those written in some kind of connexion with the Latin classics.[70]

No regular decasyllabic couplets showing clear evidence of classical influence are to be found before the period of Tottel's *Miscellany* (1557). But this collection included sixteen poems by Nicholas Grimald in couplets which are mostly closed and which have plenty of balance of a kind, together with classical allusions, rhetorical questions, and other figures such as apostrophe.[71] We are still far from the real thing; but Grimald is groping for it, and the groping continues, less markedly, for the next thirty years, during which this metre gradually established itself as the normal one to use when translating the classics for purposes of casual illustration.[72] But the first really significant step towards the Popian medium was taken in circumstances which make it certain that the decisive influence was Ovid. Marlowe, probably as an undergraduate at Cambridge before 1584,[73] made a line-for-line translation of the *Amores* in heroic couplets which achieved popularity as well as notoriety. In this every couplet was naturally closed, and the main technical features of the original were reproduced as far as possible—antithetical balance, apostrophe, rhetorical questions and so forth.†

---

* G. P. Shannon, p. 74 of an unpublished dissertation entitled *The Heroic Couplet in the Sixteenth and early Seventeenth Centuries, with Special Reference to Ovid and the Elegiac Distich* (1926), a valuable work which I have been able to use by the courtesy of Stanford University Library.

† Shannon (*op. cit.* p. 111) cites E. C. Knowlton, *Origin of the closed couplet in English,* in the New York *Nation,* 1914, as having previously expounded the claims of Marlowe to be the father of the heroic couplet.

Fool, if to keep thy wife thou hast no need,
Keep her for me, my more desire to feed.
We scorn things lawful, stolen sweets we affect;
Cruel is he that loves whom none protect.[74]

Or again:

Jove, being admonished gold had sovereign power,
To win the maid, came in a golden shower.
Till then, rough was her father, she severe,
The posts of brass, the walls of iron were,
But when in gifts the wise adulterer came,
She held her lap ope to receive the same.[75]

What is more important, Marlowe proceeded to display these features to a considerably greater extent than his predecessors had done, in a poem for which Ovid is only a secondary source, *Hero and Leander*. They had become associated with this particular metre.

The development of antithesis is most striking in *Venus and Adonis*, of which Bush remarks, 'It is hardly too much to say that the whole fabric of the poem is woven of antitheses, as if Shakespeare had fallen in love with one of Ovid's tricks and worked it to death.'[76] Lines such as

Hunting he lov'd, but love he laugh'd to scorn,
Ten kisses short as one, one long as twenty,
He red for shame, but frosty in desire,

recall immediately the poet from whom the subject-matter also was derived. And this poem had great influence, running into at least ten editions in Shakespeare's lifetime.

In Drayton's *England's Heroical Epistles* (1597) careful study of the Ovidian model is manifest from the vigorous, rhetorical style, the turns and antitheses and the closure of the couplets.[77] Who can hear the lines,

Punish my fault, or pity mine estate,
Read them for love, if not for love, for hate,

without thinking at once of

> odero, si potero, si non, invitus amabo?

All that is lacking from the original recipe is the literary allusions.
Here are some lines from Henry's lame reply to Rosamond:*

> If't be my name that doth thee so offend,
> No more myself shall be my own name's friend;
> If it be that which thou dost only hate,
> That name in my name lastly has his date.
> Say, 'tis accurst and fatal, and dispraise it;
> If written, blot it, if engraven, raze it;
> Say that of all names 'tis a name of woe,
> Once a King's name, but now it is not so.

Laboured this rhetorical conceit may be, but it can go without
much alteration into the medium of the model:

> Causa odii tanti nomen si sit tibi nostrum,
>   Nominis, en, fiam proditor ipse mei;
> Si nihil est aliud tibi quod fastidia movit,
>   Hoc et in aeternum nomine priver ego.
> Dic, fatale nefas, delendum ignobile nomen;
>   Si lapis est, scalprum, si liber, adfer aquam.
> Infaustum hoc nomen dic esse ex omnibus unum:
>   Regis erat quondam, nunc licet esse neges.

This work is likely to have had great influence; it ran into fourteen
editions by 1637.

Finally, in 1609, came Heywood's monstrous *Troia Britannica*,
of which Cantos IX and X consist in a diffuse translation of Ovid's
exchange of letters between Paris and Helen. (He had earlier
translated the *Ars* and *Remedia*.†[78]) Here once more we see the
influence of Ovid in shaping the English heroic couplet. I will

---

* Other relevant passages are quoted by Shannon, *op. cit.* p. 147. He estimates
(p. 148) that well over 20 per cent of the couplets in this work contain notable
balance, either intralinear or line against line.

† The *Ars* ran into at least eight editions.

quote some lines of Helen's, for comparison with those already given on p. 112;[79] four couplets have become seven, but the style has left its imprint:

> Yet had I rather stainless keep my fame
> Than to a stranger hazard my good name:
> Make me your instance, and forbear the fare,
> Of that which most doth please you, make most spare;
> The greatest virtue of which wise men boast
> Is to abstain from that which pleaseth most.
> How many gallant youths (think you) desire
> That which you covet, scorcht wi' the self-same fire?
> Are all the world fools, only Paris wise?
> Or is there none save you have judging eyes?
> No, no, you view no more than others see,
> But you are plainer and more bold with me;
> You are more earnest to pursue your game;
> I yield you, not more knowledge, but less shame.

Shakespeare had already put into the mouth of Iago those sudden couplets pregnant with the future beginning

> She that was ever fair and never proud,
> Had tongue at will and yet was never loud....[80]

Heywood's 'numbers' may not be conspicuously smooth or harmonious but it was now no great step to the art of Waller, Dryden and Pope; and it was Ovid who had prepared the way.

The fashion of elaborating Ovidian tales continued into the seventeenth century, with a bias towards the *risqué*. Iphis and Ianthe were the theme of *The Maid's Metamorphosis* (*c.* 1600); Beaumont may be the author of the *Salmacis and Hermaphroditus* (1602), and Barksted dealt with *Mirrha* (1607). Cowley, at the age of ten, retold the story of Pyramus and Thisbe, and published it five years later (1633). One of the last poems in the series was Shirley's *Narcissus*, which, though entered in 1618, did not appear until 1646. But by the turn of the century there were puffs of contrary wind; satire came into fashion, and with it a taste for burlesquing mythology and deflating rhetoric. Thus Nashe wrote a debunking prose version of the story of Hero and Leander entitled *Prayse of the Red Herring*, and an anonymous Jacobean composed a *Metamorphosis of Tobacco* in heroic couplets. The publication of the Frenchman Scarron's *Tryphon* in 1644 gave an impulse to the production of travesties, particularly of Ovid, which continued in England throughout the Restoration period.[81]

One product of the early seventeenth century is worth more than a passing mention, not for its intrinsic merits, but because it portends the future—Ben Jonson's *The Poetaster* (1602). This 'comicall satyre' is in dramatic form, and the scene is Augustan Rome. The earlier part is largely taken up with a sub-plot about Ovid. He is discovered by his disapproving father composing *Amores*, I, 15 (*Quid mihi, Livor edax*, here represented in English couplets). Next Tibullus brings him an invitation to a party from his mistress Corinna, *alias* the Princess Julia. There they stage a masquerade of the gods, with Ovid as Jupiter and Julia as Juno. They are surprised by Augustus, Maecenas and Horace and banished, parting in a balcony scene reminiscent of Romeo and Juliet. In the latter part of the play Virgil figures as the great poet, and together with Horace (who represents Jonson himself) arraigns and discomforts two detractors of Horace's poetry, Demetrius (=Dekker) and Crispinus (=Marston). One scene is adapted from Horace's Satire about his encounter with a bore (I, 9). Now all this is light-hearted enough; but it represents, first, a classicizing attempt to see the ancient poets and worthies in their true historical setting (though Jonson's Rome is as cardboard compared with the Rome that Shakespeare conjured up out of North's Plutarch), and secondly, a step towards the replacement of a banished Ovid by Jonson's favourite Horace in the place of honour next to Virgil. The classical attitude to antiquity is beginning to oust the romantic. When Shirley came to write his short chamber drama *The Contention of Ajax and Ulysses*, printed in 1659, the plot came from Ovid indeed, but the dirge at the end, which is all we now remember, is one of the most *Horatian* poems in the language,

The glories of our blood and state....

Nor must it be supposed that the growth of voluptuous pagan poetry in Elizabethan times took place without protest from the staider sort. John Stockwood preached at Paul's Cross against the reading of the erotic poets, including 'a great part of Ovid', and in 1582 the Privy Council prescribed patriotic literature for grammar schools instead of 'Ovide de arte amandi, de tristibus or suche lyke' (without much effect, it would seem).[82] Marlowe's translation of the *Amores* was among books ordered in 1599, by the Archbishop of Canterbury and the Bishop of London, to be publicly burnt. In Jacobean times puritanism gained momentum. Prynne's portentous *Histriomastix* (1632) denounced everything that was pagan, let alone immoral, and Cowley in 1656, grown middle-aged, turned on his fellow-poets of previous generations, for both literary and religious reasons, as handling 'confused anti-quated Dreams of senseless Fables and Metamorphoses'.[83] And so we come to the complicated and quite exceptional position of Milton.

Milton must have been introduced to Ovid at St Paul's.[84] He learnt, in the venerable European tradition, to compose in Latin verse, and faultlessly he did it.[85] With the metre he adopted, in the classical way, the turns of speech and thought that went with it. And so, in the first of his elegies, written to Diodati in 1626 while he was in rustication from Cambridge, after remarking in a rhetorical spirit that if only Ovid's exile had been as mild as his, he would have equalled Homer and Virgil, the future author of *Paradise Regained* proceeds to recount the pleasures of the London stage, and the attractions of the girls he sees in the suburban parks. The boy who could write of the theatre

> Saepe novos illic virgo mirata calores
>   quid sit amor nescit, dum quoque nescit, amat.

> *There oft a maid the unwonted ardour proves,*
> *Knows not what love is, yet unknowing loves,*

was clearly on the most familiar terms with the *Ars Amatoria*; but it would not have occurred to him that Diodati or anyone else would take him too seriously. He was simply, in the classical tradition, composing a poem in which his personal situation was made a peg for elegiac commonplaces.* In the sixth Elegy, after putting it to the same Diodati that the revelry he reports should have stimulated his lighter muse, he goes on to say that frugality and purity befit a poet with higher themes, and reveals that he himself is composing an ode *On the Morning of Christ's Nativity*. Steeped in the Latin of Ovid's works, he was a scholar of the new type, exemplified by Ben Jonson, who saw antiquity in perspective, understood its conventions, and knew exactly what he was about.

'Nothing places Milton more clearly in the Renaissance tradition', says Bush, 'than his attachment to Ovid.'[86] His early passion for the amatory elegies could not be expected to last long in so serious a puritan,[87] but his enthusiasm for 'Ovidius maior' was to remain unabated. We are told that the works he most delighted to hear read to him in his blindness were, after Homer, which he knew almost by heart, the plays of Euripides and the *Metamorphoses* of Ovid.[88] Such was the power of this great pictorial poem to 'shine inward, there plant eyes'.

The Circean passages of *Comus*, though based on Homer, owe some details to Ovid;[89] but the whole conception of this masque is in the medieval allegorizing tradition of the *Ovide moralisé*, which came down to Milton through his admired forerunner, Spenser, and perhaps through Sandys' elaborate *Ovid's Metamorphosis* of 1632.[90] We have seen how Spenser's poetic conscience impelled him to present in alluring colours the things he meant to condemn. Milton was in the same dilemma. The first utterance he gives to Comus

The Star that bids the Shepherd fold....

---

* On the other hand he carefully changes any phrase he borrows that might otherwise seem lascivious: Harding, *op. cit.*, p. 48. Who shall say whether the fair maid seen, loved and lost in Elegy VII, 61–102, ever existed?

is so beautiful in diction and imagery that it has us prejudiced in the villain's favour at once, forgetful of the previous warning given by the Attendant Spirit. But in maturity he was too rational, too sophisticated, to follow Spenser in carefree blending or juxta-position of pagan and Christian elements, yet too much im-pregnated with the classics to abjure their aid, even if he could. And so in *Paradise Lost* we find him adopting various shifts, though significantly allegory is no longer one of them. He could identify the pagan gods with the Satanic powers, a patristic and medieval notion already used in the Nativity ode.[91] He could introduce a myth with a 'fabled how', or dismiss one with a 'thus they relate, erring', refer to pagan divinities as 'feigned' or to the Muse her-self that Orpheus bore as 'an empty dream', though the con-vincing and supererogatory beauty of his treatment is apt to betray the conflict in him of poet with puritan.[92] Similes from mythology could be justified by the assertion that some storied person, place or event was here surpassed (as in the ' *Taccia*—' formula of Dante:[93] 'overgo' was the old English verb):

> Not that fair field
> Of Enna, where Proserpin gathering flowers,
> Herself a fairer flower, by gloomy Dis
> Was gathered, which cost Ceres all that pain
> To seek her through the world, nor that sweet grove
> Of Daphne by Orontes, and the inspired
> Castalian spring might with this Paradise
> Of Eden strive.[94]

Casual allusions to mythology could cause no offence. Nor could the borrowing of details in descriptive passages, where Ovid could be especially helpful. The most elaborate of Milton's evocations of dawn, at the beginning of Book VI, owes something to him:[95]

> Morn
> Waked by the circling Hours, with rosy hand
> Unbarred the gates of Light:

Ecce vigil rutilo patefecit ab ortu
purpureas Aurora fores et plena rosarum
atria.

He was invaluable, through his inventiveness which so many poets
have applauded, in the long stretches of the narrative which the
Bible did not cover; but particularly for the cosmic phenomena
described in Book 1 of the *Metamorphoses*, Chaos, Creation,
Paradise, Fall and Flood.

It is instructive to observe how the two poets deal with the
Flood. Ovid begins thus (Jupiter is the subject):[96]

Protinus Aeoliis Aquilonem claudit in antris
et quaecumque fugant inductas flamina nubes
emittitque Notum. madidis Notus evolat alis,
terribilem picea tectus caligine vultum.
barba gravis nimbis, canis fluit unda capillis;
fronte sedent nebulae, rorant pennaeque sinusque;
utque manu lata pendentia nubila pressit
fit fragor: hinc densi funduntur ab aethere nimbi.
nuntia Iunonis varios induta colores
concipit Iris aquas alimentaque nubibus adfert.
sternuntur segetes et deplorata coloni
vota iacent, longique perit labor inritus anni.

Forthwith in Aeolus' cave he prisoned fast
The North Wind and each cloud-dispelling blast,
Then let the South Wind free. His wings all wet
And awful face o'ercast with veil of jet,
Out flies the dark South Wind. His beard is hung
With heavy mist, and waters stream among
His hoary hairs. Vapour his brow enshrouds;
His breast and pinions drip. The hovering clouds
He presses with broad hand, and therewithal
A roar is heard; then down in floods they fall.
Juno's swift Iris, clad in varied hue,
Draws moisture up to feed the clouds anew.

Crops are laid low, and farmers mourn to see
Their hopes, a year's toil, ruined utterly.

Ovid is not here at his best. He lets himself be diverted from the scene by the temptation to play with the personification in a baroque way,* and his metre, 'on the hand-gallop' as ever, conflicts with the subject-matter. Milton liked the beginning, but had no use for the rest:[97]

> Meanwhile the Southwind rose, and with black wings
> Wide hovering, all the clouds together drove
> From under Heaven; the hills to their supply
> Vapour and exhalation dusk and moist
> Sent up amain; and now the thickened sky
> Like a dark ceiling stood: down rushed the rain
> Impetuous, and continued till the earth
> No more was seen.

The inspiration for that sombre sequence of gathering gloom, deathly hush, and sudden cloudburst came rather from the master of onomatopoeia, Virgil:

> Saepe etiam immensum caelo venit agmen aquarum
> et foedam glomerant tempestatem imbribus atris
> collectae ex alto nubes: ruit arduus aether
> et pluvia ingenti sata laeta boumque labores
> diluit.†

(Note especially the effect of the colon-pause at 'stood', as at 'nubes', after the long syllables have brought the gathering to a

---

* Virgil himself lapses into similar frigidity when speaking of Atlas, and Ovid may even have had the passage in mind (*Aen.* IV, 250–1):
> Nix umeros infusa tegit: tum flumina mento
> praecipitant senis, et glacie riget horrida barba.

† G. I, 322–6, tr. L. A. S. Jermyn:
> Oft advances huge
> A host of waters in the sky, and clouds,
> Gathering from the sea, marshal the storm
> Foul, dark with rain. Down pour the heavens sheer,
> In mighty floods sweeping away glad crops
> And labours of the oxen.

head.) Ovid next has an interlude equally little to Milton's purpose, in which Jupiter summons the rivers to receive their orders, but when he returns to description he can help again with suggestions of detail:

Si qua domus mansit potuitque resistere tanto
indeiecta malo, culmen tamen altior huius
unda tegit, pressaeque latent sub gurgite turres.
iamque mare et tellus nullum discrimen habebant:
omnia pontus erant, deerant quoque litora ponto.

If any house resisted and could be
Unshattered by so great calamity,
Yet o'er its roof the burying waters reared,
And towers beneath the deluge disappeared.
Now sea and land had no distinction more:
Ocean was all, an ocean without shore.

After telling of the Ark ('secure with *beakèd* prow' a few lines later echoes Ovid's 'cumba sedet alter *adunca*') Milton continues with obvious indebtedness to the above passage:

All dwellings else
Flood overwhelmed, and them with all their pomp
Deep under water rolled; Sea covered Sea,
Sea without shore, and in their palaces
Where Luxury late reigned, sea-monsters whelped
And stabled.

Even these sea-monsters come from Ovid:

et, modo qua graciles gramen carpsere capellae,
nunc ibi deformes ponunt sua corpora phocae;

Where slender goats but lately cropped the grass,
Now wallowing seals extend their shapeless mass.

but as so often, here too, *nescit quod bene cessit relinquere.*
   Another instructive comparison is provided by the scene in which Eve describes how she discovered her own beauty by

reflexion from a pool, a scene clearly suggested by Narcissus'
similar experience in the *Metamorphoses*.* Tempted by the paradoxes inherent in the situation, Ovid here again pursues his idea too
far; and again Milton borrows some details, but refines by trans-
forming or omitting others:

> Hic puer et studio venandi lasus et aestu
> procubuit faciemque loci fontemque secutus,
> dumque sitim sedare cupit, sitis altera crevit,
> dumque bibit, visae correptus imagine formae
> spem sine corpore amat, corpus putat esse, quod umbra est.
> adstupet ipse sibi vultuque immotus eodem
> haeret, ut e Pario formatum marmore signum;
> spectat humi positus geminum, sua lumina, sidus
> et dignos Baccho, dignos et Apolline crines
> impubesque genas et eburnea colla decusque
> oris et in niveo mixtum candore ruborem,
> cunctaque miratur quibus est mirabilis ipse;
> se cupit imprudens et, qui probat, ipse probatur,
> dumque petit, petitur, pariterque accendit et ardet.
> irrita fallaci quotiens dedit oscula fonti,
> in medias quotiens visum captantia collum
> bracchia mersit aquas nec se deprendit in illis!
> quid videat nescit; sed quod videt, uritur illo,
> atque oculos idem, qui decipit, incitat error.
> credule, quid frustra simulacra fugacia captas?
> quod petis, est nusquam; quod amas, avertere, perdes!
> ista repercussae, quam cernis, imaginis umbra est:
> nil habet ista sui; tecum venitque manetque;
> tecum discedet, si tu discedere possis!

> *Here, tired with heat and with the eager chase*
> *The boy lay down, attracted by the place*
> *And by its pool; and as he sought to slake*
> *His thirst, he felt another thirst awake,*

---

* III, 413–36. The pool has already been described, p. 181. Cf. *P.L.* IV, 457–69.

And as he drank, smitten by what did seem
A face, he loved an unsubstantial dream,
And what was shadow mere, did substance deem.
With fixed expression, motionless, amazed,
As if in Parian marble carved, he gazed;
Prostrate, he sees twin stars, that are his eyes,
Hair that with Bacchus' and Apollo's vies,
Smooth cheeks, an ivory neck, mouth full of grace,
And whiteness tinged with roses in that face,
What's admirable in himself admires,
Approves himself, fondly himself desires,
Seeking is sought, and burns with self-made fires.
How oft in vain he kissed the elusive pool,
Into the water plunged his arms, poor fool,
To clasp that neck, only to find it flee!
He knows not what he sees, yet burns to see;
What lures yet mocks him is the self-same thing.
Fond boy, why chase a phantom vanishing?
You seek what is not: turn away, and lo,
Your love, a mere reflected shape, will go;
Nought in itself, with you it came, it stays,
With you 'twill leave—can you but go your ways!

And now Milton's Eve:

                I thither went
With unexperienced thought, and laid me down
On the green bank, to look into the clear,
Smooth lake, that to me seemed another sky.
As I bent down to look, just opposite,
A shape within the watery gleam appeared
Bending to look on me. I started back,
It started back, but pleased I soon returned,
Pleased it returned as soon with answering looks
Of sympathy and love. There had I fixed
Mine eyes till now, and pined with vain desire,
Had not a voice thus warned me: 'What thou seest,

What there thou seest, fair creature, is thyself:
With thee it came and goes.'

Milton would feel nothing incongruous in the association of
'our general mother' with Narcissus. Giles Fletcher, in his *Christ's
Victorie and Triumph* (1610), had gravely compared the ascending
Christ with Ganymede. This mingling of pagan and Christian
elements was characteristic of the poetic tradition from Spenser to
Milton.[98] Indeed, our modern sense of incongruity may be
exceptional. Virgil puts into the mouth of Aeneas in his agony
a line altered by hardly more than a word from an utterance of
Berenice's lock in Catullus' translation of Callimachus' fanciful
burlesque.* So Milton in his third elegy, on the late lamented
Bishop of Winchester, feigns to have seen him in a dream of
Paradise, and ends with a line,

talia contingant somnia saepe mihi,

Often may I have the happiness of such dreams

which is unmistakably reminiscent of that with which Ovid concludes a very different poem.[99]

By the time he wrote *Paradise Regained* the worldly fopperies of
the Restoration had sharpened his sense of the cleavage between
pagan and Christian, which had already caused him scruples in
Paradise Lost. In the earlier poem his chief sources of ideas, apart
from the Bible, were Homer, Hesiod, Virgil and Ovid; every
book of the *Metamorphoses* except the twelfth has been found to
have contributed something.† But in the later the old mythological richness has almost disappeared. Significantly, its last

---

* *Invitus, regina, tuo de litore cessi* ('litore' for 'vertice'): *Aen.* IV, 460; Catullus
LXVI, 39. Our sensitivity about mingling architectural styles may be equally
exceptional.

† Harding, *op. cit.* ch. v; Osgood, *op. cit.* p. xlii. The final eighty-seven pages
of the latter work are an alphabetical list of names occurring in Milton with the
classical sources of the allusions.

flicker, in the description of Christ's temptations, is one of the few passages of the work that remain in the memory:

> And at a stately side-board, by the wine
> That fragrant smell diffused, in order stood
> Tall stripling youths rich clad, of fairer hue
> Than Ganymed or Hylas; distant more
> Under the trees now tripped, now solemn stood,
> Nymphs of Diana's train, and Naiades
> With fruits and flowers from Amalthea's horn,
> And ladies of the Hesperides, that seemed
> Fairer than feigned of old....[100]

Before the end of the poem he has, through the mouth of his Master, renounced his classical heritage.[101] In the year of Milton's death, 1674, Thomas Rymer remarked of the Renaissance that 'it was the vice of those Times to affect superstitiously the Allegory'; and four years later Saint Evremond expressed clearly the spirit of the dawning Age of Reason: 'The genius of our age is quite the opposite to this spirit of fables and false mysteries. We love plain truth; good sense has gained ground upon the illusions of fancy, and nothing satisfies us nowadays but solid reason.'[102] The strange, romantic marriage of Christianity and Paganism has finally been dissolved.

EPILOGUE

MOLIÈRE, like Milton, still loved the *Metamorphoses* in his old age, and had a copy always at hand in his bedroom at Auteuil.[1] But with these two the Renaissance may be said to have come to an end, and in their lifetime the reputation of Ovid began to fade. In Italy, and still more in Spain, he was eclipsed. The scholars of the Low Countries, and some of their German successors, continued to admire him; but only in France did his vogue continue, reaching its height in the age of Louis XIV.[2] His wit, his elegance and his analytical interest in the feminine heart have made him as congenial to the French as Horace has proved to the English. Racine, in 1661, read and marked the whole of his works, intending to write a play based on his life, which suggests that many passages in his works which are parallel to passages in the Roman may be ascribed to direct influence. In particular, the *Heroides* may have given him hints for the characterization of his women.[*][3]

In art Ovid had provided ideas for the garden-sculpture of the Luxembourg Palace, made for Marie de Medicis, and he continued to do so for Le Nôtre's work at the Tuileries and Versailles.[†] Frederick the Great summoned painters from France to decorate Sans Souci with scenes from the *Metamorphoses*. But after Poussin and Claude he ceased everywhere to be the painter's bible. Not that the *Metamorphoses* have failed to provide subject-matter for some far from classical artists since then, such as the Northumbrian John Martin, who painted scenes from them in the early decades of the nineteenth century, and Pablo Picasso, who in 1931 illustrated a *de luxe* translation with thirty etchings which have been recently reproduced.[4]

[*] As a young man Racine wrote Latin poems in elegiacs.

[†] It is unlikely, e.g., that the subject of the Lycians turned into frogs, figured at Versailles and therefrom in the great fountain of the Spanish royal gardens at San Ildefonso, would have occurred to anyone who had not found it in Ovid.

In England Ovid was congenial to the Restoration spirit, as we find it, for instance, in Congreve's *Way of the World*. Sir Aston Cockain wrote a play about him, *The Tragedy of Ovid*, as Racine had planned to do. Swift as a young man (1708) composed a charming adaptation of the Philemon and Baucis story, in which a village parson of Chilthorne in Somerset and his wife figure as the originals of two old yew-trees, their cottage of the church. Dryden's *Fables*, published in 1700, are largely taken from Ovid. But the translation of the *Metamorphoses* by Dryden, Congreve, Addison and others, issued in 1717, is the last great English monument of his former glory. He was now on the defensive. Gilbert Wakefield in 1799 still ventured to think him the first poet of antiquity, but his correspondent Charles James Fox was aware of temerity in putting him even next after Homer and Virgil.[5]

Of course there have been odd individuals who have shown a kindred spirit to his—Byron in *Don Juan* and *Beppo*, for instance, or Peacock; there have been odd enthusiasts even later than Wakefield, such as Landor; odd poets who have used this or that Ovidian story, as Shelley did in his *Arethusa*, Swinburne in *Atalanta in Calydon*,* Morris in the Pygmalion episode of *The Earthly Paradise*, though their spirit and intention have rarely been Ovid's; and schoolboys have read him as model for the Latin Verse Composition which until recently occupied rather too much of their time. But these instances are as nothing compared with the general neglect.

It is worth considering what causes may have contributed to the decline, at first gradual and then rapid, of Ovid's reputation. I would suggest that the following were among them, at least in England:

(*a*) He ceased to perform certain services which had been in fact largely a fortuitous by-product of his work. He was no longer the only obvious source, for writers and artists, of mythological lore, after the diffusion of handbooks such as Boccaccio's. Nor was he

---

* The main outline and some incidents come definitely from Ovid.[6]

a leading purveyor of erotic stories, after the publication of works in the vernacular such as the *Decameron* and the Spanish romances, still less after the development of novels in which these topics were treated at length, such as *Moll Flanders* or *Tom Jones*. The novels also surpassed him, at a popular level, in the portrayal of character, whereas in the Middle Ages and the Renaissance he was considered a master of psychological subtlety, particularly in the *Heroides*, but also in the *Amores*, *Ars* and *Remedia*. He had come to seem even less remarkable in this respect, owing to the general increase of awareness in the analysis and delineation of character, even before the deepening of our whole understanding of motives, and the revealing of unimagined complexities, by the discoveries of Freud and modern investigators.

(*b*) Ovid suffered a relative decline among classical authors in the seventeenth century, partly through the great advance in the study of Greek, and partly through the discovery of the more serious merits of Horace, particularly in the *Odes*. Later, the classical students of the nineteenth century, romantically preferring poetry with original rather than derivative subject-matter, intensified the study of Greek at the expense of Latin.

(*c*) The prestige of the classics as a whole began to decline in the seventeenth century. It became clear that they were of no direct help to the gentleman in fighting or managing his estate, nor yet to the middle classes for trade now that Latin was ceasing to be an international language. There was an increasing demand for an educational curriculum based on mathematics and modern languages. The latter received powerful support in the nineteenth century from the Prince Consort, when 'Modern Sides' were established in public schools. Some classical authors could be defended to utilitarians on their own ground, but Ovid was not one of these.

(*d*) In England puritan and Anglican sentiment gradually gained the upper hand. Hostility to paganism was shown by writers such as Blackmore, Addison, Watts, Spence, Johnson and Cowper;[7] and laxity in sexual matters was no longer condoned because the author was a classic. This new strictness, already operative in the age of Addison and Johnson, became a passion in the nineteenth century, which somehow managed to hush up the abusive obscenities and adultery of its favourite Catullus, 'tenderest of the Roman poets', to fall with Augustan severity on the polite flippancies of Ovid.

(e) The contrast between the fortunes of these two in that century is a pointer to the most powerful factor of all in Ovid's dethronement, the upheaval characterized by the *Sturm und Drang* in Germany, the Revolution in France, and the Romantic Movement in England. Ovid was typical of the *ancien régime*, of everything against which the spirit of the age was in revolt. The last considerable poet to make constant use of him, André Chénier, was significantly among the victims of the guillotine. In particular, his whole attitude to love was highly unromantic, a fault for which his incidental descriptions of romantic scenery could not atone.

(f) The nineteenth century also saw a broadening of men's interest in the subject-matter of the classics, as a result of which classical authors came more and more to be valued, especially at Oxford,* for their contribution to our knowledge of history, philosophy or archaeology, and less for their purely literary merit. This tendency, at first salutary, has now gone far too far. For such purposes Ovid, apart from the *Fasti*, has little to offer; he is not 'important'. Nor, on the other hand, had he special interest for the fashionable occupation of textual criticism; as Housman was to remark *à propos* the *Heroides*, there were easier tasks to hand than 'gleaning after Bentley over a stubble where Heinsius has reaped'.[8]

(g) Finally, there has been a fundamental objection to his mentality as revealed in his works, and to his works because of his mentality, which goes beyond the age-long puritan deprecation of

* Prof. M. L. Clarke, to whom I am indebted for several suggestions used in this Epilogue, tells me that at Oxford a candidate chose certain books to be examined on from a fairly long list: it did not include Ovid.

his attitude to sexual morality. I believe it can be traced to the Romantic critics, with their insistence on the sharp distinction between what is poetry and what is merely verse and their biographical approach to literature. Sometimes it is expressed by saying that he has no heart. 'The quality of heartlessness', says Mackail, 'affects the whole book (*Decameron*), and the whole of Boccaccio's work. He shares it with or inherits it from Ovid. It is consistent with the highest gifts of the story-teller, but not with the highest gifts of the poet.' It is true that the *Ars Amatoria* is heartless—one shudders to think of its being written in any other spirit; and the *Amores* are heartless—but no one should mistake them for love-poetry *manqué*. Yet when we come to the poems from exile, the only ones that bear on the real life of the poet, we surely find that he had a heart after all.

More often it is a soul he is said to lack. Ever since 'Longinus' defined sublimity as 'the echo of a great soul', a criterion has been intermittently present in men's minds which Ovid cannot satisfy. His purpose was to entertain, as Homer's was in the *Odyssey*. He is not 'sublime'; nor is he 'profound'. 'Their poetry is conceived and composed in their wits', said Matthew Arnold of Dryden and Pope; 'genuine poetry is conceived in the soul.' Palgrave voiced the general verdict of Victorian men of letters on Ovid: 'Among world-famous poets perhaps the least true to the soul of poetry.' It was left for Professor Gilbert Murray to put up a belated defence of him: 'He was a poet utterly in love with poetry; not perhaps with the soul of poetry—to be in love with souls is a feeble and somewhat morbid condition—but with the real face and voice and body and clothes and accessories of poetry.'*

That was published in 1921, and it was in the nineteen-twenties that the time was ripe for a revaluation of Ovid. T. S. Eliot, in his *Homage to John Dryden*, had staked out a claim for wit as an instrument of poetry. There was a reawakening of enthusiasm for

* See his admirable essay on 'Poesis and Mimesis' in *Essays and Addresses* (1921), pp. 115–17. Prof. Michael Grant's account of him in his *Roman Literature* (1954) is refreshingly fair to him; so indeed is Fränkel's in his book as a whole.

Dryden, and also for Pope, on whom Lytton Strachey gave his brilliant Leslie Stephen Lecture. The narrow Victorian idea of what was 'poetical' was breaking down, and long-excluded verse-writers were being re-explored. It was also a period of emancipation. Old values were being questioned. People were beginning to realize that to be shocked was not an adult response to literature; that one could appreciate it without necessarily endorsing its content; and that a man no more sublime in character than Baudelaire could be recognized as a great poet. The only sign in English classical circles of such a revaluation of Ovid was a humane essay by Mr T. F. Higham in the *Classical Review* for 1934. But classical circles are seldom in the forefront of movements in literary sensibility, and perhaps even now it is not too late.

APPENDIX OF REFERENCES

CHAPTER I

1 For the evidence concerning Ovid's life see S. G. Owen, *Tristia I*, Introduction; and for fuller discussion, A. L. Wheeler, 'Topics from the Life of Ovid', *A.J.P.* 1925, pp. 1–28.
2 *Am.* II, 16, 1–10.
3 *Am.* III, 15, 11–14.
4 *Tr.* IV, 10, 3.
5 G. Pansa, *Ovidio nel Medioevo* (1924), p. 11.
6 *Am.* III, 13, 1.
7 *Tr.* IV, 10, 5–14.
8 *Tr.* IV, 10, 7–8; *Am.* III, 8, 9–10.
9 *Am.* III, 15, 8; Schulten, *Klio*, II, p. 192; Wheeler, *op. cit.* p. 3.
10 *Am.* III, 15, 9–10.
11 Wheeler, *op. cit.* pp. 4–7.
12 See H.-J. Marrou, *Histoire de l'éducation dans l'antiquité* (1948), pp. 359–89; A. Gwynn, *Roman Education from Cicero to Quintilian* (1926), pp. 82 ff. For a short popular account see J. B. Poynton in *Greece and Rome*, Nov. 1934, pp. 1–12.
13 Marrou, *op. cit.* p. 378.
14 Cicero, *De Or.* I, 187.
15 *Part. Or.* 1–2.
16 Marrou, *op. cit.* pp. 345–58.
17 Cicero, *ap.* Suetonius, *Rhet.* 2.
18 See M. L. Clarke, *Rhetoric at Rome* (1953), pp. 12, 14.
19 Ch. 38 *fin.* For the decline see Seneca, *Contr.* I, Praef. 6–7; Vell. Pat. I, 17, 3.
20 *Rhet. ad Her.* III, 2; IV, 68.
21 See S. F. Bonner, *Roman Declamation* (1949), pp. 33 f. and n. 3.
22 *Il diritto nei retori romani* (1938).
23 *Op. cit.* chs. V and VI.
24 *Sat.* I, tr. Heseltine. For a resumé of ancient criticisms of declamation see Bonner, *op. cit.* ch. IV.
25 'The Schools of Declamation at Rome', in *Tacitus and Other Roman Studies* (1906), p. 185.
26 X, 5, 14.
27 *Contr.* II, praef. 3.
28 LL.B., Section A, 1947.
29 *Ovide* (1921), p. 17.
30 Seneca, *Contr.* II, 2, 8–9, 12.
31 *Ibid.* 9–11.
32 *Contr.* II, 2, 12.
33 *Tr.* IV, 10, 17–20.
34 Seneca, *Contr.* IX, 5, 17.
35 *P.* II, 5, 65–72.
36 *Op. cit.* pp. 167–9, n. 3.
37 *P.* IV, 2, 35–6.
38 IV, 2, 1–6.
39 *Op. cit.* p. 169.
40 *Tr.* IV, 10, 19–30.
41 Norden, *Die Antike Kunstprosa* (1898) p. 887[3] and nn.
42 *Op. cit.* pp. 149–56.
43 Wheeler, *op. cit.* pp. 4–7.
44 *Sat.* I, 6, 62–4.
45 Servius on *Aen.* VIII, 310; cf. Horace, *S.* I, 10, 85.
46 Suetonius, *Gram.* 16.
47 *A. J. P.* 1912, pp. 162–4.
48 II, 34, 66.
49 *Tr.* IV, 10, 41–56.
50 Wheeler, *op. cit.* pp. 17–25.
51 Ullman, *op. cit.* pp. 153–60.
52 *Tr.* I, 2, 77–8.
53 *P.* II, 10, 21 ff.
54 *F.* VI, 417–24.
55 *Tr.* IV, 10, 31–2.
56 *P.* I, 7, 27–8; cf. *Tr.* IV, 4, 27–30.
57 *Tr.* IV, 10, 57–60.
58 *Op. cit.* pp. 11–17.

59 *Tr.* IV, 10, 29.
60 *Tr.* II, 93–6 with S. G. Owen's note (cf. *Tr.* IV, 10, 34; *F.* IV, 384).
61 *Tr.* I, 11, 37.
62 *P.* I, 8, 43–8.
63 *Tr.* IV, 10, 69–74; Owen, *Tristia* II, pp. xvii–xviii.

CHAPTER 2

1 III, 1, 1–2.
2 65–8 and 76.
3 *Ap.* Athenaeum, 597 B, l. 77. For a summary of the controversy see Butler and Barber, Propertius edn. (1933), pp. xxvii–lv; and for a fuller discussion, A. A. Day, *The Origins of Latin Love-elegy* (1938).
4 Morel, *Frag. Poet. Lat.* pp. 42–6.
5 LXIV, 384–408.
6 LXVIII, 73–86, 105–30.
7 Cf. LXV, 13–4.
8 E.g. 1123–8, 1287–94, 1345–50; R. Reitzenstein, *Epigramm und Skolion* (1893), p. 84 n.
9 Summary in K. F. Smith, *The Elegies of Albius Tibullus* (1913), pp. 23–4 n.; see further the bibliographies in Bursian, 1911, 1923, 1926, 1932, 1939.
10 Introd. to edn. (1911), p. 12. For a full collection of echoes in Ovid of himself and other Roman poets see A. Zingerle, *Ovidius und sein Verhältniss zu den vorangegangenen und gleichzeitigen römischen Dichtern*, 3 vol. (1869–71).
11 III, 73 Pf.²
12 Servius on *E.* x, 46: 'hi autem omnes versus Galli sunt de ipsius translati carminibus.' F. Skutsch, *Aus Vergils Frühzeit* (1901), pp. 12 f.
13 *Medea*, l. 410. Cf. Horace, *Odes*, I, 29, 10; Propertius, I, 15, 29; Ovid, *Tr.* I, 8, 1. See E. Dutoit, *La Thème de l'Adynaton* (1936).
14 I, 3.
15 Seneca, *Contr.* II, 2.
16 E. Bethe, 'Die Dorische Knabenliebe', *Rh. Mus.* 1907, p. 439.
17 *A.A.* II, 683–4. Cf. III, 437–8.
18 *Ad. Fam.* IX, 26, 2.

CHAPTER 3

1 See W. Beare, *Hermathena*, 1953, p. 40.
2 Catullus LXXVI, 8; Ovid. *P.* I, 6, 26; Martial XII, 68, 6.
3 See Sturtevant, *op. cit.* p. 77.
4 Lytton Strachey, *Characters and Commentaries* (1933), pp. 288–9.
5 II, 6, 37–8.
6 M. Schuster, *Tibull-Studien* (1930), p. 58.
7 For an analysis of this expansion see O. Weinreich, *Die Distichen des Catull* (1926), pp. 70–6.
8 Diehl, *Pomp. Wand.* p. 785.
9 *Am.* I, 1, 27.
10 *Am.* III, 9, 52.
11 *A.A.* I, 300.
12 *A.A.* II, 8.
13 *F.* I, 270.
14 Psalm cxiv.
15 Pope, *Essay on Criticism*, ll. 683–6.
16 *Am.* III, 2, 80.
17 *Am.* III, 11 a, 4.
18 *Am.* III, 14, 8.
19 See R. Volkmann, *Die Rhetorik der Griechen und Römer* (1874), pp. 396 ff.
20 *Am.* II, 12, 3–4.
21 *Am.* III, 11 a, 18.
22 *Her.* VI, 127–8.
23 *Am.* II, 1, 23–8.
24 Cf. *Rhet. ad Her.* IV, 22, 31; Catullus LXIV, 19–21.
25 *Am.* III, 9, 43.
26 *R.A.* 259.
27 *R.A.* 445.
28 *Am.* I, 10, 4.
29 *Am.* I, 13, 10.

30 *Am.* II, 16, 36.
31 *Am.* III, 9, 1.
32 *Am.* III, 4, 40.
33 *Tr.* III, 8, 6.
34 *Am.* I, 2, 41–2.
35 *Am.* II, 5, 31.
36 *Am.* III, 15, 15.
37 Norden, *Aeneis* VI, p. 396³.
38 Fr. 2.
39 Fr. 10.
40 περὶ ἑξέως I, 18.
41 See Norden, *Aeneis* VI, p. 377³.
42 Norden, *Kunstprosa*, pp. 839–41³; Platnauer (who gives some figures), *op. cit.* p. 49.
43 *Am.* I, 15, 18.
44 *Am.* I, 1, 12.
45 *P.* IV, 13, 2.
46 *Am.* III, 11b, 9–12.
47 *Am.* I, 15, 33–6.
48 *Am.* III, 6, 1.
49 *A.A.* II, 56.
50 *A.A.* II, 494.
51 Horace, *Sat.* I, 10, 20; Quintilian XII, 10, 33.
52 *Am.* II, 13, 7–8.
53 *A.A.* II, 79–82.

CHAPTER 4

1 I, 6, 25–6; cf. II, 24, 6.
2 *Am.* II, 1, 2; cf. III, 1, 17–22.
3 Brooks Otis, 'Ovid and the Augustans', *T.A.P.A.*, 1938, p. 199, n. 35.
4 *Tr.* II, 353–8.
5 II, 6, 39–40.
6 *Apol.* 10.
7 I, 1, 21–4 Pf.²
8 See Propertius III, 24, 19.
9 See T. F. Higham, *C.R.* 1934, p. 113.
10 See E. Reitzenstein, *op. cit.* ('Das neue Kunstwollen in den Amores Ovids'), pp. 67–76.
11 E.g. *Am,* I, 2, 24; 51–2.
12 Cf. *A.A.* I, 139 ff.

13 XIII, 44, 1.
14 Euripides, *Bacch.* 317–18.
15 *A.P.* V, 171 and 172 St.
16 *A.P.* VII, 189–216. G. Herrlinger, *Totenklage um Tiere in der Antiken Dichtung* (1930), pp. 81–6.
17 See Leo, *Plautinische Forschungen* (1895), p. 140; E. H. Haight, *The Symbolism of the House Door in Classical Poetry* (1950), pp. 135–41.
18 III, 6, 25–45.
19 E.g. Horace, *Epode* XVI, 25–34 (the 'Phocaean' oath); *Odes* III, 3, 1–8; IV, 9, 1–28.
20 Seneca, *Contr.* IX, 5, 17.
21 *Am.* III, 8, 1.

CHAPTER 5

1 *A.J.P.* 1907, pp. 287 ff.
2 343–6.
3 For further speculation see Fränkel, *op. cit.* pp. 193–5; F. Peeters, *Les Fastes d'Ovide* (1939), p. 20. Summary in Martini, *op. cit.* p. 27.
4 *Kleinere Schriften* II, pp. 56–61 (1848).
5 'Adversarien über die sogenannten Ovidischen Heroiden', *Jahrb.* 1863, pp. 49–69. Palmer (pp. 436–7) rejected XVI–XXI, but was not followed by Purser in this (*ibid.* p. xxxii).
6 See S. B. Clark, 'The double letters in Ovid's Heroides', *Harv. Stud.* 1908, pp. 121–55.
7 Platnauer, *op. cit.* p. 17.
8 *A.A.* III, 346.
9 E.g. Catullus XIII; XXXII; Horace, *Odes* I, 20; cf. Philodemus, *A.P.* XI, 44. Kroll, *Studien*, p. 217.
10 'Der Brief in d. röm. Lit.', *Abh. Sächs. Ges.* 1903, pp. 189–90.
11 I, 2; 59–62.
12 XI, 1–6.
13 III, 1–4.
14 XVII, 266; XXI, 245–6.

15 XVIII, 1–24.
16 V, 1–2.
17 XXI, 1–2.
18 VII, 191–6.
19 IX, 143–68.
20 LXVIII, 73 ff.
21 I, 19, 7 ff.
22 65–78; 93–122; 151–166.
23 II, 128.
24 Hyginus, *Fab.* 104.
25 *Her.* III, 1–4; *Il.* I, 348.
26 5–16.
27 I, 334–8.
28 27–40; cf. *Il.* IX, 260 ff.
29 45–52; cf. *Il.* XIX, 291–6; VI, 429.
30 57–8; cf. *Il.* IX, 682–3; cf. 356–63.
31 69–76; cf. *Il.* IX, 394–400.
32 85; cf. *Il.* IX, 496.
33 91–8; cf. *Il.* IX, 590–6.
34 103–110; cf. *Il.* XIX, 258–65; XXIV, 478–9.
35 111–120; cf. *Il.* IX, 186; 665.
36 126; cf. *Il.* XVI, 140–3.
37 147–8; cf. *Il.* I, 194. For an analysis of this letter, and also of I, VII, X and XII, see J. N. Anderson, *On the Sources of Ovid's Heroides* (1896).
38 *Il.* XVI, 33; Catullus LXIV, 154–7; *Aen.* IV, 365–7; *Her.* VII, 37–40.
39 *Tr.* II, 533–6.
40 II, 75–8.
41 IX, 47–100.
42 II, 9; XV, 83.
43 XVII, 13.
44 III, 106.
45 VI, 125–8.
46 I, 77–8, *Odyssey* V, 214 ff.
47 XV, 39–40.
48 XX, 49–50.
49 XII, 171.
50 X, 107–8.
51 XIX, 167–8.
52 XII, 135–52.
53 VIII, 75–80, 89–100.
54 X, 7–36.
55 Loeb edn., Introd. p. 9.
56 Introd. p. xxiii.

57 XVIII, 75–86.
58 *Ox. Pap.* VII (1910), 1011; fr. 75 Pf².
59 *Ibid.* l. 54.
60 *R.A.* 381–2. *A.A.* I, 457; *Tr.* 3, 10, 73.
61 XXI, 77–110.
62 XVII, 65–102.
63 III–12.
64 145–6.
65 151–4.
66 177–86.
67 *Dial.* 12.
68 X, 1, 98.
69 Quintilian, VIII, 5, 6; Seneca, *Suas.* III, 7.
70 XII, 207–12.

CHAPTER 6

1 See *A.A.* III, 205.
2 *Tr.* II, 471–90.
3 II, 18, 23–6; cf. I, 2.
4 See further Holbrook Jackson, *The Eighteen Nineties,* esp. ch. VI ('The New Dandyism') and ch. VIII ('Shocking as a Fine Art').
5 See W. Gaunt, *The Aesthetic Adventure* (1945), p. 117.
6 *M.* III, 158–9.
7 Tibullus, I, 4; cf. 6. Propertius I, 10, 15 ff. Ovid, *Am.* I, 4; 8.
8 See L. P. Wilkinson, 'The Intention of Virgil's Georgics', *Greece and Rome,* 1950, pp. 19–28.
9 See F. Leo, *op. cit.* p. 146.
10 See R. Bürger, *De Ov. carm. am. inv. et arte* (1901), pp. 119 ff.
11 I, 31–4; II, 599–600; III, 611–14.
12 III, 615–16.
13 *Med. Fac.* 43–50. For the various classes of women at Rome, and the attitude of Romans towards them, with special reference to Ovid, see F. A. Wright, *The Lover's Handbook* (1924), pp. 66–92.
14 *A.A.* III, 315–28; I, 595.

15 *A.A.* III, 329–46; II, 121–4; I, 459–68.
16 I, 277–340.
17 *R.A.* 461.
18 I, 217–28.
19 P. 401 (1926 edn.); quoted by G. Hough, *The Last Romantics* (1949), pp. 207–8.
20 LXIV, 251–64.
21 I, 535–64.
22 II, 177.
23 II, 197–216.
24 III, 749–68.
25 For Roman board games see R. G. Austin in *Greece and Rome*, Oct. 1934, pp. 24–34 and Feb. 1935, pp. 76–82.
26 I, 417–36.
27 II, 281–308.
28 II, 333–6.
29 I, 241–2.
30 III, 431–2.
31 I, 485–6.
32 I, 274.
33 II, 454.
34 II, 155.
35 *R.A.* 96.
36 *R.A.* 648.
37 I, 99.
38 I, 244.
39 III, 605–10.
40 See Pohlenz, *Hermes*, 1906, pp. 321 ff.
41 1051 ff. Prinz, *op. cit.* pp. 57–61, 81–3.
42 Cf. Plato, *Rep.* V, 474 D; Lucretius IV, 1160–70; Horace, *Sat.* I, 3, 38–53. Molière, *Le Misanthrope*, act II, sc. iv.
43 I, 67–72; 255–262.
44 III, 231–2.
45 I, 159–60.
46 II, 396; III, 495–6.
47 III, 449–50.
48 I, 79–88.
49 I, 75–8.
50 III, 137–48.

51 III, 163–8.
52 III, 199–208.
53 I, 505–24.
54 III, 443–6.
55 *R.A.* 680–2.
56 III, 619–44.
57 *A.A.* I, 571–8.

CHAPTER 7

1 *Am.* III, 15, 1.
2 See M. M. Crump, *The Epyllion from Theocritus to Ovid* (1931), p. 203.
3 Probus on Virgil, G. I, 399.
4 Lafaye, *op. cit.* p. 57.
5 XI, 410–748; I, 583–747; X, 298–502; XIII, 904–XIV, 74.
6 Lafaye, *op. cit.* p. 70.
7 IV, 32–415; VIII, 547–IX, 97; VI, 313–411; XII, 146–574.
8 IX, 273–393.
9 VI, 70–128; XIII, 681–701.
10 Schefold, *op. cit.* p. 92.
11 Crump, *op. cit.* pp. 72, 76.
12 Crump, *op. cit.* p. 203.
13 X, 1–85, XI, 1–84; *Georg.* IV, 453–559. Crump, *op. cit.* pp. 132–3.
14 IV, 1, 77.
15 *Ovids elegische Erzählung*, Ber. Sächs. Akad. Leipzig (1919); see esp. p. 10.
16 C. M. Bowra, *C.Q.* 1952, pp. 125–6.
17 A. Siedow, *De elisionis usu in hexametris Latinis* (1911), p. 55.
18 R. B. Steele, *Ph. Qu.* 1926, pp. 212 ff. For further details see A. G. Lee, Edn. of *Metamorphoses* I (1953), pp. 31–6.
19 L. Mueller, *De re metrica poetarum Latinorum* (1894), pp. 144–5.
20 Review of Rex Warner's *Men and Gods* in the *Observer* for 25 June 1950.
21 Frr. 178–85 Pf.²
22 *A.P.* IX, 545, 2, on the *Hecale*.

23 75 Pf.²
24 27 Pf.²
25 41 Pf.²
26 Διηγήσεις, v, 40; fr. 110 Pf.²
27 IV, 765 ff.; VII, 494 ff.; VIII, 565 ff.; XII, 152 ff.; XIII, 636 ff.
28 VIII, 616–724; 738–878.
29 Lafaye, op. cit. pp. 32–4.
30 See L. Malten, 'Aus dem Aitia des Kallimachos', Hermes, 1918, pp. 176–7. For a detailed and judicious analysis of Ovid's debt to Callimachus see M. de Cola, Callimaco e Ovidio (1937).
31 IV, 17–30; V, 341–661; VII, 433–50; X, 17–39; XIII, 1–398; VIII, 616–724; IX, 530–63; XIV, 718–33; II, 327–8, XIV, 443–4: list from Lafaye, op. cit. pp. 89–90.
32 Am. I, 15, 13–14.
33 Shakespeare, As You Like It, III, iii, 9.
34 Wilamowitz-Moellendorf, Hellenistische Dichtung (1924), p. VI.
35 See L. P. Wilkinson, 'The Baroque Spirit in Ancient Art and Literature', in Essays by Divers Hands (Royal Society of Literature, vol. XXV, 1950, pp. 1–11).
36 I, 330–42.
37 L. P. Wilkinson, op. cit. pp. 10–11.
38 Geoffrey Scott, The Architecture of Humanism, pp. 149–50².
39 Op. cit. p. 20.
40 III, 193–9.
41 I, 548–52.
42 III, 671–682.
43 Op. cit. p. 220, n. 73. Gide, Si le grain ne meurt, ch. II.
44 IX, 786–91.
45 I, 236–9.
46 I, 414–15; Pindar, Ol. 9, 66 f.; Virgil, G. I, 63 f.
47 VI, 374–8.
48 IV, 415; V, 461.
49 XIV, 59–65.
50 With Lafaye, op. cit. p. 118, and Crump, op. cit. p. 224.

51 VI, 381–91.
52 V, 30–235.
53 XII, 210–535.
54 V, 228–30.
55 XIII, 764–7.
56 XII, 395–403.
57 I, 578.
58 I, 682–721.
59 XIV, 264–70.
60 VIII, 855–74.
61 III, 370–92.
62 II, 172.
63 IV, 195–7.
64 III, 353–5. Catullus LXII, 42–4.
65 II, 710.
66 W. Kroll, Studien zum Verständnis der röm. Literatur (1924), p. 170.
67 III, 417.
68 III, 425–6.
69 XIV, 301.
70 II, 280–1.
71 X, 156–7.
72 II, 796.
73 VI, 155–6.
74 IX, 666–8.
75 XIII, 141–7.
76 XV, 294–5.
77 VII, 589–90.
78 VIII, 195–200; 217–20.
79 VIII, 14–22.
80 I, 343–7.
81 Werke, ed. Lachmann-Muncker, vol. XV, p. 438, cited by Norden, Aeneis VI³, p. 413.
82 A. R. Bellinger, Romano-Campanian Landscape-Painting (1944), p. 141.
83 See H. Bastian, 'Brueghel und Ovid', Hum. Gym. 1934, pp. 37 ff.
84 III, 483–5; VI, 47–9.
85 I, 492–4; II, 623–5.
86 VII, 106–8.
87 IX, 220–2.
88 IV, 348–9, 354–5, 362–7 (3), 375–6.
89 XI, 24–7.
90 X, 595–6; cf. Lucretius IV, 75 ff.

91 II, 726–9; cf. Lucretius VI, 178–9.

92 III, 111–14.

93 See especially the judicious discussion of H. Bartholomé, *Ovid und die antike Kunst* (1935); also P. Grimal, 'Les Métamorphoses d'Ovide et la peinture paysagiste à l'époque d'Auguste', *Rev. Et. Lat.* 1938, pp. 145–61; W. Helbig, *Campanische Wandmalerei* (1873), pp. 18–21; Schefold, *op. cit.* pp. 94–6.

94 VIII, 727.

95 XI, 410–748.

96 *G.* III, 25.

97 *Am.* I, 14, 33–4; *A.A.* III, 224; *Tr.* II, 527; *P.* IV, 1, 29.

98 V, 585–641.

99 *Mosella*, 55–74.

100 XXXIV, 9–12.

101 *Apoc.* 2.

102 II, 112–121.

103 IX, 93.

104 XI, 97.

105 III, 150.

106 IV, 81–2.

107 *Am.* II, 16, 1–10.

108 III, 155–164.

109 Cf. Theocritus VII, 7–9; XXII, 37–43, Castiglioni, *op. cit.* pp. 223–9.

110 IX, 334–5, 341–2.

111 V, 385–91.

112 VIII, 562–4.

113 XIV, 51–3; XIII, 908–11, 924–34.

114 XI, 229–37.

115 I, 568–73.

116 XI, 352–64. *Op. cit.* p. 156.

117 *Op. cit.* p. 153.

118 II, 760–82, VIII, 788–808, XII, 39–63, XI, 592–615.

119 I, 1, 39–41 (Morpheus). Cf. Chaucer, *The Book of the Duchesse*, 153–77; *The Hous of Fame*, 69–76; Gower, *Confessio Amantis* IV, 3317 ff.

120 Acts xiv, 11–12.

121 VIII, 637–78.

122 Preface to the 'Fables', *Essays*, ed. W. P. Ker, vol. II, p. 255.

123 II, 64; IV, 7, 11–20.

124 III, 6, 17–18; 12, 21–42. See Fränkel's note 24, *op. cit.* p. 180.

125 *Op. cit.* p. 90. So does Rand, *Ovid and his Influence* (1925), pp. 73–4.

126 *Op. cit.* p. 97.

127 *Op. cit.* p. 11.

128 I, 469; II, 413; III, 370; IV, 203, 267, 326; VI, 612. Heinze, p. 18 f.

129 Schefold (*op. cit.*, p. 71) suggests that, in giving Calliope the story of Ceres, and the impious Pierid the story of the origin of the Egyptian feast-gods, he is reflecting Augustus' favour for the Eleusinian mysteries and his hostility to the Isis-cult.

130 I, 471; 546 ff.

131 IX, 239–58.

132 *Ol.* I, 52.

133 *Fr.* 75 Pf.²

134 IX, 418–27.

135 II, 846–7.

136 I, 452 ff.

137 *Op. cit.* pp. 14–15 and App. I.

138 I, 588–746.

139 II, 401–65.

140 X, 1, 88.

141 II, 843–75.

142 III, 265–6.

143 IX, 304–15.

144 III, 268.

145 III, 362–5.

146 III, 316–38.

147 I, 504–24.

148 II, 730–6.

149 V, 346–79.

150 *Od.* VIII, 266 ff.; *M.* IV, 169–89.

151 VI, 129–45.

152 V, 250 ff.

153 V, 341–661.

154 IV, 11–30.

155 Crump, *op. cit.* p. 220.

156 XI, 180–193.

157 i, 776–9.
158 xi, 150–9.
159 viii, 547 ff.; 579 ff.
160 ix, 1–97.
161 v, 409–37; 464–70.
162 v, 572.
163 v, 489–508.
164 iv, 55–166.
165 iv, 44–51.
166 vii, 690–862.
167 xi, 410–748.
168 445.
169 i, 642–50; 745–6.
170 ii, 498–504.
171 *Hipp.* 380.
172 vii, 20–1.
173 *Med.*, 1021–80.
174 vii, 169–70.
175 ix, 454–665.
176 x, 83–5; 155–61; 86–142; 162–219.
177 ii, 368–9; *Aen.* x, 189; Lafaye, *op. cit.* pp. 168–70.
178 iii, 339–510; iv, 285–388.
179 iv, 329–67.
180 ix, 669–797.
181 See Tarn-Griffith, *Hellenistic Civilisation*, pp. 100–2.[3]
182 x, 243–97.
183 iii, 435–6.
184 v, 400–1.
185 i, 755–61.
186 i, 5–150; xv, 60–478.
187 Compare e.g. *M.* vii, 517–613 (the plague at Aegina) with Lucretius vi, 1136–1285; *Am.* i, 15, 24 with Lucretius v, 95 and 1000.
188 i, 21; 32.
189 *Op. cit.* p. 219.
190 i, 85–6. Cicero, *De Leg.* i, 26; cf. *De Nat. Deor.* ii, 140; Xenophon, *Mem.* i, 4, 11.
191 i, 11 and 12 V.
192 xv, 88–90.
193 Cf. *F.* iv, 395–416; i, 337–88.
194 116–42.
195 xv, 143–52; cf. Lucretius ii, 7 ff.
196 See Fränkel, *op. cit.* p. 110.

197 xv, 262–5.
198 ii, 366; i, 560–5; ii, 259.
199 xv, 431–445.
200 *Ann.*, fr. 65 V; *M.* xiv, 805–28.
201 vii, 44–5.
202 Seneca, *Suas.* iii, 7 (referring to Ovid's *Medea*).
203 xv, 706–718.
204 *Theodor Mommsen*, by C. Bardt, p. 8; quoted by Warde Fowler, *Virgil's Gathering of the Clans*, p. 28.
205 i, 199–205.
206 xv, 444–9.
207 See Martini, *op. cit.* p. 47.
208 *Jul.* 88; *M.* xv, 745–50.
209 xv, 760–1.
210 xv, 779–802; *G.* i, 467–98.
211 xv, 832–7.
212 *G.* i, 499–510; *M.* xv, 861–70; Horace, *Odes* i, 2, 45.
213 *Horace and the Elegiac Poets* (*Roman Poets of the Augustan Age*) (1892), p. 347.
214 *Op. cit.* pp. 231, 233.
215 Preface to *Annus Mirabilis*.
216 *Aen.* iv, 328–30.
217 *Op. cit.* p. 121.
218 Seneca, *Contr.* ii, 2, 8.
219 xi, 543.
220 Stanford, *op. cit.* iii, pp. 42–3.
221 viii, 25; cf. vii, 21 ff. Stanford, *op. cit.* i, pp. 36 ff.
222 *Ibid.* i, pp. 39–45, ii, p. 41.
223 *Ibid.* ii, pp. 47–53.
224 Seneca, *Contr.* ii, 2, 8. Cf. Theon, *Progymn.* 9, 42.
225 *Aen.* i, 92, 122.
226 xiii, 5–122.
227 xiii, 128–381.
228 xiii, 361–9.
229 E.g. Callimachus, Hymn iii, 187–224.
230 ix, 182 ff. Sophocles, *Trach.* 1089 ff.
231 Hyginus, *Fab.* 181; Aeschylus, *Fr.* 245 N.; *M.* iii, 206–24; 232–3.

232 See Kroll, *op. cit.* p. 297.
233 Cicero, *Orat.* 163; Quintilian XII, 10, 33.
234 Cf. L. P. Wilkinson, 'Onomatopoeia and the Sceptics', *C.Q.* 1942, pp. 124–6.
235 VI, 422–674.
236 *Tr.* I, 7, 11–40; III, 14, 22–3. Cf. II, 63; 555.
237 Seneca, *Contr.* II, 2, 12.
238 Martini, *op. cit.* p. 39.
239 III, 141–2.
240 *Tr.* II, 63–6; 557–62.
241 *Tr.* II, 103–6; cf. III, 5, 49–50.
242 *Tr.* I, 7, 11–12.

CHAPTER 8

1 H. Herter, *A.J.P.* 1948, p. 145.
2 In 'Ἐπιτύμβιον *H. Swoboda dargebracht* (1927), pp. 165–94, esp. p. 190.
3 II, 283–380.
4 II, 1.
5 IV, 1, 69.
6 IV, 2, 4, 9 and 10.
7 II, 125 ff.
8 II, 82–118; *Her.* I, 23–4.
9 II, 193–242; 721–852; Livy II, 48–50; I, 57–9.
10 III, 13.
11 IV, 725–8.
12 III, 263–76.
13 IV, 683–713.
14 IV, 905–44.
15 Frazer, *ad loc.*
16 VI, 219–34.
17 II, 27–8.
18 V, 490.
19 *Op. cit.* p. 141.
20 VI, 395–416.
21 *Quaest. Rom.* 86; Frazer, *ad loc.*
22 VI, 295–6.
23 I, 657–60.
24 See de Cola, *op. cit.* p. 34. ὡς ἐφάμην, Κλειὼ δὲ...., *Ox. Pap.* 2080, l. 28; *Sic ego, sic Clio...*,

F. VI, 801; Pfeiffer, *Hermes,* 1928, p. 303, n. 2.
25 IV, 189–92.
26 VI, 651–6.
27 V, 447–50.
28 I, 93–8.
29 VI, 253–4.
30 IV, 947–8; V, 183–8.
31 IV, 417–620; *M.* V, 341–661.
32 II, 549–52. For the whole subject see Peeters, *op. cit.* pp. 63–87.
33 III, 57; 200; V, 147.
34 LXVIII, 31–40.
35 III, 14, 37.
36 Lactantius, *Div. Inst.* V, 5, 4.
37 See Peeters, *op. cit.* pp. 83–4.
38 III, 155–60.
39 I, 603–4.
40 III, 697–710.
41 V, 545–98.
42 I, 13.
43 I, 712–22.
44 II, 142; I, 614; IV, 953. Cf. Ripert, *op. cit.* p. 207.
45 III, 421; IV, 954; I, 608; II, 131–2.
46 IV, 407; I, 282; III, 1; 173–6.
47 II, 684; Rutilius Namatianus I, 66. Cf. *F.* I, 85–8; 515–16; 599–600; IV, 857–62.
48 I, 499–518. Cf. I, 243–6; II, 279–80; 389–92; V, 93–6; VI, 401–414; and also pp. 218–19, 258. Virgil, *Aen.* VIII, 314 ff.; cf. Propertius IV, 1, 1 ff.; Tibullus II, 5, 23–38.
49 VI, 261–4.
50 I, 199, III, 183–4; Dion. Hal., *Ant. Rom.* I, 78, 11; Plutarch, *Rom.* 20, 4.
51 I, 201–3; cf. III, 431–4.
52 III, 185–6.
53 I, 519–36.
54 IV, 19–80.
55 I, 591–606.
56 II, 139; VI, 457.
57 VI, 639–48.
58 IV, 20, 7.
59 II, 55–66; IV, 348; V, 157–8.

60 III, 704; V, 549–70; I, 709–22; V, 145–6; III, 415–28; VI, 455–60; IV, 949–54.
61 *De Civ. Dei* IV, 8.
62 IV, 203–4.
63 V, 230.
64 III, 677–94.
65 II, 45–6.
66 IV, 309–10.
67 I, 225.
68 *L'opposition sous les Césars* (1895), p. 110.
69 *De Or.* I, 69.
70 Probus on Virgil, *G.* I, 138; Lactantius, *Inst. Div.* 2, 5.
71 *Ueber den astronomischen Theil der Fasti des Ovid*, Abh. Berl. Akad. 1822–3, pp. 137–69. Peeters, *op. cit.* pp. 56–7.
72 Ideler, *op. cit.* pp. 166 ff.
73 *A.P.* IX, 75; *F.* I, 357–8. Frazer, *ad. loc.*
74 III, 87–96; VI, 59–64.
75 I, 318–32; III, 121–34; IV, 785–806.
76 I, 103, 127 (? from Verrius Flaccus); 620; 238 (cf. Virgil, *Aen.* VIII, 319–23); VI, 299.
77 *Op. cit.* p. 242, n. 18.
78 IV, 837–56; V, 469–74. II, 143.
79 V, 1–110; 427.
80 VI, 35; 88.
81 Horace, *Odes*, I, 17, 1–2. Wissowa, *Ges. Abh. zur röm. Religions- und Stadtgeschichte* (1904), p. 137.
82 Columella, *De Re Rust.* XI, 2, 98; *F.* I, 165–70.
83 Varro, *L.L.* VI, 12; *F.* I, 318.
84 Varro, *L.L.* VII, 84; *F.* I, 629.
85 I, 588; cf. I, 56 and Macrobius, *Sat.* I, 15, 16.
86 Plutarch, *Quaest. Rom.* 52; Pausanias III, 14, 9; *F.* I, 389.
87 Martial, VIII, 33, 11 f.; XIII, 27; *F.* I, 185–8.
88 *Op. cit.* pp. 15–16; 22.
89 III, 101–16: Horace, *Ep.* II, 1, 156–7.

90 I, 363–78; Virgil, *G.* IV, 315–558.
91 IV, 133–54.
92 V, 429–44.
93 II, 535–40.
94 III, 339–44.
95 Plutarch, *Numa* 15, 4.
96 II, 571–82.
97 III, 269–70.
98 II, 31.
99 IV, 725; cf. Shakespeare, *I Henry VI*, I, i, 153–4; Frazer, *ad loc.*
100 V, 182–378.
101 III, 525–42.
102 II, 303–56.
103 III, 223–4.
104 V, 673–90.
105 VI, 1–100.
106 IV, 377–86.
107 I, 539–40.
108 II, 155.
109 II, 43.
110 IV, 249–50.
111 E.g. III, 81–4; IV, 277–90; 467–80; 563–72.
112 *F.* IV, 417–620; *M.* V, 341–661.
113 Heinze, p. 10.
114 *Ibid.* p. 8.
115 *Ibid.* pp. 75–6.

CHAPTER 9

1 *Tr.* IV, 10, 71–4.
2 *P.* IV, 8, 11–12; cf. *Tr.* V, 5, 19, 'nataque *sua*' (not 'nostra').
3 *Tr.* IV, 10, 76–84.
4 *Ibid.* 75–6.
5 *Her.* VI, 93–4; *Med. Fac.*, 35–42; and more fully, *R.A.* 249–90.
6 *F.* II, 45–6.
7 *P.* I, 5, 43–6; 10, 30.
8 *A.A.* III, 101; 121–8; 133–6; I, 513–22.
9 *Med. Fac.* 43–50; *A.A.* II, 107–44.
10 *Contr.* II, 2 (10), 8.
11 *A.A.* II, 601–40.
12 *Ibid.* 473–80; *F.* IV, 107–14.
13 *A.A.* II, 158.

APPENDIX OF REFERENCES

14 *A.A.* II, 641–66; 682–4; III, 793–4.
15 *A.A.* III, 239–42.
16 *R.A.* 655–72.
17 *P.* I, 2, 139–40; *Tr.* I, 6, 25–8.
18 *P.* I, 2, 136–8.
19 *Tr.* V, 5, 19; *P.* I, 4, 47.
20 *Tr.* I, 3, 17–18, 79–102; I, 6; III,
3, 15–28; 4, 59–62; IV, 3; V, 5. *P.* I,
4, 47–58; II, 11, 13–6.
21 *P.* I, 2, 129–36.
22 *Ibid.* 115–16.
23 *P.* I, 7, 29–30.
24 *Ibid.* 15–16, 55–6.
25 *P.* III, 5, 37–44; IV, 16, 41–4.
Juvenal V, 109.
26 *P.* II, 10.
27 *Tr.* IV, 10, 41–2; *Am.* I, 15, 29–30;
III, 9, 59–64; *A.A.* III, 333–8.
28 *Tr.* V, 3, 53–6; cf. II, 467; 563–8.
29 *Tr.* IV, 10, 45–6.
30 *A.A.* III, 121–2.
31 I, 171–6; 69–72.
32 I, 31–4; II, 599–600; III, 611–14.
33 *Tr.* II, 253–4.
34 *A.A.* I, 100; 586; II, 153–6; 387–90;
III, 483–4.
35 *Tr.* II, 90; 542.
36 Tacitus, *Ann.* III, 24, IV, 71.
37 Owen, *op. cit.* pp. 12–19.
38 *P.* II, 3, 83–90.
39 *P.* II, 3, 61–8; 91–4.
40 Owen, *op. cit.* pp. 40–1.
41 *Ibid.* pp. 42–4.
42 *Tr.* III, 1, 59–82; 14, 5–18.
43 *Tr.* II, 133;
44 Owen, *op. cit.* pp. 41–2.
45 *Tr.* III, 14, 17.
46 See Owen, *op. cit.* pp. 48–9.
47 31–4. Cf. II, 599–600; III, 27; *P.* III,
3, 49–58.
48 Hyginus, *Fab.* 166.
49 *Odes* I, 6, 9–12 (to Agrippa); cf. II,
12 (to Maecenas).
50 III, 24, 58.
51 See Owen on l. 472.
52 III, 353–66.
53 I, 477.

54 Edn. of Tibullus, p. 45.
55 Suetonius, *Aug.* 69; cf. 71.
56 XI, 20.
57 Pliny, *Ep.* V, 3, 5; Macrobius,
Sat. II, 4, 21.
58 *Epit.* I, 24. Cf. Pliny, *Ep.* VIII, 22:
Owen, *op. cit.* p. 39.
59 *Tr.* I, 9, 17–20; 5, 3–6, 27–34.
60 *Tr.* I, 3.
61 *Am.* I, 13, 40.
62 *Her.* III, 68.
63 *Tr.* I, 11, 17–18.
64 *Tr.* I, 2, 19–22.
65 *Tr.* I, 10; Cat. IV. For a comparative study see Munro, *Criticisms
and Elucidations of Catullus* (1878),
pp. 12–21.
66 *Tr.* I, 10, 20–3.
67 *P.* IV, 5, 31–8.
68 *Tr.* I, 11, 9–12.

CHAPTER 10

1 *P.* I, 1, 17–18.
2 *P.* III, 6.
3 *P.* III, 9, 51–4.
4 *P.* I, 1, 19; III, 6, 45; 4, 43; *Tr.* IV,
1, 2.
5 *Tr.* V, 8, 27–30.
6 *Tr.* V, 1, 1.
7 *Tr.* I, 7, 15–22; IV, 1, 101–4; 10,
61–4; V, 12, 59–66.
8 *Tr.* III, 14, 37–44; V, 12, 53–6.
9 *P.* IV, 2, 33–4.
10 *Tr.* III, 14, 33–7; V, 12, 21–40;
P. IV, 2, 23–30.
11 *P.* I, 5, 15–24; III, 9, 7–32; *Tr.* IV,
1, 93–4.
12 *P.* I, 2, 87–8.
13 *P.* III, 1, 11–24; III, 8; *Tr.* III, 10,
69–76.
14 *Tr.* III, 10, 13–34.
15 *Tr.* III, 10, 37–50.
16 *P.* IV, 10, 35–64.
17 *Tr.* III, 3, 1–14.
18 *Tr.* IV, 6, 39–44; V, 13, 1–6.
19 *Tr.* V, 2, 1–8.

20 *P.* I, 10, 1–10; 21–36; 4, 1–10.
21 *Tr.* III, 10, 51–66.
22 *Tr.* V, 10, 15–26.
23 *Tr.* IV, 1, 71–84.
24 *P.* I, 2, 17–22.
25 *P.* I, 8, 49–50.
26 *Tr.* IV, 1, 65–6; cf. 21; V, 2, 30.
27 *Tr.* V, 10, 27–44; 7, 45–64.
28 *Tr.* III, 14, 48; V, 12, 58; *P.* III, 2, 40.
29 *P.* II, 7, 47–74.
30 *Tr.* III, 10, 35–6.
31 *P.* IV, 10, 35–6; 7, 5–12; 9, 75–88.
32 *Tr.* III, 9; cf. Apollodorus I, 9, 24.
33 *Tr.* IV, 4, 61–88; *P.* III, 2, 39–98.
34 *P.* I, 5, 73–4; II, 7, 57; *Tr.* I, 5, 61; III, 10, 3; 12.
35 1933 edn., p. 10.
36 *P.* IV, 2, 5–6.
37 *Tr.* IV, 7, 5–10; V, 13, 15–18.
38 *P.* III, 4, 59–60; IV, 11, 15–16.
39 *Tr.* V, 7, 25–8.
40 *P.* III, 5, 7–14.
41 *Tr.* III, 12, 29–44.
42 *Tr.* III, 8, 1–10.
43 *Tr.* IV, 1, 5–10.
44 *Tr.* V, 1, 53–4.
45 *P.* I, 5, 55; IV, 2, 39–46.
46 *P.* II, 10, 49–52; cf. *Tr.* V, 1, 79–80; *P.* III, 5, 41–2.
47 *P.* II, 10, 21–42.
48 *P.* IV, 15, 33.
49 *P.* I, 9, 25–34, 55–6.
50 *P.* IV, 9, 105–22.
51 *P.* II, 8.
52 *Tr.* III, 1, 39–52.
53 *Tr.* IV, 4, 15–16.
54 *Tr.* IV, 4, 20; *Odes* III, 5, 1–4.
55 *Ann.* IV, 38, 1.
56 *Tr.* II, 121–38; IV, 4, 43–8; V, 11, 9–10, 15–20; 2, 55–8.
57 *P.* II, 2, 67–84; III, 1, 133–6; 3, 85–92.
58 *P.* IV, 6, 9–10; 15–16.
59 *P.* II, 8, 37–8.
60 *P.* III, 4, 45–50.

61 *P.* IV, 6, 17–20; cf. 8, 63–4; 9, 131–4.
62 *P.* II, 5, 41–56 (written before Augustus' death).
63 *P*, IV, 13, 43–50.
64 *Di tibi sunt Caesar iuvenis*: *P.* IV, 8, 23.
65 *P.* IV, 8, 31–88.
66 *P.* II, 10, 21–42.
67 *Tr.* III, 12, 5–30.
68 *Ad. Fam.* II, 12, 2.
69 *P.* I, 8, 29–48, 65–8. *Tr.* IV, 8, 5–14, 25–8.
70 *P.* I, 3, 35–6.
71 *Tr.* III, 3, 15–24.
72 *Tr.* V, 5, 1–12; 29–30.
73 *P.* I, 4, 47–54.
74 *Tr.* I, 6; V, 5, 41–64.
75 *P.* II, 11, 13–22; III, 7, 11–2; III, 1 (illness, l. 69).
76 *Tr.* IV, 3, 1–20.
77 *Tr.* IV, 3, 31–8; III, 3, 25–8; 55.
78 *Tr.* IV, 3, 49–62.
79 See Pfeiffer I², p. 307.
80 1–10; 45–62.
81 *J.P.* 1920, p. 317.
82 *Ibid.* p. 316.
83 *Ibid.* p. 318.
84 *Tr.* III, 7, 43–54.
85 *Tr.* IV, 10, 121–32.
86 *Tr.* V, 14.
87 *P.* III, 6, 51–4.
88 In his justly much-consulted *Literary History of Rome* (1953), p. 443².
89 Loeb edn. p. xxxiii.
90 *Op. cit.* p. 132.
91 *P.* III, 9, 41–56.
92 *Tr.* IV, 6, 1–16; *P.* I, 3, 65–80.
93 *Tr.* III, 10, 41–2; 73–4.
94 Berthaut et Georgin, *Histoire illustré de la littérature latine* (1923), p. 316.
95 *Tr.* IV, 2, 25–46; *A.A.* I, 217–28; see p. 124 above.
96 *Decline and Fall*, ch. XVIII, n. 40.
97 *Tr.* III, 12, 51–4.

98 *P.* IV, 15, 31. Cf. 8, 21–4; 13, 43–50, etc.
99 *P.* I, 8.
100 11 and 152.
101 See E. Fraenkel, *J.R.S.* 1952, pp. 1–9.
102 See T. Birt, *De Halieuticis Ovidio poetae falso adscriptis*, 1878; Housman, *C.Q.* 1907, 275–8; B. Axelson, *Eine Ovidische Echtheitsfrage*, Eranos, 1945, pp. 23–35.
103 *Tr.* V, 7, 55–6.
104 *Tr.* III, 14, 48.
105 *P.* III, 2, 40; IV, 13, 17–38.
106 IV, 14, 15–44, esp. 25–6.
107 *P.* IV, 9, 89–106; 14, 15–60; cf. II, 7, 31–2; III, 2, 37–8.
108 *P.* I, 3, 37–8.
109 *Tr.* III, 3, 29–84.
110 *P.* III, 7, 19.
111 II, 10, 35–8.
112 *Tr.* III, 3, 59–64.
113 *P.* IV, 14, 49–50.

CHAPTER II

1 *Tr.* V, 7, 25–8.
2 *Tr.* II, 519–20.
3 R. Ehwald in Bursian's *Jahresbericht*, vol. 109 (1901), pp. 202–3.
4 See the index (pp. 823–4) to the *Carmina Epigraphica Latina* = *Anthologia Latina* II, 2 (Riese-Buecheler-Lommatzsch, 1926).
5 J. M. C. Toynbee in *C.R.*, 1925, p. 172.
6 For the literature see Martini, *op. cit.* pp. 91–2.
7 III, 38, 10; *Nasones Vergiliosque vides*. A. Zingerle, *Martial's Ovid-Studien* (1877).
8 L. Mueller, *op. cit.* pp. 144–5; 258–60, with statistics.
9 Martini, *op. cit.* p. 66.
10 *Contr.* III, Exc. 7, 2; X, 4, 25, etc.
11 II, 36, 3.
12 X, 1, 88; cf. 93.

13 R. R. Bolgar, *The Classical Heritage and its Beneficiaries* (1954), pp. 41–2.
14 Robinson Ellis, edn. of *Ibis* with Scholia (1881), pp. lxi–lxiii.
15 Martini (*op. cit.* p. 39), citing Ehwald, *Ad. hist. carm. Ovid. recensionemque symbolae* (1889).
16 Bolgar, *op. cit.* pp. 43–4.
17 Suetonius, *Vesp.* ch. 18.
18 Bolgar, *op. cit.* pp. 32–3.
19 *Retractationes* I, 6; Migne, *Patrologia Latina* XXXII, col. 591.
20 Bolgar, *op. cit.* pp. 42–3, 52–5.
21 M. Manitius, 'Beiträge zur Geschichte des Ovidius im Mittelalter' (*Philologus*, Suppl. 1900), p. 726.
22 Laistner, *op. cit.* pp. 28–9; Bolgar, *op. cit.* pp. 51–2.
23 Bolgar, *op. cit.* pp. 45–58; Sandys, *op. cit.* pp. 444–5.
24 Martini (*op. cit.* p. 91), citing Birt's edition (1892) and Gramlewicz, *Quaestiones Claudianeae* (1877).
25 Manitius, *op. cit.* p. 727.
26 Bolgar, *op. cit.* pp. 102–3.
27 Manitius, *op. cit.* pp. 724, 729.
28 *Poet. Lat. Aevi. Car.* I, 169 ff.; Raby, *op. cit.* I, pp. 178–9.
29 Sandys, *op. cit.* I, p. 640; R. Ellis, *Hermes*, 1880, pp. 425 f.
30 Manitius, *Geschichte der lateinischen Literatur des Mittelalters* (1911), vol. I, p. 137.
31 Bolgar, *op. cit.* pp. 106–17.
32 *Ibid.* p. 116.
33 Einhard, *Vita Karoli*, 25; Bolgar, *op. cit.* pp. 108–9.
34 *Poet. Lat. Aevi Car.* I, 483; Raby, *op. cit.* I, Ch. v. For a fuller account of the Carolingian revival see Laistner, *op. cit.* Part III.
35 Raby, *op. cit.* I, p. 247.
36 *Ibid.* pp. 253–4.
37 Raby, *op. cit.* I, p. 183. Cf. B. L. Ullman, *Cl. Phil.* 1928, p. 128; 1932, pp. 11–16, 37–42.

38 Raby, *op. cit.* I, pp. 305–6.

39 For the poetry and background of this period see, besides Raby, Helen Waddell, *The Wandering Scholars* (1927) and *Medieval Latin Lyrics* (1929); Stephen Gaselee, *The Oxford Book of Medieval Verse* (1928); C. H. Haskins, *The Renaissance of the Twelfth Century* (1927); J. Ghellinck, *L'essor de la littérature latine au XII* siècle* (1946). Concise biographies of the various poets are given in Sandys, vol. I, and Wright and Sinclair, *A History of Later Latin Literature* (1931).

40 Hauréau, *Notices et extraits des mss.* xxviii, 2, p. 415; J. H. Mozley, *Susanna and the Elders* I, 23–4, Studi Medievali, 3rd series, 1930, pp. 30 ff.

41 Raby, *op. cit.* I, pp. 343–8, 316; Haskins, *op. cit.* pp. 160–1; P. Abrahams, *Les œuvres poétiques de Baudri de Bourgueil* (1926).

42 Migne, *Pat. Lat.* CLXXI, col. 1430; Raby, *op. cit.* I, p. 353.

43 *Dist.* IV, ch. III; p. 147, ed. M. R. James.

44 Haskins, *op. cit.* pp. 156–7.

45 Raby, *op. cit.* II, p. 179.

46 See further J. H. Hanford, 'The Progenitors of Golias', *Speculum* I (1926), pp. 38 ff.; Raby, *op. cit.* II, 339–40.

47 Haskins, *op. cit.* pp. 184–5.

48 Mansi, XXIII, 33; H. Waddell, *The Wandering Scholars*, p. 259.

49 *Moral-sat. Gedichte*, no. 6, pp. 82 ff.; *Carm. Bur.* 105; Raby, *op. cit.* II, pp. 196–8, 276.

50 W. Meyer, 'Das Liebesconcil in Remiremont', *Zeitschr. für deutsches Alt.* VII (1849), pp. 160 ff.; H. Waddell, *The Wandering Scholars*, pp. 199–200.

51 Wattenbach, *N.A.* II, pp. 398 ff. ll. 37–8.

52 See, e.g., H. Unger, *De Ovidiana in Carminibus Buranis imitatione* (1914); H. Brinkmann, *Geschichte der lateinischen Liebesdichtung im Mittelalter* (1925), passim.

53 Sandys, *op. cit.* I, p. 639.

54 Details in K. Bartsch, *Albrecht von Halberstadt und Ovid* (1861), pp. iv–xi.

55 Ed. K. Breul (1915) ('The Cambridge Songs'), K. Strecker (1926) ('Die Cambridger Lieder'). Raby, *op. cit.* I, 291–306. H. Waddell, *The Wandering Scholars*, pp. 102–3; Wright and Sinclair, *op. cit.* pp. 281–6.

56 Bolgar, *op. cit.* pp. 197–8.

57 W. Schrötter, *Ovid und die Troubadours* (1908), p. 10; Rand, *op. cit.* p. 113; G. Przychocki, *Accessus Ovidiani* (1911).

58 Bolgar, *op. cit.* pp. 195–6.

59 G. Cohen, *La 'comédie' latine en France au XII* siècle* (1931), I, p. xi; Raby, *op. cit.* II, pp. 68–9.

60 In *Liber Decem Capitulorum* (Migne, *Pat. Lat.* CLXXI, col. 1695); Bolgar, *op. cit.* p. 190.

61 Raby, *op. cit.* II, 256–79; 323. Cf. H. Waddell, *The Wandering Scholars*, pp. 198–221.

62 *Opera* (ed. Giles) I, 38; 169; 227; Raby, *op. cit.* II, 323.

63 Epp. (ed. Anstruther) p. 53–7: Sandys, *op. cit.* I, p. 618. Raby, *op. cit.* II, 112.

64 Migne, *Pat. Lat.* CLXXVIII, col. 188, cf. 185–6; *Theol. Christ.* II (Migne, *Pat. Lat.* CLXXVIII, col. 1210 D); Sandys, *op. cit.* I, p. 618.

65 Bolgar, *op. cit.* pp. 190–2.

66 *Dist.* 37, c. 7; Haskins, *op. cit.* p. 97.

67 A. Jeanroy, *Les origines de la poésie lyrique en France* (1925), p. 280; Raby, *op. cit.* II, pp. 322–4.

68 Cf. p. 46. P. Abrahams, *op. cit.* p. 341.

69 See his *Chronicle*, tr. Foster (1883), II, p. 507; Rand, *op. cit.* p. 136.
70 Ripert, *op. cit.* pp. 231–2, from a thesis by V. Pieri.
71 *Am.* III, 4, 17. Rand, *op. cit.* pp. 132–3. Cf. Haskins, *op. cit.* pp. 107–9; E. Curtius, *European Literature in the Latin Middle Ages* (1953), pp. 58–9.
72 L. K. Born, 'Ovid and Allegory', *Speculum*, 1934, pp. 362–79.
73 W. Wattenbach, *Sitz. bayr. Akad.* 1873, p. 694.
74 *De Incontinentia Sacerdotum* III, 795 f.; Raby, *op. cit.* I, p. 403.
75 R. Glaber, *Hist.* II, XII (Migne, *P.L.* CXLII); H. Waddell, *The Wandering Scholars*, p. 84.
76 Printed by L. Delisle, *Le cabinet des mscr.* II, 518 ff.
77 *Inf.* IV, 82–90.
78 *Inf.* XXVI, 118; *M.* III, 543.
79 *Convivio* II, 1, 3.
80 *Inf.* XXV, 94 ff.; *M.* IV, 562 ff.; Curtius, *op. cit.* pp. 164–5.
81 *Metalogicon* I, c. 24 (Migne, *P.L.* CXCIX, col. 854); Bolgar, *op. cit.* pp. 196–7.
82 L. J. Paetow, *Two medieval satires of the University of Paris* (1927).
83 Haskins, *op. cit.* pp. 98–104.
84 H. Waddell, *op. cit.* p. 135.
85 Bolgar, *op. cit.* pp. 208–10.
86 See G. Pansa, *Ovidio nel medioevo e nella tradizione popolare* (1924), esp. pp. 18–19.
87 Ripert, *op. cit.* p. 236.
88 Bartsch, *op. cit.* pp. xii ff.; Rand, *op. cit.* pp. 142–3.
89 III, 675 ff.
90 Rand, *op. cit.* p. 130.
91 B. Bischoff, *Historisches Jahrbuch*, 1952, pp. 272–3.
92 G. Paris, *La Poésie du Moyen Age* (1885), pp. 189–209.
93 Highet, *op. cit.* pp. 61–2 and 580, n. 46.
94 W. Schrötter, *op. cit.* p. 1. For parallel passages see D. Schludenko, 'Ovid und die Trobadors', *Zeitschr. für rom. Phil.* 1934, pp. 129–74.
95 *Ibid.* p. 47.
96 E. Langlois, *Origines et Sources du Roman de la Rose* (1891), esp. pp. 69–74, 119–27; Highet, *op. cit.* pp. 62–9.
97 N. Coghill, *Chaucer* (1949), pp. 30–1.
98 *The Book of the Duchesse*, 44 ff. and Skeat's notes.
99 (D) 680 in her Prologue.
100 J. Koch, *Chaucers Belesenheit in den römischen Klassikern*, Englische Studien, 1923, p. 68.
101 *Ibid.* p. 79.
102 *Introduction to Man of Law's Prologue*, l. 92; *Anelida and Arcite*, l. 21. G. K. Kittredge, *Harvard Studies*, 1917, p. 55; 80–1.
103 *Aen.* IV, 180; *House of Fame*, 1392; Skeat, *ad loc.*
104 See p. 15 n.; Coghill, *op. cit.* p. 30; Koch, *op. cit.* pp. 82–3.
105 E.g. by S. G. Owen in *English Literature and the Classics* (ed. G. S. Gordon, 1912), pp. 175–83; Highet, *op. cit.* pp. 98–9; and at length in Shannon, *op. cit.*
106 Shannon, *op. cit.* p. 282.
107 *Ibid.* pp. 160–7.
108 VI, 2185–200.
109 Shannon, *op. cit.* pp. 35–44.
110 *Miller's Tale* (A) 3263–4. 'Preface to the Fables', *Essays*, ed. W. P. Ker, Vol. II, p. 264. Others are cited by M. A. Hill, *P.M.L.A.*, 1927, pp. 845–861.
111 III, 1225–8.
112 'Preface to the Fables', *Essays* vol. II, pp. 254 ff. See also Shannon, *op. cit.* pp. 371–6.
113 Coghill, *op. cit.* pp. 89, 93, 99–100, 103.

114 Skeat, II, p. II.

115 Koch, *op. cit.* p. 82.

116 Kittredge, *op. cit.* pp. 50–3.

CHAPTER 12

1 Quoted by E. Krause, *Die Mythen-Darstellungen in der venezianischen Ovidausgabe von 1496* (1926), p. 6.

2 G. May, *D'Ovide à Racine* (1949), pp. 31–2.

3 P. Kuntze, *Le Grand Olympe, eine alchemistische Deutung von Ovids Metamorphosen* (1912).

4 Rand, *op. cit.* p. 155.

5 P. de Nolhac, *Pétrarque et l'Humanisme* (1907), I, pp. 179–81.

6 Highet, *op. cit.* pp. 90–2; Rand, *op. cit.* pp. 151–2.

7 Martini, *op. cit.* p. 90.

8 J. Adhémar, *Influences antiques dans l'art du moyen age français* (1939), pp. 267–9.

9 *De Vita Solitaria* II, 7, 2; P. de Nolhac, *op. cit.* I, pp. 176–8.

10 M. D. Henkel, *Illustrierte Ausgaben von Ovids Metamorphosen im XV, XVI, und XVII Jahrhundert* (1930), pp. 61–71; E. Krause, *op. cit.* p. 6.

11 L. Roblot-Delondre, 'Les sujets antiques dans la tapisserie', *Rev. Archéol.* 1919, pp. 5, 10, 13–14.

12 E. Krause, *op. cit.* p. 6.

13 Ed. 1730, pp. 48–58. Seznec, *op. cit.* p. 227.

14 C. van Mander, *Het Schilderboeck* (1604); J. von Sandart, *Deutsche Akademie der Edlen Bau-, Bild-, und Malerey-Künste* (1675).

15 Schevill, *op. cit.* pp. 107–13.

16 D. Bush, *Mythology and the Renaissance Tradition* (1932), pp. 72–3.

17 Highet, *op. cit.* p. 167.

18 Vasari (ed. Milanesi) IV, p. 141. E. Panofsky, *Studies in Iconology* (1939), pp. 58–65.

19 *Op. cit.* p. 74; and see in general his chapter 'Ovid Old and New'.

20 Ripert, *op. cit.* p. 238.

21 P. de Nolhac, *Ronsard et l'Humanisme* (1921), pp. 23–6; for the influence on the *Odes* see Laumonier's edition.

22 Bolgar, *op. cit.* pp. 357–8.

23 Schevill, *op. cit.* pp. 28–9, 85–6.

24 *Ibid.* pp. 120–3.

25 *Ibid.* p. 113 n.

26 *Ibid.* pp. 89, 147.

27 E. J. Dent, 'The Baroque Opera', in *The Musical Antiquary* for 1909, p. 97. Highet, *op. cit.* p. 141.

28 E. de Sélincourt, edn. of Keats (1905), Index, p. 611, under 'Sandys'. C. Cowden Clarke, *Recollections of Writers* (1878), p. 124. Other influential English mythographies were A. Tooke's *Pantheon* (1698) and J. Spence's *Polymetis* (1747).

29 See Bush, *op. cit.* pp. 287–8. For analogous works in English see p. 428.

30 See A. A. Tilley, *The Decline of the Age of Louis XIV* (1929), Ch. x.

31 For details see S. G. Owen, 'Ovid and Romance' in *English Literature and the Classics*, ed. G. S. Gordon (1912), pp. 180–3.

32 T. A. Walker in *C.H.E.L.* vol. II, pp. 359–60.

33 Schevill, *op. cit.* p. 17.

34 T. W. Baldwin, *William Shakspere's Small Latine and Lesse Greeke* (1944), vol. I, pp. 102, 122, 338; II, 419, 193.

35 *Ibid.* I, 198, 218, 290–1; II, 383.

36 *Ibid.* I, 338; II, 419, 382.

37 *Ibid.* II, 419.

38 *Ibid.* II, 408, 418.

39 Bush, *op. cit.* pp. 78–9.

40 *Ibid.* pp. 48–9.

41 T. Warton, *History of English Poetry* (1778 edn.), p. 945.

42 Bush *op. cit.* pp. 124–9.
43 *M.* II, 1 ff.; VI, 103 ff. See p. 156 for the former.
44 I, 135–56.
45 R. K. Root, *Classical Mythology in Shakespeare* (1903), pp. 3–5; 9.
46 Bush, *op. cit.* pp. 107–16.
47 Root, *op. cit.* pp. 9–11.
48 Baldwin, *op. cit.* II, 428.
49 *M.* XI, 313.
50 Baldwin, *op. cit.* II, 408–16.
51 Baldwin, *op. cit.* II, 177–80; 193.
52 H. R. D. Anders, *Shakespeare's Books* (1904), p. 22, quoting Baynes, *Fraser's Magazine*, 1880, pp. 101–2.
53 Baldwin, *op. cit.* II, 194.
54 *Romeo and Juliet* III, ii, 1–4; *M.* II, 312.
55 *Merchant of Venice* V, i, 13–15; *M.* VII, 98.
56 IV, xiv, 54; Baldwin, *op. cit.* II, 425.
57 *Her.* VII, 153; *A. and C.* I, iii, 20–1; 89–95. T. Zielinski, 'Marginalien', *Philologus* 64 (n. F. 18), 1905, pp. 17–19.
58 *Merchant of Venice* V, i, 9–12.
59 X, 41–2; Root, *op. cit.* p. 5.
60 Bush, *op. cit.* pp. 68–72, 243–4.
61 *Ibid.* pp. 81–2.
62 *Palladis Tamia: Wits Treasury*, 280.
63 Hallett Smith, *op. cit.* p. 117.
64 *M.N.D.* V, i, 391; *M.* VII, 1–293; Baldwin, *op. cit.* II, p. 439.
65 V, i, 44–53. For this and other references see Thomson, *op. cit.* pp. 77–81.
66 *T.* V, I, 33–50; *M.* VII, 197–209.
67 Baldwin, *op. cit.* II, 444–51.
68 *Ibid.* II, 233–6.
69 *Ibid.* I, 673–7.
70 Shannon, *The Heroic Couplet*, pp. 76–108.
71 *Ibid.* pp. 77–81.
72 *Ibid.* p. 99.
73 Tucker Brooke, Introduction to the *Elegies* in Marlowe's Works, p. 15.
74 II, 19, 1–4.
75 III, 8, 29–34.
76 *Op. cit.* p. 142.
77 *Ibid.* p. 164.
78 Bush, *op. cit.* p. 187 n.
79 *Her.* XVII, 95–102.
80 *Oth.* II, i, 149–61; Lytton Strachey, *loc. cit.*
81 See p. 406, Bush, *op. cit.* pp. 288–93.
82 Baldwin, *op. cit.* I, pp. 110–12.
83 Bush, *op. cit.* pp. 246–7.
84 See D. P. Harding, *Milton and the Renaissance Ovid* (1946), ch. II.
85 E. K. Rand deals with the Elegies in a delightful essay, 'Milton in Rustication', *S.P.* 1922, pp. 109–35.
86 *Op. cit.* p. 250.
87 Cf. *Apology for Smectymnuus*, Works III, Pt. I, pp. 303–4; Harding, *op. cit.* pp. 54–7.
88 Johnson, *Life of Milton*; cf. Masson's *Life*, VI, p. 754.
89 C. G. Osgood, *The Classical Mythology of Milton's English Poems* (Yale Studies in English, 1900), p. 24.
90 See Harding, *op. cit.* ch. IV.
91 See Osgood, *op. cit.* p. XLVI.
92 Bush, *op. cit.* pp. 272–4; e.g. *P.L.* X, 580; I, 746; V, 381; VII, 39.
93 *Taccia di Cadmo e d'Aretusa Ovidio: Inf.* XXV, 94 ff.; Curtius, *op. cit.* pp. 164–5.
94 *P.L.* IV, 268–75; cf. Ovid, *M.* V, 391 ff.
95 *M.* II, 112–14. See p. 179.
96 *M.* I, 262–73. Cf. Harding, *op. cit.* pp. 81–4.
97 *P.L.* XI, 734–41.
98 Bush, *op. cit.* pp. 165–7.
99 Rand, 'Milton in Rustication', p. 133; *Am.* I, 5, 26; see p. 54.
100 *P.R.* II, 350 ff.
101 IV, 286 ff.
102 Quoted by Harding, *op. cit.* p. 26.

APPENDIX OF REFERENCES

EPILOGUE

1 W. Brewer, *op. cit.* p. 31, but with no reference.
2 Ripert, *op. cit.* pp. 237–49.
3 May, *op. cit.* pp. 25–7 and *passim.*
4 Publ. A. Skira, Lausanne; 145 copies only; etchings reproduced with A. D. Watts' translation, 1954.
5 *Correspondence of Wakefield and Fox,* pp. 83, 87.
6 C. M. Bowra, *The Romantic Imagination* (1949), p. 224.
7 See D. Bush, *Mythology and the Romantic Tradition* (1937), pp. 23–4.
8 *C.R.* 1899, p. 173.

LIST OF MODERN WORKS CITED

(For a fuller bibliography the reader should consult E. Martini, *Einleitung zu Ovid*, 1933, articles on Ovid in Bursian's *Jahresbericht* up to 1939, and *L'Année Philologique* from 1924 onwards.)

ABRAHAMS, P. *Les œuvres poétiques de Baudri de Bourgueil.* 1926.
ADHÉMAR, J. *Influences antiques dans l'art du moyen âge français.* 1939.
ALLARD, C. *La Dobroutcha.* 1859.
ALLEN, K. 'The Fasti of Ovid and the Augustan Propaganda' (*American Journal of Philology*, 1922).
ALTON, E. H. 'Ovid in the Medieval Schoolroom' (*Proceedings of the Classical Association*, 1937).
ANDERS, H. R. D. *Shakespeare's Books.* 1904.
ANDERSON, J. N. *On the Sources of Ovid's Heroides.* 1896.
AUSTIN, R. G. 'Roman Board Games' (*Greece and Rome*, Oct. 1934 and Feb. 1935).
AXELSON, B. 'Eine Ovidische Echtheitsfrage' (*Eranos*, 1945).

BAILEY, C. *Ovid, Fastorum Liber III* (edn.). 1921.
BAKKER, J. TH. *Publii Ovidii Nasonis Tristium V* (edn.). 1946.
BALDWIN, T. H. *William Shakspere's Small Latine and Lesse Greeke.* 2 vols. 1944.
BARDT, C. *Theodor Mommsen.* 1903.
BARKER, E. P. *The Lover's Manual* (Verse Translation of *Ars Amatoria*). 1931.
BARTHOLOMÉ, H. *Ovid und die antike Kunst.* 1935.
BARTSCH, K. *Albrecht von Halberstadt und Ovid.* 1861.
BASTIAN, H. 'Brueghel und Ovid' (*Humanistisches Gymnasium*, 1934).
BEARE, W. 'The meaning of ictus as applied to Latin Verse' (*Hermathena*, 1953).
BELLINGER, A. R. *Romano-Campanian Landscape-Painting.* 1944.
BENTLEY, R. 'Schediasma' prefixed to edition of Terence. 1726.
BERTHAUT ET GEORGIN. *Histoire illustré de la littérature latine.* 1923.
BETHE, E. 'Die Dorische Knabenliebe' (*Rheinisches Museum*, 1907).
BINDI, V. *Monumenti degli Abruzzi.* 1889.
BIRT, T. *De Halieuticis Ovidio poetae falso adscriptis.* 1878.
BISCHOFF, B. 'Eine mittelalterliche Ovidlegende' (*Historisches Jahrbuch*, 1952).
BOISSIER, G. *L'opposition sous les Césars.* 1885.
    'The Schools of Declamation at Rome', in *Tacitus and Other Roman Studies* (trans.), 1906.
BOLGAR, R. R. *The Classical Heritage and its Beneficiaries.* 1954.
BONNER, S. F. *Roman Declamation.* 1949.
BORN, L. K. 'Ovid and Allegory' (*Speculum*, IX, 1934).
BOWRA, Sir C. M. *The Romantic Imagination.* 1949.
    'Orpheus and Eurydice' (*Classical Quarterly*, 1952).
BRANDT, P. *De arte amatoria libri tres* (edn.). 1902.
    Amorum libri tres (edn.). 1911.

BREWER, W. *Ovid's Metamorphoses in European Culture.* 1933.

BRINKMANN, H. *Geschichte der lateinischen Liebesdichtung im Mittelalter.* 1925.

BURCK, E. 'Römische Wesenszüge in der Augusteischen Liebeselegie' (*Hermes,* 1952).

BÜRGER, R. *De Ovidii carminum amatoriorum inventione et arte.* 1901.

BURSIAN, C. (Founder.) *Jahresbericht über die Fortschritte der klassischen Altertumswissenschaft.* Since 1873.

BUSH, D. *Mythology and the Renaissance Tradition in English Poetry.* 1932.
Mythology and the Romantic Tradition in English Poetry. 1937.

BUTLER, H. E. AND BARBER, E. A. *The Elegies of Propertius* (edn.). 1933.

CAMPS, W. A. 'Critical notes on some passages in Ovid' (*Classical Review,* 1954).

CASTIGLIONI, L. 'Studi intorno alle Metamorfosi d'Ovidio' (*Annali della R. Scuola Normale Superiore di Pisa,* XX, 1907).

CHARLESWORTH, M. P. 'Tiberius and the Death of Augustus' (*American Journal of Philology,* 1923).

CHOTZEN, T. M. *Recherches sur la poésie de Dafydd ab Gwilym.* 1927.

CLARK, S. B. 'The Double Letters in Ovid's Heroides' (*Harvard Studies in Classical Philology,* 1908).

CLARKE, M. L. *Rhetoric at Rome.* 1953.

COGHILL, N. *The Poet Chaucer.* 1949.

COHEN, G. *La 'comédie' latine en France au XIIe siècle.* 1931.

COLA, M. DE. *Callimaco e Ovidio.* 1937.

COWDEN CLARKE, C. *Recollections of Writers.* 1878.

CRUMP, M. M. *The Epyllion from Theocritus to Ovid.* 1931.

CURTIUS, E. *European Literature in the Latin Middle Ages.* 1953.

DAY, A. A. *The Origins of Latin Love-elegy.* 1938.

DENT, E. J. 'The Baroque Opera' (*The Musical Antiquary,* 1909).
Mozart's Operas. 1913.

DEVILLE, A. *Essai sur l'exile d'Ovide.* 1859.

DIEHL, E. *Pompeianische Wandinschriften.* 1936.

DILLER, H. 'Die Dichterische Eigenart Ovids Metamorphosen' (*Humanistisches Gymnasium,* 1934).

DRAYTON, M. *England's Heroical Epistles.* 1597.

DRYDEN, J. *Essay of Dramatic Poesy.* 1668.
Preface to Translation of Ovid's *Epistles.* 1680.
Preface to the *Sylvae.* 1685.
Preface to the *Fables.* 1700.
Essays, ed. W. P. Ker. 2 vols. 1899.

DUTOIT, E. *La Thème de l'Adynaton.* 1936.

EHWALD, R. *Ad historiam carminum Ovidianorum recensionemque symbolae.* 1889.
Article on Ovid in Bursian's *Jahresbericht,* vol. CIX. 1901.
Die Metamorphosen (8th revision of M. Haupt's ed.). 2 vols. 1903.

ELLIS, R. 'De Artis Amatoriae Ovidianae Codice Oxoniensi' (*Hermes,* 1880).
P. Ovidii Nasonis Ibis (edn.). 1881.

FRÄNKEL, H. 'Ovid, A Poet between Two Worlds' (Sather Classical Lectures, 1945).

FRAZER, Sir J. G. The Golden Bough, 3rd edn., 1911–15. 12 vols.

Publi Ovidi Nasonis Fastorum Libri Sex, Edited with Translation and Commentary. 5 vols. 1929.

Ovid: Fasti (Loeb edn.). 1931.

GANZENMÜLLER, C. Die Elegie Nux und ihr Verfasser. 1910.

GASELEE, Sir S. Ovyde, Hys Booke of Metamorphose, Books X–XV (Reprint of Caxton's translation); with H. B. F. Brett-Smith. 1924.

The Oxford Book of Medieval Latin Verse. 1928.

GAUNT, W. The Aesthetic Adventure. 1945.

GHELLINCK, J. L'essor de la littérature latine au XIIe siècle. 1946.

GIDE, A. Si le grain ne meurt. 1926.

GOETHE, J. W. Werke (Herausgegeben im Auftrage der Grossherzogin Sophie von Sachsen). 133 vols. 1887–1918.

GORDON, G. S. (Editor). English Literature and the Classics. 1912.

Robert Bridges. 1946.

GRAEBER, G. Untersuchungen über Ovids Briefe aus der Verbannung. 1884.

GRAMLEWICZ, St. Quaestiones Claudianeae. 1877.

GRIMAL, P. 'Les Métamorphoses d'Ovide et la peinture paysagiste de l'époque d'Auguste' (Revue des études latines, 1938).

GUIDE BLEU, Roumanie-Bulgarie, Turquie. 1933.

GWYNN, A. Roman Education from Cicero to Quintilian. 1926.

HAIGHT, E. H. The Symbolism of the House Door in Classical Poetry. 1950.

HALLETT SMITH. Elizabethan Poetry. 1952.

HANFORD, J. H. 'The Progenitors of Golias' (Speculum, I, 1926).

HARDING, D. P. Milton and the Renaissance Ovid. 1946.

HASKINS, C. H. The Renaissance of the Twelfth Century. 1927.

HAURÉAU, B. Notices et extraits des mss. 1890.

HEINZE, R. 'Ovids elegische Erzählung' (Bericht über die Verhandlungen der Sächsischen Akademie der Wissenschaften zu Leipzig, 1919).

HELBIG, W. Campanische Wandmalerei. 1873.

HENKEL, M. D. Illustrierte Ausgaben von Ovids Metamorphosen im XV, XVI und XVII Jahrhundert. 1930.

HERRLINGER, G. Totenklage um Tiere in der antiken Dichtung. 1930.

HERRMANN, K. 'De Ovidii Tristium Libris V' (unprinted Leipzig dissertation). 1924.

HERTER, H. 'Ovids Kunstprinzip in den Metamorphosen' (American Journal of Philology, 1948).

HIGHAM, T. F. 'Ovid: Some Aspects of his Character and Aims' (Classical Review, 1934).

HIGHET, G. The Classical Tradition. 1949.

HILL, M. A. 'Balance in Chaucer's Poetry' (Publications of the Modern Language Association of America, 1927).

HOUGH, G. The Last Romantics. 1949.

HOUSMAN, A. E. 'Ovid's Heroides' (*Classical Review*, 1897).

'Versus Ovidi de Piscibus et Feris' (*Classical Quarterly*, 1907).

'Rostagni's Ibis' (*Classical Review*, 1921).

HUBER, G. *Lebensschilderung und Kleinmalerei im Hellenistischen Epos*. 1926.

IDELER, H. 'Ueber den astronomischen Theil der Fasti des Ovid' (*Abhandlungen der Berliner Akademie*, 1822–3).

JACKSON, H. *The Eighteen Nineties*. 1913.

JEANROY, A. *Les origines de la poésie lyrique en France*. 1925.

JOHNSON, S. 'Life of Milton' (in *Lives of the Poets*, 1779).

KEIL, H. *Grammatici Latini*. 7 vols. 1857–80.

KITTREDGE, G. K. 'Chaucer's Lollius' (*Harvard Studies in Classical Philology*, 1917).

KLEINCLAUSZ, A. *Eginhard*. 1941.

KNOWLTON, E. C. 'Origin of the Closed Couplet in English' (Article in *The Nation*, New York, 1914).

KOCH, J. *Chaucers Belesenheit in den römischen Klassikern*. 1923.

KRAUS, W. Article 'Ovidius Naso' in *Pauly-Wissowa-Kroll Real-Encyclopädie*.

KRAUSE, E. *Die Mythen-Darstellungen in der venezianischen Ovidausgabe von 1496*. 1926.

KROLL, W. *Studien zum Verständnis der römischen Literatur*. 1924.

KUNTZE, P. *Le Grande Olympe, eine alchemistische Deutung von Ovids Metamorphosen*. 1912.

LACHMANN, K. *Kleinere Schriften*, II. 1848.

LAFAYE, G. 'Les Métamorphoses d'Ovide et leurs modèles grecs' (*Bibliothèque de la Faculté des Lettres*, XIX, 1904).

LAISTNER, M. L. W. *Thought and Letters in Western Europe from A.D. 500 to 900*. 1931.

LANFRANCHI, F. *Il diritto nei retori romani*. 1938.

LANGLOIS, E. *Origines et Sources du Roman de la Rose*. 1891.

LEE, A. G. 'An appreciation of Tristia III, viii' (*Greece and Rome*, 1949).

Ovid, Metamorphoses I (edn.). 1953.

'Ovid's Lucretia' (*Greece and Rome*, 1953).

LEHRS, K. 'Adversarien über die Sogenannten Ovidischen Heroiden' (*Jahrbücher für Classische Philologie*, 1863).

LENZ (Levy), F. Article on Ovid in Bursian's *Jahresbericht* 264. 1939.

LEO, F. *Plautinische Forschungen*. 1895.

LOMBARD, A. *Un Mythe dans la Poésie et dans l'Art*. 1946.

LORENTZ, B. *De amicorum in Ovidi Tristibus personis*. 1881.

LOWES, J. L. 'The Loveres Maladye of Hereos' (*Modern Philology*, 1913–14).

The Road to Xanadu. 1927.

LUCAS, D. W. *The Medea of Euripides, Translated into English Prose with Introduction and Notes*. 1949.

LÜDKE, K. J. *Ueber Lautmalerei in Ovid's Metamorphosen.* 1871.
Ueber rhythmische Malerei in Ovid's Metamorphosen. 1878–9.

MALTEN, L. 'Aus dem Aitia des Kallimachos' (*Hermes*, 1918).
MANDER, C. VAN. *Het Schilderboeck.* 1604.
MANITIUS, M. 'Beiträge zur Geschichte des Ovidius im Mittelalter' (*Philologus*, Supplementband, 1900).
Geschichte der lateinischen Literatur des Mittelalters. 2 vols. 1911.
Handschriften antiker Autoren in mittelalterlichen Bibliothekskatalogen. 1935.
MARROU, H.-J. *Histoire de l'éducation dans l'antiquité.* 1948.
MARTINI, E. Ἐπιτύμβιον *Heinrich Swoboda dargebracht.* 1927.
'Einleitung zu Ovid' (*Schriften der deutschen Universität in Prag*, 1933).
MASSON, D. *The Life of Milton* (6 vols.). 1859–80.
MAY, G. *D'Ovide à Racine.* 1949.
MERKEL, R. *Fastorum Libri Sex* (edn.). 1841.
MEYER, W. 'Die Liebesconcil in Remiremont' (*Zeitschrift für deutsches Alterthum*, 1849).
MIGNE, J.-P. *Patrologia Latina.* 221 vols. 1846–64.
MOORE, B. P. *The Art of Love* (Translation). 1935.
MOZLEY, J. H. 'Susanna and the Elders' (*Studi Medievali*, 3rd series, 1930).
MUELLER, L. *De re metrica poetarum Latinorum.* 1894.
MUNARI, F. *P. Ovidi Nasonis Amores* (edn.). 1951.
MUNRO, H. A. J. *Criticisms and Elucidations of Catullus.* 1878.

NÉMETHY, G. *Commentarium Exegeticum ad Ovidii Tristia.* 1913.
NOGARA, B. *Antichi Affreschi del Vaticano.* 1907.
NOLHAC, P. DE. *Pétrarque et l'Humanisme.* 1907.
Ronsard et l'Humanisme. 1921.
NORDEN, E. *Die Antike Kunstprosa.* 1898.
Aeneis VI, 3rd edn. 1934.

OSGOOD, C. G. 'The Classical Mythology of Milton's English Poems' (*Yale Studies in English*, 1900).
OTIS, B. 'Ovid and the Augustans' (*Transactions of the American Philological Association*, 1938).
OWEN, S. G. *Ovid, Tristia, Book I* (edn.). 1890.
'Ovid and Romance' (in *English Literature and the Classics*, ed. G. S. Gordon, 1912).
Ovidi Tristia, Ibis, Ex Ponto, Halieutica, Fragmenta (Text). 1915.
Ovid, Tristia, Book II (edn.). 1924.
'Ovid's Use of the Simile' (*Classical Review*, 1931).

PAETOW, L. J. *Two medieval satires of the University of Paris.* 1927.
PAGE, D. L. *Euripides, Medea, edited with Introduction and Commentary.* 1938.
PALMER, A. *P. Ovidi Nasonis Heroides cum Planudis Metaphrasi* (introduction by L. C. Purser). 1898.

PALMER, H. R. *List of English Editions and Translations of Greek and Latin Classics printed before 1641*. 1911.

PANOFSKY, E. *Studies in Iconology*. 1939.

PANSA, G. *Ovidio nel medioevo e nella tradizione popolare*. 1924.

PARIS, G. *La Poésie du Moyen Age*. 1885.

PEERLKAMP, P. H.- *Quinti Horati Flacci Carmina* (edn.). 1834.

PEETERS, F. *Les Fastes d'Ovide*. 1939.

PERDRIZET, P. 'Légendes babyloniennes dans les Métamorphoses d'Ovide' (*Revue de l'histoire de la réligion*, 1932).

PETER, H. P. *Ovidi Nasonis Fasti* (edn.). 1874.
'Der Brief in der römischen Literatur' (*Abhandlungen der Sächsischen Gesellschaft*, 1903).

PFEIFFER, R. 'Ein neues Altersgedicht des Kallimachos' (*Hermes*, 1928).

PFISTER, F. 'Hat Ovid eine Gigantomachie geschrieben?' (*Rheinisches Museum*, 1915).

PLATNAUER, M. *Latin Elegiac Verse*. 1951.

PLESSIS, F. *La poésie Latine*. 1909.

POHLENZ, M. 'Das dritte und vierte Buch der Tusculanen' (*Hermes*, 1906).

POYNTON, J. B. 'Roman Education' (*Greece and Rome*, 1934).

PRINZ, K. 'Untersuchungen zu Ovids Remedia Amoris' (*Wiener Studien*, 1914).

PRZYCHOCKI, G. *Accessus Ovidiani*. 1911.

PURSER, L. C. Introduction to Palmer's edition of the *Heroides*. 1898.

PUYVELDE, L. DE. *The Sketches of Rubens*. 1947.

RABY, F. J. E. *A History of Secular Latin Poetry in the Middle Ages*. 2 vols. 1934.

RAND, E. K. 'The Chronology of Ovid's Early Works' (*American Journal of Philology*, 1907).
'Milton in Rustication' (*Studies in Philology*, 1922).
Ovid and his Influence. 1925.

REINACH, S. *La Mythologie Figurée et l'Histoire Profane dans la Peinture Italienne de la Renaissance*. 1915.

REITZENSTEIN, E. 'Das neue Kunstwollen in den Amores Ovids' (*Rheinisches Museum*, 1935).

REITZENSTEIN, R. *Epigramm und Skolion*. 1893.

RENAUDET, A. *Dante, Humaniste*. 1952.

RIPERT, E. *Ovide, Poète de l'Amour, des Dieux et de l'Exil*. 1921.

RIZZO, G. E. *La Pittura Ellenistico-Romana*. 1929.

ROBLOT-DELONDRE, L. 'Les sujets antiques dans la tapisserie' (*Revue Archéologique*, 1919).

ROOT, R. K. *Classical Mythology in Shakespeare*. 1903.

SANDART, J. VON. *Deutsche Akademie der Edlen Bau-, Bild- und Malerey-Künste*. 1675.

SANDYS, Sir J. E. *A History of Classical Scholarship*. 3 vols. 3rd edn. 1920.

SCHEFOLD, K. *Pompeianische Malerei*. 1952.

SCHEVILL, R. *Ovid and the Renascence in Spain*. 1913.

SCHLUDENKO, D. 'Ovid und die Trobadors' (*Zeitschrift für romanische Philologie*, 1934).

SCHRÖTTER, W. *Ovid und die Troubadours.* 1908.

SCHULTEN, A. 'Italische Namen und Stämme' (*Klio*, 1902).

SCHUSTER, M. *Tibull-Studien.* 1930.

SCOTT, G. *The Architecture of Humanism.* 1914.

SELLAR, W. Y. *The Roman Poets of the Augustan Age* (vol. II, *Horace and the Elegiac Poets*). 1892.

SEZNEC, J. *La Survivance des Dieux Antiques.* 1940.

SHANNON, E. F. *Chaucer and the Roman Poets.* 1929.

SHANNON, G. P. 'The Heroic Couplet in the Sixteenth and early Seventeenth Centuries, with Special Reference to Ovid and the Elegiac Distich' (Unpublished dissertation, Stanford University, California). 1926.

SHOWERMAN, G. *Ovid: Heroides and Amores* (Loeb edn.). 1921.

SHUCKBURGH, E. S. P. *Ovidii Nasonis Heroidum Epistulae* (Selection). 1879.

SIEDOW, A. *De elisionis usu in hexametris Latinis.* 1911.

SIEGMUND, A. 'Seneca und Ovidius' (*Wiener Studien*, 1900).

SIMPSON, P. 'Shakespeare's Use of Latin Authors', in *Studies in Elizabethan Drama.* 1955.

SKEAT, W. *Chaucer, The Hous of Fame* (edn.).

SKUTSCH, F. *Aus Vergils Frühzeit.* 1901.

SMITH, K. F. *The Elegies of Albius Tibullus.* 1913.

STANFORD, W. B. 'Studies in the Characterization of Ulysses, I–III' (*Hermathena*, 1949–50).

STEELE, R. B. 'Variation in the Latin Dactylic Hexameter' (*Philological Quarterly*, 1926).

STRACHEY, L. *Pope* (Leslie Stephen Lecture for 1925), reprinted in *Characters and Commentaries*, 1933.

STURTEVANT, E. 'Accent and Ictus in the Latin Hexameter' (*Transactions of the American Philological Association*, 1923).

'Accent and Ictus in the Latin Elegiac Distich' (*Transactions of the American Philological Association*, 1924).

SYMONDS, J. A. *Women, Wine and Song.* 1884.

TARN, Sir W. W. *Hellenistic Civilization.* 3rd edn. (rev. with G. T. Griffith). 1952.

THOMSON, J. A. K. *Shakespeare and the Classics.* 1952.

TILLEY, A. A. *The Decline of the Age of Louis XIV.* 1929.

TOYNBEE, J. M. C. 'Some "programme" coin-types of Antoninus Pius' (*Classical Review*, 1925).

TREVELYAN, Sir G. O. *The Life and Letters of Lord Macaulay.* 2 vols. 1876. (1908 edn.)

ULLMAN, B. L. 'Horace and Tibullus' (*American Journal of Philology*, 1912).

'Tibullus in the Medieval Florilegia' (*Classical Philology*, 1928).

'Classical Authors in Certain Medieval Florilegia' (*Classical Philology*, 1932).

UNGER, H. *De Ovidiana in Carminibus Buranis imitatione.* 1914.

VASARI, G. *Le Opere.* Ed. Milanesi, 1878.

VILLEY, P. *Les Sources et l'évolution des essais de Montaigne.* 2 vols. 1908.

VOLKMANN, R. *Die Rhetorik der Griechen und Römer.* 1874.

WADDELL, H. *The Wandering Scholars.* 1927.
Medieval Latin Lyrics. 1929.
WARDE FOWLER, W. *Virgil's Gathering of the Clans.* 1918.
The Roman Festivals. 1925.
WARNER, R. *Men and Gods.* 1950.
WARTON, T. *History of English Poetry.* 3 vols. 1774–81.
WATTENBACH, W. 'Zwei Handschriften in der königlichen Hof- und Staats-bibliothek' (*Sitzungsberichte der Bayerischen Akademie, Phil.-Hist. Classe*, 1873).
WATTS, A. D. *Ovidius, Metamorphoses, an English Version, with the etchings of Pablo Picasso.* 1954.
WEINREICH, O. *Die Distichen des Catull.* 1926.
WHEELER, A. L. 'Propertius as Praeceptor Amoris' (*Classical Philology*, 1910).
'Topics from the Life of Ovid' (*American Journal of Philology*, 1925).
WIGHT DUFF, J. *A Literary History of Rome in the Golden Age.* 3rd edn. 1953.
WILAMOWITZ-MOELLENDORF, U. VON. *Hellenistische Dichtung.* 1924.
WILKINSON, L. P. 'The Augustan Rules for Dactylic Verse' (*Classical Quarterly*, 1940).
'Onomatopoeia and the Sceptics' (*Classical Quarterly*, 1942).
Horace and his Lyric Poetry. 1945.
'The Intention of Virgil's Georgics' (*Greece and Rome*, 1950).
'The Baroque Spirit in Ancient Art and Literature', in *Essays by Divers Hands*, vol. XXV, Royal Society of Literature. 1950.
WISSOWA, G. *Gesammelte Abhandlungen zur römischen Religions und Stadtgeschichte.* 1904.
WOERMANN, K. *Die Antiken Odysseelandschaften.* 1875.
WRIGHT, F. A. *The Lover's Handbook.* 1924.
A History of Later Latin Literature (with T. A. Sinclair). 1931.

YEATS, W. B. *Autobiographies.* 1926.

ZIELINSKI, T. 'Marginalien' (*Philologus*, 1905).
ZINGERLE, A. *Ovidius und sein Verhältniss zu den vorangegangenen und gleichzeitigen römischen Dichtern.* 3 vols. 1869–71.
Martial's Ovid-Studien. 1877.

INDEXES

1. OVIDIAN PASSAGES QUOTED

2. PROPER NAMES (SELECTED)

Figures in square brackets refer to the notes in the Appendix of References